Ethical and Professional Standards

CFA® PROGRAM CURRICULUM • VOLUME 1

LEVEL III
2012

CFA INSTITUTE

PEARSON

1 2 3 4 5 6 7 8 9 10 V313 16 15 14 13 12 11

0002000010270652643

AG/JW

Please visit our website at *www.pearsoned.com*

ISBN 10: 0-558-92515-4
ISBN 13: 978-0-558-92515-4

MIX
Paper from
responsible sources
FSC® C005928

CONTENTS

HOW TO USE THE CFA PROGRAM CURRICULUM

Congratulations on passing Level II of the Chartered Financial Analyst (CFA®) Program. This exciting and rewarding program of study reflects your desire to become a serious investment professional. You are embarking on a program noted for its high ethical standards and the breadth of knowledge, skills, and abilities it develops. Your commitment to the CFA Program should be educationally and professionally rewarding.

The credential you seek is respected around the world as a mark of accomplishment and dedication. Each level of the program represents a distinct achievement in professional development. Successful completion of the program is rewarded with membership in a prestigious global community of investment professionals. CFA charterholders are dedicated to life-long learning and maintaining currency with the ever-changing dynamics of a challenging profession. The CFA Program represents the first step towards a career-long commitment to professional education.

The CFA examination measures your degree of mastery of the assigned CFA Program curriculum. Therefore, the key to your success on the examination is to master the Candidate Body of Knowledge (CBOK™), which can be accomplished by reading and studying the CFA Program curriculum. The CBOK contains the core knowledge, skills, and abilities (competencies) that are generally accepted and applied by investment professionals. These competencies are used in practice in a generalist context and are expected to be demonstrated by a recently qualified CFA charterholder. The remaining sections provide background on the CBOK, the organization of the curriculum, and tips for developing an effective study program.

Curriculum Development

The CFA Program curriculum is grounded in the practice of the investment profession. Utilizing the Global Body of Investment Knowledge (GBIK) collaborative website, CFA Institute performs a continuous practice analysis with investment professionals around the world to determine the knowledge, skills, and abilities that are relevant to the profession. Regional expert panels and targeted surveys are conducted annually to verify and reinforce the continuous feedback from the GBIK collaborative website. The practice analysis process ultimately defines the CBOK. The CBOK consists of four components:

► A broad topic outline that lists the major top-level topic areas (CBOK Topic Outline)

► Topic area weights that indicate the relative exam weightings of the top-level topic areas

► Learning Outcome Statements (LOS) that advise candidates about the specific knowledge, skills, and abilities they should acquire from readings covering a topic area (LOS are provided in online study sessions and at the beginning of each reading)

► The curriculum of material (readings and end-of-reading questions) that candidates receive upon exam registration and are expected to master

A committee consisting of practicing charterholders, in conjunction with CFA Institute staff, designs the CFA Program curriculum to deliver the CBOK to candidates. The examinations, also written by practicing charterholders, are designed to allow you to demonstrate your mastery of the CBOK as set forth in the CFA Program curriculum. As you structure your personal study program, you should emphasize mastery of the CBOK and the practical application of that knowledge. For more information on the practice analysis, CBOK, and development of the CFA Program curriculum, please visit www.cfainstitute.org.

Organization of the Curriculum

The Level III CFA Program curriculum is organized into 10 topic areas. Each topic area begins with a brief statement of the material and the depth of knowledge expected.

Each topic area is then divided into one or more study sessions. These study sessions—18 sessions in the Level III curriculum—should form the basic structure of your reading and preparation.

Each study session includes a statement of its structure and objective, and is further divided into specific reading assignments. The outline on the inside front cover of each volume illustrates the organization of these 18 study sessions.

The reading assignments are the basis for all examination questions, and are selected or developed specifically to teach the knowledge, skills, and abilities reflected in the CBOK. These readings are drawn from CFA Program-commissioned content, textbook chapters, professional journal articles, research analyst reports, and cases. All readings include problems and solutions as well as appendices to help you understand and master the topic areas.

Reading-specific Learning Outcome Statements (LOS) are listed at the beginning of each reading. These LOS indicate what you should be able to accomplish after studying the reading. The LOS, the reading, and the end-of-reading questions are dependent on each other, with the reading and questions providing context for understanding the scope of the LOS.

You should use the LOS to guide and focus your study, as each examination question is based on an assigned reading and one or more LOS. The readings provide context for the LOS and enable you to apply a principle or concept in a variety of scenarios. The candidate is responsible for the entirety of all of the required material in a study session, the assigned readings as well as the end-of-reading questions and problems.

We encourage you to review the material on LOS, including the descriptions of LOS "command words," at www.cfainstitute.org.

Features of the Curriculum

▶ **Required vs. Optional Segments** - You should read all of an assigned reading. In some cases, however, we have reprinted an entire chapter or article and marked certain parts as "optional." The CFA examination is based only on the required segments, and the optional segments are included only when they might help you to better understand the required segments (by seeing the required material in its full context). When an optional segment begins, you will see an icon and a solid vertical bar in the outside margin that will continue until the optional segment ends, accompanied by another icon. *Unless the material is specifically marked as optional, you should assume it is required.* You should rely on the required segments and the reading-specific LOS in preparing for the examination.

▶ **Problems/Solutions** - *All questions and problems in the readings as well as their solutions (which are provided directly following the problems) are part of the curriculum and required material for the exam.* When appropriate, we have included problems within and after the readings to demonstrate practical application and reinforce your understanding of the concepts presented.

The questions and problems are designed to help you learn these concepts and may serve as a basis for exam questions. Many of these questions are adapted from past CFA examinations.

▶ **Margins** - The wide margins in each volume provide space for your note-taking.

▶ **Six-volume Structure** - For portability of the curriculum, the material is spread over six volumes.

▶ **Glossary and Index** - For your convenience, we have printed a comprehensive glossary and volume-specific index in each volume. Throughout the curriculum, a **bolded blue** word in a reading denotes a term defined in the glossary.

▶ **Source Material** - The authorship, publisher, and copyright owners are given for each reading for your reference. We recommend that you use this CFA Institute curriculum rather than the original source materials because the curriculum may include only selected pages from outside readings, updated sections within the readings, and contains problems and solutions tailored to the CFA Program.

▶ **LOS Self-Check** - We have inserted checkboxes next to each LOS that you can use to track your progress in mastering the concepts in each reading.

Designing Your Personal Study Program

Create a Schedule - An orderly, systematic approach to examination preparation is critical. You should dedicate a consistent block of time every week to reading and studying. Complete all reading assignments and the associated problems and solutions in each study session. Review the LOS both before and after you study each reading to ensure that you have mastered the applicable content and can demonstrate the knowledge, skill, or ability described by the LOS and the assigned reading. Use the LOS self-check to track your progress and highlight areas of weakness for later review.

You will receive periodic e-mail communications that contain important study tips and preparation strategies. Be sure to read these carefully. Curriculum errata are periodically updated and posted on the study session page at www.cfainstitute.org. You may also sign up for an RSS feed to alert you to the latest errata update.

Successful candidates report an average of 300 hours preparing for each exam. Your preparation time will vary based on your prior education and experience. For each level of the curriculum, there are 18 study sessions, so a good plan is to devote 15–20 hours per week, for 18 weeks, to studying the material. Use the final four to six weeks before the exam to review what you've learned and practice with sample and mock exams. This recommendation, however, may substantially underestimate the hours needed for appropriate examination preparation depending on your individual circumstances, relevant experience, and academic background. You will undoubtedly adjust your study time to conform to your own strengths and weaknesses, and your educational and professional background.

You will probably spend more time on some study sessions than on others, but on average you should plan on devoting 15 hours per study session. You should allow ample time for both in-depth study of all topic areas and additional concentration on those topic areas for which you feel least prepared.

Online Sample Examinations - CFA Institute online sample examinations are intended to assess your exam preparation as you progress toward the end of your study. After each question, you will receive immediate feedback noting the correct response and indicating the relevant assigned reading, so you'll be able to identify areas of weakness for further study. The 120-minute sample examinations reflect the question formats, topics, and level of difficulty of the actual CFA examinations. Aggregate data indicate that the CFA examination pass rate was higher among candidates who took one or more online sample examinations than among candidates who did not take the online sample examinations. For more information on the online sample examinations, please visit www.cfainstitute.org.

Online Mock Examinations - In response to candidate requests, CFA Institute has developed mock examinations that mimic the actual CFA examinations not only in question format and level of difficulty, but also in length. The three-hour online mock exams simulate the morning and afternoon sessions of the actual CFA exam, and are intended to be taken after you complete your study of the full curriculum, so you can test your understanding of the CBOK and your readiness for the exam. To further differentiate, the mock exams are available in a printable PDF format with feedback provided at the end of the exam, rather than after each question as with the sample exams. CFA Institute recommends that you take these mock exams at the final stage of your preparation toward the actual CFA examination. For more information on the online mock examinations, please visit www.cfainstitute.org.

Preparatory Providers - After you enroll in the CFA Program, you may receive numerous solicitations for preparatory courses and review materials. When considering a prep course, make sure the provider is in compliance with the CFA Institute Prep Provider Guidelines Program (www.cfainstitute .org/partners/examprep/pages/cfa_prep_provider_prog_participants.aspx). Just remember, there are no shortcuts to success on the CFA examinations; reading and studying the CFA curriculum is the key to success on the examination. The CFA examinations reference only the CFA Institute assigned curriculum—no preparatory course or review course materials are consulted or referenced.

SUMMARY

Every question on the CFA examination is based on specific pages in the required readings and on one or more LOS. Frequently, an examination question is also tied to a specific example highlighted within a reading or to a specific end-of-reading question and/or problem and its solution. To make effective use of the curriculum, please remember these key points:

1. All pages printed in the Custom Curriculum are required reading for the examination except for occasional sections marked as optional. You may read optional pages as background, but you will not be tested on them.

2. All questions, problems, and their solutions - printed at the end of readings - are part of the curriculum and required study material for the examination.

3. You should make appropriate use of the online sample/mock examinations and other resources available at www.cfainstitute.org.

4. You should schedule and commit sufficient study time to cover the 18 study sessions, review the materials, and take sample/mock examinations.

5. **Note:** Some of the concepts in the study sessions may be superseded by updated rulings and/or pronouncements issued after a reading was published. Candidates are expected to be familiar with the overall analytical framework contained in the assigned readings. Candidates are not responsible for changes that occur after the material was written.

Feedback

At CFA Institute, we are committed to delivering a comprehensive and rigorous curriculum for the development of competent, ethically grounded investment professionals. We rely on candidate and member feedback as we work to incorporate content, design, and packaging improvements. You can be assured that we will continue to listen to your suggestions. Please send any comments or feedback to curriculum@cfainstitute.org. Ongoing improvements in the curriculum will help you prepare for success on the upcoming examinations, and for a lifetime of learning as a serious investment professional.

ETHICAL AND PROFESSIONAL STANDARDS

STUDY SESSIONS

Study Session 1   Code of Ethics and Standards of Professional Conduct
Study Session 2   Ethical and Professional Standards in Practice

TOPIC LEVEL LEARNING OUTCOME

The candidate should be able to demonstrate a thorough knowledge of the CFA Institute Code of Ethics and Standards of Professional Conduct.

STUDY SESSION 1
CODE OF ETHICS AND STANDARDS OF PROFESSIONAL CONDUCT

The readings in this study session establish a framework for ethical conduct in the investment profession. The principles and guidance presented in the CFA Institute *Standards of Practice Handbook (Handbook)* form the basis for the CFA Institute self-regulatory program to maintain the highest professional standards among investment practitioners. A clear understanding of the CFA Institute Code of Ethics and Standards of Professional Conduct (both found in the *Handbook*) should allow practitioners to identify and appropriately resolve ethical conflicts, leading to a reputation for integrity that benefits both the individual and the profession. Material under "Guidance" in the *Handbook* addresses the practical application of the Code and Standards. The guidance for each standard reviews its purpose and scope, presents recommended procedures for compliance, and provides examples of the standard in practice.

READING ASSIGNMENTS

Reading 1   Code of Ethics and Standards of Professional Conduct
             Standards of Practice Handbook, Tenth Edition
Reading 2   Guidance for Standards I–VII
             Standards of Practice Handbook, Tenth Edition

CODE OF ETHICS AND STANDARDS OF PROFESSIONAL CONDUCT

LEARNING OUTCOMES

The candidate should be able to:	Mastery
a. describe the structure of the CFA Institute Professional Conduct Program and the disciplinary review process for the enforcement of the Code of Ethics and Standards of Professional Conduct;	☐
b. explain the ethical responsibilities required by the Code of Ethics and the Standards of Professional Conduct, including the multiple sub-sections of each standard.	☐

PREFACE

The *Standards of Practice Handbook* (*Handbook*) provides guidance to the people who grapple with real ethical dilemmas in the investment profession on a daily basis; the *Handbook* addresses the professional intersection where theory meets practice and where the concept of ethical behavior crosses from the abstract to the concrete. The *Handbook* is intended for a diverse and global audience: CFA Institute members navigating ambiguous ethical situations; supervisors and direct/indirect reports determining the nature of their responsibilities to each other, to existing and potential clients, and to the broader financial markets; and candidates preparing for the Chartered Financial Analyst (CFA) examinations.

Recent events in the global financial markets have tested the ethical mettle of financial market participants, including CFA Institute members. The standards taught in the CFA Program and by which CFA Institute members and candidates must abide represent timeless ethical principles and professional conduct for all market conditions. Through adherence to these standards, which continue to serve as the model for ethical behavior in the investment profession globally, each market participant does his or her part to improve the integrity and efficient operations of the financial markets.

The *Handbook* provides guidance in understanding the interconnectedness of the principles and provisions of the Code of Ethics and Standards of Professional Conduct (Code and Standards). Individually, the principles outline the high level of ethical conduct required from CFA Institute members and candidates. However, applying the principles individually may not capture the complexity of ethical requirements related to the investment industry. The Code and Standards should be viewed and interpreted as an interwoven tapestry of ethical requirements. Through members' and candidates' adherence to these principles as a whole, the integrity of and trust in the capital markets are improved.

Evolution of the CFA Institute Code of Ethics and Standards of Professional Conduct

Generally, changes to the Code and Standards over the years have been minor. CFA Institute has revised the language of the Code and Standards and occasionally added a new standard to address a prominent issue of the day. For instance, in 1992, CFA Institute added the standard addressing performance presentation to the existing list of standards.

Major changes came in 2005 with the ninth edition of the *Handbook*. CFA Institute adopted new standards, revised some existing standards, and reorganized the standards. The revisions were intended to clarify the requirements of the Code and Standards and effectively convey to its global membership what constitutes "best practice" in a number of areas relating to the investment profession.

The Code and Standards must be regularly reviewed and updated if they are to remain effective and continue to represent the highest ethical standards in the global investment industry. CFA Institute strongly believes that revisions of the Code and Standards are not undertaken for cosmetic change but to add value by addressing legitimate concerns and improving comprehension.

Changes to the Code and Standards have far-reaching implications for the CFA Institute membership, the CFA Program, and the investment industry as a whole. CFA Institute members and candidates are *required* to adhere to the Code and Standards. In addition, the Code and Standards are increasingly being adopted, in whole or in part, by firms and regulatory authorities. Their relevance goes well beyond CFA Institute members and candidates.

Standards of Practice Handbook

The periodic revisions to the Code and Standards have come in conjunction with updates of the *Standards of Practice Handbook*. The *Handbook* is the fundamental element of the ethics education effort of CFA Institute and the primary resource for guidance in interpreting and implementing the Code and Standards. The *Handbook* seeks to educate members and candidates on how to apply the Code and Standards to their professional lives and thereby benefit their clients, employers, and the investing public in general. The *Handbook* explains the purpose of the Code and Standards and how they apply in a variety of situations. The sections discuss and amplify each standard and suggest procedures to prevent violations.

Examples in the "Application of the Standard" sections are meant to illustrate how the standard applies to hypothetical but factual situations. The names contained in the examples are fictional and are not meant to refer to any actual person or entity. Unless otherwise stated, individuals in each example are CFA

Institute members and holders of the CFA designation. Because factual circumstances vary so widely and often involve gray areas, the explanatory material and examples are not intended to be all inclusive. Many examples set forth in the application sections involve standards that have legal counterparts; *members are strongly urged to discuss with their supervisors and legal and compliance departments the content of the Code and Standards and the members' general obligations under the Code and Standards.*

CFA Institute recognizes that the presence of any set of ethical standards may create a false sense of security unless the documents are fully understood, enforced, and made a meaningful part of everyday professional activities. The *Handbook* is intended to provide a useful frame of reference that suggests ethical professional behavior in the investment decision-making process. This selection cannot cover every contingency or circumstance, however, and it does not attempt to do so. The development and interpretation of the Code and Standards are evolving processes; the Code and Standards will be subject to continuing refinement.

Summary of Changes in the Tenth Edition

The comprehensive review of the Code and Standards in 2005 resulted in principle requirements that remain applicable today. The review carried out for the tenth edition focused on updates to the guidance and examples within the *Handbook*. In the tenth edition, the changes relate primarily to the growing diversity of the CFA Institute membership and CFA Program candidate base and aim to make specific guidance easier to understand.

Clarification of Standard III(A)

Standard III(A) Duties to Clients—Loyalty, Prudence, and Care was shortened to improve clarity. The third sentence was deleted to avoid possible misinterpretations of the members' or candidates' required duties to their clients. The principle contained in the deleted sentence already has been established in Standard I(A) regarding the responsibility to adhere to the most strict legal, regulatory, or CFA Institute requirements.

> Deletion:
> In relationships with clients, Members and Candidates must determine applicable fiduciary duty and must comply with such duty to persons and interests to whom it is owed.

Why Ethics Matters

A new section was added to the *Handbook* to broaden the discussion of the importance of ethics to the investment profession. The chapter addresses market integrity and sustainability, the role of CFA Institute, and the importance of ongoing awareness of and education about changes in the investment industry.

Text Revisions

As the investment industry and, as a result, CFA Institute membership have become more global, the use of English that can be easily understood and translated into different languages has become critical. Therefore, in some places, CFA Institute has eliminated, modified, or added language for clarity, even though it is not the intent to change the meaning of a particular provision.

Guidance Table

To keep the *Handbook* as a primary resource for members and candidates as they tackle ethical dilemmas, bulleted tables were added to help the reader locate the guidance within a standard that is most applicable to the situations that may occur in daily professional life. The Code and Standards must not be viewed as something solely to be learned to pass the CFA examinations; its principles are intended to play an active role in everyday decision making.

Example Highlight

In a continued effort to assist readers in locating examples of situations similar to issues they are facing, this update includes a brief descriptive heading for each example in the "Application of the Standard" sections. The heading notes the principle being addressed or the nature of the example.

Cross-Standard Examples

To further highlight the applicability of multiple standards to a single set of facts, some examples are used several times. The single or slightly modified facts are accompanied by comments directed to the standard in question. The other standards using the same example are noted at the end of the comments.

CFA Institute Professional Conduct Program

All CFA Institute members and candidates enrolled in the CFA Program are required to comply with the Code and Standards. The CFA Institute Board of Governors maintains oversight and responsibility for the Professional Conduct Program (PCP), which, in conjunction with the Disciplinary Review Committee (DRC), is responsible for enforcement of the Code and Standards. The CFA Institute Bylaws and Rules of Procedure for Proceedings Related to Professional Conduct (Rules of Procedure) form the basic structure for enforcing the Code and Standards. The Rules of Procedure are based on two primary principles: 1) fair process to the member and candidate and 2) confidentiality of proceedings.

Professional Conduct staff, under the direction of the CFA Institute Designated Officer, conducts professional conduct inquiries. Several circumstances can prompt an inquiry. First, members and candidates must self-disclose on the annual Professional Conduct Statement all matters that question their professional conduct, such as involvement in civil litigation or a criminal investigation or being the subject of a written complaint. Second, written complaints received by Professional Conduct staff can bring about an investigation. Third, CFA Institute staff may become aware of questionable conduct by a member or candidate through the media or another public source. Fourth, CFA examination proctors may submit a violation report for any candidate suspected to have compromised his or her professional conduct during the examination.

When an inquiry is initiated, the Professional Conduct staff conducts an investigation that may include requesting a written explanation from the member or candidate; interviewing the member or candidate, complaining parties, and third parties; and collecting documents and records in support of its investigation. The Designated Officer, upon reviewing the material obtained during the investigation, may conclude the inquiry with no disciplinary sanction, issue a cautionary letter, or continue proceedings to discipline the member or candidate. If the Designated Officer finds that a violation of the Code and Standards occurred, the Designated Officer proposes a disciplinary sanction, which may be rejected or accepted by the member or candidate.

If the member or candidate does not accept the proposed sanction, the matter is referred to a hearing panel composed of DRC members and CFA Institute member volunteers affiliated with the DRC. The hearing panel reviews materials and presentations from the Designated Officer and from the member or candidate. The hearing panel's task is to determine whether a violation of the Code and Standards occurred and, if so, what sanction should be imposed.

Sanctions imposed by CFA Institute may have significant consequences; they include public censure, suspension of membership and use of the CFA designation, and revocation of the CFA charter. Candidates enrolled in the CFA Program who have violated the Code and Standards may be suspended from further participation in the CFA Program.

Adoption of the Code and Standards

The Code and Standards apply to individual members of CFA Institute and candidates in the CFA Program. CFA Institute does encourage firms to adopt the Code and Standards, however, as part of a firm's code of ethics. Those who claim compliance should fully understand the requirements of each of the principles of the Code and Standards.

Once a party—nonmember or firm—ensures its code of ethics meets the principles of the Code and Standards, that party should make the following statement whenever claiming compliance:

> "[Insert name of party] claims compliance with the CFA Institute Code of Ethics and Standards of Professional Conduct. This claim has not been verified by CFA Institute."

CFA Institute welcomes public acknowledgement, when appropriate, that firms are complying with the CFA Institute Code of Ethics and Standards of Professional Conduct and encourages firms to notify us of the adoption plans. For firms that would like to distribute the Code and Standards to clients and potential clients, attractive one-page copies of the Code and Standards, including translations, are available on the CFA Institute website (www. cfainstitute.org).

CFA Institute has also published the Asset Manager Code of Professional Conduct (AMC), which is designed, in part, to help asset managers comply with the regulations mandating codes of ethics for investment advisers. Whereas the Code and Standards are aimed at individual investment professionals who are members of CFA Institute or candidates in the CFA Program, the AMC was drafted specifically for firms. The AMC provides specific, practical guidelines for asset managers in six areas: loyalty to clients, the investment process, trading, compliance, performance evaluation, and disclosure. The AMC and the appropriate steps to acknowledge adoption or compliance can be found on the CFA Institute website (www.cfainstitute.org).

Acknowledgments

CFA Institute is a not-for-profit organization that is heavily dependent on the expertise and intellectual contributions of member volunteers. Members devote their time as they share a mutual interest in the organization's mission to promote and achieve ethical practice in the investment profession. CFA Institute owes much to the volunteers' abundant generosity and energy in extending ethical integrity.

The CFA Institute Standards of Practice Council (SPC), a group consisting of CFA charterholder volunteers from many different countries, is charged with maintaining and interpreting the Code and Standards and ensuring that they are effective. The SPC draws its membership from a broad spectrum of organizations in the securities field, including brokers, investment advisers, banks, and insurance companies. In most instances, the SPC members have important supervisory responsibilities within their firms.

The SPC continually evaluates the Code and Standards, as well as the guidance in the *Handbook*, to ensure that they are:

▶ representative of high standards of professional conduct;
▶ relevant to the changing nature of the investment profession;
▶ globally applicable;
▶ sufficiently comprehensive, practical, and specific;
▶ enforceable; and
▶ testable for the CFA Program.

The SPC has spent countless hours reviewing and discussing revisions to the Code and Standards and updates to the guidance that makes up the tenth edition of the *Handbook*. Following is a list of the current and former members of the SPC who generously donated their time and energy to this effort.

Christopher C. Loop, CFA, Chair	Toshihiko Saito, CFA, Prior Chair
Karin B. Bonding, CFA	Jinliang Li, CFA
Jean-Francois Bouilly, CFA	Lynn S. Mander, CFA
Terence E. Burns, CFA	James M. Meeth, CFA
Sharon Craggs, CFA	Brian O'Keefe, CFA
Mario Eichenberger, CFA	Guy G. Rutherfurd, Jr., CFA
James E. Hollis, CFA	Sunil B. Singhania, CFA
Samuel B. Jones, CFA	Peng Lian Wee, CFA
Ulrike Kaiser-Boeing, CFA	

The chair and members of the SPC would like to thank the CFA Institute staff who supported this revision for their efforts to keep the process smooth and well organized.

This tenth edition of the *Standards of Practice Handbook* is dedicated to the late Mildred Hermann, who served in a variety of capacities with the CFA Institute predecessor organizations, the Financial Analysts Federation (FAF) and the Association for Investment Management and Research (AIMR). With a work ethic that knew no limits, she possessed an unfailing sense of fairness and uncompromising integrity—attributes she expected in all investment professionals.

As FAF/AIMR staff representative to the predecessor committees to the Standards of Practice Council, Mildred was instrumental in the development of the first edition of the *Standards of Practice Handbook* and continued her direct involvement with the four subsequent editions published up to her retirement in 1991. She proved to be a passionate and skilled technician whose prodigious intellect, range of knowledge, and seasoned judgment fused seamlessly to create a deeply informed understanding of regulatory trends and their implications for FAF/AIMR members and the investment profession at large.

Mildred's tenure was marked by her special brand of leadership, vision, and commitment in promoting the highest standards of ethical conduct and professional practice. As Rossa O'Reilly, CFA, former chair of the Board of Governors, aptly observed at her retirement, "Very few professionals have contributed as much or worked as diligently toward furthering the goals of the profession of investment analysis and portfolio management as Mildred Hermann." For those of us fortunate enough to have worked with Mildred, she is fondly remembered as a unique talent, quick wit, valued colleague, model of human decency, and a humble, beloved friend.

WHY ETHICS MATTERS

The adherence of investment professionals to ethical practices benefits all market participants and increases investor confidence in global financial markets. Clients are reassured that the investment professionals they hire operate with the clients' best interests in mind, and investment professionals benefit from the more efficient and transparent operation of the market that integrity promotes. Ethical practices instill public trust in markets and support the development of markets. Sound ethics is fundamental to capital markets and the investment profession.

The first decade of the 21st century has been but one of many times of crisis for the investment industry. This period, unfortunately, has encompassed many instances of unethical behavior—by business executives and investment professionals. The newspapers and airwaves have brimmed with a succession of accounting frauds and manipulations, Ponzi schemes, insider trading, and other misdeeds. Each case has resulted in heavy financial losses and stained reputations. Equally important has been the terrible toll these actions have taken on investors' trust. Trust is hard earned and easily lost; corporations and individuals can safeguard themselves by committing to the highest standards of ethics and professional conduct.

Ethics is not merely a virtue to be demonstrated by CFA Institute members and candidates. Ethics must permeate all levels of our profession. Serving the best interests of the investing clients and employers lies at the heart of what collectively must be done to ensure a sense of trust and integrity in the financial markets. Although the drive to achieve such a lofty collective objective is critically important, the drive must ultimately start in the workplace. It is imperative that top management foster a strong culture of ethics not just among CFA charterholders and candidates but among all staff members who are involved directly or indirectly with client relations, the investment process, record keeping, and beyond. In such a culture, all participants can see clear evidence of how extremely important ethics is when woven into the fabric of an organization, or in other words, all participants in the process will know that ethics genuinely matters.

Ethics and CFA Institute

An important goal of CFA Institute is to ensure that the organization and its members develop, promote, and follow the highest ethical standards in the investment industry. The CFA Institute Code of Ethics (Code) and Standards of Professional Conduct (Standards) are the foundation supporting the organization's quest to advance the interests of the global investment community by establishing and maintaining the highest standards of professional excellence and integrity. The Code is a set of principles that define the professional conduct CFA Institute expects from its members and candidates in the CFA Program. The Code works in tandem with the Standards, which outline conduct that constitutes fair and ethical business practices.

For more than 40 years, CFA Institute members and candidates in the CFA Program have been required to abide by the organization's Code and Standards. Periodically, CFA Institute has revised and updated its Code and Standards to ensure that they remain relevant to the changing nature of the investment profession and representative of the "highest standard" of professional conduct. Recent events have highlighted unethical actions in the areas of governance, investment ratings, financial product packaging and distribution, and outright investment fraud. Finance is a sophisticated and interconnected global industry; new investment opportunities and new financial instruments to make the most of those opportunities are constantly developing. Although the investment world has become a far more complex place since the first publication of the *Handbook*, distinguishing right from wrong remains the paramount principle of the Code and Standards.

Ethics and Market Sustainability

The increasingly interconnected nature of global finance brings to the fore an added consideration that was, perhaps, less relevant in years past. This consideration is that of *market sustainability*. In addition to committing to the highest levels of ethical behavior, today's investment professional, when making decisions, should consider the long-term health of the market as a whole. As recent events have demonstrated, the sum of apparently isolated and unrelated decisions, however innocuous when considered on an individual basis, when aggregated, can precipitate a market crisis. In an interconnected global economy and marketplace, each participant should strive to be aware of how his or her actions or products may be distributed to, used in, or have an impact on other regions or countries.

The much-discussed credit crisis that buffeted global financial markets highlights these concerns. Relying on esoteric structures, certain banks developed financial instruments that extended credit to consumers and companies that otherwise would not have had access to those monies. Clients purchased these instruments in a quest for yield in a low-interest-rate environment. But some of the higher-risk borrowers could not afford their loans and were not able to refinance them. Defaults soared, and some of the instruments collapsed. Many of the institutions that had purchased the instruments or retained stakes in them had not completed sufficient diligence on the instruments' structures and suffered horrendous losses. Established institutions toppled into ruin, wrecking lives and reputations. Had members of the investment profession considered with greater foresight the question of market sustainability in tandem with the needs and expectations of their clients, the magnitude of the crisis might have been lessened.

CFA Institute encourages all members and candidates to consider in their investment decision-making process the promotion and protection of the global financial markets as an aspect of the broader context of the application of the Code and Standards. Those in positions of authority have a special responsibility to consider the broader context of market sustainability in their development and approval of corporate policies, particularly those involving risk management and product development. In addition, corporate compensation strategies should not encourage otherwise ethically sound individuals to engage in unethical or questionable conduct for financial gain. Ethics, sustainability, and properly functioning capital markets are components of the same concept of protecting the interests of all.

Ethics and Regulation

Regulation alone will never fully anticipate and eliminate the causes of financial crises. Some individuals will try to and may well be able to circumvent the regulatory rules. Only strong ethical principles, at the level of the individual and the level of the firm, will limit abuses. Knowing the rules or regulations to apply in a particular situation, although important, is not sufficient to ensure ethical decision making. Individuals must be able both to recognize areas that are prone to ethical pitfalls and to identify those circumstances and influences that can impair ethical judgment.

The Code and Standards, as well as other voluntary ethical standards of the CFA Institute (e.g., the Global Investment Performance Standards, Soft Dollar Standards, Trade Management Guidelines, Research Objectivity Standards, and the Asset Manager Code of Professional Conduct), offer a foundation to adopt and build on in promoting an ethical corporate culture. The adoption of these standards is not limited to investment professionals and their firms affiliated with CFA Institute. National regulators might consider the *Handbook*'s guidance in fostering ethical identities within organizations and national systems.

In the future, the nature and level of regulation will depend on how companies comply with the rules already in place. Greater adherence to the spirit of current rules may well require fewer regulatory changes. Conversely, continued short-sightedness and disregard for the outcomes of particularly adverse practices may necessitate more stringent regulation. In this respect, the investment industry can have a positive effect on evolving regulation and, in that way, on its own operational environment. Through continuing education, investment professionals can reinforce and evaluate their personal ethical conduct.

Ethics Education and Awareness

New challenges will continually arise for members and candidates in applying the Code and Standards because ethical dilemmas are not unambiguously right or wrong. The dilemma exists because the choice between right and wrong is not always clear. Even well-intentioned investment professionals can find themselves in circumstances that may tempt them to cut corners. Situational influences can overpower the best of intentions.

To assist members and candidates in adhering to the principles of the Code and Standards, CFA Institute has made a significant commitment to provide members and candidates with the resources to extend and deepen their understanding of the principles' applications. The publications from CFA Institute offer a wealth of material. *CFA Magazine* contains a section on ethics in most issues. The magazine contains not only vignettes describing potentially questionable situations and guidance related to the Code and Standards but also frequent articles on broad topics relevant to current and developing ethical issues. The *Financial Analysts Journal* also publishes articles related to ethics and professional conduct. Archived issues of these publications are available on the CFA Institute website (www.cfainstitute.org).

CFA Institute includes presentations on ethics in many of its sponsored conferences. These presentations vary as widely as the articles do, from staff-led training courses to discussion of market events by outside professionals with a view toward ethical education. These presentations highlight current trends and how improved ethical decision making may lead to different or even preferred outcomes in the future.

These various resources are available to members and candidates and the investment community at large. Those unable to attend an actual conference will find podcasts, webcasts, or transcripts available on the CFA Institute website (www.cfainstitute.org). Conferences and the presentations offered in the *CFA Institute Conference Proceedings Quarterly* also provide continuing education credits for those members participating in the program.

The Research Foundation of CFA Institute, a not-for-profit organization established to promote the development and dissemination of relevant research for investment practitioners worldwide, has contributed to continued ethical education through the commission and publication in 2007 of *The Psychology of Ethics in the Finance and Investment Industry*. In this monograph, Thomas Oberlechner, professor of psychology at Webster University in Vienna, discusses the role psychology plays in individuals' ethical or unethical decision making. He concludes that understanding the dynamic nature of ethical decision making allows us to understand why unethical decisions can be made by anyone and, hence, how to manage our ethical conduct.

Markets function to an important extent on trust. Recent events have shown the fragility of this foundation and the devastating consequences that can ensue when this foundation is fundamentally questioned. Investment professionals should remain mindful of the long-term health of financial markets and incorporate this concern for the market's sustainability in their investment decision making. CFA Institute and the Standards of Practice Council hope this edition of the *Handbook* will assist and guide investment professionals in meeting the ethical demands of the highly interconnected global capital markets.

CFA INSTITUTE CODE OF ETHICS AND STANDARDS OF PROFESSIONAL CONDUCT

Preamble

The CFA Institute Code of Ethics and Standards of Professional Conduct are fundamental to the values of CFA Institute and essential to achieving its mission to lead the investment profession globally by setting high standards of education, integrity, and professional excellence. High ethical standards are critical to maintaining the public's trust in financial markets and in the investment profession. Since their creation in the 1960s, the Code and Standards have promoted the integrity of CFA Institute members and served as a model for measuring the ethics of investment professionals globally, regardless of job function, cultural differences, or local laws and regulations. All CFA Institute members (including holders of the Chartered Financial Analyst [CFA] designation) and CFA candidates must abide by the Code and Standards and are encouraged to notify their employer of this responsibility. Violations may result in disciplinary sanctions by CFA Institute. Sanctions can include revocation of membership, revocation of candidacy in the CFA Program, and revocation of the right to use the CFA designation.

The Code of Ethics

Members of CFA Institute (including CFA charterholders) and candidates for the CFA designation ("Members and Candidates") must:

▶ Act with integrity, competence, diligence, respect, and in an ethical manner with the public, clients, prospective clients, employers, employees, colleagues in the investment profession, and other participants in the global capital markets.

▶ Place the integrity of the investment profession and the interests of clients above their own personal interests.

▶ Use reasonable care and exercise independent professional judgment when conducting investment analysis, making investment recommendations, taking investment actions, and engaging in other professional activities.

▶ Practice and encourage others to practice in a professional and ethical manner that will reflect credit on themselves and the profession.

▶ Promote the integrity of and uphold the rules governing capital markets.

▶ Maintain and improve their professional competence and strive to maintain and improve the competence of other investment professionals.

Standards of Professional Conduct

I. PROFESSIONALISM

A. Knowledge of the Law. Members and Candidates must understand and comply with all applicable laws, rules, and regulations (including the CFA Institute Code of Ethics and Standards of Professional Conduct) of any government, regulatory organization, licensing agency, or professional association governing their professional activities. In the event of conflict, Members and Candidates must comply with the more strict law, rule, or regulation. Members and Candidates must not knowingly participate or assist in and must dissociate from any violation of such laws, rules, or regulations.

B. Independence and Objectivity. Members and Candidates must use reasonable care and judgment to achieve and maintain independence and objectivity in their professional activities. Members and Candidates must not offer, solicit, or accept any gift, benefit, compensation, or consideration that reasonably could be expected to compromise their own or another's independence and objectivity.

C. Misrepresentation. Members and Candidates must not knowingly make any misrepresentations relating to investment analysis, recommendations, actions, or other professional activities.

D. Misconduct. Members and Candidates must not engage in any professional conduct involving dishonesty, fraud, or deceit or commit any act that reflects adversely on their professional reputation, integrity, or competence.

II. INTEGRITY OF CAPITAL MARKETS

A. Material Nonpublic Information. Members and Candidates who possess material nonpublic information that could affect the value of an investment must not act or cause others to act on the information.

B. Market Manipulation. Members and Candidates must not engage in practices that distort prices or artificially inflate trading volume with the intent to mislead market participants.

III. DUTIES TO CLIENTS

A. Loyalty, Prudence, and Care. Members and Candidates have a duty of loyalty to their clients and must act with reasonable care and exercise prudent judgment. Members and Candidates must act for the benefit of their clients and place their clients' interests before their employer's or their own interests.

B. Fair Dealing. Members and Candidates must deal fairly and objectively with all clients when providing investment analysis, making investment recommendations, taking investment action, or engaging in other professional activities.

C. Suitability.

1. When Members and Candidates are in an advisory relationship with a client, they must:

   a. Make a reasonable inquiry into a client's or prospective client's investment experience, risk and return objectives, and financial constraints prior to making any investment recommendation or taking investment action and must reassess and update this information regularly.

   b. Determine that an investment is suitable to the client's financial situation and consistent with the client's written objectives, mandates, and constraints before making an investment recommendation or taking investment action.

   c. Judge the suitability of investments in the context of the client's total portfolio.

2. When Members and Candidates are responsible for managing a portfolio to a specific mandate, strategy, or style, they must make only investment recommendations or take only investment actions that are consistent with the stated objectives and constraints of the portfolio.

D. Performance Presentation. When communicating investment performance information, Members and Candidates must make reasonable efforts to ensure that it is fair, accurate, and complete.

E. Preservation of Confidentiality. Members and Candidates must keep information about current, former, and prospective clients confidential unless:

1. The information concerns illegal activities on the part of the client or prospective client,

2. Disclosure is required by law, or

3. The client or prospective client permits disclosure of the information.

IV. DUTIES TO EMPLOYERS

A. Loyalty. In matters related to their employment, Members and Candidates must act for the benefit of their employer and not deprive their employer of the advantage of their skills and abilities, divulge confidential information, or otherwise cause harm to their employer.

B. Additional Compensation Arrangements. Members and Candidates must not accept gifts, benefits, compensation, or consideration that competes with or might reasonably be expected to create a conflict of interest with their employer's interest unless they obtain written consent from all parties involved.

C. Responsibilities of Supervisors. Members and Candidates must make reasonable efforts to detect and prevent violations of applicable laws, rules, regulations, and the Code and Standards by anyone subject to their supervision or authority.

V. INVESTMENT ANALYSIS, RECOMMENDATIONS, AND ACTIONS

A. Diligence and Reasonable Basis. Members and Candidates must:

1. Exercise diligence, independence, and thoroughness in analyzing investments, making investment recommendations, and taking investment actions.

2. Have a reasonable and adequate basis, supported by appropriate research and investigation, for any investment analysis, recommendation, or action.

B. Communication with Clients and Prospective Clients. Members and Candidates must:

1. Disclose to clients and prospective clients the basic format and general principles of the investment processes they use to analyze investments, select securities, and construct portfolios and must promptly disclose any changes that might materially affect those processes.

2. Use reasonable judgment in identifying which factors are important to their investment analyses, recommendations, or actions and include those factors in communications with clients and prospective clients.

3. Distinguish between fact and opinion in the presentation of investment analysis and recommendations.

C. Record Retention. Members and Candidates must develop and maintain appropriate records to support their investment analyses, recommendations, actions, and other investment-related communications with clients and prospective clients.

VI. CONFLICTS OF INTEREST

A. Disclosure of Conflicts. Members and Candidates must make full and fair disclosure of all matters that could reasonably be expected to impair their independence and objectivity or interfere with respective duties to their clients, prospective clients, and employer. Members and Candidates must ensure that such disclosures are prominent, are delivered in plain language, and communicate the relevant information effectively.

B. Priority of Transactions. Investment transactions for clients and employers must have priority over investment transactions in which a Member or Candidate is the beneficial owner.

C. Referral Fees. Members and Candidates must disclose to their employer, clients, and prospective clients, as appropriate, any compensation, consideration, or benefit received from or paid to others for the recommendation of products or services.

VII. RESPONSIBILITIES AS A CFA INSTITUTE MEMBER OR CFA CANDIDATE

A. Conduct as Members and Candidates in the CFA Program. Members and Candidates must not engage in any conduct that compromises the reputation or integrity of CFA Institute or the CFA designation or the integrity, validity, or security of the CFA examinations.

B. Reference to CFA Institute, the CFA Designation, and the CFA Program. When referring to CFA Institute, CFA Institute membership, the CFA designation, or candidacy in the CFA Program, Members and Candidates must not misrepresent or exaggerate the meaning or implications of membership in CFA Institute, holding the CFA designation, or candidacy in the CFA program.

GUIDANCE FOR STANDARDS I–VII

LEARNING OUTCOMES

The candidate should be able to:	Mastery
a. demonstrate a thorough knowledge of the Code of Ethics and Standards of Professional Conduct by interpreting the Code and Standards in various situations involving issues of professional integrity;	☐
b. recommend practices and procedures designed to prevent violations of the Code of Ethics and Standards of Professional Conduct.	☐

STANDARD I—PROFESSIONALISM

A. Knowledge of the Law

Members and Candidates must understand and comply with all applicable laws, rules, and regulations (including the CFA Institute Code of Ethics and Standards of Professional Conduct) of any government, regulatory organization, licensing agency, or professional association governing their professional activities. In the event of conflict, Members and Candidates must comply with the more strict law, rule, or regulation. Members and Candidates must not knowingly participate or assist in and must dissociate from any violation of such laws, rules, or regulations.

Guidance

Highlights:

▶ *Relationship between the Code and Standards and Applicable Law*
▶ *Participation in or Association with Violations by Others*
▶ *Investment Products and Applicable Laws*

Members and candidates must understand the applicable laws and regulations of all the countries in which they trade securities or provide investment advice or other investment services. On the basis of their understanding, members and candidates must comply with the laws and regulations that directly govern their work. When questions arise, members and candidates should know their firm's policies and procedures for accessing compliance guidance. This standard does not require members and candidates to become experts, however, in compliance. Additionally, investment professionals are not required to have detailed knowledge of or be experts on all the laws that could potentially govern the member's or candidate's activities.

During times of changing regulations, members and candidates must remain vigilant in maintaining their knowledge of the requirements for their professional activities. The financial and ethical missteps in the first decade of the 21st century created an environment for swift and wide-ranging regulatory changes. As new local, regional, and global requirements are updated, members, candidates, and their firms must adjust their procedures and practices to remain in compliance.

Relationship between the Code and Standards and Applicable Law

Some members or candidates may live, work, or provide investment services to clients living in a country that has no law or regulation governing a particular action or that has laws or regulations that differ from the requirements of the Code and Standards. When applicable law and the Code and Standards require different conduct, members and candidates must follow the more strict of the applicable law or the Code and Standards.

"Applicable law" is the law that governs the member's or candidate's conduct. Which law applies will depend on the particular facts and circumstances of each case. The "more strict" law or regulation is the law or regulation that imposes greater restrictions on the action of the member or candidate or calls for the member or candidate to exert a greater degree of action that protects the interests of investors. For example, applicable law or regulation may not require members and candidates to disclose referral fees received from or paid to others for the recommendation of investment products or services. Because the Code and Standards impose this obligation, however, members and candidates must disclose the existence of such fees.

Members and candidates must adhere to the following principles:

▶ Members and candidates must comply with applicable law or regulation related to their professional activities.

▶ Members and candidates must not engage in conduct that constitutes a violation of the Code and Standards, even though it may otherwise be legal.

▶ In the absence of any applicable law or regulation or when the Code and Standards impose a higher degree of responsibility than applicable laws and regulations, members and candidates must adhere to the Code and Standards. Applications of these principles are outlined in Exhibit 1.

CFA Institute members are obligated to abide by the CFA Institute Articles of Incorporation, Bylaws, Code of Ethics, Standards of Professional Conduct,

Rules of Procedure, Membership Agreement, and other applicable rules promulgated by CFA Institute, all as amended from time to time. CFA candidates who are not members must also abide by these documents (except for the Membership Agreement) as well as rules and regulations related to the administration of the CFA examination, the Candidate Responsibility Statement, and the Candidate Pledge.

Participation in or Association with Violations by Others

Members and candidates are responsible for violations in which they *knowingly* participate or assist. Although members and candidates are presumed to have knowledge of all applicable laws, rules, and regulations, CFA Institute acknowledges that members may not recognize violations if they are not aware of all the facts giving rise to the violations. Standard I(A) applies when members and candidates know or should know that their conduct may contribute to a violation of applicable laws, rules, regulations, or the Code and Standards.

If a member or candidate has reasonable grounds to believe that imminent or ongoing client or employer activities are illegal or unethical, the member or candidate must dissociate, or separate, from the activity. In extreme cases, dissociation may require a member or candidate to leave his or her employment. Members and candidates may take the following intermediate steps to dissociate from ethical violations of others when direct discussions with the person or persons committing the violation are unsuccessful. The first step should be to attempt to stop the behavior by bringing it to the attention of the employer through a supervisor or the firm's compliance department. If this attempt is unsuccessful, then members and candidates have a responsibility to step away and dissociate from the activity. Dissociation practices will differ on the basis of the member's or candidate's role in the investment industry. It may include removing one's name from written reports or recommendations, asking for a different assignment, or refusing to accept a new client or continue to advise a current client. Inaction combined with continuing association with those involved in illegal or unethical conduct may be construed as participation or assistance in the illegal or unethical conduct.

CFA Institute strongly encourages members and candidates to report potential violations of the Code and Standards committed by fellow members and candidates. Although a failure to report is less likely to be construed as a violation than a failure to dissociate from unethical conduct, the impact of inactivity on the integrity of capital markets can be significant. Although the Code and Standards do not compel members and candidates to report violations to their governmental or regulatory organizations unless such disclosure is mandatory under applicable law, such disclosure may be prudent under certain circumstances. Members and candidates should consult their legal and compliance advisers for guidance.

Additionally, CFA Institute encourages members, nonmembers, clients, and the investing public to report violations of the Code and Standards by CFA Institute members or CFA candidates by submitting a complaint in writing to the CFA Institute Professional Conduct Program via e-mail (pcprogram@cfainstitute.org) or the CFA Institute website (www.cfainstitute.org).

Investment Products and Applicable Laws

Members and candidates involved in creating or maintaining investment services or investment products or packages of securities and/or derivatives should be mindful of where these products or packages will be sold as well as their places of origination. The applicable laws and regulations of the countries or regions of origination and expected sale should be understood by those responsible for the supervision of the services or creation and maintenance of the products or packages. Members and candidates should make reasonable efforts to review whether associated firms that are distributing products or services developed by their employing firm also abide by the laws and regulations of the countries and regions of distribution. Members and candidates should undertake the necessary due diligence when transacting cross-border business to understand the multiple applicable laws and regulations in order to protect the reputation of their firm and themselves.

EXHIBIT 1	Global Application of the Code and Standards

Members and candidates who practice in multiple jurisdictions may be subject to varied securities laws and regulations. If applicable law is stricter than the requirements of the Code and Standards, members and candidates must adhere to applicable law; otherwise, they must adhere to the Code and Standards. The following chart provides illustrations involving a member who may be subject to the securities laws and regulations of three different types of countries:

NS: country with no securities laws or regulations
LS: country with *less* strict securities laws and regulations than the Code and Standards
MS: country with *more* strict securities laws and regulations than the Code and Standards

Applicable Law	Duties	Explanation
Member resides in NS country, does business in LS country; LS law applies.	Member must adhere to the Code and Standards.	Because applicable law is less strict than the Code and Standards, the member must adhere to the Code and Standards.
Member resides in NS country, does business in MS country; MS law applies.	Member must adhere to the law of MS country.	Because applicable law is stricter than the Code and Standards, member must adhere to the more strict applicable law.
Member resides in LS country, does business in NS country; LS law applies.	Member must adhere to the Code and Standards.	Because applicable law is less strict than the Code and Standards, member must adhere to the Code and Standards.
Member resides in LS country, does business in MS country; MS law applies.	Member must adhere to the law of MS country.	Because applicable law is stricter than the Code and Standards, member must adhere to the more strict applicable law.

(Exhibit continued on next page . . .)

EXHIBIT 1   (continued)

Applicable Law	Duties	Explanation
Member resides in LS country, does business in NS country; LS law applies, but it states that law of locality where business is conducted governs.	Member must adhere to the Code and Standards.	Because applicable law states that the law of the locality where the business is conducted governs and there is no local law, the member must adhere to the Code and Standards.
Member resides in LS country, does business in MS country; LS law applies, but it states that law of locality where business is conducted governs.	Member must adhere to the law of MS country.	Because applicable law of the locality where the business is conducted governs and local law is stricter than the Code and Standards, member must adhere to the more strict applicable law.
Member resides in MS country, does business in LS country; MS law applies.	Member must adhere to the law of MS country.	Because applicable law is stricter than the Code and Standards, member must adhere to the more strict applicable law.
Member resides in MS country, does business in LS country; MS law applies, but it states that law of locality where business is conducted governs.	Member must adhere to the Code and Standards.	Because applicable law states that the law of the locality where the business is conducted governs and local law is less strict than the Code and Standards, member must adhere to the Code and Standards.
Member resides in MS country, does business in LS country with a client who is a citizen of LS country; MS law applies, but it states that the law of the client's home country governs.	Member must adhere to the Code and Standards.	Because applicable law states that the law of the client's home country governs (which is less strict than the Code and Standards), member must adhere to the Code and Standards.
Member resides in MS country, does business in LS country with a client who is a citizen of MS country; MS law applies, but it states that the law of the client's home country governs.	Member must adhere to the law of MS country.	Because applicable law states that the law of the client's home country governs and the law of the client's home country is stricter than the Code and Standards, the member must adhere to the more strict applicable law.

Recommended Procedures for Compliance

Members and Candidates

Suggested methods by which members and candidates can acquire and maintain understanding of applicable laws, rules, and regulations include the following:

▶ *Stay informed*: Members and candidates should establish or encourage their employers to establish a procedure by which employees are regularly informed about changes in applicable laws, rules, regulations, and case law. In many instances, the employer's compliance department or legal counsel can provide such information in the form of memorandums distributed to employees in the organization. Also, participation in an internal or external continuing education program is a practical method of staying current.

▶ *Review procedures*: Members and candidates should review, or encourage their employers to review, the firm's written compliance procedures on a regular basis to ensure that the procedures reflect current law and provide adequate guidance to employees about what is permissible conduct under the law and/or the Code and Standards. Recommended compliance procedures for specific items of the Code and Standards are discussed in this *Handbook* in the "Guidance" sections associated with each standard.

▶ *Maintain current files*: Members and candidates should maintain or encourage their employers to maintain readily accessible current reference copies of applicable statutes, rules, regulations, and important cases.

Distribution Area Laws

Members and candidates should make reasonable efforts to understand the applicable laws—both country and regional—for the countries and regions where their investment products are developed and are most likely to be distributed to clients.

Legal Counsel

When in doubt about the appropriate action to undertake, it is recommended that a member or candidate seek the advice of compliance personnel or legal counsel concerning legal requirements. If a potential violation is being committed by a fellow employee, it may also be prudent for the member or candidate to seek the advice of the firm's compliance department or legal counsel.

Dissociation

When dissociating from an activity that violates the Code and Standards, members and candidates should document the violation and urge their firms to attempt to persuade the perpetrator(s) to cease such conduct. To dissociate from the conduct, a member or candidate may have to resign his or her employment.

Firms

The formality and complexity of compliance procedures for firms depend on the nature and size of the organization and the nature of its investment operations. Members and candidates should encourage their firms to consider the following policies and procedures to support the principles of Standard I(A):

▶ *Develop and/or adopt a code of ethics*: The ethical culture of an organization starts at the top. Members and candidates should encourage their supervisors or managers to adopt a code of ethics. Adhering to a code of ethics facilitates solutions when people face ethical dilemmas and can prevent the need for employees to resort to a "whistleblowing" solution publicly alleging concealed misconduct. CFA Institute has published the *Asset Manager Code of Professional Conduct,* which firms may adopt or use as the basis for their codes (visit www.cfapubs.org/loi/ccb).

▶ *Provide information on applicable laws*: Pertinent information that highlights applicable laws and regulations might be distributed to employees or made available in a central location. Information sources might include primary information developed by the relevant government, governmental agencies, regulatory organizations, licensing agencies, and professional associations (e.g., from their websites); law firm memorandums or newsletters; and association memorandums or publications (e.g., *CFA Magazine*).

▶ *Establish procedures for reporting violations*: Firms might provide written protocols for reporting suspected violations of laws, regulations, or company policies.

Application of the Standard

Example 1 (Notification of Known Violations): Michael Allen works for a brokerage firm and is responsible for an underwriting of securities. A company official gives Allen information indicating that the financial statements Allen filed with the regulator overstate the issuer's earnings. Allen seeks the advice of the brokerage firm's general counsel, who states that it would be difficult for the regulator to prove that Allen has been involved in any wrongdoing.

Comment: Although it is recommended that members and candidates seek the advice of legal counsel, the reliance on such advice does not absolve a member or candidate from the requirement to comply with the law or regulation. Allen should report this situation to his supervisor, seek an independent legal opinion, and determine whether the regulator should be notified of the error.

Example 2 (Dissociating from a Violation): Lawrence Brown's employer, an investment banking firm, is the principal underwriter for an issue of convertible debentures by the Courtney Company. Brown discovers that the Courtney Company has concealed severe third-quarter losses in its foreign operations. The preliminary prospectus has already been distributed.

Comment: Knowing that the preliminary prospectus is misleading, Brown should report his findings to the appropriate supervisory persons in his firm. If the matter is not remedied and Brown's employer does not dissociate from the underwriting, Brown should sever all his connections with the underwriting. Brown should also seek legal advice to determine whether additional reporting or other action should be taken.

Example 3 (Dissociating from a Violation): Kamisha Washington's firm advertises its past performance record by showing the 10-year return of a composite of its client accounts. Washington discovers, however, that the composite omits the performance of accounts that have left the firm during the 10-year period, whereas the description of the composite indicates the inclusion of all firm accounts. This omission has led to an inflated performance figure. Washington is asked to use promotional material that includes the erroneous performance number when soliciting business for the firm.

> *Comment*: Misrepresenting performance is a violation of the Code and Standards. Although she did not calculate the performance herself, Washington would be assisting in violating Standard I(A) if she were to use the inflated performance number when soliciting clients. She must dissociate herself from the activity. If discussing the misleading number with the person responsible is not an option for correcting the problem, she can bring the situation to the attention of her supervisor or the compliance department at her firm. If her firm is unwilling to recalculate performance, she must refrain from using the misleading promotional material and should notify the firm of her reasons. If the firm insists that she use the material, she should consider whether her obligation to dissociate from the activity requires her to seek other employment.

Example 4 (Following the Highest Requirements): James Collins is an investment analyst for a major Wall Street brokerage firm. He works in a developing country with a rapidly modernizing economy and a growing capital market. Local securities laws are minimal—in form and content—and include no punitive prohibitions against insider trading.

> *Comment*: Collins must abide by the requirements of the Code and Standards that might be more strict than the rules of the developing country. He should be aware of the risks that a small market and the absence of a fairly regulated flow of information to the market represent to his ability to obtain information and make timely judgments. He should include this factor in formulating his advice to clients. In handling material nonpublic information that accidentally comes into his possession, he must follow Standard II(A)—Material Nonpublic Information.

Example 5 (Following the Highest Requirements): Laura Jameson works for a multinational investment adviser based in the United States. Jameson lives and works as a registered investment adviser in the tiny, but wealthy, island nation of Karramba. Karramba's securities laws state that no investment adviser registered and working in that country can participate in initial public offerings (IPOs) for the adviser's personal account. Jameson, believing that as a U.S. citizen working for a U.S.-based company she should comply only with U.S. law, has ignored this Karrambian law. In addition, Jameson believes that, as a charterholder, as long as she adheres to the Code and Standards requirement that she disclose her participation in any IPO to her employer and clients when such ownership creates a conflict of interest, she is meeting the highest ethical requirements.

> *Comment*: Jameson is in violation of Standard I(A). As a registered investment adviser in Karramba, Jameson is prevented by Karrambian securities law from participating in IPOs regardless of the law of her home country. In addition, because the law of the country where she is working is stricter than the Code and Standards, she must follow the stricter requirements of the local law rather than the requirements of the Code and Standards.

Example 6 (Laws and Regulations Based on Religious Tenets): Amanda Janney is employed as a fixed-income portfolio manager for a large international firm. She is on a team within her firm that is responsible for creating and managing a fixed-income hedge fund to be sold throughout the firm's distribution centers to high-net-worth clients. Her firm receives expressions of interest from potential clients from the Middle East who are seeking investments that comply with Islamic law. The marketing and promotional materials for the fixed-income hedge fund do not specify whether or not the fund is a suitable investment for an investor seeking compliance with Islamic law. Because the fund is being distributed globally, Janney is concerned about the reputation of the fund and the firm and believes disclosure of whether or not the fund complies with Islamic law could help minimize potential mistakes with placing this investment.

> *Comment*: As the financial market continues to become globalized, members and candidates will need to be aware of the differences between cultural and religious laws and requirements as well as the different governmental laws and regulations. Janney and the firm could be proactive in their efforts to acknowledge areas where the new fund may not be suitable for clients.

Example 7 (Reporting Potential Unethical Actions): Krista Blume is a junior portfolio manager for high-net-worth portfolios at a large global investment manager. She observes a number of new portfolios and relationships coming from a country in Europe where the firm did not have previous business and is told that a broker in that country is responsible for this new business. At a meeting on allocation of research resources to third-party research firms, Blume notes that this broker has been added to the list and is allocated payments for research. However, she knows the portfolios do not invest in securities in the broker's country. And she has not seen any research come from this broker. Blume asks her supervisor about the name being on the list and is told that someone in marketing is receiving the research and that the name being on the list is OK. She believes that what is going on may be that the broker is being paid for new business through the inappropriate research payments and wishes to dissociate from the misconduct.

> *Comment*: Blume should follow the firm's policies and procedures for reporting potential unethical activity, which may include discussions with her supervisor or someone in a designated compliance department. She should communicate her concerns appropriately while advocating for disclosure between the new broker relationship and the research payments.

B. Independence and Objectivity

Members and Candidates must use reasonable care and judgment to achieve and maintain independence and objectivity in their professional activities. Members and Candidates must not offer, solicit, or accept any gift, benefit, compensation, or consideration that reasonably could be expected to compromise their own or another's independence and objectivity.

Guidance

Highlights:

- ▶ *Buy-Side Clients*
- ▶ *Fund Manager Relationships*
- ▶ *Investment Banking Relationships*

▶ *Public Companies*

▶ *Credit Rating Agency Opinions*

▶ *Issuer-Paid Research*

▶ *Travel Funding*

Standard I(B) states the responsibility of CFA Institute members and candidates in the CFA Program to maintain independence and objectivity so that their clients will have the benefit of their work and opinions unaffected by any potential conflict of interest or other circumstance adversely affecting their judgment. Every member and candidate should endeavor to avoid situations that could cause or be perceived to cause a loss of independence or objectivity in recommending investments or taking investment action.

External sources may try to influence the investment process by offering analysts and portfolio managers a variety of benefits. Corporations may seek expanded research coverage; issuers and underwriters may wish to promote new securities offerings; brokers may want to increase commission business; and independent rating agencies may be influenced by the company requesting the rating. Benefits may include gifts, invitations to lavish functions, tickets, favors, or job referrals. One type of benefit is the allocation of shares in oversubscribed IPOs to investment managers for their personal accounts. This practice affords managers the opportunity to make quick profits that may not be available to their clients. Such a practice is prohibited under Standard I(B). Modest gifts and entertainment are acceptable, but special care must be taken by members and candidates to resist subtle and not-so-subtle pressures to act in conflict with the interests of their clients. Best practice dictates that members and candidates reject any offer of gift or entertainment that could be expected to threaten their independence and objectivity.

Receiving a gift, benefit, or consideration from a *client* can be distinguished from gifts given by entities seeking to influence a member or candidate to the detriment of other clients. In a client relationship, the client has already entered some type of compensation arrangement with the member, candidate, or his or her firm. A gift from a client could be considered supplementary compensation. The potential for obtaining influence to the detriment of other clients, although present, is not as great as in situations where no compensation arrangement exists. When possible, prior to accepting "bonuses" or gifts from clients, members and candidates should disclose to their employers such benefits offered by clients. If notification is not possible prior to acceptance, members and candidates must disclose to their employers benefits previously accepted from clients. Disclosure allows the employer of a member or candidate to make an independent determination about the extent to which the gift may affect the member's or candidate's independence and objectivity.

Members and candidates may also come under pressure from their own firms to, for example, issue favorable research reports or recommendations for certain companies with potential or continuing business relationships with the firm. The situation may be aggravated if an executive of the company sits on the bank or investment firm's board and attempts to interfere in investment decision making. Members and candidates acting in a sales or marketing capacity must be especially mindful of their objectivity in promoting appropriate investments for their clients.

Left unmanaged, pressures that threaten independence place research analysts in a difficult position and may jeopardize their ability to act independently and objectively. One of the ways that research analysts have coped with these pressures in the past is to use subtle and ambiguous language in their recommendations or to temper the tone of their research reports. Such subtleties are lost on some investors, however, who reasonably expect research reports and recommendations to be straightforward and transparent, and to communicate clearly an analyst's views based on unbiased analysis and independent judgment.

Members and candidates are personally responsible for maintaining independence and objectivity when preparing research reports, making investment recommendations, and taking investment action on behalf of clients. Recommendations must convey the member's or candidate's true opinions, free of bias from internal or external pressures, and be stated in clear and unambiguous language.

Members and candidates also should be aware that some of their professional or social activities within CFA Institute or its member societies may subtly threaten their independence or objectivity. When seeking corporate financial support for conventions, seminars, or even weekly society luncheons, the members or candidates responsible for the activities should evaluate both the actual effect of such solicitations on their independence and whether their objectivity might be perceived to be compromised in the eyes of their clients.

Buy-Side Clients

One source of pressure on sell-side analysts is buy-side clients. Institutional clients are traditionally the primary users of sell-side research, either directly or with soft dollar brokerage. Portfolio managers may have significant positions in the security of a company under review. A rating downgrade may adversely affect the portfolio's performance, particularly in the short term, because the sensitivity of stock prices to ratings changes has increased in recent years. A downgrade may also affect the manager's compensation, which is usually tied to portfolio performance. Moreover, portfolio performance is subject to media and public scrutiny, which may affect the manager's professional reputation. Consequently, some portfolio managers implicitly or explicitly support sell-side ratings inflation.

Portfolio managers have a responsibility to respect and foster the intellectual honesty of sell-side research. Therefore, it is improper for portfolio managers to threaten or engage in retaliatory practices, such as reporting sell-side analysts to the covered company in order to instigate negative corporate reactions. Although most portfolio managers do not engage in such practices, the perception by the research analyst that a reprisal is possible may cause concern and make it difficult for the analyst to maintain independence and objectivity.

Fund Manager Relationships

Research analysts are not the only people who must be concerned with maintaining their independence. Members and candidates who are responsible for hiring and retaining outside managers should not accepts gifts, entertainment, or travel funding that may be perceived as impairing their decisions. The use of secondary fund managers has evolved into a common practice to manage specific asset allocations. Both the primary and secondary fund managers often arrange educational and marketing events to inform others about their business strategies or investment process. Members and candidates must review the merits of each offer individually in determining whether they may attend yet maintain their independence.

Investment Banking Relationships

Some sell-side firms may exert pressure on their analysts to issue favorable research reports on current or prospective investment banking clients. For many of these firms, income from investment banking has become increasingly important to overall firm profitability because brokerage income has declined as a result of price competition. Consequently, firms offering investment banking services work hard to develop and maintain relationships with investment banking clients and prospects. These companies are often covered by the firm's research analysts because companies often select their investment banks on the basis of the reputation of their research analysts, the quality of their work, and their standing in the industry.

In some countries, research analysts frequently work closely with their investment banking colleagues to help evaluate prospective investment banking clients. In other countries, because of past abuses in managing the obvious conflicts of interest, regulators have established clear rules prohibiting the interaction of these groups. Although collaboration between research analysts and investment banking colleagues may benefit the firm and enhance market efficiency (e.g., by allowing firms to assess risks more accurately and make better pricing assumptions), it requires firms to carefully balance the conflicts of interest inherent in the collaboration. Having analysts work with investment bankers is appropriate only when the conflicts are adequately and effectively managed and disclosed. Firm managers have a responsibility to provide an environment in which analysts are neither coerced nor enticed into issuing research that does not reflect their true opinions. Firms should require public disclosure of actual conflicts of interest to investors.

Members, candidates, and their firms must adopt and follow perceived best practices in maintaining independence and objectivity in the corporate culture and protecting analysts from undue pressure by their investment banking colleagues. The "firewalls" traditionally built between these two functions must be managed to minimize conflicts of interest; indeed, enhanced firewall policies may go as far as prohibiting all communications between these groups. A key element of an enhanced firewall is separate reporting structures for personnel on the research side and personnel on the investment banking side. For example, investment banking personnel should not have any authority to approve, disapprove, or make changes to research reports or recommendations. Another element should be a compensation arrangement that minimizes the pressures on research analysts and rewards objectivity and accuracy. Compensation arrangements should not link analyst remuneration directly to investment banking assignments in which the analyst may participate as a team member. Firms should also regularly review their policies and procedures to determine whether analysts are adequately safeguarded and to improve the transparency of disclosures relating to conflicts of interest. The highest level of transparency is achieved when disclosures are prominent and specific rather than marginalized and generic.

Public Companies

Analysts may be pressured to issue favorable reports and recommendations by the companies they follow. Not every stock is a "buy," and not every research report is favorable—for many reasons, including the cyclical nature of many business activities and market fluctuations. For instance, a "good company" does not always translate into a "good stock" rating if the current stock price is fully valued. In making an investment recommendation, the analyst is responsible for anticipating, interpreting, and assessing a company's prospects and stock price performance in a factual manner. Many company managers, however, believe that their company's stock is undervalued, and these managers may find it difficult to accept critical research reports or ratings downgrades. Company managers' compensation may also be dependent on stock performance.

Due diligence in financial research and analysis involves gathering information from a wide variety of sources, including public disclosure documents (such as proxy statements, annual reports, and other regulatory filings) and also company management and investor-relations personnel, suppliers, customers, competitors, and other relevant sources. Research analysts may justifiably fear that companies will limit their ability to conduct thorough research by denying analysts who have "negative" views direct access to company managers and/or barring them from conference calls and other communication venues. Retaliatory practices include companies bringing legal action against analysts personally and/or their firms to seek monetary damages for the economic effects of negative reports and recommendations. Although few companies engage in such behavior, the perception that a reprisal is possible is a reasonable concern for analysts. This concern may make it difficult for them to conduct the comprehensive research needed to make objective recommendations. For further information and guidance, members and candidates should refer to the CFA Institute publication *Best Practice Guidelines Governing Analyst/Corporate Issuer Relations* (www.cfainstitute.org).

Credit Rating Agency Opinions

Credit rating agencies provide a service by grading the fixed-income products offered by companies. Analysts face challenges related to incentives and compensation schemes that may be tied to the final rating and successful placement of the product. Members and candidates employed at rating agencies should ensure that procedures and processes at the agencies prevent undue influences from a sponsoring company during the analysis. Members and candidates should abide by their agencies' and the industry's standards of conduct regarding the analytical process and the distribution of their reports.

The work of credit rating agencies also raises concerns similar to those inherent in investment banking relationships. Analysts may face pressure to issue ratings at a specific level because of other services the agency offers companies, namely, advising on the development of structured products. The rating agencies need to develop the necessary firewalls and protections to allow the independent operations of their different business lines.

When using information provided by credit rating agencies, members and candidates should be mindful of the potential conflicts of interest. And because of the potential conflicts, members and candidates may need to independently validate the rating granted.

Issuer-Paid Research

In light of the recent reduction of sell-side research coverage, many companies, seeking to increase visibility both in the financial markets and with potential investors, have hired analysts to produce research reports analyzing their companies. These reports bridge the gap created by the lack of coverage and can be an effective method of communicating with investors.

Issuer-paid research conducted by independent analysts, however, is fraught with potential conflicts. Depending on how the research is written and distributed, investors may be misled into believing that the research is from an independent source when, in reality, it has been paid for by the subject company.

Members and candidates must adhere to strict standards of conduct that govern how the research is to be conducted and what disclosures must be made in the report. Analysts must engage in thorough, independent, and unbiased analysis and must fully disclose potential conflicts of interest, including the nature of their compensation. Otherwise, analysts risk misleading investors.

Investors need clear, credible, and thorough information about companies, and they need research based on independent thought. At a minimum, issuer-paid research should include a thorough analysis of the company's financial statements based on publicly disclosed information, benchmarking within a peer group, and industry analysis. Analysts must exercise diligence, independence, and thoroughness in conducting their research in an objective manner. Analysts must distinguish between fact and opinion in their reports. Conclusions must have a reasonable and adequate basis and must be supported by appropriate research.

Independent analysts must also strictly limit the type of compensation that they accept for conducting issuer-paid research. Otherwise, the content and conclusions of the reports could reasonably be expected to be determined or affected by compensation from the sponsoring companies. Compensation that might influence the research report could be direct, such as payment based on the conclusions of the report, or indirect, such as stock warrants or other equity instruments that could increase in value on the basis of positive coverage in the report. In such instances, the independent analyst has an incentive to avoid including negative information or making negative conclusions. Best practice is for independent analysts, prior to writing their report, to negotiate only a flat fee for their work that is not linked to their conclusions or recommendations.

Travel Funding

The benefits related to accepting paid travel extend beyond the cost savings to the member or candidate, such as the chance to talk exclusively with the executives of a company. The problem is that members and candidates may be influenced by these discussions when flying on a corporate or chartered jet. Best practice dictates that members and candidates always use commercial transportation rather than accept paid travel arrangements from an outside company. Should commercial transportation be unavailable, members and candidates may accept modestly arranged travel to participate in appropriate information-gathering events, such as a property tour.

Recommended Procedures for Compliance

Members and candidates should adhere to the following practices and should encourage their firms to establish procedures to avoid violations of Standard I(B):

▶ *Protect the integrity of opinions*: Members, candidates, and their firms should establish policies stating that every research report concerning the securities of a corporate client should reflect the unbiased opinion of the analyst. Firms should also design compensation systems that protect the integrity of the investment decision process by maintaining the independence and objectivity of analysts.

▶ *Create a restricted list*: If the firm is unwilling to permit dissemination of adverse opinions about a corporate client, members and candidates should encourage the firm to remove the controversial company from the research universe and put it on a restricted list so that the firm disseminates only factual information about the company.

▶ *Restrict special cost arrangements*: When attending meetings at an issuer's headquarters, members and candidates should pay for commercial transportation and hotel charges. No corporate issuer should reimburse members or candidates for air transportation. Members and candidates should encourage issuers to limit the use of corporate aircraft to situations in which commercial transportation is not available or in which efficient movement could not otherwise be arranged. Members and candidates should take particular care that when frequent meetings are held between an individual issuer and an individual member or candidate, the issuer should not always host the member or candidate.

▶ *Limit gifts*: Members and candidates must limit the acceptance of gratuities and/or gifts to token items. Standard I(B) does not preclude customary, ordinary business-related entertainment as long as its purpose is not to influence or reward members or candidates. Firms should consider a strict value limit for acceptable gifts that is based on the local or regional customs and should address whether the limit is per gift or an aggregate annual value.

▶ *Restrict investments*: Members and candidates should encourage their investment firms to develop formal polices related to employee purchases of equity or equity-related IPOs. Firms should require prior approval for employee participation in IPOs, with prompt disclosure of investment actions taken following the offering. Strict limits should be imposed on investment personnel acquiring securities in private placements.

▶ *Review procedures*: Members and candidates should encourage their firms to implement effective supervisory and review procedures to ensure that analysts and portfolio managers comply with policies relating to their personal investment activities.

▶ *Independence policy*: Members, candidates, and their firms should establish a formal written policy on the independence and objectivity of research and implement reporting structures and review procedures to ensure that research analysts do not report to and are not supervised or controlled by any department of the firm that could compromise the independence of the analyst. More detailed recommendations related to a firm's policies regarding research objectivity are set forth in the CFA Institute statement *Research Objectivity Standards* (www.cfainstitute.org).

▶ *Appointed officer*: Firms should appoint a senior officer with oversight responsibilities for compliance with the firm's code of ethics and all regulations concerning its business. Firms should provide every employee with the procedures and policies for reporting potentially unethical behavior, violations of regulations, or other activities that may harm the firm's reputation.

Application of the Standard

Example 1 (Travel Expenses): Steven Taylor, a mining analyst with Bronson Brokers, is invited by Precision Metals to join a group of his peers in a tour of mining facilities in several western U.S. states. The company arranges for chartered group flights from site to site and for accommodations in Spartan Motels, the only chain with accommodations near the mines, for three nights. Taylor allows Precision Metals to pick up his tab, as do the other analysts, with one exception—John Adams, an employee of a large trust company who insists on following his company's policy and paying for his hotel room himself.

> *Comment*: The policy of the company where Adams works complies closely with Standard I(B) by avoiding even the appearance of a conflict of interest, but Taylor and the other analysts were not necessarily violating Standard I(B).

In general, when allowing companies to pay for travel and/or accommodations in these circumstances, members and candidates must use their judgment. They must be on guard that such arrangements not impinge on a member's or candidate's independence and objectivity. In this example, the trip was strictly for business and Taylor was not accepting irrelevant or lavish hospitality. The itinerary required chartered flights, for which analysts were not expected to pay. The accommodations were modest. These arrangements are not unusual and did not violate Standard I(B) as long as Taylor's independence and objectivity were not compromised. In the final analysis, members and candidates should consider both whether they can remain objective and whether their integrity might be perceived by their clients to have been compromised.

Example 2 (Research Independence): Susan Dillon, an analyst in the corporate finance department of an investment services firm, is making a presentation to a potential new business client that includes the promise that her firm will provide full research coverage of the potential client.

> *Comment*: Dillon may agree to provide research coverage, but she must not commit her firm's research department to providing a favorable recommendation. The firm's recommendation (favorable, neutral, or unfavorable) must be based on an independent and objective investigation and analysis of the company and its securities.

Example 3 (Research Independence and Intrafirm Pressure): Walter Fritz is an equity analyst with Hilton Brokerage who covers the mining industry. He has concluded that the stock of Metals & Mining is overpriced at its current level, but he is concerned that a negative research report will hurt the good relationship between Metals & Mining and the investment banking division of his firm. In fact, a senior manager of Hilton Brokerage has just sent him a copy of a proposal his firm has made to Metals & Mining to underwrite a debt offering. Fritz needs to produce a report right away and is concerned about issuing a less-than-favorable rating.

> *Comment*: Fritz's analysis of Metals & Mining must be objective and based solely on consideration of company fundamentals. Any pressure from other divisions of his firm is inappropriate. This conflict could have been eliminated if, in anticipation of the offering, Hilton Brokerage had placed Metals & Mining on a restricted list for its sales force.

Example 4 (Research Independence and Issuer Relationship Pressure): As in Example 3, Walter Fritz has concluded that Metals & Mining stock is overvalued at its current level, but he is concerned that a negative research report might jeopardize a close rapport that he has nurtured over the years with Metals & Mining's CEO, chief finance officer, and investment relations officer. Fritz is concerned that a negative report might result also in management retaliation—for instance, cutting him off from participating in conference calls when a quarterly earnings release is made, denying him the ability to ask questions on such calls, and/or denying him access to top management for arranging group meetings between Hilton Brokerage clients with top Metals & Mining managers.

> *Comment*: As in Example 3, Fritz's analysis must be objective and based solely on consideration of company fundamentals. Any pressure from Metals & Mining is inappropriate. Fritz should reinforce the integrity of his conclusions by stressing that his investment recommendation is based on relative valuation, which may include qualitative issues with respect to Metals & Mining's management.

Example 5 (Research Independence and Sales Pressure): As support for the sales effort of her corporate bond department, Lindsey Warner offers credit guidance to purchasers of fixed-income securities. Her compensation is closely linked to the performance of the corporate bond department. Near the quarter's end, Warner's firm has a large inventory position in the bonds of Milton, Ltd., and has been unable to sell the bonds because of Milton's recent announcement of an operating problem. Salespeople have asked her to contact large clients to push the bonds.

> *Comment*: Unethical sales practices create significant potential violations of the Code and Standards. Warner's opinion of the Milton bonds must not be affected by internal pressure or compensation. In this case, Warner must refuse to push the Milton bonds unless she is able to justify that the market price has already adjusted for the operating problem.

Example 6 (Research Independence and Prior Coverage): Jill Jorund is a securities analyst following airline stocks and a rising star at her firm. Her boss has been carrying a "buy" recommendation on International Airlines and asks Jorund to take over coverage of that airline. He tells Jorund that under no circumstances should the prevailing buy recommendation be changed.

> *Comment*: Jorund must be independent and objective in her analysis of International Airlines. If she believes that her boss's instructions have compromised her, she has two options: Tell her boss that she cannot cover the company under these constraints or take over coverage of the company, reach her own independent conclusions, and if they conflict with her boss's opinion, share the conclusions with her boss or other supervisors in the firm so that they can make appropriate recommendations. Jorund must issue only recommendations that reflect her independent and objective opinion.

Example 7 (Gifts and Entertainment from Related Party): Edward Grant directs a large amount of his commission business to a New York-based brokerage house. In appreciation for all the business, the brokerage house gives Grant two tickets to the World Cup in South Africa, two nights at a nearby resort, several meals, and transportation via limousine to the game. Grant fails to disclose receiving this package to his supervisor.

> *Comment*: Grant has violated Standard I(B) because accepting these substantial gifts may impede his independence and objectivity. Every member and candidate should endeavor to avoid situations that might cause or be perceived to cause a loss of independence or objectivity in recommending investments or taking investment action. By accepting the trip, Grant has opened himself up to the accusation that he may give the broker favored treatment in return.

Example 8 (Gifts and Entertainment from Client): Theresa Green manages the portfolio of Ian Knowlden, a client of Tisbury Investments. Green achieves an annual return for Knowlden that is consistently better than that of the benchmark she and the client previously agreed to. As a reward, Knowlden offers Green two tickets to Wimbledon and the use of Knowlden's flat in London for a week. Green discloses this gift to her supervisor at Tisbury.

> *Comment*: Green is in compliance with Standard I(B) because she disclosed the gift from one of her clients in accordance with the firm's policies. Members and candidates may accept bonuses or gifts from clients as long as they disclose them to their employers, because gifts in a client relationship are deemed less likely to affect a member's or candidate's objectivity and

independence than gifts in other situations. Disclosure is required, however, so that supervisors can monitor such situations to guard against employees favoring a gift-giving client to the detriment of other fee-paying clients (such as by allocating a greater proportion of IPO stock to the gift-giving client's portfolio).

Best practices for monitoring include comparing the transaction costs of the Knowlden account with the costs of other accounts managed by Green and other similar accounts within Tisbury. The supervisor could also compare the performance returns with the returns of other clients with the same mandate. This comparison will assist in determining whether a pattern of favoritism by Green is disadvantaging other Tisbury clients or the possibility that this favoritism could affect her future behavior.

Example 9 (Travel Expenses from External Manager): Tom Wayne is the investment manager of the Franklin City Employees Pension Plan. He recently completed a successful search for a firm to manage the foreign equity allocation of the plan's diversified portfolio. He followed the plan's standard procedure of seeking presentations from a number of qualified firms and recommended that his board select Penguin Advisors because of its experience, well-defined investment strategy, and performance record. The firm claims compliance with the Global Investment Performance Standards (GIPS) and has been verified. Following the selection of Penguin, a reporter from the *Franklin City Record* calls to ask if there was any connection between this action and the fact that Penguin was one of the sponsors of an "investment fact-finding trip to Asia" that Wayne made earlier in the year. The trip was one of several conducted by the Pension Investment Academy, which had arranged the itinerary of meetings with economic, government, and corporate officials in major cities in several Asian countries. The Pension Investment Academy obtains support for the cost of these trips from a number of investment managers, including Penguin Advisors; the Academy then pays the travel expenses of the various pension plan managers on the trip and provides all meals and accommodations. The president of Penguin Advisors was also one of the travelers on the trip.

> *Comment*: Although Wayne can probably put to good use the knowledge he gained from the trip in selecting portfolio managers and in other areas of managing the pension plan, his recommendation of Penguin Advisors may be tainted by the possible conflict incurred when he participated in a trip partly paid for by Penguin Advisors and when he was in the daily company of the president of Penguin Advisors. To avoid violating Standard I(B), Wayne's basic expenses for travel and accommodations should have been paid by his employer or the pension plan; contact with the president of Penguin Advisors should have been limited to informational or educational events only; and the trip, the organizer, and the sponsor should have been made a matter of public record. Even if his actions were not in violation of Standard I(B), Wayne should have been sensitive to the public perception of the trip when reported in the newspaper and the extent to which the subjective elements of his decision might have been affected by the familiarity that the daily contact of such a trip would encourage. This advantage would probably not be shared by firms competing with Penguin Advisors.

Example 10 (Research Independence and Compensation Arrangements): Javier Herrero recently left his job as a research analyst for a large investment adviser. While looking for a new position, he was hired by an investor-relations firm to write a research report on one of its clients, a small educational software company. The investor-relations firm hopes to generate investor interest in the technology company. The firm will pay Herrero a flat fee plus a bonus if any new investors buy stock in the company as a result of Herrero's report.

> *Comment*: If Herrero accepts this payment arrangement, he will be in violation of Standard I(B) because the compensation arrangement can reasonably be expected to compromise his independence and objectivity. Herrero will receive a bonus for attracting investors, which provides an incentive to draft a positive report regardless of the facts and to ignore or play down any negative information about the company. Herrero should accept only a flat fee that is not tied to the conclusions or recommendations of the report. Issuer-paid research that is objective and unbiased can be done under the right circumstances as long as the analyst takes steps to maintain his or her objectivity and includes in the report proper disclosures regarding potential conflicts of interest.

Example 11 (Recommendation Objectivity and Service Fees): Two years ago, Bob Wade, trust manager for Central Midas Bank, was approached by Western Funds about promoting its family of funds, with special interest in the service-fee class of funds. To entice Central to promote this class, Western Funds offered to pay the bank a service fee of 0.25 percent. Without disclosing the fee being offered to the bank, Wade asked one of the investment managers to review Western's funds to determine whether they were suitable for clients of Central Midas Bank. The manager completed the normal due diligence review and determined that the new funds were fairly valued in the market with fee structures on a par with competitors. Wade decided to accept Western's offer and instructed the team of portfolio managers to exclusively promote these funds and the service-fee class to clients seeking to invest new funds or transfer from their current investments.

Now, two years later, the funds managed by Western begin to underperform their peers. Wade is counting on the fees to reach his profitability targets and continues to push these funds as acceptable investments for Central's clients.

> *Comment*: Wade is violating Standard I(B) because the fee arrangement has affected the objectivity of his recommendations. Wade is relying on the fee as a component of the department's profitability and is unwilling to offer other products that may affect the fees received.
>
> See also Standard VI(A)—Disclosure of Conflicts.

Example 12 (Recommendation Objectivity): Bob Thompson has been doing research for the portfolio manager of the fixed-income department. His assignment is to do sensitivity analysis on securitized subprime mortgages. He has discussed with the manager possible scenarios to use to calculate expected returns. A key assumption in such calculations is housing price appreciation (HPA) because it drives "prepays" (prepayments of mortgages) and losses. Thompson is concerned with the significant appreciation experienced over the previous five years as a result of the increased availability of funds from subprime mortgages. Thompson insists that the analysis should include a scenario run with negative 10 percent for the first year, negative 5 percent for the second year, and then (to project a worst-case scenario) 0 percent for Years 3 through 5. The manager replies that these assumptions are too dire because there has never been a time in their available database when HPA was negative.

Thompson conducts his research to better understand the risks inherent in these securities and evaluates these securities in the worst-case scenario, an unlikely but possible environment. Based on the results of the enhanced scenarios, Thompson does not recommend the purchase of the securitization. Against the general market trends, the manager follows Thompson's recommendation and does not invest. The following year, the housing market collapses. In avoiding the subprime investments, the manager's portfolio outperforms its peer group that year.

> *Comment*: Thompson's actions in running the worst-case scenario against the protests of the portfolio manager are in alignment with the principles of Standard I(B). Thompson did not allow his research to be pressured by the general trends of the market or the manager's desire to limit the research to historical norms.
>
> See also Standard V(A)—Diligence and Reasonable Basis.

C. Misrepresentation

Members and Candidates must not knowingly make any misrepresentations relating to investment analysis, recommendations, actions, or other professional activities.

Guidance

Highlights:

▶ *Impact on Investment Practice*

▶ *Plagiarism*

▶ *Work Completed for Employer*

Trust is the foundation of the investment profession. Investors must be able to rely on the statements and information provided to them by those with whom the investors have trusted their financial well-being. Investment professionals who make false or misleading statements not only harm investors but also reduce the level of investor confidence in the investment profession and threaten the integrity of capital markets as a whole.

A misrepresentation is any untrue statement or omission of a fact or any statement that is otherwise false or misleading. A member or candidate must not knowingly omit or misrepresent information or give a false impression of a firm, organization, or security in the member's or candidate's oral representations, advertising (whether in the press or through brochures), electronic communications, or written materials (whether publicly disseminated or not). In this context, "knowingly" means that the member or candidate either knows or should have known that the misrepresentation was being made or that omitted information could alter the investment decision-making process.

Written materials include, but are not limited to, research reports, underwriting documents, company financial reports, market letters, newspaper columns, and books. Electronic communications include, but are not limited to, internet communications, webpages, chat rooms, and e-mails. Members and candidates who use webpages should regularly monitor materials posted on the site to ensure that the site contains current information. Members and candidates should also ensure that all reasonable precautions have been taken to protect the site's integrity and security and that the site does not misrepresent any information and does provide full disclosure.

The omission of a fact or outcome has increased in importance because of the growing use of technical analysis. Many members and candidates rely on models to scan for new investment opportunities, to develop investment vehicles, and to produce investment recommendations and ratings. Although not every model can test for every factor or outcome, members and candidates should ensure that their analyses incorporate a broad range of assumptions—from very positive scenarios to extremely negative scenarios. The omission from the analysis of potentially negative outcomes or of levels of risk outside the norm may misrepresent the true economic value of the investment.

Impact on Investment Practice

Members and candidates must not misrepresent any aspect of their practice, including (but not limited to) their qualifications or credentials, the qualifications or services provided by their firm, their performance record and the record of their firm, and the characteristics of an investment. Any misrepresentation made by a member or candidate relating to the member's or candidate's professional activities is a breach of this standard.

Members and candidates should exercise care and diligence when incorporating third-party information. Misrepresentations resulting from the use of the credit ratings, research, testimonials, or marketing materials of these outside parties become the responsibility of the investment professional when it affects that professional's business practices.

Investing through outside managers continues to expand as an acceptable method of investing in areas outside a firm's core competencies. Members and candidates must disclose their intended use of external managers and must not represent those managers' investment practices as their own. Although the level of involvement of outside managers may change over time, appropriate disclosures by members and candidates are important to avoiding misrepresentations, especially if the primary activity is to invest directly with a single external manager. Standard V(B)—Communication with Clients and Prospective Clients discusses in further detail communicating the firm's investment practices.

Standard I(C) prohibits members and candidates from guaranteeing clients any specific return on volatile investments. Most investments contain some element of risk that makes their return inherently unpredictable. For these investments, guaranteeing either a particular rate of return or a guaranteed preservation of investment capital (e.g., "I can guarantee that you will earn 8 percent on equities this year" or "I can guarantee that you will not lose money on this investment") is misleading to investors. Standard I(C) does not prohibit members and candidates from providing clients with information on investment products that have guarantees built into the structure of the product itself or for which an institution has agreed to cover any losses.

Plagiarism

Standard I(C) also prohibits plagiarism in the preparation of material for distribution to employers, associates, clients, prospects, or the general public. Plagiarism is defined as copying or using in substantially the same form materials prepared by others without acknowledging the source of the material or identifying the author and publisher of such material. Members and candidates must not copy (or represent as their own) original ideas or material without permission and must acknowledge and identify the source of ideas or material that is not their own.

The investment profession uses a myriad of financial, economic, and statistical data in the investment decision-making process. Through various publications and presentations, the investment professional is constantly exposed to the work of others and to the temptation to use that work without proper acknowledgment.

Misrepresentation through plagiarism in investment management can take various forms. The simplest and most flagrant example is to take a research report or study done by another firm or person, change the names, and release the material as one's own original analysis. This action is a clear violation of Standard I(C). Other practices include 1) using excerpts from articles or reports prepared by others either verbatim or with only slight changes in wording without acknowledgment, 2) citing specific quotations as attributable to "leading analysts" and "investment experts" without naming the specific references, 3) presenting statistical estimates of forecasts prepared by others and identifying the sources but without including the qualifying statements or caveats that may have been used, 4) using charts and graphs without stating their sources, and 5) copying proprietary computerized spreadsheets or algorithms without seeking the cooperation or authorization of their creators.

In the case of distributing third-party, outsourced research, members and candidates may use and distribute these reports as long as they do not represent themselves as the authors of such a report. Indeed, the member or candidate may add value for the client by sifting through research and repackaging it for clients. In such cases, clients should be fully informed that they are paying for the ability of the member or candidate to find the best research from a wide variety of sources. Members and candidates must not misrepresent their abilities, the extent of their expertise, or the extent of their work in a way that would mislead their clients or prospective clients. Members and candidates should disclose whether the research being presented to clients comes from another source, from either within or outside the member's or candidate's firm. This allows clients to understand who has the expertise behind the report or if the work is being done by the analyst, other members of the firm, or an outside party.

Standard I(C) also applies to plagiarism in oral communications, such as through group meetings; visits with associates, clients, and customers; use of audio/video media (which is rapidly increasing); and telecommunications, including electronic data transfer and the outright copying of electronic media.

One of the most egregious practices in violation of this standard is the preparation of research reports based on multiple sources of information without acknowledging the sources. Examples of information from such sources include ideas, statistical compilations, and forecasts combined to give the appearance of original work. Although there is no monopoly on ideas, members and candidates must give credit where it is clearly due. Analysts should not use undocumented forecasts, earnings projections, asset values, and so on. Sources must be revealed to bring the responsibility directly back to the author of the report or the firm involved.

Work Completed for Employer

The preceding paragraphs address actions that would constitute a violation of Standard I(C). In some situations, however, members or candidates may use research conducted or models developed by others within the same firm without committing a violation. The most common example relates to the situation in which one (or more) of the original analysts is no longer with the firm. Research and models developed while employed by a firm are the property of the firm. The firm retains the right to continue using the work completed after a member or candidate has left the organization. The firm may issue future reports without providing attribution to the prior analysts. A member or candidate cannot, however, reissue a previously released report solely under his or her name.

Recommended Procedures for Compliance

Factual Presentations

Members and candidates can prevent unintentional misrepresentations of the qualifications or services they or their firms provide if each member and candidate understands the limit of the firm's or individual's capabilities and the need to be accurate and complete in presentations. Firms can provide guidance for employees who make written or oral presentations to clients or potential clients by providing a written list of the firm's available services and a description of the firm's qualifications. This list should suggest ways of describing the firm's services, qualifications, and compensation that are both accurate and suitable for client or customer presentations. Firms can also help prevent misrepresentation by specifically designating which employees are authorized to speak on behalf of the firm. Whether or not the firm provides guidance, members and candidates should make certain that they understand the services the firm can perform and its qualifications.

Qualification Summary

In addition, to ensure accurate presentations to clients, each member and candidate should prepare a summary of his or her own qualifications and experience and a list of the services the member or candidate is capable of performing. Firms can assist member and candidate compliance by periodically reviewing employee correspondence and documents that contain representations of individual or firm qualifications.

Verify Outside Information

When providing information to clients from third parties, members and candidates share a responsibility for the accuracy of the marketing and distribution materials that pertain to the third party's capabilities, services, and products. Misrepresentation by third parties can damage the member's or candidate's reputation, the reputation of the firm, and the integrity of the capital markets. Members and candidates should encourage their employers to develop procedures for verifying information of third-party firms.

Maintain Webpages

Members and candidates who publish webpages should regularly monitor materials posted on the site to ensure that the site contains current information. Members and candidates should also ensure that all reasonable precautions have been taken to protect the site's integrity, confidentiality, and security and that the site does not misrepresent any information and provides full disclosure.

Plagiarism Policy

To avoid plagiarism in preparing research reports or conclusions of analysis, members and candidates should take the following steps:

▶ *Maintain copies*: Keep copies of all research reports, articles containing research ideas, material with new statistical methodologies, and other materials that were relied on in preparing the research report.

▶ *Attribute quotations*: Attribute to their sources any direct quotations, including projections, tables, statistics, model/product ideas, and new methodologies prepared by persons other than recognized financial and statistical reporting services or similar sources.

▶ *Attribute summaries*: Attribute to their sources any paraphrases or summaries of material prepared by others. For example, to support his analysis of Brown Company's competitive position, the author of a research report on Brown might summarize another analyst's report on Brown's chief competitor, but the author of the Brown report must acknowledge in his own report the reliance on the other analyst's report.

Application of the Standard

Example 1 (Representing the Firm's Abilities): Allison Rogers is a partner in the firm of Rogers and Black, a small firm offering investment advisory services. She assures a prospective client who has just inherited US$1 million that "we can perform all the financial and investment services you need." Rogers and Black is well equipped to provide investment advice but, in fact, cannot provide asset allocation assistance or a full array of financial and investment services.

Comment: Rogers has violated Standard I(C) by orally misrepresenting the services her firm can perform for the prospective client. She must limit herself to describing the range of investment advisory services Rogers and Black can provide and offer to help the client obtain elsewhere the financial and investment services that her firm cannot provide.

Example 2 (Disclosure of Issuer-Paid Research): Anthony McGuire is an issuer-paid analyst hired by publicly traded companies to electronically promote their stocks. McGuire creates a website that promotes his research efforts as a seemingly independent analyst. McGuire posts a profile and a strong buy recommendation for each company on the website indicating that the stock is expected to increase in value. He does not disclose the contractual relationships with the companies he covers on his website, in the research reports he issues, or in the statements he makes about the companies in internet chat rooms.

Comment: McGuire has violated Standard I(C) because the internet site is misleading to potential investors. Even if the recommendations are valid and supported with thorough research, his omissions regarding the true relationship between himself and the companies he covers constitute a misrepresentation. McGuire has also violated Standard VI(A)—Disclosure of Conflicts by not disclosing the existence of an arrangement with the companies through which he receives compensation in exchange for his services.

Example 3 (Correction of Unintentional Errors): Hijan Yao is responsible for the creation and distribution of the marketing materials for his firm, which claims compliance with the GIPS standards. Yao creates and distributes a presentation of performance by the firm's Asian equity composite that states the composite has ¥350 billion in assets. In fact, the composite has only ¥35 billion in assets, and the higher figure on the presentation is a result of a typographical error. Nevertheless, the erroneous material is distributed to a number of clients before Yao catches the mistake.

Comment: Once the error is discovered, Yao must take steps to cease distribution of the incorrect material and correct the error by informing those who have received the erroneous information. Because Yao did not knowingly make the misrepresentation, however, he did not violate Standard I(C). Since his firm claims compliance with the GIPS standards, it must also comply with the GIPS Guidance Statement on Error Correction in relation to the error.

Example 4 (Noncorrection of Known Errors): Syed Muhammad is the president of an investment management firm. The promotional material for the firm, created by the firm's marketing department, incorrectly claims that Muhammad has an advanced degree in finance from a prestigious business school in addition to the CFA designation. Although Muhammad attended the school for a short period of time, he did not receive a degree. Over the years, Muhammad and others in the firm have distributed this material to numerous prospective clients and consultants.

Comment: Even though Muhammad may not have been directly responsible for the misrepresentation of his credentials in the firm's promotional material, he used this material numerous times over an extended period and should have known of the misrepresentation. Thus, Muhammad has violated Standard I(C).

Example 5 (Plagiarism): Cindy Grant, a research analyst for a Canadian brokerage firm, has specialized in the Canadian mining industry for the past 10 years. She recently read an extensive research report on Jefferson Mining, Ltd., by Jeremy Barton, another analyst. Barton provided extensive statistics on the mineral reserves, production capacity, selling rates, and marketing factors affecting Jefferson's operations. He also noted that initial drilling results on a new ore body, which had not been made public, might show the existence of mineral zones that could increase the life of Jefferson's main mines, but Barton cited no specific data as to the initial drilling results. Grant called an officer of Jefferson, who gave her the initial drilling results over the telephone. The data indicated that the expected life of the main mines would be tripled. Grant added these statistics to Barton's report and circulated it as her own report within her firm.

Comment: Grant plagiarized Barton's report by reproducing large parts of it in her own report without acknowledgment.

Example 6 (Misrepresentation of Information): When Ricki Marks sells mortgage-backed derivatives called "interest-only strips" (IOs) to public pension plan clients, she describes them as "guaranteed by the U.S. government." Purchasers of the IOs are entitled only to the interest stream generated by the mortgages, however, not the notional principal itself. One particular municipality's investment policies and local law require that securities purchased by its public pension plans be guaranteed by the U.S. government. Although the underlying mortgages are guaranteed, neither the investor's investment nor the interest stream on the IOs is guaranteed. When interest rates decline, causing an increase in prepayment of mortgages, interest payments to the IOs' investors decline, and these investors lose a portion of their investment.

Comment: Marks violated Standard I(C) by misrepresenting the terms and character of the investment.

Example 7 (Potential Information Misrepresentation): Khalouck Abdrabbo manages the investments of several high-net-worth individuals in the United States who are approaching retirement. Abdrabbo advises these individuals that a portion of their investments be moved from equity to bank-sponsored certificates of deposit and money market accounts so that the principal will be "guaranteed" up to a certain amount. The interest is not guaranteed.

Comment: Although there is risk that the institution offering the certificates of deposits and money market accounts could go bankrupt, in the United States, these accounts are insured by the U.S. government through the Federal Deposit Insurance Corporation. Therefore, using the term "guaranteed" in this context is not inappropriate as long as the amount is within the government-insured limit. Abdrabbo should explain these facts to the clients.

Example 8 (Plagiarism): Steve Swanson is a senior analyst in the investment research department of Ballard and Company. Apex Corporation has asked Ballard to assist in acquiring the majority ownership of stock in the Campbell Company, a financial consulting firm, and to prepare a report recommending that stockholders of Campbell agree to the acquisition. Another investment firm, Davis and Company, had already prepared a report for Apex analyzing both Apex and Campbell and recommending an exchange ratio. Apex has given the Davis report to Ballard officers, who have passed it on to Swanson. Swanson reviews the Davis report and other available material on Apex and Campbell companies. From his analysis, he concludes that the common stocks of Campbell and Apex represent good value at their current prices; he believes, however, that the Davis report does not consider all the factors a Campbell stockholder would need to know to make a decision. Swanson reports his conclusions to the partner in charge, who tells him to "use the Davis report, change a few words, sign your name, and get it out."

Comment: If Swanson does as requested, he will violate Standard I(C). He could refer to those portions of the Davis report that he agrees with if he identifies Davis as the source; he could then add his own analysis and conclusions to the report before signing and distributing it.

Example 9 (Plagiarism): Claude Browning, a quantitative analyst for Double Alpha, Inc., returns in great excitement from a seminar. In that seminar, Jack Jorrely, a well-publicized quantitative analyst at a national brokerage firm, discussed one of his new models in great detail, and Browning is intrigued by the new concepts. He proceeds to test the model, making some minor mechanical changes but retaining the concepts, until he produces some very positive results. Browning quickly announces to his supervisors at Double Alpha that he has discovered a new model and that clients and prospective clients should be informed of this positive finding as ongoing proof of Double Alpha's continuing innovation and ability to add value.

Comment: Although Browning tested Jorrely's model on his own and even slightly modified it, he must still acknowledge the original source of the idea. Browning can certainly take credit for the final, practical results; he can also support his conclusions with his own test. The credit for the innovative thinking, however, must be awarded to Jorrely.

Example 10 (Plagiarism): Fernando Zubia would like to include in his firm's marketing materials some "plain-language" descriptions of various concepts, such as the price-to-earnings (P/E) multiple and why standard deviation is used as a measure of risk. The descriptions come from other sources, but Zubia wishes to use them without reference to the original authors. Would this use of material be a violation of Standard I(C)?

Comment: Copying verbatim any material without acknowledgement, including plain-language descriptions of the P/E multiple and standard deviation, violates Standard I(C). Even though these concepts are general, best practice would be for Zubia to describe them in his own words or cite the sources from which the descriptions are quoted. Members and candidates would be violating Standard I(C) if they were either responsible for creating marketing materials without attribution or knowingly use plagiarized materials.

Example 11 (Plagiarism): Through a mainstream media outlet, Erika Schneider learns about a study that she would like to cite in her research. Should she cite both the mainstream intermediary source as well as the author of the study itself when using that information?

Comment: In all instances, a member or candidate must cite the actual source of the information. Best practice for Schneider would be to obtain the information directly from the author and review it before citing it in a report. In that case, Schneider would not need to report how she found out about the information. For example, suppose Schneider read in the *Financial Times* about a study issued by CFA Institute; best practice for Schneider would be to obtain a copy of the study from CFA Institute, review it, and then cite it in her report. If she does not use any interpretation of the report from the *Financial Times* and the newspaper does not add value to the report itself, the newspaper is merely a conduit to the original information and does not need to be cited. If she does not obtain the report and review the information, Schneider runs the risk of relying on second-hand information that may misstate facts. If, for example, the *Financial Times* erroneously reported some information from the original CFA Institute study and Schneider copied that erroneous information without acknowledging CFA Institute, she could be the object of complaints. Best practice would be either to obtain the complete study from its original author and cite only that author or to use the information provided by the intermediary and cite both sources.

Example 12 (Misrepresentation of Information): Paul Ostrowski runs a two-person investment management firm. Ostrowski's firm subscribes to a service from a large investment research firm that provides research reports that can be repackaged by smaller firms for those firms' clients. Ostrowski's firm distributes these reports to clients as its own work.

Comment: Ostrowski can rely on third-party research that has a reasonable and adequate basis, but he cannot imply that he is the author of such research. If he does, Ostrowski is misrepresenting the extent of his work in a way that misleads the firm's clients or prospective clients.

Example 13 (Misrepresentation of Information): Tom Stafford is part of a team within Appleton Investment Management responsible for managing a pool of assets for Open Air Bank, which distributes structured securities to offshore clients. He becomes aware that Open Air is promoting the structured securities as a much less risky investment than the investment management policy followed by him and the team to manage the original pool of assets. Also, Open Air has procured an independent rating for the pool that significantly overstates the quality of the investments. Stafford communicates his concerns to his team leader and supervisor, who responds that Open Air owns the product and is responsible for all marketing and distribution. Stafford's supervisor goes on to say that the product is outside of the U.S. regulatory regime that Appleton follows and that all risks of the product are disclosed at the bottom of page 184 of the prospectus.

Comment: As a member of the investment team, Stafford is qualified to recognize the degree of accuracy of the materials that characterize the portfolio, and he is correct to be worried about Appleton's responsibility for a misrepresentation of the risks. Thus, he should continue to pursue the issue of Open Air's inaccurate promotion of the portfolio according to the firm's policies and procedures.

The Code and Standards stress protecting the reputation of the firm and the sustainability and integrity of the capital markets. Misrepresenting the quality and risks associated with the investment pool may lead to negative consequences for others well beyond the direct investors.

Example 14 (Avoiding a Misrepresentation): Trina Smith is a fixed-income portfolio manager at a pension fund. She has observed that the market for highly structured mortgages is the focus of salespeople she meets and that these products represent a significant number of trading opportunities. In discussions about this topic with her team, Smith learns that calculating yields on changing cash flows within the deal structure requires very specialized vendor software. After more research, they find out that each deal is unique and that deals can have more than a dozen layers and changing cash flow priorities. Smith comes to the conclusion that, because of the complexity of these securities, the team cannot effectively distinguish between potentially good and bad investment options. To avoid misrepresenting their understanding, the team decides that the highly structured mortgage segment of the securitized market should not become part of the core of the fund's portfolio; they will allow some of the less complex securities to be part of the core.

> *Comment*: Smith is in compliance with Standard I(C) by not investing in securities that she and her team cannot effectively understand. Because she is not able to describe the risk and return profile of the securities to the pension fund beneficiaries and trustees, she appropriately limits the fund's exposure to this sector.

D. Misconduct

Members and Candidates must not engage in any professional conduct involving dishonesty, fraud, or deceit or commit any act that reflects adversely on their professional reputation, integrity, or competence.

Guidance

Whereas Standard I(A) addresses the obligation of members and candidates to comply with applicable law that governs their professional activities, Standard I(D) addresses *all* conduct that reflects poorly on the professional integrity, good reputation, or competence of members and candidates. Any act that involves lying, cheating, stealing, or other dishonest conduct is a violation of this standard if the offense reflects adversely on a member's or candidate's professional activities. Although CFA Institute discourages any sort of unethical behavior by members and candidates, the Code and Standards are primarily aimed at conduct and actions related to a member's or candidate's professional life.

Conduct that damages trustworthiness or competence may include behavior that, although it is not illegal, nevertheless negatively affects a member's or candidate's ability to perform his or her responsibilities. For example, abusing alcohol during business hours might constitute a violation of this standard because it could have a detrimental effect on the member's or candidate's ability to fulfill his or her professional responsibilities. Personal bankruptcy may not reflect on the integrity or trustworthiness of the person declaring bankruptcy, but if the circumstances of the bankruptcy involve fraudulent or deceitful business conduct, the bankruptcy may be a violation of this standard.

In some cases, the absence of appropriate conduct or the lack of sufficient effort may be a violation of Standard I(D). The integrity of the investment profession is built on trust. A member or candidate—whether an investment banker, rating or research analyst, or portfolio manager—is expected to conduct the necessary due diligence to properly understand the nature and risks of an investment before making an investment recommendation. By not taking these steps and, instead, relying on someone else in the process to have performed them, members or candidates may violate the trust their clients have placed in them. This loss of trust may have a significant impact on the reputation of the member or candidate and the operations of the financial market as a whole.

Individuals may attempt to abuse the CFA Institute Professional Conduct Program by actively seeking CFA Institute enforcement of the Code and Standards, and Standard I(D) in particular, as a method of settling personal, political, or other disputes unrelated to professional ethics. CFA Institute is aware of this issue, and appropriate disciplinary policies, procedures, and enforcement mechanisms are in place to address misuse of the Code and Standards and the Professional Conduct Program in this way.

Recommended Procedures for Compliance

In addition to ensuring that their own behavior is consistent with Standard I(D), to prevent general misconduct, members and candidates should encourage their firms to adopt the following policies and procedures to support the principles of Standard I(D):

▶ *Code of ethics*: Develop and/or adopt a code of ethics to which every employee must subscribe and make clear that any personal behavior that reflects poorly on the individual involved, the institution as a whole, or the investment industry will not be tolerated.

▶ *List of violations*: Disseminate to all employees a list of potential violations and associated disciplinary sanctions, up to and including dismissal from the firm.

▶ *Employee references*: Check references of potential employees to ensure that they are of good character and not ineligible to work in the investment industry because of past infractions of the law.

Application of the Standard

Example 1 (Professionalism and Competence): Simon Sasserman is a trust investment officer at a bank in a small affluent town. He enjoys lunching every day with friends at the country club, where his clients have observed him having numerous drinks. Back at work after lunch, he clearly is intoxicated while making investment decisions. His colleagues make a point of handling any business with Sasserman in the morning because they distrust his judgment after lunch.

Comment: Sasserman's excessive drinking at lunch and subsequent intoxication at work constitute a violation of Standard I(D) because this conduct has raised questions about his professionalism and competence. His behavior reflects poorly on him, his employer, and the investment industry.

Example 2 (Fraud and Deceit): Howard Hoffman, a security analyst at ATZ Brothers, Inc., a large brokerage house, submits reimbursement forms over a two-year period to ATZ's self-funded health insurance program for more than two dozen bills, most of which have been altered to increase the amount due. An investigation by the firm's director of employee benefits uncovers the inappropriate conduct. ATZ subsequently terminates Hoffman's employment and notifies CFA Institute.

> *Comment*: Hoffman violated Standard I(D) because he engaged in intentional conduct involving fraud and deceit in the workplace that adversely reflected on his integrity.

Example 3 (Fraud and Deceit): Jody Brink, an analyst covering the automotive industry, volunteers much of her spare time to local charities. The board of one of the charitable institutions decides to buy five new vans to deliver hot lunches to low-income elderly people. Brink offers to donate her time to handle purchasing agreements. To pay a long-standing debt to a friend who operates an automobile dealership—and to compensate herself for her trouble—she agrees to a price 20 percent higher than normal and splits the surcharge with her friend. The director of the charity ultimately discovers the scheme and tells Brink that her services, donated or otherwise, are no longer required.

> *Comment*: Brink engaged in conduct involving dishonesty, fraud, and misrepresentation and has violated Standard I(D).

Example 4 (Personal Actions and Integrity): Carmen Garcia manages a mutual fund dedicated to socially responsible investing. She is also an environmental activist. As the result of her participation in nonviolent protests, Garcia has been arrested on numerous occasions for trespassing on the property of a large petrochemical plant that is accused of damaging the environment.

> *Comment*: Generally, Standard I(D) is not meant to cover legal transgressions resulting from acts of civil disobedience in support of personal beliefs because such conduct does not reflect poorly on the member's or candidate's professional reputation, integrity, or competence.

Example 5 (Professional Misconduct): Meredith Rasmussen works on a buy-side trading desk of an investment management firm and concentrates on in-house trades for a hedge fund subsidiary managed by a team at the investment management firm. The hedge fund has been very successful and is marketed globally by the firm. From her experience as the trader for much of the activity of the fund, Rasmussen has become quite knowledgeable about the hedge fund's strategy, tactics, and performance. When a distinct break in the market occurs, however, and many of the securities involved in the hedge fund's strategy decline markedly in value, Rasmussen observes that the reported performance of the hedge fund does not reflect this decline. In her experience, the lack of effect is a very unlikely occurrence. She approaches the head of trading about her concern and is told that she should not ask any questions, that the fund is big and successful and is not her concern. She is fairly sure something is not right, so she contacts the compliance officer, who also tells her to stay away from the issue of the hedge fund's reporting.

> *Comment*: Rasmussen has clearly come upon an error in policies, procedures, and compliance practices within the firm's operations. According to the firm's procedures for reporting potentially unethical activity, she should pursue the issue by gathering some proof of her reason for doubt. Should all internal communications within the firm not satisfy her concerns, Rasmussen should consider reporting the potential unethical activity to the appropriate regulator.
>
> See also Standard IV(A) for guidance on whistleblowing and Standard IV(C) for the duties of a supervisor.

STANDARD II—INTEGRITY OF CAPITAL MARKETS

A. Material Nonpublic Information

Members and Candidates who possess material nonpublic information that could affect the value of an investment must not act or cause others to act on the information.

Guidance

Highlights:

- ▶ *What Is "Material" Information?*
- ▶ *What Constitutes "Nonpublic" Information?*
- ▶ *Mosaic Theory*
- ▶ *Investment Research Reports*

Trading or inducing others to trade on material nonpublic information erodes confidence in capital markets, institutions, and investment professionals by supporting the idea that those with inside information and special access can take unfair advantage of the general investing public. Although trading on inside information may lead to short-term profits, in the long run, individuals and the profession as a whole will suffer from such trading. It will cause investors to avoid capital markets because the markets are perceived to be "rigged" in favor of the knowledgeable insider. Standard II(A) promotes and maintains a high level of confidence in market integrity, which is one of the foundations of the investment profession.

The prohibition on using this information goes beyond the direct buying and selling of individual securities or bonds. Members and candidates must not use material nonpublic information to influence their investment actions related to derivatives (e.g., swaps or option contracts), mutual funds, or other alternative investments. *Any* trading based on material nonpublic information constitutes a violation of Standard II(A). The expansion of financial products and the increasing interconnectivity of financial markets globally have resulted in new potential opportunities for trading on material nonpublic information.

What Is "Material" Information?

Information is "material" if its disclosure would probably have an impact on the price of a security or if reasonable investors would want to know the information before making an investment decision. In other words, information is material if it would significantly alter the total mix of information currently available about a security in such a way that the price of the security would be affected.

The specificity of the information, the extent of its difference from public information, its nature, and its reliability are key factors in determining whether a particular piece of information fits the definition of material. For example, material information may include, but is not limited to, information on the following:

- ▶ earnings;
- ▶ mergers, acquisitions, tender offers, or joint ventures;
- ▶ changes in assets or asset quality;

- ▶ innovative products, processes, or discoveries;
- ▶ new licenses, patents, registered trademarks, or regulatory approval/rejection of a product;
- ▶ developments regarding customers or suppliers (e.g., the acquisition or loss of a contract);
- ▶ changes in management;
- ▶ change in auditor notification or the fact that the issuer may no longer rely on an auditor's report or qualified opinion;
- ▶ events regarding the issuer's securities (e.g., defaults on senior securities, calls of securities for redemption, repurchase plans, stock splits, changes in dividends, changes to the rights of security holders, public or private sales of additional securities, and changes in credit ratings);
- ▶ bankruptcies;
- ▶ significant legal disputes;
- ▶ government reports of economic trends (employment, housing starts, currency information, etc.);
- ▶ orders for large trades before they are executed.

In addition to the substance and specificity of the information, the source or relative reliability of the information also determines materiality. The less reliable a source, the less likely the information provided would be considered material. For example, factual information from a corporate insider regarding a significant new contract for a company is likely to be material, whereas an assumption based on speculation by a competitor about the same contract is likely to be less reliable and, therefore, not material.

Also, the more ambiguous the effect of the information on price, the less material that information is considered. If it is unclear whether the information will affect the price of a security and to what extent, the information may not be considered material. The passage of time may also render information that was once important immaterial.

What Constitutes "Nonpublic" Information?

Information is "nonpublic" until it has been disseminated or is available to the marketplace in general (as opposed to a select group of investors). Dissemination can be defined as "made known to." For example, a company report of profits that is posted on the internet and distributed widely through a press release or accompanied by a filing has been effectively disseminated to the marketplace. Members and candidates must have a reasonable expectation that people have received the information before it can be considered public. It is not necessary, however, to wait for the slowest method of delivery. Once the information is disseminated to the market, it is public information that is no longer covered by this standard.

Members and candidates must be particularly aware of information that is selectively disclosed by corporations to a small group of investors, analysts, or other market participants. Information that is made available to analysts remains nonpublic until it is made available to investors in general. Corporations that disclose information on a limited basis create the potential for insider-trading violations.

Issues of selective disclosure often arise when a corporate insider provides material information to analysts in a briefing or conference call before that information is released to the public. Analysts must be aware that a disclosure made to a room full of analysts does not necessarily make the disclosed information "public." Analysts should also be alert to the possibility that they are selectively receiving material nonpublic information when a company provides them with guidance or interpretation of such publicly available information as financial statements or regulatory filings.

Mosaic Theory

A financial analyst gathers and interprets large quantities of information from many sources. The analyst may use significant conclusions derived from the analysis of public and nonmaterial nonpublic information as the basis for investment recommendations and decisions even if those conclusions would have been material inside information had they been communicated directly to the analyst by a company. Under the "mosaic theory," financial analysts are free to act on this collection, or mosaic, of information without risking violation.

The practice of financial analysis depends on the free flow of information. For the fair and efficient operation of the capital markets, analysts and investors must have the greatest amount of information possible to facilitate making well-informed investment decisions about how and where to invest capital. Accurate, timely, and intelligible communication is essential if analysts and investors are to obtain the data needed to make informed decisions about how and where to invest capital. These disclosures must go beyond the information mandated by the reporting requirements of the securities laws and should include specific business information about items used to guide a company's future growth, such as new products, capital projects, and the competitive environment. Analysts seek and use such information to compare and contrast investment alternatives.

Much of the information used by analysts comes directly from companies. Analysts often receive such information through contacts with corporate insiders, especially investor-relations staff and financial officers. Information may be disseminated in the form of press releases, through oral presentations by company executives in analysts' meetings or conference calls, or during analysts' visits to company premises. In seeking to develop the most accurate and complete picture of a company, analysts should also reach beyond contacts with companies themselves and collect information from other sources, such as customers, contractors, suppliers, and the companies' competitors.

Analysts are in the business of formulating opinions and insights that are not obvious to the general investing public about the attractiveness of particular securities. In the course of their work, analysts actively seek out corporate information not generally known to the market for the express purpose of analyzing that information, forming an opinion on its significance, and informing their clients, who can be expected to trade on the basis of the recommendation. Analysts' initiatives to discover and analyze information and communicate their findings to their clients significantly enhance market efficiency, thus benefiting all investors (see *Dirks v. Securities and Exchange Commission*). Accordingly, violations of Standard II(A) will *not* result when a perceptive analyst reaches a conclusion about a corporate action or event through an analysis of public information and items of nonmaterial nonpublic information.

Investment professionals should note, however, that although analysts are free to use mosaic information in their research reports, they should save and document all their research [see Standard V(C)—Record Retention]. Evidence of the analyst's knowledge of public and nonmaterial nonpublic information about a corporation strengthens the assertion that the analyst reached his or her conclusions solely through appropriate methods rather than through the use of material nonpublic information.

Investment Research Reports

When a particularly well-known or respected analyst issues a report or makes changes to his or her recommendation, that information alone may have an effect on the market and thus may be considered material. Theoretically, under Standard II(A), such a report would have to be made public before it was distributed to clients. The analyst is not a company insider, however, and does not have access to inside information. Presumably, the analyst created the report from information available to the public (mosaic theory) and by using his or her expertise to interpret the information. The analyst's hard work, paid for by the client, generated the conclusions. Simply because the public in general would find the conclusions material does not require that the analyst make his or her work public. Investors who are not clients of the analyst can either do the work themselves or become clients of the analyst for access to the analyst's expertise.

Recommended Procedures for Compliance

Achieve Public Dissemination

If a member or candidate determines that information is material, the member or candidate should make reasonable efforts to achieve public dissemination of the information. This effort usually entails encouraging the issuer company to make the information public. If public dissemination is not possible, the member or candidate must communicate the information only to the designated supervisory and compliance personnel within the member's or candidate's firm and must not take investment action or alter current investment recommendations on the basis of the information. Moreover, members and candidates must not knowingly engage in any conduct that may induce company insiders to privately disclose material nonpublic information.

Adopt Compliance Procedures

Members and candidates should encourage their firms to adopt compliance procedures to prevent the misuse of material nonpublic information. Particularly important is improving compliance in such areas as the review of employee and proprietary trading, documentation of firm procedures, and the supervision of interdepartmental communications in multiservice firms. Compliance procedures should suit the particular characteristics of a firm, including its size and the nature of its business.

Adopt Disclosure Procedures

Members and candidates should encourage their firms to develop and follow disclosure policies designed to ensure that information is disseminated to the marketplace in an equitable manner. For example, analysts from small firms should receive the same information and attention from a company as analysts from large firms receive. Similarly, companies should not provide certain information to buy-side analysts but not to sell-side analysts, or vice versa. Furthermore, a company should not discriminate among analysts in the provision of information or "blackball" particular analysts who have given negative reports on the company in the past.

Issue Press Releases

Companies should consider issuing press releases prior to analyst meetings and conference calls and scripting those meetings and calls to decrease the chance that further information will be disclosed. If material nonpublic information is disclosed for the first time in an analyst meeting or call, the company should promptly issue a press release or otherwise make the information publicly available.

Firewall Elements

An information barrier commonly referred to as a "firewall" is the most widely used approach to preventing the communication of material nonpublic information within firms. It restricts the flow of confidential information to those who need to know the information to perform their jobs effectively. The minimum elements of such a system include, but are not limited to, the following:

▶ substantial control of relevant interdepartmental communications, preferably through a clearance area within the firm in either the compliance or legal department;

▶ review of employee trading through the maintenance of "watch," "restricted," and "rumor" lists;

▶ documentation of the procedures designed to limit the flow of information between departments and of the actions taken to enforce those procedures;

▶ heightened review or restriction of proprietary trading while a firm is in possession of material nonpublic information.

Appropriate Interdepartmental Communications

Although documentation requirements must, for practical reasons, take into account the differences between the activities of small firms and those of large, multiservice firms, firms of all sizes and types benefit by improving the documentation of their internal enforcement of firewall procedures. Therefore, even at small firms, procedures concerning interdepartmental communication, the review of trading activity, and the investigation of possible violations should be compiled and formalized.

Physical Separation of Departments

As a practical matter, to the extent possible, firms should consider the physical separation of departments and files to prevent the communication of sensitive information that should not be shared. For example, the investment banking and corporate finance areas of a brokerage firm should be separated from the sales and research departments, and a bank's commercial lending department should be segregated from its trust and research departments.

Prevention of Personnel Overlap

There should be no overlap of personnel between the investment banking and corporate finance areas of a brokerage firm and the sales and research departments or between a bank's commercial lending department and its trust and research departments. For a firewall to be effective in a multiservice firm, an employee can be allowed to be on only one side of the firewall at any time. Inside knowledge may not be limited to information about a specific offering or the current financial condition of a company. Analysts may be exposed to much information about the company, including new product developments or future budget projections that clearly constitute inside knowledge and thus preclude the analyst from returning to his or her research function. For example, an analyst who follows a particular company may provide limited assistance to the investment bankers under carefully controlled circumstances when the firm's investment banking department is involved in a deal with the company. That analyst must then be treated as though he or she were an investment banker; the analyst must remain on the investment banking side of the wall until any information he or she learns is publicly disclosed. In short, the analyst cannot use any information learned in the course of the project for research purposes and cannot share that information with colleagues in the research department.

A Reporting System

A primary objective of an effective firewall procedure is to establish a reporting system in which authorized people review and approve communications between departments. If an employee behind a firewall believes that he or she needs to share confidential information with someone on the other side of the wall, the employee should consult a designated compliance officer to determine whether sharing the information is necessary and how much information should be shared. If the sharing is necessary, the compliance officer should coordinate the process of "looking over the wall" so that the necessary information will be shared and the integrity of the procedure will be maintained.

A single supervisor or compliance officer should have the specific authority and responsibility of deciding whether or not information is material and whether it is sufficiently public to be used as the basis for investment decisions. Ideally, the supervisor or compliance officer responsible for communicating information to a firm's research or brokerage area would not be a member of that area.

Personal Trading Limitations

Firms should consider restrictions or prohibitions on personal trading by employees and should carefully monitor both proprietary trading and personal trading by employees. Firms should require employees to make periodic reports (to the extent that such reporting is not already required by securities laws) of their own transactions and transactions made for the benefit of family members. Securities should be placed on a restricted list when a firm has or may have material nonpublic information. The broad distribution of a restricted list often triggers the sort of trading the list was developed to avoid. Therefore, a watch list shown to only the few people responsible for compliance should be used to monitor transactions in specified securities. The use of a watch list in combination with a restricted list is an increasingly common means of ensuring effective control of personal trading.

Record Maintenance

Multiservice firms should maintain written records of the communications between various departments. Firms should place a high priority on training and should consider instituting comprehensive training programs, particularly for employees in sensitive areas.

Proprietary Trading Procedures

Procedures concerning the restriction or review of a firm's proprietary trading while it possesses material nonpublic information will necessarily depend on the types of proprietary trading in which a firm may engage. A prohibition on all types of proprietary activity when a firm comes into possession of material nonpublic information is *not* appropriate. For example, when a firm acts as a market maker, a prohibition on proprietary trading may be counterproductive to the goals of maintaining the confidentiality of information and market liquidity. This concern is particularly important in the relationships between small, regional broker/dealers and small issuers. In many situations, a firm will take a small issuer public with the understanding that the firm will continue to be a market maker in the stock. In such instances, a withdrawal by the firm from market-making acts would be a clear tip to outsiders. Firms that continue market-making activity while in the possession of material nonpublic information should, however, instruct their market makers to remain passive to the market—that is, to take only the contra side of unsolicited customer trades.

In risk-arbitrage trading, the case for a trading prohibition is more compelling than it is in the case of market making. The impetus for arbitrage trading is neither passive nor reactive, and the potential for illegal profits is greater than in market making. The most prudent course for firms is to suspend arbitrage activity when a security is placed on the watch list. Those firms that continue arbitrage activity face a high hurdle in proving the adequacy of their internal procedures for preventing trading on material nonpublic information and must demonstrate a stringent review and documentation of firm trades.

Communication to All Employees

Written compliance policies and guidelines should be circulated to all employees of a firm. Policies and guidelines should be used in conjunction with training programs aimed at enabling employees to recognize material nonpublic information. Such information is not always clearly identifiable. Employees must be given sufficient training to either make an informed decision or to realize they need to consult a supervisor or compliance officer before engaging in questionable transactions.

Application of the Standard

Example 1 (Acting on Nonpublic Information): Frank Barnes, the president and controlling shareholder of the SmartTown clothing chain, decides to accept a tender offer and sell the family business at a price almost double the market price of its shares. He describes this decision to his sister (SmartTown's treasurer), who conveys it to her daughter (who owns no stock in the family company at present), who tells her husband, Staple. Staple, however, tells his stockbroker, Alex Halsey, who immediately buys SmartTown stock for himself.

> *Comment*: The information regarding the pending sale is both material and nonpublic. Staple has violated Standard II(A) by communicating the inside information to his broker. Halsey also has violated the standard by buying the shares on the basis of material nonpublic information.

Example 2 (Acting on Nonpublic Information): Josephine Walsh is riding an elevator up to her office when she overhears the chief financial officer (CFO) for the Swan Furniture Company tell the president of Swan that he has just calculated the company's earnings for the past quarter and they have unexpectedly and significantly dropped. The CFO adds that this drop will not be released to the public until next week. Walsh immediately calls her broker and tells him to sell her Swan stock.

> *Comment*: Walsh has sufficient information to determine that the information is both material and nonpublic. By trading on the inside information, she has violated Standard II(A).

Example 3 (Controlling Nonpublic Information): Samuel Peter, an analyst with Scotland and Pierce Incorporated, is assisting his firm with a secondary offering for Bright Ideas Lamp Company. Peter participates, via telephone conference call, in a meeting with Scotland and Pierce investment banking employees and Bright Ideas' CEO. Peter is advised that the company's earnings projections for the next year have significantly dropped. Throughout the telephone conference call, several Scotland and Pierce salespeople and portfolio managers walk in and out of Peter's office, where the telephone call is taking place. As a result, they are aware of the drop in projected earnings for Bright Ideas. Before the conference call is concluded, the salespeople trade the stock of the company on behalf of the firm's clients and other firm personnel trade the stock in a firm proprietary account and in employee personal accounts.

> *Comment*: Peter has violated Standard II(A) because he failed to prevent the transfer and misuse of material nonpublic information to others in his firm. Peter's firm should have adopted information barriers to prevent the communication of nonpublic information between departments of the firm. The salespeople and portfolio managers who traded on the information have also violated Standard II(A) by trading on inside information.

Example 4 (Acting on Nonpublic Information): Madison & Lambeau, a well-respected broker/dealer, submits a weekly column to *Securities Weekly* magazine. Once published, the column usually affects the value of the stocks discussed. Ron George, an employee of Madison & Lambeau, knows that *Securities Weekly* is published by Ziegler Publishing, for which his nephew is the night foreman. George's nephew faxes him an advance copy of the weekly column before it is printed. George regularly trades in the securities mentioned in the Madison & Lambeau column prior to its distribution, and to date, he has realized a personal profit of US$42,000 as well as significant profits for his clients.

> *Comment*: George has violated Standard II(A) by trading on material nonpublic information. The Madison & Lambeau article is considered nonpublic until the magazine is distributed through the normal channels.

Example 5 (Acting on Nonpublic Information): Greg Newman and his wife, Nancy Newman, volunteer at a local charitable organization that delivers meals to the elderly. One morning, Nancy Newman receives a telephone call from Betsy Sterling, another volunteer, who asks if the Newmans can fill in for her and her husband that afternoon. Betsy Sterling indicates that her husband is busy at work because his company has just fired its chief financial officer for misappropriation of funds. Nancy Newman agrees to perform the volunteer work for the Sterlings and advises her husband of the situation. Greg Newman knows that Betsy Sterling's husband is the CEO at O'Hara Brothers Incorporated, and he determines that this information is not public. Then, he sells his entire holding of 3,000 shares of O'Hara Brothers. Three days later, the firing is announced and O'Hara Brothers stock drops in value.

> *Comment*: Because the information is material and nonpublic, Greg Newman has violated Standard II(A) by trading on this information.

Example 6 (Selective Disclosure of Material Information): Elizabeth Levenson is based in Taipei and covers the Taiwanese market for her firm, which is based in Singapore. She is invited, together with the other 10 largest shareholders of a manufacturing company, to meet the finance director of that company. During the meeting, the finance director states that the company expects its workforce to strike next Friday, which will cripple productivity and distribution. Can Levenson use this information as a basis to change her rating on the company from "buy" to "sell"?

> *Comment*: Levenson must first determine whether the material information is public. According to Standard II(A), if the company has not made this information public (a small-group forum does not qualify as a method of public dissemination), she cannot use the information.

Example 7 (Determining Materiality): Leah Fechtman is trying to decide whether to hold or sell shares of an oil-and-gas exploration company that she owns in several of the funds she manages. Although the company has underperformed the index for some time already, the trends in the industry sector signal that companies of this type might become takeover targets. While she is considering her decision, her doctor, who casually follows the markets, mentions that she thinks that the company in question will soon be bought out by a large multinational conglomerate and that it would be a good idea to buy the stock right now. After talking to various investment professionals and checking their opinions on the company as well as checking industry trends, Fechtman decides the next day to accumulate more stock in the oil-and-gas exploration company.

> *Comment*: Although information on an expected takeover bid may be of the type that is generally material and nonpublic, in this case, the source of information is unreliable, so the information cannot be considered material. Therefore, Fechtman is not prohibited from trading the stock on the basis of this information.

Example 8 (Applying the Mosaic Theory): Jagdish Teja is a buy-side analyst covering the furniture industry. Looking for an attractive company to recommend as a buy, he analyzes several furniture makers by studying their financial reports and visiting their operations. He also talks to some designers and retailers to find out which furniture styles are trendy and popular. Although none of the companies that he analyzes are a clear buy, he discovers that one of them, Swan Furniture Company (SFC), may be in trouble financially. Swan's extravagant new designs have been introduced at substantial cost. Even though these designs initially attracted attention, in the long run, the public is buying more conservative furniture from other makers. Based on this information and on a profit-and-loss analysis, Teja believes that Swan's next quarter's earnings will drop substantially. He issues a sell recommendation for SFC. Immediately after receiving that recommendation, investment managers start reducing the SFC stock in their portfolios.

> *Comment*: Information on quarterly earnings data is material and nonpublic. Teja arrived at his conclusion about the earnings drop on the basis of public information and on pieces of nonmaterial nonpublic information (such as opinions of designers and retailers). Therefore, trading based on Teja's correct conclusion is not prohibited by Standard II(A).

Example 9 (Applying the Mosaic Theory): Roger Clement is a senior financial analyst who specializes in the European automobile sector at Rivoli Capital. Because he has been repeatedly nominated by many leading industry magazines and newsletters as "best analyst" for the automobile industry, he is widely regarded as an authority on the sector. After speaking with representatives of Tur-got Chariots, a European auto manufacturer with sales primarily in South Korea, as well as interviews with salespeople, labor leaders, his firm's Korean currency ana-lysts, and banking officials, Clement has analyzed Turgot Chariots and concluded that 1) its newly introduced model will probably not meet sales anticipation, 2) its corporate restructuring strategy may well face serious opposition from the unions, 3) the depreciation of the Korean won should lead to pressure on margins for the industry in general and Turgot's market segment in particular, and 4) banks could take a tougher-than-expected stance in the upcoming round of credit renegotia-tions with the company. For these reasons, he changes his conclusion about the company from "market outperform" to "market underperform."

> *Comment*: To reach a conclusion about the value of the company, Clement has pieced together a number of nonmaterial or public bits of information that affect Turgot Chariots. Therefore, under the mosaic theory, Clement has not violated Standard II(A) in drafting the report.

Example 10 (Analyst Recommendations as Material Nonpublic Information): The next day, Clement is preparing to be interviewed on a global financial news television program where he will discuss his changed recommendation on Tur-got Chariots for the first time in public. While preparing for the program, he mentions to the show's producers and Mary Zito, the journalist who will be inter-viewing him, the information he will be discussing. Just prior to going on the air, Zito sells her holdings in Turgot Chariots.

> *Comment*: When Zito receives advance notice of Clement's change of opin-ion, she knows it will have a material impact on the stock price, even if she is not totally aware of Clement's underlying reasoning. She is not a client of Clement but obtains early access to the material nonpublic information prior to publication. Her trades are thus based on material nonpublic infor-mation and violate Standard II(A).

Example 11 (Acting on Nonpublic Information): Timothy Holt is a portfolio manager for the Toro Aggressive Growth Fund, a large mutual fund with an aggressive-growth mandate. Because of its mandate, the fund is heavily invested in small-cap companies with strong growth potential. Based on an unfavorable analysis of McCardell Industries by his research department, Holt decides to liq-uidate the fund's holdings in this company. Holt knows that this action will be widely viewed as negative by the market and that the company's stock is likely to plunge. He contacts several family members to tell them to liquidate any of their holdings before Toro's holdings are sold.

> *Comment*: When Holt tells his family to sell stock in advance of Toro's trade, he is violating Standard II(A) by causing others to trade on material non-public information.

Example 12 (Acting on Nonpublic Information): Holt executes his sell order of McCardell Industries with Toro's broker, Karim Ahmed. Ahmed immediately recognizes the likely effect this order will have on the stock price of McCardell and sells his own holdings in the company prior to placing the order.

> *Comment*: Ahmed has violated Standard II(A) by trading on material non-public information.

Example 13 (Acting on Nonpublic Information): Ashton Kellogg is a retired investment professional who manages his own portfolio. He owns shares in National Savings, a large local bank. A close friend and golfing buddy, John May-field, is a senior executive at National. National has seen its stock drop consider-ably, and the news and outlook are not good. In a conversation about the economy and the banking industry on the golf course, Mayfield drops the information that National will surprise the investment community in a few days when it announces excellent earnings for the quarter. Kellogg is pleasantly surprised by this information, and thinking that Mayfield, as a senior executive, knows the law and would not disclose inside information, he doubles his position in the bank. Subsequently, National announces that it had good operating earnings but had to set aside reserves for anticipated significant losses on its loan portfolio. The combined news causes the stock to go down 60 percent.

> *Comment*: Even though Kellogg believes that Mayfield would not break the law by disclosing insider information and money was lost on the purchase, Kellogg should not have purchased additional shares of National. It is the member's or candidate's responsibility to make sure, before executing investment actions, that comments about earnings are not material nonpublic information. Kellogg has violated Standard II(A).

B. Market Manipulation

Members and Candidates must not engage in practices that distort prices or artificially inflate trading volume with the intent to mislead market participants.

Guidance

Highlights:

▶ *Information-Based Manipulation*
▶ *Transaction-Based Manipulation*

Standard II(B) requires that members and candidates uphold market integrity by prohibiting market manipulation. Market manipulation includes practices that distort security prices or trading volume with the intent to deceive people or entities that rely on information in the market. Market manipulation damages the interests of all investors by disrupting the smooth functioning of financial markets and lowering investor confidence. Although market manipulation may be less likely to occur in mature financial markets than in emerging markets, cross-border investing increasingly exposes all global investors to the potential for such practices.

Market manipulation includes 1) the dissemination of false or misleading information and 2) transactions that deceive or would be likely to mislead market participants by distorting the price-setting mechanism of financial instruments. The development of new products and technologies increases the incentives, means, and opportunities for market manipulation.

Information-Based Manipulation

Information-based manipulation includes, but is not limited to, spreading false rumors to induce trading by others. For example, members and candidates must refrain from "pumping up" the price of an investment by issuing misleading positive information or overly optimistic projections of a security's worth only to later "dump" the investment (sell ownership in it) once the price of the stock, fueled by the misleading information's effect on other market participants, reaches an artificially high level.

Transaction-Based Manipulation

Transaction-based manipulation involves instances where the member or candidate knew or should have known that his or her actions could very well affect the pricing of a security. This includes, but is not limited to, the following:

▶ transactions that artificially affect prices or volume to give the impression of activity or price movement in a financial instrument, which represent a diversion from the expectations of a fair and efficient market; and

▶ securing a controlling, dominant position in a financial instrument to exploit and manipulate the price of a related derivative and/or the underlying asset.

Standard II(B) is not intended to preclude transactions undertaken on legitimate trading strategies based on perceived market inefficiencies. The intent of the action is critical to determining whether it is a violation of this standard.

Application of the Standard

Example 1 (Independent Analysis and Company Promotion): The principal owner of Financial Information Services (FIS) entered into an agreement with two microcap companies to promote the companies' stock in exchange for stock and cash compensation. The principal owner caused FIS to disseminate e-mails, design and maintain several internet sites, and distribute an online investment newsletter—all of which recommended investment in the two companies. The systematic publication of purportedly independent analyses and recommendations containing inaccurate and highly promotional and speculative statements increased public investment in the companies and led to dramatically higher stock prices.

> *Comment*: The principal owner of FIS violated Standard II(B) by using inaccurate reporting and misleading information under the guise of independent analysis to artificially increase the stock price of the companies. Furthermore, the principal owner violated Standard V(A)—Diligence and Reasonable Basis by not having a reasonable and adequate basis for recommending the two companies and violated Standard VI(A)—Disclosure of Conflicts by not disclosing to investors the compensation agreements (which constituted a conflict of interest).

Example 2 (Personal Trading Practices and Price): An employee of a broker/dealer acquired a significant ownership interest in several publicly traded microcap stocks and held the stock in various brokerage accounts in which the broker/dealer had a controlling interest. The employee orchestrated the manipulation of the stock price by artificially increasing the bid price for the stock through transactions among the various accounts.

> *Comment*: The employee of the broker/dealer violated Standard II(B) by distorting the price of the stock through false trading and manipulative sales practices.

Example 3 (Creating Artificial Price Volatility): Matthew Murphy is an analyst at Divisadero Securities & Co., which has a significant number of hedge funds among its most important brokerage clients. Some of the hedge funds hold short positions on Wirewolf Semiconductor. Two trading days before the publication of the quarter-end report, Murphy alerts his sales force that he is about to issue a research report on Wirewolf that will include the following opinion:

▶ quarterly revenues are likely to fall short of management's guidance;

▶ earnings will be as much as 5 cents per share (or more than 10 percent) below consensus; and

▶ Wirewolf's highly respected chief financial officer may be about to join another company.

Knowing that Wirewolf has already entered its declared quarter-end "quiet period" before reporting earnings (and thus would be reluctant to respond to rumors), Murphy times the release of his research report specifically to sensationalize the negative aspects of the message in order to create significant downward pressure on Wirewolf's stock—to the distinct advantage of Divisadero's hedge fund clients. The report's conclusions are based on speculation, not on fact. The next day, the research report is broadcast to all of Divisadero's clients and to the usual newswire services.

Before Wirewolf's investor-relations department can assess the damage on the final trading day of the quarter and refute Murphy's report, its stock opens trading sharply lower, allowing Divisadero's clients to cover their short positions at substantial gains.

Comment: Murphy violated Standard II(B) by aiming to create artificial price volatility designed to have a material impact on the price of an issuer's stock. Moreover, by lacking an adequate basis for the recommendation, Murphy also violated Standard V(A)—Diligence and Reasonable Basis.

Example 4 (Personal Trading and Volume): Rajesh Sekar manages two funds—an equity fund and a balanced fund—whose equity components are supposed to be managed in accordance with the same model. According to that model, the funds' holdings in stock of Digital Design Inc. (DD) are excessive. Reduction of the DD holdings would not be easy, however, because the stock has low liquidity in the stock market. Sekar decides to start trading larger portions of DD stock back and forth between his two funds to slowly increase the price; he believes market participants will see growing volume and increasing price and become interested in the stock. If other investors are willing to buy the DD stock because of such interest, then Sekar will be able to get rid of at least some of his overweight position without inducing price decreases. In this way, the whole transaction will be for the benefit of fund participants, even if additional brokers' commissions are incurred.

Comment: Sekar's plan would be beneficial for his funds' participants but is based on artificial distortion of both trading volume and the price of the DD stock and thus constitutes a violation of Standard II(B).

Example 5 ("Pump-Priming" Strategy): Sergei Gonchar is chairman of the ACME Futures Exchange, which is launching a new bond futures contract. To convince investors, traders, arbitrageurs, hedgers, and so on, to use its contract, the exchange attempts to demonstrate that it has the best liquidity. To do so, it enters into agreements with members in which they commit to a substantial minimum trading volume on the new contract over a specific period in exchange for substantial reductions of their regular commissions.

Comment: The formal liquidity of a market is determined by the obligations set on market makers, but the actual liquidity of a market is better estimated by the actual trading volume and bid–ask spreads. Attempts to mislead participants about the actual liquidity of the market constitute a violation of Standard II(B). In this example, investors have been intentionally misled to believe they chose the most liquid instrument for some specific purpose, but they could eventually see the actual liquidity of the contract significantly reduced after the term of the agreement expires. If the ACME Futures Exchange fully discloses its agreement with members to boost transactions over some initial launch period, it will not violate Standard II(B). ACME's intent is not to harm investors but, on the contrary, to give them a better service. For that purpose, it may engage in a liquidity-pumping strategy, but the strategy must be disclosed.

Example 6 (Creating Artificial Price Volatility): Emily Gordon, an analyst of household products companies, is employed by a research boutique, Picador & Co. Based on information that she has gathered during a trip through Latin America, she believes that Hygene, Inc., a major marketer of personal care products, has generated better-than-expected sales from its new product initiatives in South America. After modestly boosting her projections for revenue and for gross profit margin in her worksheet models for Hygene, Gordon estimates that her earnings projection of US$2.00 per diluted share for the current year may be as much as 5 percent too low. She contacts the chief financial officer (CFO) of Hygene to try to gain confirmation of her findings from her trip and to get some feedback regarding her revised models. The CFO declines to comment and reiterates management's most recent guidance of US$1.95 to US$2.05 for the year.

Gordon decides to try to force a comment from the company by telling Picador & Co. clients who follow a momentum investment style that consensus earnings projections for Hygene are much too low; she explains that she is considering raising her published estimate by an ambitious US$0.15 to US$2.15 per share. She believes that when word of an unrealistically high earnings projection filters back to Hygene's investor-relations department, the company will feel compelled to update its earnings guidance. Meanwhile, Gordon hopes that she is at least correct with respect to the earnings direction and that she will help clients who act on her insights to profit from a quick gain by trading on her advice.

Comment: By exaggerating her earnings projections in order to try to fuel a quick gain in Hygene's stock price, Gordon is in violation of Standard II(B). Furthermore, by virtue of previewing her intentions of revising upward her earnings projections to only a select group of clients, she is in violation of Standard III(B)—Fair Dealing. Instead of what she did, it would have been acceptable for Gordon to write a report that:

- ▶ framed her earnings projection in a range of possible outcomes;
- ▶ outlined clearly the assumptions used in her Hygene models that took into consideration the findings from her trip through Latin America; and
- ▶ distributed the report to all Picador & Co. clients in an equitable manner.

Example 7 (Pump and Dump Strategy): In an effort to pump up the price of his holdings in Moosehead & Belfast Railroad Company, Steve Weinberg logs on to several investor chat rooms on the internet to start rumors that the company is about to expand its rail network in anticipation of receiving a large contract for shipping lumber.

Comment: Weinberg has violated Standard II(B) by disseminating false information about Moosehead & Belfast with the intent to mislead market participants.

Example 8 (Manipulating Model Inputs): Bill Mandeville supervises a structured financing team for Superior Investment Bank. His responsibilities include packaging new structured investment products and managing Superior's relationship with relevant rating agencies. To achieve the best rating possible, Mandeville uses mostly positive scenarios as model inputs—scenarios that reflect minimal downside risk in the assets underlying the structured products. The resulting output statistics in the rating request and underwriting prospectus support the idea that the new structured products have minimal potential downside risk. Additionally, Mandeville's compensation from Superior is partially based on both the level of the rating assigned and the successful sale of new structured investment products but does not have a link to the long-term performance of the instruments.

Mandeville is extremely successful and leads Superior as the top originator of structured investment products for the next two years. In the third year, the economy experiences difficulties and the values of the assets underlying structured products significantly decline. The subsequent defaults lead to major turmoil in the capital markets, the demise of Superior Investment Bank, and Mandeville's loss of employment.

Comment: Mandeville manipulates the inputs of a model to minimize associated risk to achieve higher ratings. His understanding of structured products allows him to skillfully decide which inputs to include in support of the desired rating and price. This information manipulation for short-term gain, which is in violation of Standard II(B), ultimately causes significant damage to many parties and the capital markets as a whole. Mandeville should have realized that promoting a rating and price with inaccurate information could cause not only a loss of price confidence in the particular structured product but also a loss of investor trust in the system. Such loss of confidence affects the ability of the capital markets to operate efficiently.

STANDARD III—DUTIES TO CLIENTS

A. Loyalty, Prudence, and Care

Members and Candidates have a duty of loyalty to their clients and must act with reasonable care and exercise prudent judgment. Members and Candidates must act for the benefit of their clients and place their clients' interests before their employer's or their own interests.

Guidance

Highlights:

▶ *Identifying the Actual Investment Client*
▶ *Developing the Client's Portfolio*
▶ *Soft Commission Policies*
▶ *Proxy Voting Policies*

Standard III(A) clarifies that client interests are paramount. A member's or candidate's responsibility to a client includes a duty of loyalty and a duty to exercise reasonable care. Investment actions must be carried out for the sole benefit of the client and in a manner the member or candidate believes, given the known facts and circumstances, to be in the best interest of the client. Members and candidates must exercise the same level of prudence, judgment, and care that they would apply in the management and disposition of their own interests in similar circumstances.

Prudence requires caution and discretion. The exercise of prudence by investment professionals requires that they act with the care, skill, and diligence in the circumstances that a reasonable person acting in a like capacity and familiar with such matters would use. In the context of managing a client's portfolio, prudence requires following the investment parameters set forth by the client and balancing risk and return. Acting with care requires members and candidates to act in a prudent and judicious manner in avoiding harm to clients.

Standard III(A) sets minimum expectations for members and candidates when fulfilling their responsibilities to their clients. Regulatory and legal requirements for such duties can vary across the investment industry depending on a variety of factors, including job function of the investment professional, the existence of an adviser/client relationship, and the nature of the recommendations being offered. From the perspective of the end user of financial services, these different standards can be arcane and confusing, leaving investors unsure of what level of service to expect from investment professionals they employ. The single standard of conduct described in Standard III(A) benefits investors by establishing a benchmark for the duties of loyalty, prudence, and care and clarifies that all CFA Institute members and candidates, regardless of job title, local laws, or cultural differences, are required to comply with these fundamental responsibilities. Investors hiring members or candidates who must adhere to the duty of loyalty, prudence, and care set forth in this standard can be confident that these responsibilities are a requirement regardless of any legally imposed fiduciary duties.

Standard III(A), however, is not a substitute for a member's or candidate's legal or regulatory obligations. Members and candidates must also understand and adhere to any legally imposed fiduciary responsibility they assume with each client. Fiduciary duties are often imposed by law or regulation when an individual or institution is charged with the duty of acting for the benefit of another party, such as managing investment assets. The duty required in fiduciary relationships exceeds what is acceptable in many other business relationships because a fiduciary is in an enhanced position of trust.

As stated in Standard I(A), members and candidates must abide by the most strict requirements imposed on them by regulators or the Code and Standards, including any legally imposed fiduciary duty. Standard III(A) establishes a minimum benchmark for the duties of loyalty, prudence, and care that are required of all members and candidates regardless of whether a legal fiduciary duty applies.

Members and candidates must also be aware of whether they have "custody" or effective control of client assets. If so, a heightened level of responsibility arises. Members and candidates are considered to have custody if they have any direct or indirect access to client funds. Members and candidates must manage any pool of assets in their control in accordance with the terms of the governing documents (such as trust documents and investment management agreements), which are the primary determinant of the manager's powers and duties. Whenever their actions are contrary to provisions of those instruments or applicable law, members and candidates are at risk of violating Standard III(A).

Identifying the Actual Investment Client

The first step for members and candidates in fulfilling their duty of loyalty to clients is to determine the identity of the "client" to whom the duty of loyalty is owed. In the context of an investment manager managing the personal assets of an individual, the client is easily identified. When the manager is responsible for the portfolios of pension plans or trusts, however, the client is not the person or entity who hires the manager but, rather, the beneficiaries of the plan or trust. The duty of loyalty is owed to the ultimate beneficiaries.

In some situations, an actual client or group of beneficiaries may not exist. Members and candidates managing a fund to an index or an expected mandate owe the duty of loyalty, prudence, and care to invest in a manner consistent with the stated mandate. The decisions of a fund's manager, although benefiting all fund investors, do not have to be based on an individual investor's requirements and risk profile. Client loyalty and care for those investing in the fund are the responsibility of members and candidates who have an advisory relationship with those individuals.

Situations involving potential conflicts of interest with respect to responsibilities to clients may be extremely complex because they may involve a number of competing interests. The duty of loyalty, prudence, and care applies to a large number of persons in varying capacities, but the exact duties may differ in many respects in accord with the relationship with each client or each type of account in which the assets are managed. Members and candidates must not only put their obligations to clients first in all dealings but must also endeavor to avoid all real or potential conflicts of interest.

Members and candidates with positions whose responsibilities do not include direct investment management also have "clients" that must be considered. Just as there are various types of advisory relationships, members and candidates must look at their roles and responsibilities when making a determination of who their clients are. Sometimes the client is easily identifiable; such is the case in the relationship between a company executive and the firm's public shareholders. At other times, the client may be the investing public as a whole, in which case, the goals of independence and objectivity of research surpass the goal of loyalty to a single organization.

Developing the Client's Portfolio

The duty of loyalty, prudence, and care owed to the individual client is especially important because the professional investment manager typically possesses greater knowledge in the investment arena than the client does. This disparity places the individual client in a vulnerable position; the client must trust the manager. The manager in these situations should ensure that the client's objectives and expectations for the performance of the account are realistic and suitable to the client's circumstances and that the risks involved are appropriate. In most circumstances, recommended investment strategies should relate to the long-term objectives and circumstances of the client.

Particular care must be taken to detect whether the goals of the investment manager or the firm in placing business, selling products, and executing security transactions potentially conflict with the best interests and objectives of the client. When members and candidates cannot avoid potential conflicts between their firm and clients' interests, they must provide clear and factual disclosures of the circumstances to the clients.

Members and candidates must follow any guidelines set by their clients for the management of their assets. Some clients, such as charitable organizations and pension plans, have strict investment policies that limit investment options to certain types or classes of investment or prohibit investment in certain securities. Other organizations have aggressive policies that do not prohibit investments by type but, instead, set criteria on the basis of the portfolio's total risk and return.

Investment decisions must be judged in the context of the total portfolio rather than by individual investment within the portfolio. The member's or candidate's duty is satisfied with respect to a particular investment if the individual has thoroughly considered the investment's place in the overall portfolio, the risk of loss and opportunity for gains, tax implications, and the diversification, liquidity, cash flow, and overall return requirements of the assets or the portion of the assets for which the manager is responsible.

Soft Commission Policies

An investment manager often has discretion over the selection of brokers executing transactions. Conflicts arise when an investment manager uses client brokerage to purchase research services that benefit the investment manager, a practice commonly called "soft dollars" or "soft commissions." Whenever members or candidates use client brokerage to purchase goods or services that do not benefit the client, they should disclose to clients the methods or policies followed in addressing the potential conflict. A member or candidate who pays a higher commission than he or she would normally pay to purchase goods or services, without corresponding benefit to the client, violates the duty of loyalty to the client.

From time to time, a client will direct a manager to use the client's brokerage to purchase goods or services for the client, a practice that is commonly called "directed brokerage." Because brokerage commission is an asset of the client and is used to benefit that client, not the manager, such a practice does not violate any duty of loyalty. A member or candidate is obligated to seek "best price" and "best execution," however, and be assured by the client that the goods or services purchased from the brokerage will benefit the account beneficiaries. "Best execution" refers to a trading process that seeks to maximize the value of the client's portfolio within the client's stated investment objectives and constraints. In addition, the member or candidate should disclose to the client that the client may not be getting best execution from the directed brokerage.

Proxy Voting Policies

The duty of loyalty, prudence, and care may apply in a number of situations facing the investment professional other than issues related directly to investing assets.

Part of a member's or candidate's duty of loyalty includes voting proxies in an informed and responsible manner. Proxies have economic value to a client, and members and candidates must ensure that they properly safeguard and maximize this value. An investment manager who fails to vote, casts a vote without considering the impact of the question, or votes blindly with management on nonroutine governance issues (e.g., a change in company capitalization) may violate this standard. Voting of proxies is an integral part of the management of investments.

A cost–benefit analysis may show that voting all proxies may not benefit the client, so voting proxies may not be necessary in all instances. Members and candidates should disclose to clients their proxy voting policies.

Recommended Procedures for Compliance

Regular Account Information

Members and candidates with control of client assets should submit to each client, at least quarterly, an itemized statement showing the funds and securities in the custody or possession of the member or candidate plus all debits, credits, and transactions that occurred during the period; should disclose to the client where the assets are to be maintained, as well as where or when they are moved; and should separate the client's assets from any other party's assets, including the member's or candidate's own assets.

Client Approval

If a member or candidate is uncertain about the appropriate course of action with respect to a client, the member or candidate should ask what he or she would expect or demand if the member or candidate were the client. If in doubt, a member or candidate should disclose the questionable matter in writing to the client and obtain client approval.

Firm Policies

Members and candidates should address and encourage their firms to address the following topics when drafting the statements or manuals containing their policies and procedures regarding responsibilities to clients:

▶ *Follow all applicable rules and laws*: Members and candidates must follow all legal requirements and applicable provisions of the Code and Standards.

▶ *Establish the investment objectives of the client*: Make a reasonable inquiry into a client's investment experience, risk and return objectives, and financial constraints prior to making investment recommendations or taking investment actions.

▶ *Consider all the information when taking actions*: When taking investment actions, members and candidates must consider the appropriateness and suitability of the investment relative to 1) the client's needs and circumstances, 2) the investment's basic characteristics, and 3) the basic characteristics of the total portfolio.

▶ *Diversify*: Members and candidates should diversify investments to reduce the risk of loss, unless diversification is not consistent with plan guidelines or is contrary to the account objectives.

▶ *Carry out regular reviews*: Members and candidates should establish regular review schedules to ensure that the investments held in the account adhere to the terms of the governing documents.

▶ *Deal fairly with all clients with respect to investment actions*: Members and candidates must not favor some clients over others and should establish policies for allocating trades and disseminating investment recommendations.

▶ *Disclose conflicts of interest*: Members and candidates must disclose all actual and potential conflicts of interest so that clients can evaluate those conflicts.

▶ *Disclose compensation arrangements*: Members and candidates should make their clients aware of all forms of manager compensation.

▶ *Vote proxies*: In most cases, members and candidates should determine who is authorized to vote shares and vote proxies in the best interests of the clients and ultimate beneficiaries.

▶ *Maintain confidentiality*: Members and candidates must preserve the confidentiality of client information.

▶ *Seek best execution*: Unless directed by the client as ultimate beneficiary, members and candidates must seek best execution for their clients. (Best execution is defined in the preceding text.)

▶ *Place client interests first*: Members and candidates must serve the best interests of clients.

Application of the Standard

Example 1 (Identifying the Client—Plan Participants): First Country Bank serves as trustee for the Miller Company's pension plan. Miller is the target of a hostile takeover attempt by Newton, Inc. In attempting to ward off Newton, Miller's managers persuade Julian Wiley, an investment manager at First Country Bank, to purchase Miller common stock in the open market for the employee pension plan. Miller's officials indicate that such action would be favorably received and would probably result in other accounts being placed with the bank. Although Wiley believes the stock to be overvalued and would not ordinarily buy it, he purchases the stock to support Miller's managers, to maintain Miller's good favor toward the bank, and to realize additional new business. The heavy stock purchases cause Miller's market price to rise to such a level that Newton retracts its takeover bid.

> *Comment*: Standard III(A) requires that a member or candidate, in evaluating a takeover bid, act prudently and solely in the interests of plan participants and beneficiaries. To meet this requirement, a member or candidate must carefully evaluate the long-term prospects of the company against the short-term prospects presented by the takeover offer and by the ability to invest elsewhere. In this instance, Wiley, acting on behalf of his employer, which was the trustee for a pension plan, clearly violated Standard III(A). He used the pension plan to perpetuate existing management, perhaps to the detriment of plan participants and the company's shareholders, and to benefit himself. Wiley's responsibilities to the plan participants and beneficiaries should have taken precedence over any ties of his bank to corporate managers and over his self-interest. Wiley had a duty to examine the takeover offer on its own merits and to make an independent decision. The guiding principle is the appropriateness of the investment decision to the pension plan, not whether the decision benefited Wiley or the company that hired him.

Example 2 (Client Commission Practices): JNI, a successful investment counseling firm, serves as investment manager for the pension plans of several large regionally based companies. Its trading activities generate a significant amount of commission-related business. JNI uses the brokerage and research services of many firms, but most of its trading activity is handled through a large brokerage company, Thompson, Inc. The reason is that the executives of the two firms have a close friendship. Thompson's commission structure is high in comparison with charges for similar brokerage services from other firms. JNI considers Thompson's research services and execution capabilities average. In exchange for JNI directing its brokerage to Thompson, Thompson absorbs a number of JNI overhead expenses, including those for rent.

Comment: JNI executives are breaching their responsibilities by using client brokerage for services that do not benefit JNI clients and by not obtaining best price and best execution for their clients. Because JNI executives are not upholding their duty of loyalty, they are violating Standard III(A).

Example 3 (Brokerage Arrangements): Charlotte Everett, a struggling independent investment adviser, serves as investment manager for the pension plans of several companies. One of her brokers, Scott Company, is close to consummating management agreements with prospective new clients whereby Everett would manage the new client accounts and trade the accounts exclusively through Scott. One of Everett's existing clients, Crayton Corporation, has directed Everett to place securities transactions for Crayton's account exclusively through Scott. But to induce Scott to exert efforts to send more new accounts to her, Everett also directs transactions to Scott from other clients without their knowledge.

Comment: Everett has an obligation at all times to seek best price and best execution on all trades. Everett may direct new client trades exclusively through Scott Company as long as Everett receives best price and execution on the trades or receives a written statement from new clients that she is *not* to seek best price and execution and that they are aware of the consequence for their accounts. Everett may trade other accounts through Scott as a reward for directing clients to Everett only if the accounts receive best price and execution and the practice is disclosed to the accounts. Because Everett does not disclose the directed trading, Everett has violated Standard III(A).

Example 4 (Brokerage Arrangements): Emilie Rome is a trust officer for Paget Trust Company. Rome's supervisor is responsible for reviewing Rome's trust account transactions and her monthly reports of personal stock transactions. Rome has been using Nathan Gray, a broker, almost exclusively for trust account brokerage transactions. When Gray makes a market in stocks, he has been giving Rome a lower price for personal purchases and a higher price for sales than he gives to Rome's trust accounts and other investors.

Comment: Rome is violating her duty of loyalty to the bank's trust accounts by using Gray for brokerage transactions simply because Gray trades Rome's personal account on favorable terms. Rome is placing her own interests before those of her clients.

Example 5 (Client Commission Practices): Lauren Parker, an analyst with Provo Advisors, covers South American equities for her firm. She likes to travel to the markets for which she is responsible and decides to go on a trip to Chile, Argentina, and Brazil. The trip is sponsored by SouthAM, Inc., a research firm with a small broker/dealer affiliate that uses the clearing facilities of a larger New York brokerage house. SouthAM specializes in arranging South American trips for analysts during which they can meet with central bank officials, government ministers, local economists, and senior executives of corporations. SouthAM accepts commission dollars at a ratio of 2 to 1 against the hard dollar costs of the research fee for the trip. Parker is not sure that SouthAM's execution is competitive, but without informing her supervisor, she directs the trading desk at Provo to start giving commission business to SouthAM so she can take the trip. SouthAM has conveniently timed the briefing trip to coincide with the beginning of Carnival season, so Parker also decides to spend five days of vacation in Rio de Janeiro at the end of the trip. Parker uses commission dollars to pay for the five days of hotel expenses.

Comment: Parker is violating Standard III(A) by not exercising her duty of loyalty to her clients. She should have determined whether the commissions charged by SouthAM are reasonable in relation to the benefit of the research provided by the trip. She also should have determined whether best execution and prices could be received from SouthAM. In addition, the five extra days are not part of the research effort because they do not assist in the investment decision making. Thus, the hotel expenses for the five days should not be paid for with client assets.

Example 6 (Excessive Trading): Vida Knauss manages the portfolios of a number of high-net-worth individuals. A major part of her investment management fee is based on trading commissions. Knauss engages in extensive trading for each of her clients to ensure that she attains the minimum commission level set by her firm. Although the securities purchased and sold for the clients are appropriate and fall within the acceptable asset classes for the clients, the amount of trading for each account exceeds what is necessary to accomplish the client's investment objectives.

Comment: Knauss has violated Standard III(A) because she is using the assets of her clients to benefit her firm and herself.

Example 7 (Managing Family Accounts): Adam Dill recently joined New Investments Asset Managers. To assist Dill in building a book of clients, both his father and brother opened new fee-paying accounts. Dill followed all the firm's procedures in noting his relationships with these clients and in developing their investment policy statements.

After several years, the number of Dill's clients has grown, but he still manages the original accounts of his family members. An IPO is coming to market that is a suitable investment for many of his clients, including his brother. Dill does not receive the amount of stock he requested, so to avoid any appearance of a conflict of interest, he does not allocate any shares to his brother's account.

Comment: Dill has violated Standard III(A) because he is not acting for the benefit of his brother's account as well as his other accounts. The brother's account is a regular fee-paying account comparable to the accounts of his other clients. By not allocating the shares proportionately across *all* accounts for which he thought the IPO was suitable, Dill is disadvantaging specific clients.

Dill would have been correct in not allocating shares to his brother's account if that account was being managed outside the normal fee structure of the firm.

Example 8 (Identifying the Client): Donna Hensley has been hired by a law firm to testify as an expert witness. Although the testimony is intended to represent impartial advice, she is concerned that her work may have negative consequences for the law firm. If the law firm is Hensley's client, how does she ensure that her testimony will not violate the required duty of loyalty, prudence, and care to one's client?

Comment: In this situation, the law firm represents Hensley's employer and the aspect of "who is the client" is not well defined. When acting as an expert witness, Hensley is bound by the standard of independence and objectivity in the same manner as an independent research analyst would be bound. Hensley must not let the law firm influence the testimony she is to provide in the legal proceedings.

Example 9 (Identifying the Client): Jon Miller is a mutual fund portfolio manager. The fund is focused on the global financial services sector. Wanda Spears is a private wealth manager in the same city as Miller and is a friend of Miller. At a local CFA Institute society meeting, Spears mentions to Miller that her new client is an investor in Miller's fund. She states that the two of them now share a responsibility to this client.

> *Comment*: Spears' statement is not totally correct. Because she provides the advisory services to her new client, she alone is bound by the duty of loyalty to this client. Miller's responsibility is to manage the fund according to the investment policy statement of the fund. His actions should not be influenced by the needs of any particular fund investor.

B. Fair Dealing

Members and Candidates must deal fairly and objectively with all clients when providing investment analysis, making investment recommendations, taking investment action, or engaging in other professional activities.

Guidance

Highlights:

- ▶ *Investment Recommendations*
- ▶ *Investment Action*

Standard III(B) requires members and candidates to treat all clients fairly when disseminating investment recommendations or making material changes to prior investment recommendations or when taking investment action with regard to general purchases, new issues, or secondary offerings. Only through the fair treatment of all parties can the investment management profession maintain the confidence of the investing public.

When an investment adviser has multiple clients, the potential exists for the adviser to favor one client over another. This favoritism may take various forms—from the quality and timing of services provided to the allocation of investment opportunities.

The term "fairly" implies that the member or candidate must take care not to discriminate against any clients when disseminating investment recommendations or taking investment action. Standard III(B) does not state "equally" because members and candidates could not possibly reach all clients at exactly the same time—whether by printed mail, telephone (including text messaging), computer (including internet updates and e-mail distribution), facsimile (fax), or wire. Each client has unique needs, investment criteria, and investment objectives, so not all investment opportunities are suitable for all clients. In addition, members and candidates may provide more personal, specialized, or in-depth service to clients who are willing to pay for premium services through higher management fees or higher levels of brokerage. Members and candidates may differentiate their services to clients, but different levels of service must not disadvantage or negatively affect clients. In addition, the different service levels should be disclosed to clients and prospective clients and should be available to everyone (i.e., different service levels should not be offered selectively).

Standard III(B) covers conduct in two broadly defined categories—investment recommendations and investment action.

Investment Recommendations

The first category of conduct involves members and candidates whose primary function is the preparation of investment recommendations to be disseminated either to the public or within a firm for the use of others in making investment decisions. This group includes members and candidates employed by investment counseling, advisory, or consulting firms as well as banks, brokerage firms, and insurance companies. The criterion is that the member's or candidate's primary responsibility is the preparation of recommendations to be acted on by others, including those in the member's or candidate's organization.

An investment recommendation is any opinion expressed by a member or candidate in regard to purchasing, selling, or holding a given security or other investment. The opinion may be disseminated to customers or clients through an initial detailed research report, through a brief update report, by addition to or deletion from a list of recommended securities, or simply by oral communication. A recommendation that is distributed to anyone outside the organization is considered a communication for general distribution under Standard III(B).

Standard III(B) addresses the manner in which investment recommendations or changes in prior recommendations are disseminated to clients. Each member or candidate is obligated to ensure that information is disseminated in such a manner that all clients have a fair opportunity to act on every recommendation. Communicating with all clients on a uniform basis presents practical problems for members and candidates because of differences in timing and methods of communication with various types of customers and clients. Members and candidates should encourage their firms to design an equitable system to prevent selective or discriminatory disclosure and should inform clients about what kind of communications they will receive.

The duty to clients imposed by Standard III(B) may be more critical when members or candidates change their recommendations than when they make initial recommendations. Material changes in a member's or candidate's prior investment recommendations because of subsequent research should be communicated to all current clients; particular care should be taken that the information reaches those clients who the member or candidate knows have acted on or been affected by the earlier advice. Clients who do not know that the member or candidate has changed a recommendation and who, therefore, place orders contrary to a current recommendation should be advised of the changed recommendation before the order is accepted.

Investment Action

The second category of conduct includes those members and candidates whose primary function is taking investment action (portfolio management) on the basis of recommendations prepared internally or received from external sources. Investment action, like investment recommendations, can affect market value. Consequently, Standard III(B) requires that members or candidates treat all clients fairly in light of their investment objectives and circumstances. For example, when making investments in new offerings or in secondary financings, members and candidates should distribute the issues to all customers for whom the investments are appropriate in a manner consistent with the policies of the firm for allocating blocks of stock. If the issue is oversubscribed, then the issue should be prorated to all subscribers. This action should be taken on a round-lot basis to avoid odd-lot distributions. In addition, if the issue is oversubscribed, members and candidates should forgo any sales to themselves or their immediate families in order to free up additional shares for clients. If the investment professional's family-member accounts are managed similarly to the accounts of other clients of the firm, however, the family-member accounts should not be excluded from buying such shares.

Members and candidates must make every effort to treat all individual and institutional clients in a fair and impartial manner. A member or candidate may have multiple relationships with an institution; for example, the member or candidate may be a corporate trustee, pension fund manager, manager of funds for individuals employed by the customer, loan originator, or creditor. A member or candidate must exercise care to treat all clients fairly.

Members and candidates should disclose to clients and prospective clients the documented allocation procedures they or their firms have in place and how the procedures would affect the client or prospect. The disclosure should be clear and complete so that the client can make an informed investment decision. Even when complete disclosure is made, however, members and candidates must put client interests ahead of their own. A member's or candidate's duty of fairness and loyalty to clients can never be overridden by client consent to patently unfair allocation procedures.

Treating clients fairly also means that members and candidates should not take advantage of their position in the industry to the detriment of clients. For instance, in the context of IPOs, members and candidates must make bona fide public distributions of "hot issue" securities (defined as securities of a public offering that are trading at a premium in the secondary market whenever such trading commences because of the great demand for the securities). Members and candidates are prohibited from withholding such securities for their own benefit and must not use such securities as a reward or incentive to gain benefit.

Recommended Procedures for Compliance

Develop Firm Policies

Although Standard III(B) refers to a member's or candidate's responsibility to deal fairly and objectively with clients, members and candidates should also encourage their firms to establish compliance procedures requiring all employees who disseminate investment recommendations or take investment actions to treat customers and clients fairly. At the very least, a member or candidate should recommend appropriate procedures to management if none are in place. And the member or candidate should make management aware of possible violations of fair-dealing practices within the firm when they come to the attention of the member or candidate.

The extent of the formality and complexity of such compliance procedures depends on the nature and size of the organization and the type of securities involved. An investment adviser who is a sole proprietor and handles only discretionary accounts might not disseminate recommendations to the public, but that adviser should have formal written procedures to ensure that all clients receive fair investment action.

Good business practice dictates that initial recommendations be made available to all customers who indicate an interest. Although a member or candidate need not communicate a recommendation to all customers, the selection process by which customers receive information should be based on suitability and known interest, not on any preferred or favored status. A common practice to assure fair dealing is to communicate recommendations simultaneously within the firm and to customers.

Members and candidates should consider the following points when establishing fair-dealing compliance procedures:

▶ *Limit the number of people involved*: Members and candidates should make reasonable efforts to limit the number of people who are privy to the fact that a recommendation is going to be disseminated.

▶ *Shorten the time frame between decision and dissemination*: Members and candidates should make reasonable efforts to limit the amount of time that elapses between the decision to make an investment recommendation and the time the actual recommendation is disseminated. If a detailed institutional recommendation is in preparation that might take two or three weeks to publish, a short summary report including the conclusion might be published in advance. In an organization where both a research committee and an investment policy committee must approve a recommendation, the meetings should be held on the same day if possible. The process of reviewing, printing, and mailing reports or faxing or distributing them by e-mail necessarily involves the passage of time, sometimes long periods of time. In large firms with extensive review processes, the time factor is usually not within the control of the analyst who prepares the report. Thus, many firms and their analysts communicate to customers and firm personnel the new or changed recommendations by an update or "flash" report. The communication technique might be fax, e-mail, wire, or short written report.

▶ *Publish guidelines for pre-dissemination behavior*: Guidelines are needed that prohibit personnel who have prior knowledge of an investment recommendation from discussing or taking any action on the pending recommendation.

▶ *Simultaneous dissemination*: Members and candidates should establish procedures for the timing of dissemination of investment recommendations so that all clients are treated fairly—that is, are informed at approximately the same time. For example, if a firm is going to announce a new recommendation, supervisory personnel should time the announcement to avoid placing any client or group of clients at unfair advantage relative to other clients. A communication to all branch offices should be sent at the time of the general announcement. (When appropriate, the firm should accompany the announcement of a new recommendation with a statement that trading restrictions for the firm's employees are now in effect.) The trading restrictions should stay in effect until the recommendation is widely distributed to all relevant clients. Once this distribution has occurred, the member or candidate may follow up separately with individual clients, but members and candidates should not give favored clients advance information when such advance notification may disadvantage other clients.

▶ *Maintain a list of clients and their holdings*: Members and candidates should maintain a list of all clients and the securities or other investments each client holds in order to facilitate notification of customers or clients of a change in an investment recommendation. If a particular security or other investment is to be sold, such a list can be used to ensure that all holders are treated fairly in the liquidation of that particular investment.

▶ *Develop and document trade allocation procedures*: When formulating procedures for allocating trades, members and candidates should develop a set of guiding principles that ensure:

　▶ fairness to advisory clients, both in priority of execution of orders and in the allocation of the price obtained in execution of block orders or trades;

- ► timeliness and efficiency in the execution of orders; and
- ► accuracy of the member's or candidate's records as to trade orders and client account positions.

With these principles in mind, members and candidates should develop or encourage their firm to develop written allocation procedures, with particular attention to procedures for block trades and new issues. Procedures to consider are as follows:

- ► requiring orders and modifications or cancellations of orders to be documented and time stamped;
- ► processing and executing orders on a first-in, first-out basis with consideration of bundling orders for efficiency as appropriate for the asset class or the security;
- ► developing a policy to address such issues as calculating execution prices and "partial fills" when trades are grouped, or in a block, for efficiency;
- ► giving all client accounts participating in a block trade the same execution price and charging the same commission;
- ► when the full amount of the block order is not executed, allocating partially executed orders among the participating client accounts pro rata on the basis of order size while not going below an established minimum lot size for some securities (e.g., bonds);
- ► when allocating trades for new issues, obtaining advance indications of interest, allocating securities by client (rather than portfolio manager), and providing a method for calculating allocations.

Disclose Trade Allocation Procedures

Members and candidates should disclose to clients and prospective clients how they select accounts to participate in an order and how they determine the amount of securities each account will buy or sell. Trade allocation procedures must be fair and equitable, and disclosure of inequitable allocation methods does not relieve the member or candidate of this obligation.

Establish Systematic Account Review

Member and candidate supervisors should review each account on a regular basis to ensure that no client or customer is being given preferential treatment and that the investment actions taken for each account are suitable for each account's objectives. Because investments should be based on individual needs and circumstances, an investment manager may have good reasons for placing a given security or other investment in one account while selling it from another account and should fully document the reasons behind both sides of the transaction. Members and candidates should encourage firms to establish review procedures, however, to detect whether trading in one account is being used to benefit a favored client.

Disclose Levels of Service

Members and candidates should disclose to all clients whether the organization offers different levels of service to clients for the same fee or different fees. Different levels of service should not be offered to clients selectively.

Application of the Standard

Example 1 (Selective Disclosure): Bradley Ames, a well-known and respected analyst, follows the computer industry. In the course of his research, he finds that a small, relatively unknown company whose shares are traded over the counter has just signed significant contracts with some of the companies he follows. After a considerable amount of investigation, Ames decides to write a research report on the small company and recommend purchase of its shares. While the report is being reviewed by the company for factual accuracy, Ames schedules a luncheon with several of his best clients to discuss the company. At the luncheon, he mentions the purchase recommendation scheduled to be sent early the following week to all the firm's clients.

> *Comment*: Ames has violated Standard III(B) by disseminating the purchase recommendation to the clients with whom he has lunch a week before the recommendation is sent to all clients.

Example 2 (Fair Dealing between Funds): Spencer Rivers, president of XYZ Corporation, moves his company's growth-oriented pension fund to a particular bank primarily because of the excellent investment performance achieved by the bank's commingled fund for the prior five-year period. Later, Rivers compares the results of his pension fund with those of the bank's commingled fund. He is startled to learn that, even though the two accounts have the same investment objectives and similar portfolios, his company's pension fund has significantly underperformed the bank's commingled fund. Questioning this result at his next meeting with the pension fund's manager, Rivers is told that, as a matter of policy, when a new security is placed on the recommended list, Morgan Jackson, the pension fund manager, first purchases the security for the commingled account and then purchases it on a pro rata basis for all other pension fund accounts. Similarly, when a sale is recommended, the security is sold first from the commingled account and then sold on a pro rata basis from all other accounts. Rivers also learns that if the bank cannot get enough shares (especially of hot issues) to be meaningful to all the accounts, its policy is to place the new issues only in the commingled account.

Seeing that Rivers is neither satisfied nor pleased by the explanation, Jackson quickly adds that nondiscretionary pension accounts and personal trust accounts have a lower priority on purchase and sale recommendations than discretionary pension fund accounts. Furthermore, Jackson states, the company's pension fund had the opportunity to invest up to 5 percent in the commingled fund.

> *Comment*: The bank's policy does not treat all customers fairly, and Jackson has violated her duty to her clients by giving priority to the growth-oriented commingled fund over all other funds and to discretionary accounts over nondiscretionary accounts. Jackson must execute orders on a systematic basis that is fair to all clients. In addition, trade allocation procedures should be disclosed to all clients when they become clients. Of course, in this case, disclosure of the bank's policy would not change the fact that the policy is unfair.

Example 3 (Fair Dealing and IPO Distribution): Dominic Morris works for a small regional securities firm. His work consists of corporate finance activities and investing for institutional clients. Arena, Ltd., is planning to go public. The partners have secured rights to buy an arena football league franchise and are planning to use the funds from the issue to complete the purchase. Because arena football is the current rage, Morris believes he has a hot issue on his hands.

He has quietly negotiated some options for himself for helping convince Arena to do the financing through his securities firm. When he seeks expressions of interest, the institutional buyers oversubscribe the issue. Morris, assuming that the institutions have the financial clout to drive the stock up, then fills all orders (including his own) and decreases the institutional blocks.

> *Comment*: Morris has violated Standard III(B) by not treating all customers fairly. He should not have taken any shares himself and should have prorated the shares offered among all clients. In addition, he should have disclosed to his firm and to his clients that he received options as part of the deal [see Standard VI(A)—Disclosure of Conflicts].

Example 4 (Fair Dealing and Transaction Allocation): Eleanor Preston, the chief investment officer of Porter Williams Investments (PWI), a medium-sized money management firm, has been trying to retain a client, Colby Company. Management at Colby, which accounts for almost half of PWI's revenues, recently told Preston that if the performance of its account did not improve, it would find a new money manager. Shortly after this threat, Preston purchases mortgage-backed securities (MBS) for several accounts, including Colby's. Preston is busy with a number of transactions that day, so she fails to allocate the trades immediately or write up the trade tickets. A few days later, when Preston is allocating trades, she notes that some of the MBS have significantly increased in price and some have dropped. Preston decides to allocate the profitable trades to Colby and spread the losing trades among several other PWI accounts.

> *Comment*: Preston has violated Standard III(B) by failing to deal fairly with her clients in taking these investment actions. Preston should have allocated the trades prior to executing the orders, or she should have had a systematic approach to allocating the trades, such as pro rata, as soon as practical after they were executed. Among other things, Preston must disclose to the client that the adviser may act as broker for, receive commissions from, and have a potential conflict of interest regarding both parties in agency cross-transactions. After the disclosure, she should obtain from the client consent authorizing such transactions in advance.

Example 5 (Selective Disclosure): Saunders Industrial Waste Management (SIWM) publicly indicates to analysts that it is comfortable with the somewhat disappointing earnings per share projection of US$1.16 for the quarter. Bernard Roberts, an analyst at Coffey Investments, is confident that SIWM management has understated the forecasted earnings so that the real announcement will cause an "upside surprise" and boost the price of SIWM stock. The "whisper number" (rumored) estimate based on extensive research and discussed among knowledgeable analysts is higher than US$1.16. Roberts repeats the US$1.16 figure in his research report to all Coffey clients but informally tells his large clients that he expects the earnings per share to be higher, making SIWM a good buy.

> *Comment*: By not sharing his opinion regarding the potential for a significant upside earnings surprise with all clients, Roberts is not treating all clients fairly and has violated Standard III(B).

Example 6 (Additional Services for Select Clients): Jenpin Weng uses e-mail to issue a new recommendation to all his clients. He then calls his three largest institutional clients to discuss the recommendation in detail.

> *Comment*: Weng has not violated Standard III(B) because he widely disseminated the recommendation and provided the information to all his clients prior to discussing it with a select few. Weng's largest clients received

additional personal service because they presumably pay higher fees or because they have a large amount of assets under Weng's management. If Weng had discussed the report with a select group of clients prior to distributing it to all his clients, he would have violated Standard III(B).

Example 7 (Minimum Lot Allocations): Lynn Hampton is a well-respected private wealth manager in her community with a diversified client base. She determines that a new 10-year bond being offered by Healthy Pharmaceuticals is appropriate for five of her clients. Three clients request to purchase US$10,000 each, and the other two request US$50,000 each. The minimum lot size is established at US$5,000, and the issue is oversubscribed at the time of placement. Her firm's policy is that odd-lot allocations, especially those below the minimum, should be avoided because they may affect the liquidity of the security at the time of sale.

Hampton is informed she will receive only US$55,000 of the offering for all accounts. Hampton distributes the bond investments as follows: The three accounts that requested US$10,000 are allocated US$5,000 each, and the two accounts that requested US$50,000 are allocated US$20,000 each.

Comment: Hampton has not violated Standard III(B), even though the distribution is not on a complete pro rata basis because of the required minimum lot size. With the total allocation being significantly below the amount requested, Hampton ensured that each client received at least the minimum lot size of the issue. This approach allowed the clients to efficiently sell the bond later if necessary.

C. Suitability

1. **When Members and Candidates are in an advisory relationship with a client, they must:**

   a. **Make a reasonable inquiry into a client's or prospective client's investment experience, risk and return objectives, and financial constraints prior to making any investment recommendation or taking investment action and must reassess and update this information regularly.**

   b. **Determine that an investment is suitable to the client's financial situation and consistent with the client's written objectives, mandates, and constraints before making an investment recommendation or taking investment action.**

   c. **Judge the suitability of investments in the context of the client's total portfolio.**

2. **When Members and Candidates are responsible for managing a portfolio to a specific mandate, strategy, or style, they must make only investment recommendations or take only investment actions that are consistent with the stated objectives and constraints of the portfolio.**

Guidance

Highlights:

► *Developing an Investment Policy*
► *Understanding the Client's Risk Profile*

▶ *Updating an Investment Policy*

▶ *The Need for Diversification*

▶ *Managing to an Index or Mandate*

Standard III(C) requires that members and candidates who are in an investment advisory relationship with clients consider carefully the needs, circumstances, and objectives of the clients when determining the appropriateness and suitability of a given investment or course of investment action. An appropriate suitability determination will not, however, prevent some investments or investment actions from losing value.

In judging the suitability of a potential investment, the member or candidate should review many aspects of the client's knowledge, experience related to investing, and financial situation. These aspects include, but are not limited to, the risk profile of the investment as compared with the constraints of the client, the impact of the investment on the diversity of the portfolio, and whether the client has the means or net worth to assume the associated risk. The investment professional's determination of suitability should reflect only the investment recommendations or actions that a prudent person would be willing to undertake. Not every investment opportunity will be suitable for every portfolio, regardless of the potential return being offered.

The responsibilities of members and candidates to gather information and make a suitability analysis prior to making a recommendation or taking investment action fall on those members and candidates who provide investment advice in the course of an advisory relationship with a client. Other members and candidates may be simply executing specific instructions for retail clients when buying or selling securities, such as shares in mutual funds. These members and candidates and some others, such as sell-side analysts, may not have the opportunity to judge the suitability of a particular investment for the ultimate client. In cases of unsolicited trade requests that a member or candidate knows are unsuitable for the client, the member or candidate should refrain from making the trade or should seek an affirmative statement from the client that suitability is not a consideration.

Developing an Investment Policy

When an advisory relationship exists, members and candidates must gather client information at the inception of the relationship. Such information includes the client's financial circumstances, personal data (such as age and occupation) that are relevant to investment decisions, attitudes toward risk, and objectives in investing. This information should be incorporated into a written investment policy statement (IPS) that addresses the client's risk tolerance, return requirements, and all investment constraints (including time horizon, liquidity needs, tax concerns, legal and regulatory factors, and unique circumstances). Without identifying such client factors, members and candidates cannot judge whether a particular investment or strategy is suitable for a particular client. The IPS also should identify and describe the roles and responsibilities of the parties to the advisory relationship and investment process, as well as schedules for review and evaluation of the IPS. After formulating long-term capital market expectations, members and candidates can assist in developing an appropriate strategic asset allocation and investment program for the client, whether these are presented in separate documents or incorporated in the IPS or in appendices to the IPS.

Understanding the Client's Risk Profile

One of the most important factors to be considered in matching appropriateness and suitability of an investment with a client's needs and circumstances is measuring that client's tolerance for risk. The investment professional must consider the possibilities of rapidly changing investment environments and their likely impact on a client's holdings, both individual securities and the collective portfolio. The risk of many investment strategies can and should be analyzed and quantified in advance.

The use of synthetic investment vehicles and derivative investment products has introduced particular issues of risk. Members and candidates should pay careful attention to the leverage inherent in many of these vehicles or products when considering them for use in a client's investment program. Such leverage and limited liquidity, depending on the degree to which they are hedged, bear directly on the issue of suitability for the client.

Updating an Investment Policy

Updating the IPS should be repeated at least annually and also prior to material changes to any specific investment recommendations or decisions on behalf of the client. The effort to determine the needs and circumstances of each client is not a one-time occurrence. Investment recommendations or decisions are usually part of an ongoing process that takes into account the diversity and changing nature of portfolio and client characteristics. The passage of time is bound to produce changes that are important with respect to investment objectives.

For an individual client, important changes might include the number of dependents, personal tax status, health, liquidity needs, risk tolerance, amount of wealth beyond that represented in the portfolio, and extent to which compensation and other income provide for current-income needs. With respect to an institutional client, such changes might relate to the magnitude of unfunded liabilities in a pension fund, the withdrawal privileges in an employee savings plan, or the distribution requirements of a charitable foundation. Without efforts to update information concerning client factors, one or more factors could change without the investment manager's knowledge.

Suitability review can be done effectively only if the client fully discloses his or her complete financial portfolio, including those portions not managed by the member or candidate. If clients withhold information about their financial portfolio, the suitability analysis conducted by members and candidates cannot be expected to be complete; it must be based on the information provided.

The Need for Diversification

The investment profession has long recognized that the combination of several different investments is likely to provide a more acceptable level of risk exposure than having all assets in a single investment. The unique characteristics (or risks) of an individual investment may become partially or entirely neutralized when it is combined with other individual investments within a portfolio. Some reasonable amount of diversification is thus the norm for many portfolios, especially those managed by individuals or institutions that have some degree of legal fiduciary responsibility.

An investment with high relative risk on its own may be a suitable investment in the context of the entire portfolio or when the client's stated objectives contemplate speculative or risky investments. The manager may be responsible for only a portion of the client's total portfolio, or the client may not have provided a full financial picture. Members and candidates can be responsible for assessing the suitability of an investment only on the basis of the information and criteria actually provided by the client.

Managing to an Index or Mandate

Some members and candidates do not manage money for individuals but are responsible for managing a fund to an index or an expected mandate. The responsibility of these members and candidates is to invest in a manner consistent with the stated mandate. For example, a member or candidate who serves as the fund manager for a large-cap income fund would not be following the fund mandate by investing heavily in small-cap or start-up companies whose stock is speculative in nature. Members and candidates who manage pooled assets to a specific mandate are not responsible for determining the suitability of the fund as an investment for investors who may be purchasing shares in the fund. The responsibility for determining the suitability of an investment for clients can only be conferred on members and candidates who have an advisory relationship with clients.

Recommended Procedures for Compliance

Investment Policy Statement

To fulfill the basic provisions of Standard III(C), a member or candidate should put the needs and circumstances of each client and the client's investment objectives into a written investment policy statement. In formulating an investment policy for the client, the member or candidate should take the following into consideration:

- ▶ client identification—1) type and nature of client, 2) the existence of separate beneficiaries, and 3) approximate portion of total client assets that the member or candidate is managing;
- ▶ investor objectives—1) return objectives (income, growth in principal, maintenance of purchasing power) and 2) risk tolerance (suitability, stability of values);
- ▶ investor constraints—1) liquidity needs, 2) expected cash flows (patterns of additions and/or withdrawals), 3) investable funds (assets and liabilities or other commitments), 4) time horizon, 5) tax considerations, 6) regulatory and legal circumstances, 7) investor preferences, prohibitions, circumstances, and unique needs, and 8) proxy voting responsibilities and guidance;
- ▶ performance measurement benchmarks.

Regular Updates

The investor's objectives and constraints should be maintained and reviewed periodically to reflect any changes in the client's circumstances. Members and candidates should regularly compare client constraints with capital market expectations to arrive at an appropriate asset allocation. Changes in either factor may result in a fundamental change in asset allocation. Annual review is reasonable unless business or other reasons, such as a major change in market conditions, dictate more frequent review. Members and candidates should document attempts to carry out such a review if circumstances prevent it.

Suitability Test Policies

With the increase in regulatory required suitability tests, members and candidates should encourage their firms to develop related policies and procedures. The procedures will differ according to the size of the firm and scope of the services offered to its clients.

The test procedures should require the investment professional to look beyond the potential return of the investment and include the following:

▶ an analysis on the impact on the portfolio's diversification;

▶ a comparison of the investment risks with the client's assessed risk tolerance; and

▶ the fit of the investment with the required investment strategy.

Application of the Standard

Example 1 (Investment Suitability—Risk Profile): Caleb Smith, an investment adviser, has two clients: Larry Robertson, 60 years old, and Gabriel Lanai, 40 years old. Both clients earn roughly the same salary, but Robertson has a much higher risk tolerance because he has a large asset base. Robertson is willing to invest part of his assets very aggressively; Lanai wants only to achieve a steady rate of return with low volatility to pay for his children's education. Smith recommends investing 20 percent of both portfolios in zero-yield, small-cap, high-technology equity issues.

> *Comment*: In Robertson's case, the investment may be appropriate because of his financial circumstances and aggressive investment position, but this investment is not suitable for Lanai. Smith is violating Standard III(C) by applying Robertson's investment strategy to Lanai because the two clients' financial circumstances and objectives differ.

Example 2 (Investment Suitability—Entire Portfolio): Jessica Walters, an investment adviser, suggests to Brian Crosby, a risk-averse client, that covered call options be used in his equity portfolio. The purpose would be to enhance Crosby's income and partially offset any untimely depreciation in the portfolio's value should the stock market or other circumstances affect his holdings unfavorably. Walters educates Crosby about all possible outcomes, including the risk of incurring an added tax liability if a stock rises in price and is called away and, conversely, the risk of his holdings losing protection on the downside if prices drop sharply.

> *Comment*: When determining suitability of an investment, the primary focus should be on the characteristics of the client's entire portfolio, not the characteristics of single securities on an issue-by-issue basis. The basic characteristics of the entire portfolio will largely determine whether investment recommendations are taking client factors into account. Therefore, the most important aspects of a particular investment are those that will affect the characteristics of the total portfolio. In this case, Walters properly considers the investment in the context of the entire portfolio and thoroughly explains the investment to the client.

Example 3 (IPS Updating): In a regular meeting with client Seth Jones, the portfolio managers at Blue Chip Investment Advisors are careful to allow some time to review his current needs and circumstances. In doing so, they learn that some significant changes have recently taken place in his life. A wealthy uncle left Jones an inheritance that increased his net worth fourfold, to US$1,000,000.

Comment: The inheritance has significantly increased Jones's ability (and possibly his willingness) to assume risk and has diminished the average yield required to meet his current-income needs. Jones's financial circumstances have definitely changed, so Blue Chip managers must update Jones's investment policy statement to reflect how his investment objectives have changed. Accordingly, the Blue Chip portfolio managers should consider a somewhat higher equity ratio for his portfolio than was called for by the previous circumstances, and the managers' specific common stock recommendations might be heavily tilted toward low-yield, growth-oriented issues.

Example 4 (Following an Investment Mandate): Louis Perkowski manages a high-income mutual fund. He purchases zero-dividend stock in a financial services company because he believes the stock is undervalued and is in a potential growth industry, which makes it an attractive investment.

Comment: A zero-dividend stock does not seem to fit the mandate of the fund that Perkowski is managing. Unless Perkowski's investment fits within the mandate or is within the realm of allowable investments the fund has made clear in its disclosures, Perkowski has violated Standard III(C).

Example 5 (IPS Requirements and Limitations): Max Gubler, chief investment officer of a property/casualty insurance subsidiary of a large financial conglomerate, wants to improve the diversification of the subsidiary's investment portfolio and increase its returns. The subsidiary's investment policy statement provides for highly liquid investments, such as large-cap equities and government, supranational, and corporate bonds with a minimum credit rating of AA and maturity of no more than five years. In a recent presentation, a venture capital group offered very attractive prospective returns on some of its private equity funds that provide seed capital to ventures. An exit strategy was already contemplated, but investors would have to observe a minimum three-year lock-up period and a subsequent laddered exit option for a maximum of one-third of their shares per year. Gubler does not want to miss this opportunity. After extensive analysis, with the intent to optimize the return on the equity assets within the subsidiary's current portfolio, he invests 4 percent in this seed fund, leaving the portfolio's total equity exposure still well below its upper limit.

Comment: Gubler is violating Standard III(A)—Loyalty, Prudence, and Care as well as Standard III(C). His new investment locks up part of the subsidiary's assets for at least three years and up to as many as five years and possibly beyond. The IPS requires investments in highly liquid investments and describes accepted asset classes; private equity investments with a lock-up period certainly do not qualify. Even without a lock-up period, an asset class with only an occasional, and thus implicitly illiquid, market may not be suitable for the portfolio. Although an IPS typically describes objectives and constraints in great detail, the manager must also make every effort to understand the client's business and circumstances. Doing so should enable the manager to recognize, understand, and discuss with the client other factors that may be or may become material in the investment management process.

Example 6 (Submanager and IPS Reviews): Paul Ostrowski's investment management business has grown significantly over the past couple of years, and some clients want to diversify internationally. Ostrowski decides to find a submanager to handle the expected international investments. Because this will be his first subadviser, Ostrowski uses the CFA Institute model "request for proposal" to design a questionnaire for his search. By his deadline, he receives seven completed questionnaires from a variety of domestic and international firms trying to gain his business. Ostrowski reviews all the applications in detail and decides to select the firm that charges the lowest fees because doing so will have the least impact on his firm's bottom line.

> *Comment*: When selecting an external or subadviser, Ostrowski needs to ensure that the new manager's services are appropriate for his clients. This due diligence includes comparing the risk profile of the clients with the investment strategy of the manager. In basing the decision on the fee structure alone, Ostrowski may be violating Standard III(C).
>
> When clients ask to diversify into international products, it is an appropriate time to review and update the clients' IPS. Ostrowski's review may determine that the risk of international investments modifies the risk profiles of the clients or does not represent an appropriate investment.
>
> See also Standard V(A)—Diligence and Reasonable Basis for further discussion of the review process needed in selecting appropriate submanagers.

Example 7 (Investment Suitability—Risk Profile): Samantha Snead, a portfolio manager for Thomas Investment Counsel, Inc., specializes in managing public retirement funds and defined-benefit pension plan accounts, all of which have long-term investment objectives. A year ago, Snead's employer, in an attempt to motivate and retain key investment professionals, introduced a bonus compensation system that rewards portfolio managers on the basis of quarterly performance relative to their peers and to certain benchmark indices. In an attempt to improve the short-term performance of her accounts, Snead changes her investment strategy and purchases several high-beta stocks for client portfolios. These purchases are seemingly contrary to the clients' investment policy statements. Following their purchase, an officer of Griffin Corporation, one of Snead's pension fund clients, asks why Griffin Corporation's portfolio seems to be dominated by high-beta stocks of companies that often appear among the most actively traded issues. No change in objective or strategy has been recommended by Snead during the year.

> *Comment*: Snead violated Standard III(C) by investing the clients' assets in high-beta stocks. These high-risk investments are contrary to the long-term risk profile established in the clients' IPS. Snead has changed the investment strategy of the clients in an attempt to reap short-term rewards offered by her firm's new compensation arrangement, not in response to changes in clients' investment policy statements.
>
> See also Standard VI(A)—Disclosure of Conflicts.

Example 8 (Investment Suitability): Andre Shrub owns and operates Conduit, an investment advisory firm. Prior to opening Conduit, Shrub was an account manager with Elite Investment, a hedge fund managed by his good friend Adam Reed. To attract clients to a new Conduit fund, Shrub offers lower-than-normal management fees. He can do so because the fund consists of two top-performing funds managed by Reed. Given his personal friendship with Reed and the prior performance record of these two funds, Shrub believes this new fund is a winning combination for all parties. Clients quickly invest with Conduit to gain access to the Elite funds. No one is turned away because Conduit is seeking to expand its assets under management.

> *Comment*: Shrub has violated Standard III(C) because the risk profile of the new fund may not be suitable for every client. As an investment adviser, Shrub needs to establish an investment policy statement for each client and recommend only investments that match that client's risk and return profile in that client's IPS. Shrub is required to act as more than a simple sales agent for Elite.

Although Shrub cannot disobey the direct request of a client to purchase a specific security, he should fully discuss the risks of a planned purchase and provide reasons why it might not be suitable for a client. This requirement may lead members and candidates to decline new customers if those customers' requested investment decisions are significantly out of line with their stated requirements.

See also Standard V(A)—Diligence and Reasonable Basis.

D. Performance Presentation

When communicating investment performance information, Members and Candidates must make reasonable efforts to ensure that it is fair, accurate, and complete.

Guidance

Standard III(D) requires members and candidates to provide credible performance information to clients and prospective clients and to avoid misstating performance or misleading clients and prospective clients about the investment performance of members or candidates or their firms. This standard encourages full disclosure of investment performance data to clients and prospective clients.

Standard III(D) covers any practice that would lead to misrepresentation of a member's or candidate's performance record, whether the practice involves performance presentation or performance measurement. This standard prohibits misrepresentations of past performance or reasonably expected performance. A member or candidate must give a fair and complete presentation of performance information whenever communicating data with respect to the performance history of individual accounts, composites or groups of accounts, or composites of an analyst's or firm's performance results. Furthermore, members and candidates should not state or imply that clients will obtain or benefit from a rate of return that was generated in the past.

The requirements of this standard are not limited to members and candidates managing separate accounts. Whenever a member or candidate provides performance information for which the manager is claiming responsibility, such as for pooled funds, the history must be accurate. Research analysts promoting the success or accuracy of their recommendations must ensure that their claims are fair, accurate, and complete.

If the presentation is brief, the member or candidate must make available to clients and prospects, on request, the detailed information supporting that communication. Best practice dictates that brief presentations include a reference to the limited nature of the information provided.

Recommended Procedures for Compliance

Apply GIPS Standards. For members and candidates who are showing the performance history of the assets they manage, compliance with the GIPS standards is the best method to meet their obligations under Standard III(D). Members and candidates should encourage their firms to comply with the GIPS standards.

Compliance without Applying GIPS Standards

Members and candidates can also meet their obligations under Standard III(D) by:

▶ considering the knowledge and sophistication of the audience to whom a performance presentation is addressed;

▶ presenting the performance of the weighted composite of similar portfolios rather than using a single representative account;

▶ including terminated accounts as part of performance history with a clear indication of when the accounts were terminated;

▶ including disclosures that fully explain the performance results being reported (for example, stating, when appropriate, that results are simulated when model results are used, clearly indicating when the performance record is that of a prior entity, or disclosing whether the performance is gross of fees, net of fees, or after tax); and

▶ maintaining the data and records used to calculate the performance being presented.

Application of the Standard

Example 1 (Performance Calculation and Length of Time): Kyle Taylor of Taylor Trust Company, noting the performance of Taylor's common trust fund for the past two years, states in a brochure sent to his potential clients, "You can expect steady 25 percent annual compound growth of the value of your investments over the year." Taylor Trust's common trust fund did increase at the rate of 25 percent per year for the past year, which mirrored the increase of the entire market. The fund has never averaged that growth for more than one year, however, and the average rate of growth of all of its trust accounts for five years is 5 percent per year.

> *Comment*: Taylor's brochure is in violation of Standard III(D). Taylor should have disclosed that the 25 percent growth occurred only in one year. Additionally, Taylor did not include client accounts other than those in the firm's common trust fund. A general claim of firm performance should take into account the performance of all categories of accounts. Finally, by stating that clients can expect a steady 25 percent annual compound growth rate, Taylor is also violating Standard I(C)—Misrepresentation, which prohibits assurances or guarantees regarding an investment.

Example 2 (Performance Calculation and Asset Weighting): Anna Judd, a senior partner of Alexander Capital Management, circulates a performance report for the capital appreciation accounts for the years 1988 through 2004. The firm claims compliance with the GIPS standards. Returns are not calculated in accordance with the requirements of the GIPS standards, however, because the composites are not asset weighted.

> *Comment*: Judd is in violation of Standard III(D). When claiming compliance with GIPS standards, firms must meet all of the requirements, make mandatory disclosures, and meet any other requirements that apply to that firm's specific situation. Judd's violation is not from any misuse of the data but from a false claim of GIPS compliance.

Example 3 (Performance Presentation and Prior Fund/Employer): Aaron McCoy is vice president and managing partner of the equity investment group of

Mastermind Financial Advisors, a new business. Mastermind recruited McCoy because he had a proven six-year track record with G&P Financial. In developing Mastermind's advertising and marketing campaign, McCoy prepares an advertisement that includes the equity investment performance he achieved at G&P Financial. The advertisement for Mastermind does not identify the equity performance as being earned while at G&P. The advertisement is distributed to existing clients and prospective clients of Mastermind.

> *Comment*: McCoy has violated Standard III(D) by distributing an advertisement that contains material misrepresentations about the historical performance of Mastermind. Standard III(D) requires that members and candidates make every reasonable effort to ensure that performance information is a fair, accurate, and complete representation of an individual's or firm's performance. As a general matter, this standard does not prohibit showing past performance of funds managed at a prior firm as part of a performance track record as long as showing that record is accompanied by appropriate disclosures about where the performance took place and the person's specific role in achieving that performance. If McCoy chooses to use his past performance from G&P in Mastermind's advertising, he should make full disclosure of the source of the historical performance.

Example 4 (Performance Presentation and Simulated Results): Jed Davis has developed a mutual fund selection product based on historical information from the 1990–95 period. Davis tested his methodology by applying it retroactively to data from the 1996–2003 period, thus producing simulated performance results for those years. In January 2004, Davis's employer decided to offer the product and Davis began promoting it through trade journal advertisements and direct dissemination to clients. The advertisements included the performance results for the 1996–2003 period but did not indicate that the results were simulated.

> *Comment*: Davis violated Standard III(D) by failing to clearly identify simulated performance results. Standard III(D) prohibits members and candidates from making any statements that misrepresent the performance achieved by them or their firms and requires members and candidates to make every reasonable effort to ensure that performance information presented to clients is fair, accurate, and complete. Use of simulated results should be accompanied by full disclosure as to the source of the performance data, including the fact that the results from 1995 through 2003 were the result of applying the model retroactively to that time period.

Example 5 (Performance Calculation and Selected Accounts Only): In a presentation prepared for prospective clients, William Kilmer shows the rates of return realized over a five-year period by a "composite" of his firm's discretionary accounts that have a "balanced" objective. This composite consisted of only a few of the accounts, however, that met the balanced criterion set by the firm, excluded accounts under a certain asset level without disclosing the fact of their exclusion, and included accounts that did not have the balanced mandate because those accounts would boost the investment results. In addition, to achieve better results, Kilmer manipulated the narrow range of accounts included in the composite by changing the accounts that made up the composite over time.

> *Comment*: Kilmer violated Standard III(D) by misrepresenting the facts in the promotional material sent to prospective clients, distorting his firm's performance record, and failing to include disclosures that would have clarified the presentation.

E. Preservation of Confidentiality

Members and Candidates must keep information about current, former, and prospective clients confidential unless:

1. **The information concerns illegal activities on the part of the client;**
2. **Disclosure is required by law; or**
3. **The client or prospective client permits disclosure of the information.**

Guidance

Highlights:

▶ *Status of Client*
▶ *Compliance with Laws*
▶ *Electronic Information and Security*
▶ *Professional Conduct Investigations by CFA Institute*

Standard III(E) requires that members and candidates preserve the confidentiality of information communicated to them by their clients, prospective clients, and former clients. This standard is applicable when 1) the member or candidate receives information because of his or her special ability to conduct a portion of the client's business or personal affairs and 2) the member or candidate receives information that arises from or is relevant to that portion of the client's business that is the subject of the special or confidential relationship. If disclosure of the information is required by law or the information concerns illegal activities by the client, however, the member or candidate may have an obligation to report the activities to the appropriate authorities.

Status of Client

This standard protects the confidentiality of client information even if the person or entity is no longer a client of the member or candidate. Therefore, members and candidates must continue to maintain the confidentiality of client records even after the client relationship has ended. If a client or former client expressly authorizes the member or candidate to disclose information, however, the member or candidate may follow the terms of the authorization and provide the information.

Compliance with Laws

As a general matter, members and candidates must comply with applicable law. If applicable law requires disclosure of client information in certain circumstances, members and candidates must comply with the law. Similarly, if applicable law requires members and candidates to maintain confidentiality, even if the information concerns illegal activities on the part of the client, members and candidates should not disclose such information. When in doubt, members and candidates should consult with their employer's compliance personnel or legal counsel before disclosing confidential information about clients.

Electronic Information and Security

Because of the ever increasing volume of electronically stored information, members and candidates need to be particularly aware of possible accidental disclosures. Many employers have strict policies about storing client information on personal laptops or portable drives. Standard III(E) does not require members or candidates to become experts in information security technology, but they should have a thorough understanding of the policies of their employers. The size and operations of the firm will lead to differing policies for ensuring the security of confidential information maintained within the firm.

Professional Conduct Investigations by CFA Institute

The requirements of Standard III(E) are not intended to prevent members and candidates from cooperating with an investigation by the CFA Institute Professional Conduct Program (PCP). When permissible under applicable law, members and candidates shall consider the PCP an extension of themselves when requested to provide information about a client in support of a PCP investigation into their own conduct. Members and candidates are encouraged to cooperate with investigations into the conduct of others. Any information turned over to the PCP is kept in the strictest confidence. Members and candidates will not be considered in violation of this standard by forwarding confidential information to the PCP.

Recommended Procedures for Compliance

The simplest, most conservative, and most effective way to comply with Standard III(E) is to avoid disclosing any information received from a client except to authorized fellow employees who are also working for the client. In some instances, however, a member or candidate may want to disclose information received from clients that is outside the scope of the confidential relationship and does not involve illegal activities. Before making such a disclosure, a member or candidate should ask the following:

▶ In what context was the information disclosed? If disclosed in a discussion of work being performed for the client, is the information relevant to the work?

▶ Is the information background material that, if disclosed, will enable the member or candidate to improve service to the client?

Members and candidates need to understand and follow their firm's electronic information storage procedures. If the firm does not have procedures in place, members and candidates should encourage the development of procedures that appropriately reflect the firm's size and business operations.

Application of the Standard

Example 1 (Possessing Confidential Information): Sarah Connor, a financial analyst employed by Johnson Investment Counselors, Inc., provides investment advice to the trustees of City Medical Center. The trustees have given her a number of internal reports concerning City Medical's needs for physical plant renovation and expansion. They have asked Connor to recommend investments that would generate capital appreciation in endowment funds to meet projected capital expenditures. Connor is approached by a local businessman, Thomas Kasey, who is considering a substantial contribution either to City Medical Center or to another local hospital. Kasey wants to find out the building plans of both institutions before making a decision, but he does not want to speak to the trustees.

Comment: The trustees gave Connor the internal reports so she could advise them on how to manage their endowment funds. Because the information in the reports is clearly both confidential and within the scope of the confidential relationship, Standard III(E) requires that Connor refuse to divulge information to Kasey.

Example 2 (Disclosing Confidential Information): Lynn Moody is an investment officer at the Lester Trust Company. She has an advisory customer who has talked to her about giving approximately US$50,000 to charity to reduce her income taxes. Moody is also treasurer of the Home for Indigent Widows (HIW), which is planning its annual giving campaign. HIW hopes to expand its list of prospects, particularly those capable of substantial gifts. Moody recommends that HIW's vice president for corporate gifts call on her customer and ask for a donation in the US$50,000 range.

Comment: Even though the attempt to help the Home for Indigent Widows was well intended, Moody violated Standard III(E) by revealing confidential information about her client.

Example 3 (Disclosing Possible Illegal Activity): Government officials approach Casey Samuel, the portfolio manager for Garcia Company's pension plan, to examine pension fund records. They tell her that Garcia's corporate tax returns are being audited and the pension fund is being reviewed. Two days earlier, Samuel had learned in a regular investment review with Garcia officers that potentially excessive and improper charges were being made to the pension plan by Garcia. Samuel consults her employer's general counsel and is advised that Garcia has probably violated tax and fiduciary regulations and laws.

Comment: Samuel should inform her supervisor of these activities, and her employer should take steps, with Garcia, to remedy the violations. If that approach is not successful, Samuel and her employer should seek advice of legal counsel to determine the appropriate steps to be taken. Samuel may well have a duty to disclose the evidence she has of the continuing legal violations and to resign as asset manager for Garcia.

Example 4 (Disclosing Possible Illegal Activity): David Bradford manages money for a family-owned real estate development corporation. He also manages the individual portfolios of several of the family members and officers of the corporation, including the chief financial officer (CFO). Based on the financial records of the corporation and some questionable practices of the CFO that Bradford has observed, Bradford believes that the CFO is embezzling money from the corporation and putting it into his personal investment account.

Comment: Bradford should check with his firm's compliance department or appropriate legal counsel to determine whether applicable securities regulations require reporting the CFO's financial records.

STANDARD IV—DUTIES TO EMPLOYERS

A. Loyalty

In matters related to their employment, Members and Candidates must act for the benefit of their employer and not deprive their employer of the advantage of their skills and abilities, divulge confidential information, or otherwise cause harm to their employer.

Guidance

Highlights:

▶ *Employer Responsibilities*
▶ *Independent Practice*
▶ *Leaving an Employer*
▶ *Whistleblowing*
▶ *Nature of Employment*

Standard IV(A) requires members and candidates to protect the interests of their firm by refraining from any conduct that would injure the firm, deprive it of profit, or deprive it of the member's or candidate's skills and ability. Members and candidates must always place the interests of clients above the interests of their employer but should also consider the effects of their conduct on the sustainability and integrity of the employer firm. In matters related to their employment, members and candidates must not engage in conduct that harms the interests of their employer. Implicit in this standard is the obligation of members and candidates to comply with the policies and procedures established by their employers that govern the employer–employee relationship—to the extent that such policies and procedures do not conflict with applicable laws, rules, regulations, or the Code and Standards.

This standard is not meant to be a blanket requirement to place employer interests ahead of personal interests in all matters. The standard does not require members and candidates to subordinate important personal and family obligations to their work. Members and candidates should enter into a dialogue with their employer about balancing personal and employment obligations when personal matters may interfere with their work on a regular or significant basis.

Employer Responsibilities

The employer–employee relationship imposes duties and responsibilities on both parties. Employers must recognize the duties and responsibilities that they owe to their employees if they expect to have contented and productive employees.

Members and candidates are encouraged to provide their employers with a copy of the Code and Standards. These materials will inform the employer of the responsibilities of a CFA Institute member or candidate in the CFA Program. The Code and Standards also serve as a basis for questioning employer policies and practices that conflict with these responsibilities.

Employers are not obligated to adhere to the Code and Standards. In expecting to retain competent employees who are members and candidates, however, they should not develop conflicting policies and procedures. The employer is responsible for a positive working environment, which includes an ethical workplace. Senior management has the additional responsibility to devise compensation structures and incentive arrangements that do not encourage unethical behavior.

Independent Practice

Included in Standard IV(A) is the requirement that members and candidates abstain from independent competitive activity that could conflict with the interests of their employer. Although Standard IV(A) does not preclude members or candidates from entering into an independent business while still employed, members and candidates who plan to engage in independent practice for compensation must notify their employer and describe the types of services the members or candidates will render to prospective independent clients, the expected duration of the services, and the compensation for the services. Members and candidates should not render services until they receive consent from their employer to all of the terms of the arrangement. "Practice" means any service that the employer currently makes available for remuneration. "Undertaking independent practice" means engaging in competitive business, as opposed to making preparations to begin such practice.

Leaving an Employer

When members and candidates are planning to leave their current employer, they must continue to act in the employer's best interest. They must not engage in any activities that would conflict with this duty until their resignation becomes effective. It is difficult to define specific guidelines for those members and candidates who are planning to compete with their employer as part of a new venture. The circumstances of each situation must be reviewed to distinguish permissible preparations from violations of duty. Activities that might constitute a violation, especially in combination, include the following:

▶ misappropriation of trade secrets;

▶ misuse of confidential information;

▶ solicitation of employer's clients prior to cessation of employment;

▶ self-dealing (appropriating for one's own property a business opportunity or information belonging to one's employer); and

▶ misappropriation of clients or client lists.

A departing employee is generally free to make arrangements or preparations to go into a competitive business before terminating the relationship with his or her employer as long as such preparations do not breach the employee's duty of loyalty. Members and candidates who are contemplating seeking other employment must not contact existing clients or potential clients prior to leaving their employer for purposes of soliciting their business for the new employer. Once notice is provided to the employer of the intent to resign, the member or candidate must follow the employer's policies and procedures related to notifying clients of his or her planned departure. In addition, the member or candidate must not take records or files to a new employer without the written permission of the previous employer.

Once an employee has left the firm, the skills and experience that an employee obtained while employed are not "confidential" or "privileged" information. Similarly, simple knowledge of the names and existence of former clients is generally not confidential information unless deemed such by an agreement or by law. Standard IV(A) does not prohibit experience or knowledge gained at one employer from being used at another employer. Firm records, however, or work performed on behalf of the firm that is stored in paper copy or electronically for the member's or candidate's convenience while employed should be erased or returned to the employer unless the firm gives permission to keep those records after employment ends.

The standard does not prohibit former employees from contacting clients of their previous firm as long as the contact information does not come from the records of the former employer or violate an applicable "noncompete agreement." Members and candidates are free to use public information after departing to contact former clients without violating Standard IV(A) as long as there is no specific agreement not to do so.

Employers often require employees to sign noncompete agreements that preclude a departing employee from engaging in certain conduct. Members and candidates should take care to review the terms of any such agreement when leaving their employer to determine what, if any, conduct those agreements may prohibit.

Whistleblowing

A member's or candidate's personal interests, as well as the interests of his or her employer, are secondary to protecting the integrity of capital markets and the interests of clients. Therefore, circumstances may arise (e.g., when an employer is engaged in illegal or unethical activity) in which members and candidates must act contrary to their employer's interests in order to comply with their duties to the market and clients. In such instances, activities that would normally violate a member's or candidate's duty to his or her employer (such as contradicting employer instructions, violating certain policies and procedures, or preserving a record by copying employer records) may be justified. Such action would be permitted only if the intent is clearly aimed at protecting clients or the integrity of the market, not for personal gain.

Nature of Employment

A wide variety of business relationships exists within the investment industry. For instance, a member or candidate may be an employee or an independent contractor. Members and candidates must determine whether they are employees or independent contractors in order to determine the applicability of Standard IV(A). This issue will be decided largely by the degree of control exercised by the employing entity over the member or candidate. Factors determining control include whether the member's or candidate's hours, work location, and other parameters of the job are set; whether facilities are provided to the member or candidate; whether the member's or candidate's expenses are reimbursed; whether the member or candidate seeks work from other employers; and the number of clients or employers the member or candidate works for.

A member's or candidate's duties within an independent contractor relationship are governed by the oral or written agreement between the member and the client. Members and candidates should take care to define clearly the scope of their responsibilities and the expectations of each client within the context of each relationship. Once the member or candidate establishes a relationship with a client, the member or candidate has a duty to abide by the terms of the agreement.

Recommended Procedures for Compliance

Employers may establish codes of conduct and operating procedures for their employees to follow. Members and candidates should fully understand the policies to ensure that they are not in conflict with the Code and Standards. The following topics identify policies that members and candidates should encourage their firms to adopt if the policies are not currently in their procedures.

Competition Policy

Members and candidates must understand any restrictions placed by the employer on offering similar services outside the firm while employed by the firm. The policy may outline the procedures for requesting approval to undertake the outside service or may be a strict prohibition of such service. If a member's or candidate's employer elects to have its employees sign a noncompete agreement as part of the employment agreement, members and candidates should ensure that the details are clear and fully explained prior to signing the agreement.

Termination Policy

Members and candidates should clearly understand the termination policies of their employer. The policy should establish clear procedures regarding the resignation process, including addressing how the termination will be disclosed to clients and staff. The firm's policy may also outline the procedures for transferring responsibilities of ongoing research responsibilities and account management.

Incident-Reporting Procedures

Members and candidates should be aware of their firm's policies related to whistleblowing and encourage their firms to adopt industry best practices in this area. Many firms are required by regulatory mandates to establish confidential and anonymous reporting procedures that allow employees to report potentially unethical and illegal activities in the firm.

Employee Classification

Members and candidates should understand their status within their employer firm. Firms are encouraged to adopt a standardized classification structure—e.g., part time, full time, outside contractor—for their employees and indicate how each of the firm's policies applies to each employee class.

Application of the Standard

Example 1 (Soliciting Former Clients): Samuel Magee manages pension accounts for Trust Assets, Inc., but has become frustrated with the working environment and has been offered a position with Fiduciary Management. Before resigning from Trust Assets, Magee asks four big accounts to leave that firm and open accounts with Fiduciary. Magee also persuades several prospective clients to sign agreements with Fiduciary Management. Magee had previously made presentations to these prospects on behalf of Trust Assets.

> *Comment*: Magee violated the employee–employer principle requiring him to act solely for his employer's benefit. Magee's duty is to Trust Assets as long as he is employed there. The solicitation of Trust Assets' current clients and prospective clients is unethical and violates Standard IV(A).

Example 2 (Former Employer's Documents and Files): James Hightower has been employed by Jason Investment Management Corporation for 15 years. He began as an analyst but assumed increasing responsibilities and is now a senior portfolio manager and a member of the firm's investment policy committee. Hightower has decided to leave Jason Investment and start his own investment management business. He has been careful not to tell any of Jason's clients that he is leaving; he does not want to be accused of breaching his duty to Jason by soliciting Jason's clients before his departure. Hightower is planning to copy and take with him the following documents and information he developed or worked on while at Jason: 1) the client list, with addresses, telephone numbers, and other pertinent client information; 2) client account statements; 3) sample marketing presentations to prospective clients containing Jason's performance record; 4) Jason's recommended list of securities; 5) computer models to determine asset allocations for accounts with various objectives; 6) computer models for stock selection; and 7) personal computer spreadsheets for Hightower's major corporate recommendations, which he developed when he was an analyst.

> *Comment*: Except with the consent of their employer, departing members and candidates may not take employer property, which includes books, records, reports, and other materials, because taking such materials may interfere with their employer's business opportunities. Taking any employer records, even those the member or candidate prepared, violates Standard IV(A). Employer records include items stored in hard copy or any other medium (e.g., home computers, portable storage devices, cell phones).

Example 3 (Addressing Rumors): Reuben Winston manages all-equity portfolios at Target Asset Management (TAM), a large, established investment counselor. Ten years previously, Philpott & Company, which manages a family of global bond mutual funds, acquired TAM in a diversification move. After the merger, the combined operations prospered in the fixed-income business but the equity management business at TAM languished. Lately, a few of the equity pension accounts that had been with TAM before the merger have terminated their relationships with TAM. One day, Winston finds on his voice mail a message from a concerned client, "Hey! I just heard that Philpott is close to announcing the sale of your firm's equity management business to Rugged Life. What is going on?" Not being aware of any such deal, Winston and his associates are stunned. Their internal inquiries are met with denials from Philpott management, but the rumors persist. Feeling left in the dark, Winston contemplates leading an employee buyout of TAM's equity management business.

> *Comment*: An employee-led buyout of TAM's equity asset management business would be consistent with Standard IV(A) because it would rest on the permission of the employer and, ultimately, the clients. In this case, however, in which employees suspect the senior managers or principals are not truthful or forthcoming, Winston should consult legal counsel to determine appropriate action.

Example 4 (Ownership of Completed Prior Work): Laura Clay, who is unemployed, wants part-time consulting work while seeking a full-time analyst position. During an interview at Bradley Associates, a large institutional asset manager, Clay is told that the firm has no immediate research openings but would be willing to pay her a flat fee to complete a study of the wireless communications industry within a given period of time. Clay would be allowed unlimited access to Bradley's research files and would be welcome to come to the offices and use whatever support facilities are available during normal working hours. Bradley's research director does not seek any exclusivity for Clay's output, and the two agree to the arrangement on a handshake. As Clay nears completion of the study, she is offered an analyst job in the research department of Winston & Company, a brokerage firm, and she is pondering submitting the draft of her wireless study for publication by Winston.

Comment: Although she is under no written contractual obligation to Bradley, Clay has an obligation to let Bradley act on the output of her study before Winston & Company or Clay use the information to their advantage. That is, unless Bradley gives permission to Clay and waives its rights to her wireless report, Clay would be in violation of Standard IV(A) if she were to immediately recommend to Winston the same transactions recommended in the report to Bradley. Furthermore, Clay must not take from Bradley any research file material or other property that she may have used.

Example 5 (Ownership of Completed Prior Work): Emma Madeline, a recent college graduate and a candidate in the CFA Program, spends her summer as an unpaid intern at Murdoch and Lowell. The senior managers at Murdoch are attempting to bring the firm into compliance with the GIPS standards, and Madeline is assigned to assist in its efforts. Two months into her internship, Madeline applies for a job at McMillan & Company, which has plans to become GIPS compliant. Madeline accepts the job with McMillan. Before leaving Murdoch, she copies the firm's software that she helped develop because she believes this software will assist her in her new position.

Comment: Even though Madeline does not receive monetary compensation for her services at Murdoch, she has used firm resources in creating the software and is considered an employee because she receives compensation and benefits in the form of work experience and knowledge. By copying the software, Madeline violated Standard IV(A) because she misappropriated Murdoch's property without permission.

Example 6 (Soliciting Former Clients): Dennis Elliot has hired Sam Chisolm, who previously worked for a competing firm. Chisolm left his former firm after 18 years of employment. When Chisolm begins working for Elliot, he wants to contact his former clients because he knows them well and is certain that many will follow him to his new employer. Is Chisolm in violation of Standard IV(A) if he contacts his former clients?

Comment: Because client records are the property of the firm, contacting former clients for any reason through the use of client lists or other information taken from a former employer without permission would be a violation of Standard IV(A). In addition, the nature and extent of the contact with former clients may be governed by the terms of any noncompete agreement signed by the employee and the former employer that covers contact with former clients after employment.

Simple knowledge of the names and existence of former clients is not confidential information, just as skills or experience that an employee obtains while employed are not "confidential" or "privileged" information. The Code and Standards do not impose a prohibition on the use of experience or knowledge gained at one employer from being used at another employer. The Code and Standards also do not prohibit former employees from contacting clients of their previous firm, in the absence of a noncompete agreement. Members and candidates are free to use public information about their former firm after departing to contact former clients without violating Standard IV(A).

In the absence of a noncompete agreement, as long as Chisolm maintains his duty of loyalty to his employer before joining Elliot's firm, does not take steps to solicit clients until he has left his former firm, and does not make use of material from his former employer without its permission after he has left, he is not in violation of the Code and Standards.

Example 7 (Starting a New Firm): Geraldine Allen currently works at a registered investment company as an equity analyst. Without notice to her employer, she registers with government authorities to start an investment company that will compete with her employer, but she does not actively seek clients. Does registration of this competing company with the appropriate regulatory authorities constitute a violation of Standard IV(A)?

Comment: Allen's preparation for the new business by registering with the regulatory authorities does not conflict with the work for her employer if the preparations have been done on Allen's own time outside the office and if Allen will not be soliciting clients for the business or otherwise operating the new company until she has left her current employer.

Example 8 (Competing with Current Employer): Several employees are planning to depart their current employer within a few weeks and have been careful to not engage in any activities that would conflict with their duty to their current employer. They have just learned that one of their employer's clients has undertaken a request for proposal (RFP) to review and possibly hire a new investment consultant. The RFP has been sent to the employer and all of its competitors. The group believes that the new entity to be formed would be qualified to respond to the RFP and be eligible for the business. The RFP submission period is likely to conclude before the employees' resignations are effective. Is it permissible for the group of departing employees to respond to the RFP for their anticipated new firm?

Comment: A group of employees responding to an RFP that their employer is also responding to would lead to direct competition between the employees and the employer. Such conduct violates Standard IV(A) unless the group of employees receives permission from their employer as well as the entity sending out the RFP.

Example 9 (Externally Compensated Assignments): Alfonso Mota is a research analyst with Tyson Investments. He works part time as a mayor for his hometown, a position for which he receives compensation. Must Mota seek permission from Tyson to serve as mayor?

Comment: If Mota's mayoral duties are so extensive and time-consuming that they might detract from his ability to fulfill his responsibilities at Tyson, he should discuss his outside activities with his employer and come to a mutual agreement regarding how to manage his personal commitments with his responsibilities to his employer.

Example 10 (Soliciting Former Clients): After leaving her employer, Shawna McQuillen establishes her own money management business. While with her former employer, she did not sign a noncompete agreement that would have prevented her from soliciting former clients. Upon her departure, she does not take any of her client lists or contact information and she clears her personal computer of any employer records, including client contact information. She obtains the phone numbers of her former clients through public records and contacts them to solicit their business.

Comment: McQuillen is not in violation of Standard IV(A) because she has not used information or records from her former employer and is not prevented by an agreement with her former employer from soliciting her former clients.

Example 11 (Whistleblowing Actions): Meredith Rasmussen works on a buy-side trading desk and concentrates on in-house trades for a hedge fund subsidiary managed by a team at the investment management firm. The hedge fund has been very successful and is marketed globally by the firm. From her experience as the trader for much of the activity of the fund, Rasmussen has become quite knowledgeable about the hedge fund's strategy, tactics, and performance. When a distinct break in the market occurs, however, and many of the securities involved in the hedge fund's strategy decline markedly in value, Rasmussen observes that the reported performance of the hedge fund does not reflect this decline. In her experience, the lack of any effect is a very unlikely occurrence. She approaches the head of trading about her concern and is told that she should not ask any questions, that the fund is big and successful and is not her concern. She is fairly sure something is not right, so she contacts the compliance officer, who also tells her to stay away from the issue of this hedge fund's reporting.

> *Comment*: Rasmussen has clearly come upon an error in policies, procedures, and compliance practices in the firm's operations. Having been unsuccessful in finding a resolution with her supervisor and the compliance officer, Rasmussen should consult the firm's whistleblowing policy to determine the appropriate next step toward informing management of her concerns. The potentially unethical actions of the investment management division are appropriate grounds for further disclosure, so Rasmussen's whistleblowing would not represent a violation of Standard IV(A).
>
> See also Standard I(D)—Misconduct and Standard IV(C)—Responsibilities of Supervisors.

Example 12 (Soliciting Former Clients): Angel Crome has been a private banker for YBSafe Bank for the past eight years. She has been very successful and built a considerable client portfolio during that time but is extremely frustrated by the recent loss of reputation by her current employer and subsequent client insecurity. A locally renowned headhunter contacted Crome a few days ago and offered her an interesting job with a competing private bank. This bank offers a substantial signing bonus for advisers with their own client portfolios. Crome figures that she can solicit at least 70 percent of her clients to follow her and gladly enters into the new employment contract.

> *Comment*: Crome may contact former clients upon termination of her employment with YBSafe Bank, but she is prohibited from using client records built and kept with her in her capacity as an employee of YBSafe Bank. Client lists are proprietary information of her former employer and must not be used for her or her new employer's benefit. The use of written, electronic, or any other form of records, other than publicly available information, to contact her former clients at YBSafe Bank will be a violation of Standard IV(A).

Example 13 (Notification of Code and Standards): Krista Smith is a relatively new assistant trader for the fixed-income desk of a major investment bank. She is on a team responsible for structuring collateralized debt obligations (CDOs) made up of securities in the inventory of the trading desk. At a meeting of the team, senior executives explain the opportunity to eventually separate the CDO into various risk-rated tranches to be sold to the clients of the firm. After the senior executives leave the meeting, the head trader announces various responsibilities of each member of the team and then says, "This is a good time to unload some of the junk we have been stuck with for a while and disguise it with ratings and a thick, unreadable prospectus, so don't be shy in putting this CDO together. Just kidding." Smith is worried by this remark and asks some of her colleagues what the head trader meant. They all respond that he was just kidding but that there is some truth in the remark because the CDO is seen by management as an opportunity to improve the quality of the securities in the firm's inventory.

Concerned about the ethical environment of the workplace, Smith decides to talk to her supervisor about her concerns and provides the head trader with a copy of the Code and Standards. Smith discusses the principle of placing the client above the interest of the firm and the possibility that the development of the new CDO will not adhere to this responsibility. The head trader assures Smith that the appropriate analysis will be conducted when determining the appropriate securities for collateral. Furthermore, the ratings are assigned by an independent firm and the prospectus will include full and factual disclosures. Smith is reassured by the meeting, but she also reviews the company's procedures and requirements for reporting potential violations of company policy and securities laws.

> *Comment*: Smith's review of the company policies and procedures for reporting violations allows her to be prepared to report through the appropriate whistleblower process if she decides that the CDO development process involves unethical actions by others. Smith's actions comply with the Code and Standards principles of placing the clients' interests first and being loyal to her employer. In providing her supervisor with a copy of the Code and Standards, Smith is highlighting the high level of ethical conduct she is required to adhere to in her professional activities.

B. Additional Compensation Arrangements

Members and Candidates must not accept gifts, benefits, compensation, or consideration that competes with or might reasonably be expected to create a conflict of interest with their employer's interest unless they obtain written consent from all parties involved.

Guidance

Standard IV(B) requires members and candidates to obtain permission from their employer before accepting compensation or other benefits from third parties for the services rendered to the employer or for any services that might create a conflict with their employer's interest. Compensation and benefits include direct compensation by the client and any indirect compensation or other benefits received from third parties. "Written consent" includes any form of communication that can be documented (for example, communication via computer e-mail that can be retrieved and documented).

Members and candidates must obtain permission for additional compensation/benefits because such arrangements may affect loyalties and objectivity and create potential conflicts of interest. Disclosure allows an employer to consider the outside arrangements when evaluating the actions and motivations of members and candidates. Moreover, the employer is entitled to have full knowledge of all compensation/benefit arrangements so as to be able to assess the true cost of the services members or candidates are providing.

Recommended Procedures for Compliance

Members and candidates should make an immediate written report to their employer specifying any compensation they propose to receive for services in addition to the compensation or benefits received from their employer. The details of the report should be confirmed by the party offering the additional compensation, including performance incentives offered by clients. This written report should state the terms of any agreement under which a member or candidate will receive additional compensation; "terms" include the nature of the compensation, the approximate amount of compensation, and the duration of the agreement.

Application of the Standard

Example 1 (Notification of Client Bonus Compensation): Geoff Whitman, a portfolio analyst for Adams Trust Company, manages the account of Carol Cochran, a client. Whitman is paid a salary by his employer, and Cochran pays the trust company a standard fee based on the market value of assets in her portfolio. Cochran proposes to Whitman that "any year that my portfolio achieves at least a 15 percent return before taxes, you and your wife can fly to Monaco at my expense and use my condominium during the third week of January." Whitman does not inform his employer of the arrangement and vacations in Monaco the following January as Cochran's guest.

> *Comment*: Whitman violated Standard IV(B) by failing to inform his employer in writing of this supplemental, contingent compensation arrangement. The nature of the arrangement could have resulted in partiality to Cochran's account, which could have detracted from Whitman's performance with respect to other accounts he handles for Adams Trust. Whitman must obtain the consent of his employer to accept such a supplemental benefit.

Example 2 (Notification of Outside Compensation): Terry Jones sits on the board of directors of Exercise Unlimited, Inc. In return for his services on the board, Jones receives unlimited membership privileges for his family at all Exercise Unlimited facilities. Jones purchases Exercise Unlimited stock for the client accounts for which it is appropriate. Jones does not disclose this arrangement to his employer because he does not receive monetary compensation for his services to the board.

> *Comment*: Jones has violated Standard IV(B) by failing to disclose to his employer benefits received in exchange for his services on the board of directors. The nonmonetary compensation may create a conflict of interest in the same manner as being paid to serve as a director.

Example 3 (Prior Approval for Outside Compensation): Jonathan Hollis is an analyst of oil-and-gas companies for Specialty Investment Management. He is currently recommending the purchase of ABC Oil Company shares and has published a long, well-thought-out research report to substantiate his recommendation. Several weeks after publishing the report, Hollis received a call from the investor-relations office of ABC Oil saying that Thomas Andrews, CEO of the company, saw the report and really liked the analyst's grasp of the business and his company. The investor-relations officer invited Hollis to visit ABC Oil to discuss the industry further. ABC Oil offers to send a company plane to pick Hollis up and arrange for his accommodations while visiting. Hollis, after gaining the appropriate approvals, accepts the meeting with the CEO but declines the offered travel arrangements.

Several weeks later, Andrews and Hollis meet to discuss the oil business and Hollis's report. Following the meeting, Hollis joins Andrews and the investment relations officer for dinner at an upscale restaurant near ABC Oil's headquarters.

Upon returning to Specialty Investment Management, Hollis provides a full review of the meeting to the director of research, including a disclosure of the dinner attended.

Comment: Hollis's actions did not violate Standard IV(B). Through gaining approval before accepting the meeting and declining the offered travel arrangements, Hollis sought to avoid any potential conflicts of interest between his company and ABC Oil. Because the location of the dinner was not available prior to arrival and Hollis notified his company of the dinner upon his return, accepting the dinner should not impair his objectivity. By disclosing the dinner, Hollis has enabled Specialty Investment Management to assess whether it has any impact on future reports and recommendations by Hollis related to ABC Oil.

C. Responsibilities of Supervisors

Members and Candidates must make reasonable efforts to detect and prevent violations of applicable laws, rules, regulations, and the Code and Standards by anyone subject to their supervision or authority.

Guidance

Highlights:

▶ *Detection Procedures*

▶ *Compliance Procedures*

▶ *Inadequate Procedures*

▶ *Enforcement of Non-Investment-Related Policies*

Standard IV(C) states that members and candidates must take steps to prevent persons acting under their supervision from violating laws, rules, regulations, firm policies, or the Code and Standards.

Any investment professional who has employees subject to her or his control or influence—whether or not the employees are CFA Institute members, CFA charterholders, or candidates in the CFA Program—exercises supervisory responsibility. Members and candidates acting as supervisors must also have in-depth knowledge of the Code and Standards so that they can apply this knowledge in discharging their supervisory responsibilities.

The conduct that constitutes reasonable supervision in a particular case depends on the number of employees supervised and the work performed by those employees. Members and candidates who supervise large numbers of employees cannot personally evaluate the conduct of their employees on a continuing basis. Although these members and candidates may delegate supervisory duties, such delegation does not relieve them of their supervisory responsibility. Their responsibilities under Standard IV(C) include instructing those subordinates to whom supervision is delegated about methods to prevent and detect violations of laws, rules, regulations, firm policies, and the Code and Standards.

Detection Procedures

Members and candidates with supervisory responsibility must make reasonable efforts to detect violations of laws, rules, regulations, firm policies, and the Code and Standards. They exercise reasonable supervision by establishing and implementing written compliance procedures and ensuring that those procedures are followed through periodic review. If a member or candidate has adopted reasonable procedures and taken steps to institute an effective compliance program, then the member or candidate may not be in violation of Standard IV(C) if he or she does not detect violations that occur despite these efforts. The fact that violations do occur may indicate, however, that the compliance procedures are inadequate. In addition, in some cases, merely enacting such procedures may not be sufficient to fulfill the duty required by Standard IV(C). A member or candidate may be in violation of Standard IV(C) if he or she knows or should know that the procedures designed to detect and prevent violations are not being followed.

Compliance Procedures

Members and candidates with supervisory responsibility must understand what constitutes an adequate compliance system for their firms and make reasonable efforts to see that appropriate compliance procedures are established, documented, communicated to covered personnel, and followed. "Adequate" procedures are those designed to meet industry standards, regulatory requirements, the requirements of the Code and Standards, and the circumstances of the firm. Once compliance procedures are established, the supervisor must also make reasonable efforts to ensure that the procedures are monitored and enforced.

To be effective, compliance procedures must be in place prior to the occurrence of a violation of the law or the Code and Standards. Although compliance procedures cannot be designed to anticipate every potential violation, they should be designed to anticipate the activities most likely to result in misconduct. Each compliance program must be appropriate for the size and nature of the organization. The member or candidate should review model compliance procedures or other industry programs to ensure that the firm's procedures meet the minimum industry standards.

Once a supervisor learns that an employee has violated or may have violated the law or the Code and Standards, the supervisor must promptly initiate an investigation to ascertain the extent of the wrongdoing. Relying on an employee's statements about the extent of the violation or assurances that the wrongdoing will not recur is not enough. Reporting the misconduct up the chain of command and warning the employee to cease the activity are also not enough. Pending the outcome of the investigation, a supervisor should take steps to ensure that the violation will not be repeated, such as placing limits on the employee's activities or increasing the monitoring of the employee's activities.

Inadequate Procedures

A member or candidate with supervisory responsibility should bring an inadequate compliance system to the attention of the firm's senior managers and recommend corrective action. If the member or candidate clearly cannot discharge supervisory responsibilities because of the absence of a compliance system or because of an inadequate compliance system, the member or candidate should decline in writing to accept supervisory responsibility until the firm adopts reasonable procedures to allow adequate exercise of supervisory responsibility.

Enforcement of Non-Investment-Related Policies

A member or candidate with supervisory responsibility should enforce policies related to investment and non-investment-related activities equally. Firms regularly establish policies related to attendance and acceptable workplace actions, such as mandatory vacations for specific positions. The equal enforcement of all firm policies assists in creating a strong ethical work environment where all rules are demonstrated to be important.

Recommended Procedures for Compliance

Codes of Ethics or Compliance Procedures

Members and candidates are encouraged to recommend that their employers adopt a code of ethics. Adoption of a code of ethics is critical to establishing a strong ethical foundation for investment advisory firms and their employees. Codes of ethics formally emphasize and reinforce the client loyalty responsibilities of investment firm personnel, protect investing clients by deterring misconduct, and protect the firm's reputation for integrity.

There is a distinction, however, between codes of ethics and the specific policies and procedures needed to ensure compliance with the codes and with securities laws and regulations. Although both are important, codes of ethics should consist of fundamental, principle-based ethical and fiduciary concepts that are applicable to all of the firm's employees. In this way, firms can best convey to employees and clients the ethical ideals that investment advisers strive to achieve. These concepts need to be implemented, however, by detailed, firmwide compliance policies and procedures. Compliance procedures assist the firm's personnel in fulfilling the responsibilities enumerated in the code of ethics and make probable that the ideals expressed in the code of ethics will be adhered to in the day-to-day operation of the firm.

Stand-alone codes of ethics should be written in plain language and should address general fiduciary concepts. They should be unencumbered by numerous detailed procedures. Codes presented in this way are the most effective in stressing to employees that they are in positions of trust and must act with integrity at all times. Mingling compliance procedures in the firm's code of ethics goes against the goal of reinforcing the ethical obligations of employees.

Separating the code of ethics from compliance procedures will also reduce, if not eliminate, the legal terminology and "boilerplate" language that can make the underlying ethical principles incomprehensible to the average person. Above all, to ensure that a culture of ethics and integrity is created rather than merely a focus on following the rules, the principles in the code of ethics must be stated in a way that is accessible and understandable to everyone in the firm.

Members and candidates should encourage their employers to provide their codes of ethics to clients. In this case also, a simple, straightforward code of ethics will be best understood by clients. Unencumbered by the compliance procedures, the code of ethics will be effective in conveying that the firm is committed to conducting business in an ethical manner and in the best interests of the clients.

Adequate Compliance Procedures

A supervisor complies with Standard IV(C) by identifying situations in which legal violations or violations of the Code and Standards are likely to occur and by establishing and enforcing compliance procedures to prevent such violations. Adequate compliance procedures should:

▶ be contained in a clearly written and accessible manual that is tailored to the firm's operations;

- be drafted so that the procedures are easy to understand;
- designate a compliance officer whose authority and responsibility are clearly defined and who has the necessary resources and authority to implement the firm's compliance procedures;
- describe the hierarchy of supervision and assign duties among supervisors;
- implement a system of checks and balances;
- outline the scope of the procedures;
- outline procedures to document the monitoring and testing of compliance procedures;
- outline permissible conduct; and
- delineate procedures for reporting violations and sanctions.

Once a compliance program is in place, a supervisor should:

- disseminate the contents of the program to appropriate personnel;
- periodically update procedures to ensure that the measures are adequate under the law;
- continually educate personnel regarding the compliance procedures;
- issue periodic reminders of the procedures to appropriate personnel;
- incorporate a professional conduct evaluation as part of an employee's performance review;
- review the actions of employees to ensure compliance and identify violators; and
- take the necessary steps to enforce the procedures once a violation has occurred.

Once a violation is discovered, a supervisor should:

- respond promptly;
- conduct a thorough investigation of the activities to determine the scope of the wrongdoing; and
- increase supervision or place appropriate limitations on the wrongdoer pending the outcome of the investigation.

Application of the Standard

Example 1 (Supervising Research Activities): Jane Mattock, senior vice president and head of the research department of H&V, Inc., a regional brokerage firm, has decided to change her recommendation for Timber Products from buy to sell. In line with H&V's procedures, she orally advises certain other H&V executives of her proposed actions before the report is prepared for publication. As a result of Mattock's conversation with Dieter Frampton, one of the executives of H&V accountable to Mattock, Frampton immediately sells Timber's stock from his own account and from certain discretionary client accounts. In addition, other personnel inform certain institutional customers of the changed recommendation before it is printed and disseminated to all H&V customers who have received previous Timber reports.

Comment: Mattock has violated Standard IV(C) by failing to reasonably and adequately supervise the actions of those accountable to her. She did not prevent or establish reasonable procedures designed to prevent dissemination of or trading on the information by those who knew of her changed recommendation. She must ensure that her firm has procedures for reviewing or recording any trading in the stock of a corporation that has been the subject of an unpublished change in recommendation. Adequate procedures would have informed the subordinates of their duties and detected sales by Frampton and selected customers.

Example 2 (Supervising Research Activities): Deion Miller is the research director for Jamestown Investment Programs. The portfolio managers have become critical of Miller and his staff because the Jamestown portfolios do not include any stock that has been the subject of a merger or tender offer. Georgia Ginn, a member of Miller's staff, tells Miller that she has been studying a local company, Excelsior, Inc., and recommends its purchase. Ginn adds that the company has been widely rumored to be the subject of a merger study by a well-known conglomerate and discussions between them are under way. At Miller's request, Ginn prepares a memo recommending the stock. Miller passes along Ginn's memo to the portfolio managers prior to leaving for vacation, and he notes that he has not reviewed the memo. As a result of the memo, the portfolio managers buy Excelsior stock immediately. The day Miller returns to the office, he learns that Ginn's only sources for the report were her brother, who is an acquisitions analyst with Acme Industries, the "well-known conglomerate," and that the merger discussions were planned but not held.

> *Comment*: Miller violated Standard IV(C) by not exercising reasonable supervision when he disseminated the memo without checking to ensure that Ginn had a reasonable and adequate basis for her recommendations and that Ginn was not relying on material nonpublic information.

Example 3 (Supervising Trading Activities): David Edwards, a trainee trader at Wheeler & Company, a major national brokerage firm, assists a customer in paying for the securities of Highland, Inc., by using anticipated profits from the immediate sale of the same securities. Despite the fact that Highland is not on Wheeler's recommended list, a large volume of its stock is traded through Wheeler in this manner. Roberta Ann Mason is a Wheeler vice president responsible for supervising compliance with the securities laws in the trading department. Part of her compensation from Wheeler is based on commission revenues from the trading department. Although she notices the increased trading activity, she does nothing to investigate or halt it.

> *Comment*: Mason's failure to adequately review and investigate purchase orders in Highland stock executed by Edwards and her failure to supervise the trainee's activities violate Standard IV(C). Supervisors should be especially sensitive to actual or potential conflicts between their own self-interests and their supervisory responsibilities.

Example 4 (Supervising Trading Activities and Record Keeping): Samantha Tabbing is senior vice president and portfolio manager for Crozet, Inc., a registered investment advisory and registered broker/dealer firm. She reports to Charles Henry, the president of Crozet. Crozet serves as the investment adviser and principal underwriter for ABC and XYZ public mutual funds. The two funds' prospectuses allow Crozet to trade financial futures for the funds for the limited purpose of hedging against market risks. Henry, extremely impressed by Tabbing's performance in the past two years, directs Tabbing to act as portfolio manager for the funds. For the benefit of its employees, Crozet has also organized the Crozet Employee Profit-Sharing Plan (CEPSP), a defined-contribution retirement plan. Henry assigns Tabbing to manage 20 percent of the assets of CEPSP.

Tabbing's investment objective for her portion of CEPSP's assets is aggressive growth. Unbeknownst to Henry, Tabbing frequently places S&P 500 Index purchase and sale orders for the funds and the CEPSP without providing the futures commission merchants (FCMs) who take the orders with any prior or simultaneous designation of the account for which the trade has been placed. Frequently, neither Tabbing nor anyone else at Crozet completes an internal trade ticket to record the time an order was placed or the specific account for which the order was intended. FCMs often designate a specific account only after the trade, when Tabbing provides such designation. Crozet has no written operating procedures or compliance manual concerning its futures trading, and its compliance department does not review such trading. After observing the market's movement, Tabbing assigns to CEPSP the S&P 500 positions with more-favorable execution prices and assigns positions with less-favorable execution prices to the funds.

> *Comment*: Henry violated Standard IV(C) by failing to adequately supervise Tabbing with respect to her S&P 500 trading. Henry further violated Standard IV(C) by failing to establish record-keeping and reporting procedures to prevent or detect Tabbing's violations.

Example 5 (Accepting Responsibility): Meredith Rasmussen works on a buy-side trading desk and concentrates on in-house trades for a hedge fund subsidiary managed by a team at the investment management firm. The hedge fund has been very successful and is marketed globally by the firm. From her experience as the trader for much of the activity of the fund, Rasmussen has become quite knowledgeable about the hedge fund's strategy, tactics, and performance. When a distinct break in the market occurs and many of the securities involved in the hedge fund's strategy decline markedly in value, however, Rasmussen observes that the reported performance of the hedge fund does not at all reflect this decline. From her experience, this lack of an effect is a very unlikely occurrence. She approaches the head of trading about her concern and is told that she should not ask any questions, that the fund is too big and successful and is not her concern. She is fairly sure something is not right, so she contacts the compliance officer and is again told to stay away from the hedge fund reporting issue.

> *Comment*: Rasmussen has clearly come upon an error in policies, procedures, and compliance practices within the firm's operations. According to Standard IV(C), the supervisor and the compliance officer have the responsibility to review the concerns brought forth by Rasmussen. Supervisors have the responsibility of establishing and encouraging an ethical culture in the firm. The dismissal of Rasmussen's question violates Standard IV(C) and undermines the firm's ethical operations.
>
> See also Standard I(D)—Misconduct and, for guidance on whistleblowing, Standard IV(A)—Loyalty.

Example 6 (Inadequate Procedures): Brendan Witt, a former junior sell-side technology analyst, decided to return to school to earn an MBA. To keep his research skills and industry knowledge sharp, Witt accepted a position with On-line and Informed, an independent internet-based research company. The position requires the publication of a recommendation and report on a different company every month. Initially, Witt is a regular contributor of new research and a participant in the associated discussion boards that generally have positive comments on the technology sector. Over time, his ability to manage his educational requirements and his work requirements begin to conflict with one another. Knowing a recommendation is due the next day for On-line, Witt creates a report based on a few news articles and what the conventional wisdom of the markets has deemed the "hot" security of the day.

Comment: Allowing the report submitted by Witt to be posted highlights a lack of compliance procedures by the research firm. Witt's supervisor needs to work with the management of On-line to develop an appropriate review process to ensure that all contracted analysts comply with the requirements.

See also Standard V(A)—Diligence and Reasonable Basis, as it relates to Witt's responsibility for substantiating a recommendation.

Example 7 (Inadequate Supervision): Michael Papis is the chief investment officer of his state's retirement fund. The fund has always used outside advisers for the real estate allocation, and this information is clearly presented in all fund communications. Thomas Nagle, a recognized sell-side research analyst and Papis's business school classmate, recently left the investment bank he worked for to start his own asset management firm, Accessible Real Estate. Nagle is trying to build his assets under management and contacts Papis about gaining some of the retirement fund's allocation. In the previous few years, the performance of the retirement fund's real estate investments was in line with the fund's benchmark but was not extraordinary. Papis decides to help out his old friend and also to seek better returns by moving the real estate allocation to Accessible. The only notice of the change in adviser appears in the next annual report in the listing of associated advisers.

Comment: Papis's actions highlight the need for supervision and review at all levels in an organization. His responsibilities may include the selection of external advisers, but the decision to change advisers appears arbitrary. Members and candidates should ensure that their firm has appropriate policies and procedures in place to detect inappropriate actions such as the action taken by Papis.

See also Standard V(A)—Diligence and Reasonable Basis, Standard V(B)—Communication with Clients and Prospective Clients, and Standard VI(A)—Disclosure of Conflicts.

STANDARD V—INVESTMENT ANALYSIS, RECOMMENDATIONS, AND ACTIONS

A. Diligence and Reasonable Basis

Members and Candidates must:

1. **Exercise diligence, independence, and thoroughness in analyzing investments, making investment recommendations, and taking investment actions.**
2. **Have a reasonable and adequate basis, supported by appropriate research and investigation, for any investment analysis, recommendation, or action.**

Guidance

Highlights:

▶ *Defining Diligence and Reasonable Basis*
▶ *Using Secondary or Third-Party Research*

▶ *Quantitatively Oriented Research*

▶ *Selecting External Advisers and Subadvisers*

▶ *Group Research and Decision Making*

The application of Standard V(A) depends on the investment philosophy the member, candidate, or firm is following, the role of the member or candidate in the investment decision-making process, and the support and resources provided by the member's or candidate's employer. These factors will dictate the nature of the diligence and thoroughness of the research and the level of investigation required by Standard V(A).

The requirements for issuing conclusions based on research will vary in relation to the member's or candidate's role in the investment decision-making process, but the member or candidate must make reasonable efforts to cover all pertinent issues when arriving at a recommendation. Members and candidates enhance transparency by providing or offering to provide supporting information to clients when recommending a purchase or sale or when changing a recommendation.

Defining Diligence and Reasonable Basis

Every investment decision is based on a set of facts known and understood at the time. Clients turn to members and candidates for advice and expect these advisers to have more information and knowledge than they do. This information and knowledge is the basis from which members and candidates apply their professional judgment in taking investment actions and making recommendations.

At a basic level, clients want assurance that members and candidates are putting forth the necessary effort to support the recommendations they are making. Communicating the level and thoroughness of the information reviewed before the member or candidate makes a judgment allows clients to understand the reasonableness of the recommended investment actions.

As with determining the suitability of an investment for the client, the necessary level of research and analysis will differ with the product, security, or service being offered. In providing an investment service, members and candidates typically use a variety of resources, including company reports, third-party research, and results from quantitative models. A reasonable basis is formed through a balance of these resources appropriate for the security or decision being analyzed.

The following list provides some, but definitely not all, examples of attributes to consider while forming the basis for a recommendation:

▶ company's operating and financial history;

▶ current stage of the industry's business cycle;

▶ mutual fund's fee structure and management history;

▶ output and potential limitations of quantitative models;

▶ quality of the assets included in a securitization; and

▶ appropriateness of selected peer-group comparisons.

Even though an investment recommendation may be well-informed, downside risk remains for any investment. Members and candidates can base their decision only on the information available at the time the decision is made. The steps taken in developing a diligent and reasonable recommendation should minimize unexpected downside events.

Using Secondary or Third-Party Research

If members and candidates rely on secondary or third-party research, they must make reasonable and diligent efforts to determine whether such research is sound. Secondary research is defined as research conducted by someone else in the member's or candidate's firm. Third-party research is research conducted by entities outside the member's or candidate's firm, such as a brokerage firm, bank, or research firm. If a member or candidate has reason to suspect that either secondary or third-party research or information comes from a source that lacks a sound basis, the member or candidate must not rely on that information. Criteria that a member or candidate can use in forming an opinion on whether research is sound include the following:

- ▶ assumptions used;
- ▶ rigor of the analysis performed;
- ▶ date/timeliness of the research; and
- ▶ evaluation of the objectivity and independence of the recommendations.

A member or candidate may rely on others in his or her firm to determine whether secondary or third-party research is sound and use the information in good faith unless the member or candidate has reason to question its validity or the processes and procedures used by those responsible for the research. For example, a portfolio manager may not have a choice of a data source because the firm's senior managers conducted due diligence to determine which vendor would provide services; the member or candidate can use the information in good faith assuming the due diligence process was deemed adequate.

A member or candidate should verify that the firm has a policy about the timely and consistent review of approved research providers to ensure that the quality of the research continues to meet the necessary standards. If such a policy is not in place at the firm, the member or candidate should encourage the development and adoption of a formal review practice.

Quantitatively Oriented Research

Standard V(A) applies to the rapidly expanding use of quantitatively oriented research models, such as computer-generated screening and ranking of equity securities and the creation or valuation of derivative instruments. Models are being used for more than the back testing of investment strategies, and the continued development of models is an important part of capital market developments.

The importance and limitations of financial models became clear as the credit crisis unfolded in 2007 and 2008. In many cases the financial models used to value collateralized debt securities and related derivative products were poorly understood. Members and candidates need to have an understanding of the parameters used in the model or quantitative research. Although they are not required to become experts in the technical aspects of the models, they must be able to explain to their clients the importance of the quantitative research and how the results were used in the decision-making process.

Members and candidates need to consider the time horizon of the data used as inputs in financial models. The information from many commercially available databases may not effectively incorporate both positive and negative market cycles. In the development of a recommendation, the member or candidate may need to test the models by using volatility and performance expectations that represent scenarios outside the observable databases. In reviewing the computer models or the resulting output, members and candidates need to pay particular attention to the assumptions used in the analysis and the rigor of the analysis to ensure that the model incorporates negative market events.

Selecting External Advisers and Subadvisers

Financial instruments and asset allocation techniques continue to develop and evolve. This progression has led to the use of specialized managers to invest in specific asset classes or diversification strategies that complement a firm's in-house expertise. Standard V(A) applies to the level of review necessary in selecting an external adviser or subadviser.

Members and candidates need to ensure that their firms have standardized criteria for reviewing external advisers. Such criteria would include, but would not be limited to, the following:

▶ reviewing the adviser's established code of ethics;

▶ understanding the adviser's compliance and internal control procedures;

▶ assessing the quality of the published return information; and

▶ reviewing the adviser's adherence to its stated strategy.

CFA Institute published codes, standards, and guides to best practice provide members and candidates with examples of acceptable practices for external advisers and advice in selecting a new adviser. The following guides are available at the CFA Institute website (www.cfainstitute.org): Asset Manager Code of Professional Conduct, Global Investment Performance Standards, and Model Request for Proposal (for equity, credit, or real estate managers).

Group Research and Decision Making

Commonly, members and candidates are part of a group or team that is collectively responsible for producing investment analysis or research. The conclusions or recommendations of the group report represent the consensus of the group and are not necessarily the views of the member or candidate, even though the name of the member or candidate is included on the report. In some instances, the member or candidate will not agree with the view of the group. If, however, the member or candidate believes that the consensus opinion has a reasonable and adequate basis and is independent and objective, the member or candidate need not decline to be identified with the report. If the member or candidate is confident in the process, the member or candidate does not need to dissociate from the report even if it does not reflect his or her opinion.

Recommended Procedures for Compliance

Members and candidates should encourage their firms to consider the following policies and procedures to support the principles of Standard V(A):

▶ Establish a policy requiring that research reports, credit ratings, and investment recommendations have a basis that can be substantiated as reasonable and adequate. An individual employee (a supervisory analyst) or a group of employees (a review committee) should be appointed to review and approve such items prior to external circulation to determine whether the criteria established in the policy have been met.

▶ Develop detailed, written guidance for analysts (research, investment, or credit), supervisory analysts, and review committees that establishes the due diligence procedures for judging whether a particular recommendation has a reasonable and adequate basis.

▶ Develop measurable criteria for assessing the quality of research, the reasonableness and adequacy of the basis for any recommendation or rating, and the accuracy of recommendations over time. In some cases, firms may consider implementing compensation arrangements that depend on these measurable criteria and that are applied consistently to all related analysts.

▶ Develop detailed, written guidance that establishes minimum levels of scenario testing of all computer-based models used in developing, rating, and evaluating financial instruments. The policy should contain criteria related to the breadth of the scenarios tested, the accuracy of the output over time, and the analysis of cash flow sensitivity to inputs.

▶ Develop measurable criteria for assessing outside providers, including the quality of information being provided, the reasonableness and adequacy of the provider's collection practices, and the accuracy of the information over time. The established policy should outline how often the provider's products are reviewed.

▶ Adopt a standardized set of criteria for evaluating the adequacy of external advisers. The policy should include how often and on what basis the allocation of funds to the adviser will be reviewed.

Application of the Standard

Example 1 (Sufficient Due Diligence): Helen Hawke manages the corporate finance department of Sarkozi Securities, Ltd. The firm is anticipating that the government will soon close a tax loophole that currently allows oil-and-gas exploration companies to pass on drilling expenses to holders of a certain class of shares. Because market demand for this tax-advantaged class of stock is currently high, Sarkozi convinces several companies to undertake new equity financings at once before the loophole closes. Time is of the essence, but Sarkozi lacks sufficient resources to conduct adequate research on all the prospective issuing companies. Hawke decides to estimate the IPO prices on the basis of the relative size of each company and to justify the pricing later when her staff has time.

> *Comment*: Sarkozi should have taken on only the work that it could adequately handle. By categorizing the issuers by general size, Hawke has bypassed researching all the other relevant aspects that should be considered when pricing new issues and thus has not performed sufficient due diligence. Such an omission can result in investors purchasing shares at prices that have no actual basis. Hawke has violated Standard V(A).

Example 2 (Sufficient Scenario Testing): Babu Dhaliwal works for Heinrich Brokerage in the corporate finance group. He has just persuaded Feggans Resources, Ltd., to allow his firm to do a secondary equity financing at Feggans Resources' current stock price. Because the stock has been trading at higher multiples than similar companies with equivalent production, Dhaliwal presses the Feggans Resources managers to project what would be the maximum production they could achieve in an optimal scenario. Based on these numbers, he is able to justify the price his firm will be asking for the secondary issue. During a sales pitch to the brokers, Dhaliwal then uses these numbers as the base-case production levels that Feggans Resources will achieve.

Comment: When presenting information to the brokers, Dhaliwal should have given a range of production scenarios and the probability of Feggans Resources achieving each level. By giving the maximum production level as the likely level of production, he has misrepresented the chances of achieving that production level and seriously misled the brokers. Dhaliwal has violated Standard V(A).

Example 3 (Developing a Reasonable Basis): Brendan Witt, a former junior sell-side technology analyst, decided to return to school to earn an MBA. To keep his research skills and industry knowledge sharp, Witt accepted a position with On-line and Informed, an independent internet-based research company. The position requires the publication of a recommendation and report on a different company every month. Initially, Witt is a regular contributor of new research and a participant in the associated discussion boards that generally have positive comments on the technology sector. Over time, his ability to manage his educational requirements and his work requirements begin to conflict with one another. Knowing a recommendation is due the next day for On-line, Witt creates a report based on a few news articles and what the conventional wisdom of the markets has deemed the "hot" security of the day.

Comment: Witt's knowledge of and exuberance for technology stocks, a few news articles, and the conventional wisdom of the markets do not constitute, without more information, a reasonable and adequate basis for a stock recommendation that is supported by appropriate research and investigation. Therefore, Witt has violated Standard V(A).

See also Standard IV(C)—Responsibilities of Supervisors as it relates to the firm's inadequate procedures.

Example 4 (Timely Client Updates): Kristen Chandler is an investment consultant in the London office of Dalton Securities, a major global investment consultant firm. One of her U.K. pension funds has decided to appoint a specialist U.S. equity manager. Dalton's global manager of research relies on local consultants to cover managers within their regions and, after conducting thorough due diligence, puts their views and ratings in Dalton's manager database. Chandler accesses Dalton's global manager research database and conducts a screen of all U.S. equity managers on the basis of a match with the client's desired philosophy/ style, performance, and tracking-error targets. She selects the five managers that meet these criteria and puts them in a briefing report that is delivered to the client 10 days later. Between the time of Chandler's database search and the delivery of the report to the client, Chandler is told that Dalton has updated the database with the information that one of the firms that Chandler has recommended for consideration lost its chief investment officer, the head of its U.S. equity research, and the majority of its portfolio managers on the U.S. equity product—all of whom have left to establish their own firm. Chandler does not revise her report with this updated information.

Comment: Chandler has failed to satisfy the requirement of Standard V(A). Although Dalton updated the manager ratings to reflect the personnel turnover at one of the firms, Chandler did not update her report to reflect the new information.

Example 5 (Group Research Opinions): Evelyn Mastakis is a junior analyst who has been asked by her firm to write a research report predicting the expected interest rate for residential mortgages over the next six months. Mastakis submits her report to the fixed-income investment committee of her firm for review, as required by firm procedures. Although some committee members support Mastakis's conclusion, the majority of the committee disagrees with her conclusion, and the report is significantly changed to indicate that interest rates are likely to increase more than originally predicted by Mastakis. Should Mastakis ask that her name be taken off the report when it is disseminated?

> *Comment*: The results of research are not always clear, and different people may have different opinions based on the same factual evidence. In this case, the committee may have valid reasons for issuing a report that differs from the analyst's original research. The firm can issue a report that is different from the original report of an analyst as long as there is a reasonable or adequate basis for its conclusions.
>
> Generally, analysts must write research reports that reflect their own opinion and can ask the firm not to put their name on reports that ultimately differ from that opinion. When the work is a group effort, however, not all members of the team may agree with all aspects of the report. Ultimately, members and candidates can ask to have their names removed from the report, but if they are satisfied that the process has produced results or conclusions that have a reasonable or adequate basis, members or candidates do not have to dissociate from the report even when they do not agree with its contents. If Mastakis is confident in the process, she does not need to dissociate from the report even if it does not reflect her opinion.

Example 6 (Reliance on Third-Party Research): Gary McDermott runs a two-person investment management firm. McDermott's firm subscribes to a service from a large investment research firm that provides research reports. McDermott's firm makes investment recommendations on the basis of these reports.

> *Comment*: Members and candidates can rely on third-party research but must make reasonable and diligent efforts to determine that such research is sound. If McDermott undertakes due diligence efforts on a regular basis to ensure that the research produced by the large firm is objective and reasonably based, McDermott can rely on that research when making investment recommendations to clients.

Example 7 (Due Diligence in Submanager Selection): Paul Ostrowski's business has grown significantly over the past couple of years, and some clients want to diversify internationally. Ostrowski decides to find a submanager to handle the expected international investments. Because this will be his first subadviser, Ostrowski uses the CFA Institute model "request for proposal" to design a questionnaire for his search. By his deadline, he receives seven completed questionnaires from a variety of domestic and international firms trying to gain his business. Ostrowski reviews all the applications in detail and decides to select the firm that charges the lowest fees because doing so will have the least impact on his firm's bottom line.

> *Comment*: The selection of an external adviser or subadviser should be based on a full and complete review of the advisers' services, performance history, and cost structure. In basing the decision on the fee structure alone, Ostrowski may be violating Standard V(A).
>
> See also Standard III(C)—Suitability as it relates to the ability of the selected adviser to meet the needs of the clients.

Example 8 (Sufficient Due Diligence): Michael Papis is the chief investment officer of his state's retirement fund. The fund has always used outside advisers for the real estate allocation, and this information is clearly presented in all fund communications. Thomas Nagle, a recognized sell-side research analyst and Papis's business school classmate, recently left the investment bank he worked for to start his own asset management firm, Accessible Real Estate. Nagle is trying to build his assets under management and contacts Papis about gaining some of the retirement fund's allocation. In the previous few years, the performance of the retirement fund's real estate investments was in line with the fund's benchmark but was not extraordinary. Papis decides to help out his old friend and also to seek better returns by moving the real estate allocation to Accessible. The only notice of the change in adviser appears in the next annual report in the listing of associated advisers.

> *Comment*: Papis violated Standard V(A) in this example. His responsibilities may include the selection of the external advisers, but the decision to change advisers appears to have been arbitrary. If Papis was dissatisfied with the current real estate adviser, he should have conducted a proper solicitation to select the most appropriate adviser.
>
> See also Standard IV(C)—Responsibilities of Supervisors, Standard V(B)—Communication with Clients and Prospective Clients, and Standard VI(A)—Disclosure of Conflicts.

Example 9 (Sufficient Due Diligence): Andre Shrub owns and operates Conduit, an investment advisory firm. Prior to opening Conduit, Shrub was an account manager with Elite Investment, a hedge fund managed by his good friend Adam Reed. To attract clients to a new Conduit fund, Shrub offers lower-than-normal management fees. He can do so because the fund consists of two top-performing funds managed by Reed. Given his personal friendship with Reed and the prior performance record of these two funds, Shrub believes this new fund is a winning combination for all parties. Clients quickly invest with Conduit to gain access to the Elite funds. No one is turned away because Conduit is seeking to expand its assets under management.

> *Comment*: Shrub violated Standard V(A) by not conducting a thorough analysis of the funds managed by Reed before developing the new Conduit fund. Due diligence must be applied more deeply than review of a single security. It includes a review of outside managers and investment funds. Shrub's reliance on his personal relationship with Reed and his prior knowledge of Elite are insufficient justification for the investments. The funds may be appropriately considered, but a full review of their operating procedures, reporting practices, and transparency are some elements of the necessary due diligence.
>
> See also Standard III(C)—Suitability.

Example 10 (Sufficient Due Diligence): Bob Thompson has been doing research for the portfolio manager of the fixed-income department. His assignment is to do sensitivity analysis on securitized subprime mortgages. He has discussed with the manager possible scenarios to use to calculate expected returns. A key assumption in such calculations is housing price appreciation (HPA) because it drives "prepays" (prepayments of mortgages) and losses. Thompson is concerned with the significant appreciation experienced over the previous five years as a result of the increased availability of funds from subprime mortgages. Thompson insists that the analysis should include a scenario run with negative 10 percent for the first year, negative 5 percent for the second year, and then (to project a worst-case scenario) 0 percent for Years 3 through 5. The manager replies that these assumptions are too dire because there has never been a time in their available database when HPA was negative.

Thompson conducts his research to better understand the risks inherent in these securities and evaluates these securities in the worst-case scenario, an unlikely but possible environment. Based on the results of the enhanced scenarios, Thompson does not recommend the purchase of the securitization. Against the general market trends, the manager follows Thompson's recommendation and does not invest. The following year, the housing market collapses. In avoiding the subprime investments, the manager's portfolio outperforms its peer group that year.

> *Comment*: Thompson's actions in running the scenario test with inputs beyond the historical trends available in the firm's databases adheres to the principles of Standard V(A). His concerns over recent trends provide a sound basis for further analysis. Thompson understands the limitations of his model, when combined with the limited available historical information, to accurately predict the performance of the funds if market conditions change negatively.
>
> See also Standard I(B)—Independence and Objectivity.

Example 11 (Use of Quantitatively Oriented Models): Espacia Liakos works in sales for Hellenica Securities, a firm specializing in developing intricate derivative strategies to profit from particular views on market expectations. One of her clients is Eugenie Carapalis, who has become convinced that commodity prices will become more volatile over the coming months. Carapalis asks Liakos to quickly engineer a strategy that will benefit from this expectation. Liakos turns to Hellenica's modelling group to fulfil this request. Because of the tight deadline, the modelling group outsources parts of the work to several trusted third parties. Liakos implements the disparate components of the strategy as the firms complete them.

Within a month, Carapalis is proven correct: Volatility across a range of commodities increases sharply. But her derivatives position with Hellenica returns huge losses, and the losses increase daily. Liakos investigates and realizes that, although each of the various components of the strategy had been validated, they had never been evaluated as an integrated whole. In extreme conditions, portions of the model worked at cross-purposes with other portions, causing the overall strategy to fail dramatically.

> *Comment*: Liakos violated Standard V(A). Members and candidates must understand the statistical significance of the results of the models they recommend and must be able to explain them to clients. Liakos did not take adequate care to ensure a thorough review of the whole model; its components were evaluated only individually. Because Carapalis clearly intended to implement the strategy as a whole rather than as separate parts, Liakos should have tested how the components of the strategy interacted as well as how they performed individually.

Example 12 (Successful Due Diligence/Failed Investment): Alton Newbury is an investment adviser to high-net-worth clients. A client with an aggressive risk profile in his investment policy statement asks about investing in the Top Shelf hedge fund. This fund, based in Calgary, Alberta, Canada, has reported 20 percent returns for the first three years. The fund prospectus states that its strategy involves long and short positions in the energy sector and extensive leverage. Based on his analysis of the fund's track record, the principals involved in managing the fund, the fees charged, and the fund's risk profile, Newbury recommends the fund to the client and secures a position in it. The next week, the fund announces that it has suffered a loss of 60 percent of its value and is suspending operations and redemptions until after a regulatory review. Newbury's client calls him in a panic and asks for an explanation.

> *Comment*: Newbury's actions were consistent with Standard V(A). Analysis of an investment that results in a reasonable basis for recommendation does not guarantee that the investment will have no downside risk. Newbury should discuss the analysis process with the client while reminding him or her that past performance does not lead to guaranteed future gains and that losses in an aggressive investment portfolio should be expected.

B. Communication with Clients and Prospective Clients

Members and Candidates must:

1. **Disclose to clients and prospective clients the basic format and general principles of the investment processes they use to analyze investments, select securities, and construct portfolios and must promptly disclose any changes that might materially affect those processes.**
2. **Use reasonable judgment in identifying which factors are important to their investment analyses, recommendations, or actions and include those factors in communications with clients and prospective clients.**
3. **Distinguish between fact and opinion in the presentation of investment analyses and recommendations.**

Guidance

Highlights:

▶ *Informing Clients of the Investment Process*
▶ *Different Forms of Communication*
▶ *Identifying Limitations of Analysis*
▶ *Distinction between Facts and Opinions in Reports*

Standard V(B) addresses member and candidate conduct with respect to communicating with clients. Developing and maintaining clear, frequent, and thorough communication practices is critical to providing high-quality financial services to clients. When clients understand the information communicated to them, they also can understand exactly how members and candidates are acting on their behalf, which gives clients the opportunity to make well-informed decisions about their investments. Such understanding can be accomplished only through clear communication.

Standard V(B) states that members and candidates should communicate in a recommendation the factors that were instrumental in making the investment recommendation. A critical part of this requirement is to distinguish clearly between opinions and facts. In preparing a research report, the member or candidate must present the basic characteristics of the security(ies) being analyzed, which will allow the reader to evaluate the report and incorporate information the reader deems relevant to his or her investment decision-making process.

Similarly, in preparing a recommendation about, for example, an asset allocation strategy, alternative investment vehicle, or structured investment product, the member or candidate should include factors that are relevant to whatever asset classes are being discussed. In all cases, the upside potential and downside risk expressed in terms of expected total returns should be among the factors communicated. Follow-on communication of any changes in the risk characteristics of a security or asset strategy would also be advisable.

Informing Clients of the Investment Process

Members and candidates must adequately describe to clients and prospective clients the manner in which the member or candidate conducts the investment decision-making process. The member or candidate must keep clients and other interested parties informed on an ongoing basis about changes to the investment process. Only by thoroughly understanding the nature of the investment product or service can a client determine whether changes to that product or service could materially affect his or her investment objectives.

Understanding the basic characteristics of an investment is of great importance in judging the suitability of that investment on a stand-alone basis, but it is especially important in determining the impact each investment will have on the characteristics of a portfolio. Although the risk and return characteristics of a common stock might seem to be essentially the same for any investor when the stock is viewed in isolation, the effects of those characteristics greatly depend on the other investments held. For instance, if the particular stock will represent 90 percent of an individual's investments, the stock's importance in the portfolio is vastly different from what it would be to an investor with a highly diversified portfolio for whom the stock will represent only 2 percent of the holdings.

A firm's investment policy may include the use of outside advisers to manage various portions of the clients' assets under management. Members and candidates should inform the clients about the specialization or diversification expertise provided by the external adviser(s). This information allows clients to understand the full mix of products and strategies being applied that may affect their investment objectives.

Different Forms of Communication

For purposes of Standard V(B), communication is not confined to a written report of the type traditionally generated by an analyst researching a security, company, or industry. A presentation of information can be made via any means of communication, including in-person recommendation or description, telephone conversation, media broadcast, or transmission by computer (e.g., on the internet). Furthermore, the nature of these communications is highly diverse— from one word ("buy" or "sell") to in-depth reports of more than 100 pages.

A communication may contain a general recommendation about the market, asset allocations, or classes of investments (e.g., stocks, bonds, real estate) or may relate to a specific security. If recommendations are contained in capsule form (such as a recommended stock list), members and candidates should notify clients that additional information and analyses are available from the producer of the report.

Identifying Limitations of Analysis

Investment advice based on quantitative research and analysis must be supported by readily available reference material and should be applied in a manner consistent with previously applied methodology; if changes in methodology are made, they should be highlighted. Members and candidates should outline known limitations of the analysis and conclusions contained in their investment advice. In evaluating the basic characteristics of the investment being recommended, members and candidates should consider in the report the potential total returns and the principal risks inherent in the expected returns, which may include credit risk, financial risk (specifically, the use of leverage or financial derivatives), and overall market risk.

Once the process has been completed, the member or candidate who prepares the report must include those elements that are important to the analysis and conclusions of the report so that the reader can follow and challenge the report's reasoning. A report writer who has done adequate investigation may emphasize certain areas, touch briefly on others, and omit certain aspects deemed unimportant. For instance, a report may dwell on a quarterly earnings release or new-product introduction and omit other matters as long as the analyst clearly stipulates the limits to the scope of the report.

Distinction between Facts and Opinions in Reports

Standard V(B) requires that opinion be separated from fact. Violations often occur when reports fail to separate the past from the future by not indicating that earnings estimates, changes in the outlook for dividends, and/or future market price information are *opinions* subject to future circumstances. In the case of complex quantitative analyses, analysts must clearly separate fact from statistical conjecture and should identify the known limitations of an analysis. Analysts may violate Standard V(B) by failing to identify the limits of statistically developed projections, because this omission leaves readers unaware of the limits of the published projections.

Recommended Procedures for Compliance

Because the selection of relevant factors is an analytical skill, determination of whether a member or candidate has used reasonable judgment in excluding and including information in research reports depends heavily on case-by-case review rather than a specific checklist. To assist in the after-the-fact review of a report, the member or candidate must maintain records indicating the nature of the research and should, if asked, be able to supply additional information to the client (or any user of the report) covering factors not included in the report.

Application of the Standard

Example 1 (Sufficient Disclosure of Investment System): Sarah Williamson, director of marketing for Country Technicians, Inc., is convinced that she has found the perfect formula for increasing Country Technician's income and diversifying its product base. Williamson plans to build on Country Technician's reputation as a leading money manager by marketing an exclusive and expensive investment advice letter to high-net-worth individuals. One hitch in the plan is the complexity of Country Technician's investment system—a combination of technical trading rules (based on historical price and volume fluctuations) and portfolio construction rules designed to minimize risk. To simplify the newsletter, she decides to include only each week's top-five "buy" and "sell" recommendations and to leave out details of the valuation models and the portfolio structuring scheme.

> *Comment*: Williamson's plans for the newsletter violate Standard V(B). Williamson need not describe the investment system in detail in order to implement the advice effectively, but she must inform clients of Country Technician's basic process and logic. Without understanding the basis for a recommendation, clients cannot possibly understand its limitations or its inherent risks.

Example 2 (Providing Opinions as Facts): Richard Dox is a mining analyst for East Bank Securities. He has just finished his report on Boisy Bay Minerals. Included in his report is his own assessment of the geological extent of mineral reserves likely to be found on the company's land. Dox completed this calculation on the basis of the core samples from the company's latest drilling. According to Dox's calculations, the company has more than 500,000 ounces of gold on the property. Dox concludes his research report as follows: "Based on the fact that the company has 500,000 ounces of gold to be mined, I recommend a strong BUY."

> *Comment*: If Dox issues the report as written, he will violate Standard V(B). His calculation of the total gold reserves for the property is an opinion, not a fact. Opinion must be distinguished from fact in research reports.

Example 3 (Proper Description of a Security): Olivia Thomas, an analyst at Government Brokers, Inc., which is a brokerage firm specializing in government bond trading, has produced a report that describes an investment strategy designed to benefit from an expected decline in U.S. interest rates. The firm's derivative products group has designed a structured product that will allow the firm's clients to benefit from this strategy. Thomas's report describing the strategy indicates that high returns are possible if various scenarios for declining interest rates are assumed. Citing the proprietary nature of the structured product underlying the strategy, the report does not describe in detail how the firm is able to offer such returns or the related risks in the scenarios, nor does the report address the likely returns of the strategy if, contrary to expectations, interest rates rise.

> *Comment*: Thomas has violated Standard V(B) because her report fails to describe properly the basic characteristics of the actual and implied risks of the investment strategy, including how the structure was created and the degree to which leverage was embedded in the structure. The report should include a balanced discussion of how the strategy would perform in the case of rising as well as falling interest rates, preferably illustrating how the strategies might be expected to perform in the event of a reasonable variety of interest rate and credit-risk-spread scenarios. If liquidity issues are relevant with regard to the valuation of either the derivatives or the underlying securities, provisions the firm has made to address those risks should also be disclosed.

Example 4 (Notification of Fund Mandate Change): May & Associates is an aggressive-growth manager that has represented itself since its inception as a specialist at investing in small-cap U.S. stocks. One of May's selection criteria is a maximum capitalization of US$250 million for any given company. After a string of successful years of superior performance relative to its peers, May has expanded its client base significantly, to the point at which assets under management now exceed $3 billion. For liquidity purposes, May's chief investment officer (CIO) decides to lift the maximum permissible market-cap ceiling to US$500 million and change the firm's sales and marketing literature accordingly to inform prospective clients and third-party consultants.

> *Comment*: Although May's CIO is correct about informing potentially interested parties as to the change in investment process, he must also notify May's existing clients. Among the latter group might be a number of clients who not only retained May as a small-cap manager but also retained midcap and large-cap specialists in a multiple-manager approach. Such clients could regard May's change of criteria as a style change that distorts their overall asset allocations.

Example 5 (Notification of Fund Mandate Change): Rather than lifting the ceiling for its universe from US$250 million to US$500 million, May & Associates extends its small-cap universe to include a number of non-U.S. companies.

Comment: Standard V(B) requires that May's CIO advise May's clients of this change because the firm may have been retained by some clients specifically for its prowess at investing in U.S. small-cap stocks. Other changes that require client notification are introducing derivatives to emulate a certain market sector or relaxing various other constraints, such as portfolio beta. In all such cases, members and candidates must disclose changes to all interested parties.

Example 6 (Notification of Changes to the Investment Process): RJZ Capital Management is an active value-style equity manager that selects stocks by using a combination of four multifactor models. The firm has found favorable results when back testing the most recent 10 years of available market data in a new dividend discount model (DDM) designed by the firm. This model is based on projected inflation rates, earnings growth rates, and interest rates. The president of RJZ decides to replace its simple model that uses price to trailing 12-months earnings with the new DDM.

Comment: Because the introduction of a new and different valuation model represents a material change in the investment process, RJZ's president must communicate the change to the firm's clients. RJZ is moving away from a model based on hard data toward a new model that is at least partly dependent on the firm's forecasting skills. Clients would likely view such a model as a significant change rather than a mere refinement of RJZ's process.

Example 7 (Notification of Changes to the Investment Process): RJZ Capital Management loses the chief architect of its multifactor valuation system. Without informing its clients, the president of RJZ decides to redirect the firm's talents and resources toward developing a product for passive equity management—a product that will emulate the performance of a major market index.

Comment: By failing to disclose to clients a substantial change to its investment process, the president of RJZ has violated Standard V(B).

Example 8 (Notification of Changes to the Investment Process): At Fundamental Asset Management, Inc., the responsibility for selecting stocks for addition to the firm's "approved" list has just shifted from individual security analysts to a committee consisting of the research director and three senior portfolio managers. Eleanor Morales, a portfolio manager with Fundamental Asset Management, thinks this change is not important enough to communicate to her clients.

Comment: Morales must disclose the process change to all her clients. Some of Fundamental's clients might be concerned about the morale and motivation among the firm's best research analysts after such a change. Moreover, clients might challenge the stock-picking track record of the portfolio managers and might even want to monitor the situation closely.

Example 9 (Sufficient Disclosure of Investment System): Amanda Chinn is the investment director for Diversified Asset Management, which manages the endowment of a charitable organization. Because of recent staff departures, Diversified has decided to limit its direct investment focus to large-cap securities and supplement the needs for small-cap and midcap management by hiring outside fund managers. In describing the planned strategy change to the charity, Chinn's update letter states, "As investment director, I will directly oversee the investment team managing the endowment's large-capitalization allocation. I will coordinate the selection and ongoing review of external managers responsible for allocations to other classes." The letter also describes the reasons for the change and the characteristics external managers must have to be considered.

>   *Comment*: Standard V(B) requires the disclosure of the investment process used to construct the portfolio of the fund. Changing the investment process from managing all classes of investments within the firm to the use of external managers is one example of information that needs to be communicated to clients. Chinn and her firm have embraced the principles of Standard V(B) by providing their client with relevant information. The charity can now make a reasonable decision about whether Diversified Asset Management remains the appropriate manager for its fund.

Example 10 (Notification of Changes to the Investment Process): Michael Papis is the chief investment officer of his state's retirement fund. The fund has always used outside advisers for the real estate allocation, and this information is clearly presented in all fund communications. Thomas Nagle, a recognized sell-side research analyst and Papis's business school classmate, recently left the investment bank he worked for to start his own asset management firm, Accessible Real Estate. Nagle is trying to build his assets under management and contacts Papis about gaining some of the retirement fund's allocation. In the previous few years, the performance of the retirement fund's real estate investments was in line with the fund's benchmark but was not extraordinary. Papis decides to help out his old friend and also to seek better returns by moving the real estate allocation to Accessible. The only notice of the change in adviser appears in the next annual report in the listing of associated advisers.

>   *Comment*: Papis has violated Standard V(B). He attempted to hide the nature of his decision to change external managers by making only a limited disclosure. The plan recipients and the fund's trustees need to be aware when changes are made to ensure that operational procedures are being followed.
>
>   See also Standard IV(C)—Responsibilities of Supervisors, Standard V(A)—Diligence and Reasonable Basis, and Standard VI(A)—Disclosure of Conflicts.

C. Record Retention

Members and Candidates must develop and maintain appropriate records to support their investment analyses, recommendations, actions, and other investment-related communications with clients and prospective clients.

Guidance

Highlights:

▶ *Records Are Property of the Firm*
▶ *Local Requirements*

Members and candidates must retain records that substantiate the scope of their research and reasons for their actions or conclusions. Which records are required to support recommendations and/or investment actions depends on the role of the member or candidate in the investment decision-making process. Records may be maintained either in hard copy or electronic form.

Some examples of supporting documentation that assists the member or candidate in meeting the requirements for retention are as follows:

- ▶ personal notes from meetings with the covered company;
- ▶ press releases or presentations issued by the covered company;
- ▶ computer-based model outputs and analyses;
- ▶ computer-based model input parameters;
- ▶ risk analyses of securities' impacts on a portfolio;
- ▶ selection criteria for external advisers;
- ▶ notes from clients from meetings to review investment policy statements;
- ▶ outside research reports.

Records Are Property of the Firm

As a general matter, records created as part of a member's or candidate's professional activity on behalf of his or her employer are the property of the firm. When a member or candidate leaves a firm to seek other employment, the member or candidate cannot take the property of the firm, including originals or copies of supporting records of the member's or candidate's work, to the new employer without the express consent of the previous employer. The member or candidate cannot use historical recommendations or research reports created at the previous firm because the supporting documentation is unavailable. For future use, the member or candidate must re-create the supporting records at the new firm with information gathered through public sources or directly from the covered company and not from memory or sources obtained at the previous employer.

Local Requirements

Local regulators often impose requirements on members, candidates, and their firms related to record retention that must be followed. Fulfilling such regulatory requirements also may satisfy the requirements of Standard V(C), but members and candidates should explicitly determine whether it does. In the absence of regulatory guidance, CFA Institute recommends maintaining records for at least seven years.

Recommended Procedures for Compliance

The responsibility to maintain records that support investment action generally falls with the firm rather than individuals. Members and candidates must, however, archive research notes and other documents, either electronically or in hard copy, that support their current investment-related communications. Doing so will assist their firms in complying with requirements for preservation of internal or external records.

Application of the Standard

Example 1 (Record Retention and IPS Objectives and Recommendations): One of Nikolas Lindstrom's clients is upset by the negative investment returns in his equity portfolio. The investment policy statement for the client requires that the portfolio manager follow a benchmark-oriented approach. The benchmark for the client includes a 35 percent investment allocation in the technology sector. The client acknowledges that this allocation was appropriate, but over the past three years, technology stocks have suffered severe losses. The client complains to the investment manager that so much money was allocated to this sector.

> *Comment*: For Lindstrom, having appropriate records is important to show that over the past three years the percentage of technology stocks in the benchmark index was 35 percent as called for in the IPS. Lindstrom should also have the IPS for the client stating that the benchmark was appropriate for the client's investment objectives. He should also have records indicating that the investment has been explained appropriately to the client and that the IPS was updated on a regular basis. Taking these actions, Lindstrom would be in compliance with Standard V(C).

Example 2 (Record Retention and Research Process): Malcolm Young is a research analyst who writes numerous reports rating companies in the luxury retail industry. His reports are based on a variety of sources, including interviews with company managers, manufacturers, and economists; onsite company visits; customer surveys; and secondary research from analysts covering related industries.

> *Comment*: Young must carefully document and keep copies of all the information that goes into his reports, including the secondary or third-party research of other analysts. Failure to maintain such files would violate Standard V(C).

Example 3 (Records as Firm, Not Employee, Property): Martin Blank develops an analytical model while he is employed by Grosse Point Investment Management, LLP (GPIM). While at the firm, he systematically documents the assumptions that make up the model as well as his reasoning behind the assumptions. As a result of the success of his model, Blank is hired to be the head of the research department of one of GPIM's competitors. Blank takes copies of the records supporting his model to his new firm.

> *Comment*: The records created by Blank supporting the research model he developed at GPIM are the records of GPIM. Taking the documents with him to his new employer without GPIM's permission violates Standard V(C). To use the model in the future, Blank must re-create the records supporting his model at the new firm.

STANDARD VI—CONFLICTS OF INTEREST

A. Disclosure of Conflicts

Members and Candidates must make full and fair disclosure of all matters that could reasonably be expected to impair their independence and objectivity or interfere with respective duties to their clients, prospective clients, and employer. Members and Candidates must ensure that such disclosures are prominent, are delivered in plain language, and communicate the relevant information effectively.

Guidance

Highlights:

▶ *Disclosure of Conflicts to Employers*

▶ *Disclosure to Clients*

▶ *Cross-Departmental Conflicts*

▶ *Conflicts with Stock Ownership*

▶ *Conflicts as a Director*

Best practice is to avoid actual conflicts or the appearance of conflicts of interest when possible. Conflicts of interest often arise in the investment profession. Conflicts can occur between the interests of clients, the interests of employers, and the member's or candidate's own personal interests. Common sources for conflict are compensation structures, especially incentive and bonus structures that provide immediate returns for members and candidates with little or no consideration of long-term value creation.

Identifying and managing these conflicts is a critical part of working in the investment industry and can take many forms. When conflicts cannot be reasonably avoided, clear and complete disclosure of their existence is necessary.

Standard VI(A) protects investors and employers by requiring members and candidates to fully disclose to clients, potential clients, and employers all actual and potential conflicts of interest. Once a member or candidate has made full disclosure, the member's or candidate's employer, clients, and prospective clients will have the information needed to evaluate the objectivity of the investment advice or action taken on their behalf.

To be effective, disclosures must be prominent and must be made in plain language and in a manner designed to effectively communicate the information. Members and candidates have the responsibility of determining how often, in what manner, and in what particular circumstances the disclosure of conflicts must be made. Best practices dictate updating disclosures when the nature of a conflict of interest changes materially—for example, if the nature of a conflict of interest deepens through the introduction of bonuses based on each quarter's profits as opposed to the previous review based on annual profits. In making and updating disclosures of conflicts of interest, members and candidates should err on the side of caution to ensure that conflicts are effectively communicated.

Disclosure of Conflicts to Employers

Disclosure of conflicts to employers may be appropriate in many instances. When reporting conflicts of interest to employers, members and candidates should give their employers enough information to assess the impact of the conflict. By complying with employer guidelines, members and candidates allow their employers to avoid potentially embarrassing and costly ethical or regulatory violations.

Reportable situations include conflicts that would interfere with rendering unbiased investment advice and conflicts that would cause a member or candidate to act not in the employer's best interest. The same circumstances that generate conflicts to be reported to clients and prospective clients also would dictate reporting to employers. Ownership of stocks analyzed or recommended, participation on outside boards, and financial or other pressures that could influence a decision are to be promptly reported to the employer so that their impact can be assessed and a decision made on how to resolve the conflict.

The mere appearance of a conflict of interest may create problems for members, candidates, and their employers. Therefore, many of the conflicts previously mentioned could be explicitly prohibited by an employer. For example, many employers restrict personal trading, outside board membership, and related activities to prevent situations that might not normally be considered problematic from a conflict-of-interest point of view but that could give the appearance of a conflict of interest. Members and candidates must comply with these restrictions. Members and candidates must take reasonable steps to avoid conflicts and, if they occur inadvertently, must report them promptly so that the employer and the member or candidate can resolve them as quickly and effectively as possible.

Standard VI(A) also deals with a member's or candidate's conflicts of interest that might be detrimental to the employer's business. Any potential conflict situation that could prevent clear judgment about or full commitment to the execution of the member's or candidate's duties to the employer should be reported to the member's or candidate's employer and promptly resolved.

Disclosure to Clients

Members and candidates must maintain their objectivity when rendering investment advice or taking investment action. Investment advice or actions may be perceived to be tainted in numerous situations. Can a member or candidate remain objective if, on behalf of the firm, the member or candidate obtains or assists in obtaining fees for services? Can a member or candidate give objective advice if he or she owns stock in the company that is the subject of an investment recommendation or if the member or candidate has a close personal relationship with the company managers? Requiring members and candidates to disclose all matters that reasonably could be expected to impair the member's or candidate's objectivity allows clients and prospective clients to judge motives and possible biases for themselves.

Often in the investment industry, a conflict, or the perception of a conflict, cannot be avoided. The most obvious conflicts of interest, which should always be disclosed, are relationships between an issuer and the member, candidate, or their firm (such as a directorship or consultancy by a member; investment banking, underwriting, and financial relationships; broker/dealer market-making activities; and material beneficial ownership of stock). For the purposes of Standard VI(A), members and candidates beneficially own securities or other investments if they have a direct or indirect pecuniary interest in the securities; have the power to vote or direct the voting of the shares of the securities or investments; or have the power to dispose or direct the disposition of the security or investment.

A member or candidate must take reasonable steps to determine whether a conflict of interest exists and disclose to clients any known conflicts of the member's or candidate's firm. Disclosure of broker/dealer market-making activities alerts clients that a purchase or sale might be made from or to the firm's principal account and that the firm has a special interest in the price of the stock.

Additionally, disclosures should be made to clients of fee arrangements, subadvisory agreements, or other situations involving nonstandard fee structures. Equally important is the disclosure of arrangements in which the firm benefits directly from investment recommendations. An obvious conflict of interest is the rebate of a portion of the service fee some classes of mutual funds charge to investors. Members and candidates should ensure that their firms disclose such relationships so clients can fully understand the costs of their investments and the benefits received by their investment manager's employer.

Cross-Departmental Conflicts

Other circumstances can give rise to actual or potential conflicts of interest. For instance, a sell-side analyst working for a broker/dealer may be encouraged, not only by members of her or his own firm but by corporate issuers themselves, to write research reports about particular companies. The buy-side analyst is likely to be faced with similar conflicts as banks exercise their underwriting and security-dealing powers. The marketing division may ask an analyst to recommend the stock of a certain company in order to obtain business from that company.

The potential for conflicts of interest also exists with broker-sponsored limited partnerships formed to invest venture capital. Increasingly, members and candidates are expected not only to follow issues from these partnerships once they are offered to the public but also to promote the issues in the secondary market after public offerings. Members, candidates, and their firms should attempt to resolve situations presenting potential conflicts of interest or disclose them in accordance with the principles set forth in Standard VI(A).

Conflicts with Stock Ownership

The most prevalent conflict requiring disclosure under Standard VI(A) is a member's or candidate's ownership of stock in companies that he or she recommends to clients and/or that clients hold. Clearly, the easiest method for preventing a conflict is to prohibit members and candidates from owning any such securities, but this approach is overly burdensome and discriminates against members and candidates.

Therefore, sell-side members and candidates should disclose any materially beneficial ownership interest in a security or other investment that the member or candidate is recommending. Buy-side members and candidates should disclose their procedures for reporting requirements for personal transactions. Conflicts arising from personal investing are discussed more fully in the guidance for Standard VI(B).

Conflicts as a Director

Service as a director poses three basic conflicts of interest. First, a conflict may exist between the duties owed to clients and the duties owed to shareholders of the company. Second, investment personnel who serve as directors may receive the securities or options to purchase securities of the company as compensation for serving on the board, which could raise questions about trading actions that might increase the value of those securities. Third, board service creates the opportunity to receive material nonpublic information involving the company. Even though the information is confidential, the perception could be that information not available to the public is being communicated to a director's firm—whether a broker, investment adviser, or other type of organization. When members or candidates providing investment services also serve as directors, they should be isolated from those making investment decisions by the use of firewalls or similar restrictions.

Recommended Procedures for Compliance

Members or candidates should disclose special compensation arrangements with the employer that might conflict with client interests, such as bonuses based on short-term performance criteria, commissions, incentive fees, performance fees, and referral fees. If the member's or candidate's firm does not permit such disclosure, the member or candidate should document the request and may consider dissociating from the activity.

Members' and candidates' firms are encouraged to include information on compensation packages in firms' promotional literature. If a member or candidate manages a portfolio for which the fee is based on capital gains or capital appreciation (a performance fee), this information should be disclosed to clients. If a member, candidate, or a member's or candidate's firm has outstanding agent options to buy stock as part of the compensation package for corporate financing activities, the amount and expiration date of these options should be disclosed as a footnote to any research report published by the member's or candidate's firm.

Application of the Standard

Example 1 (Conflict of Interest and Business Relationships): Hunter Weiss is a research analyst with Farmington Company, a broker and investment banking firm. Farmington's merger and acquisition department has represented Vimco, a conglomerate, in all of Vimco's acquisitions for 20 years. From time to time, Farmington officers sit on the boards of directors of various Vimco subsidiaries. Weiss is writing a research report on Vimco.

> *Comment*: Weiss must disclose in his research report Farmington's special relationship with Vimco. Broker/dealer management of and participation in public offerings must be disclosed in research reports. Because the position of underwriter to a company entails a special past and potential future relationship with a company that is the subject of investment advice, it threatens the independence and objectivity of the report writer and must be disclosed.

Example 2 (Conflict of Interest and Business Stock Ownership): The investment management firm of Dover & Roe sells a 25 percent interest in its partnership to a multinational bank holding company, First of New York. Immediately after the sale, Margaret Hobbs, president of Dover & Roe, changes her recommendation for First of New York's common stock from "sell" to "buy" and adds First of New York's commercial paper to Dover & Roe's approved list for purchase.

> *Comment*: Hobbs must disclose the new relationship with First of New York to all Dover & Roe clients. This relationship must also be disclosed to clients by the firm's portfolio managers when they make specific investment recommendations or take investment actions with respect to First of New York's securities.

Example 3 (Conflict of Interest and Personal Stock Ownership): Carl Fargmon, a research analyst who follows firms producing office equipment, has been recommending purchase of Kincaid Printing because of its innovative new line of copiers. After his initial report on the company, Fargmon's wife inherits from a distant relative US$3 million of Kincaid stock. He has been asked to write a follow-up report on Kincaid.

> *Comment*: Fargmon must disclose his wife's ownership of the Kincaid stock to his employer and in his follow-up report. Best practice would be to avoid the conflict by asking his employer to assign another analyst to draft the follow-up report.

Example 4 (Conflict of Interest and Personal Stock Ownership): Betty Roberts is speculating in penny stocks for her own account and purchases 100,000 shares of Drew Mining, Inc., for 30 cents a share. She intends to sell these shares at the sign of any substantial upward price movement of the stock. A week later, her employer asks her to write a report on penny stocks in the mining industry to be published in two weeks. Even without owning the Drew stock, Roberts would recommend it in her report as a "buy." A surge in the price of the stock to the US$2 range is likely to result once the report is issued.

> *Comment*: Although this holding may not be material, Roberts must disclose it in the report and to her employer before writing the report because the gain for her will be substantial if the market responds strongly to her recommendation. The fact that she has only recently purchased the stock adds to the appearance that she is not entirely objective.

Example 5 (Conflict of Interest and Compensation Arrangement): Samantha Snead, a portfolio manager for Thomas Investment Counsel, Inc., specializes in managing public retirement funds and defined-benefit pension plan accounts, all of which have long-term investment objectives. A year ago, Snead's employer, in an attempt to motivate and retain key investment professionals, introduced a bonus compensation system that rewards portfolio managers on the basis of quarterly performance relative to their peers and to certain benchmark indices. In an attempt to improve the short-term performance of her accounts, Snead changes her investment strategy and purchases several high-beta stocks for client portfolios. These purchases are seemingly contrary to the clients' investment policy statements. Following their purchase, an officer of Griffin Corporation, one of Snead's pension fund clients, asks why Griffin Corporation's portfolio seems to be dominated by high-beta stocks of companies that often appear among the most actively traded issues. No change in objective or strategy has been recommended by Snead during the year.

> *Comment*: Snead has violated Standard VI(A) by failing to inform her clients of the changes in her compensation arrangement with her employer, which created a conflict of interest between her compensation and her clients' IPS. Firms may pay employees on the basis of performance, but pressure by Thomas Investment Counsel to achieve short-term performance goals is in basic conflict with the objectives of Snead's accounts.
>
> See also Standard III(C)—Suitability.

Example 6 (Conflict of Interest and Options and Compensation Arrangements): Wayland Securities works with small companies doing IPOs and/or secondary offerings. Typically, these deals are in the US$10 million to US$50 million range, and as a result, the corporate finance fees are quite small. To compensate for the small fees, Wayland Securities usually takes "agents options"—that is, rights (exercisable within a two-year time frame) to acquire up to an additional 10 percent of the current offering. Following an IPO performed by Wayland for Falk Resources, Ltd., Darcy Hunter, the head of corporate finance at Wayland, is concerned about receiving value for her Falk Resources options. The options are one month from expiring, and the stock is not doing well. She contacts John Fitzpatrick in the research department of Wayland Securities, reminds him that he is eligible for 30 percent of these options, and indicates that now would be a good time to give some additional coverage to Falk Resources. Fitzpatrick agrees and immediately issues a favorable report.

> *Comment*: For Fitzpatrick to avoid being in violation of Standard VI(A), he must indicate in the report the volume and expiration date of agent options outstanding. Furthermore, because he is personally eligible for some of the options, Fitzpatrick must disclose the extent of this compensation. He also must be careful that he does not violate his duty of independence and objectivity under Standard I(B).

Example 7 (Conflict of Interest and Compensation Arrangements): Gary Carter is a representative with Bengal International, a registered broker/dealer. Carter is approached by a stock promoter for Badger Company, who offers to pay Carter additional compensation for sales of Badger Company's stock to Carter's clients. Carter accepts the stock promoter's offer but does not disclose the arrangements to his clients or to his employer. Carter sells shares of the stock to his clients.

Comment: Carter has violated Standard VI(A) by failing to disclose to clients that he is receiving additional compensation for recommending and selling Badger stock. Because he did not disclose the arrangement with Badger to his clients, the clients were unable to evaluate whether Carter's recommendations to buy Badger were affected by this arrangement. Carter's conduct also violated Standard VI(A) by failing to disclose to his employer monetary compensation received in addition to the compensation and benefits conferred by his employer. Carter was required by Standard VI(A) to disclose the arrangement with Badger to his employer so that his employer could evaluate whether the arrangement affected Carter's objectivity and loyalty.

Example 8 (Conflict of Interest and Directorship): Carol Corky, a senior portfolio manager for Universal Management, recently became involved as a trustee with the Chelsea Foundation, a large not-for-profit foundation in her hometown. Universal is a small money manager (with assets under management of approximately US$100 million) that caters to individual investors. Chelsea has assets in excess of US$2 billion. Corky does not believe informing Universal of her involvement with Chelsea is necessary.

Comment: By failing to inform Universal of her involvement with Chelsea, Corky violated Standard VI(A). Given the large size of the endowment at Chelsea, Corky's new role as a trustee can reasonably be expected to be time-consuming, to the possible detriment of Corky's portfolio responsibilities with Universal. Also, as a trustee, Corky may become involved in the investment decisions at Chelsea. Therefore, Standard VI(A) obligates Corky to discuss becoming a trustee at Chelsea with her compliance officer or supervisor at Universal before accepting the position, and she should have disclosed the degree to which she would be involved in investment decisions at Chelsea.

Example 9 (Conflict of Interest and Personal Trading): Bruce Smith covers East European equities for Marlborough Investments, an investment management firm with a strong presence in emerging markets. While on a business trip to Russia, Smith learns that investing in Russian equity directly is difficult but that equity-linked notes that replicate the performance of the underlying Russian equity can be purchased from a New York–based investment bank. Believing that his firm would not be interested in such a security, Smith purchases a note linked to a Russian telecommunications company for his own account without informing Marlborough. A month later, Smith decides that the firm should consider investing in Russian equities by way of the equity-linked notes. He prepares a write-up on the market that concludes with a recommendation to purchase several of the notes. One note he recommends is linked to the same Russian telecom company that Smith holds in his personal account.

Comment: Smith has violated Standard VI(A) by failing to disclose his purchase and ownership of the note linked to the Russian telecom company. Smith is required by the standard to disclose the investment opportunity to his employer and look to his company's policies on personal trading to determine whether it was proper for him to purchase the note for his own account. By purchasing the note, Smith may or may not have impaired his ability to make an unbiased and objective assessment of the appropriateness of the derivative instrument for his firm, but Smith's failure to disclose the purchase to his employer impaired his employer's ability to decide whether his ownership of the security is a conflict of interest that might affect Smith's future recommendations. Then, when he recommended the particular telecom notes to his firm, Smith compounded his problems by not disclosing that he owned the notes in his personal account—a clear conflict of interest.

Example 10 (Conflict of Interest and Requested Favors): Michael Papis is the chief investment officer of his state's retirement fund. The fund has always used outside advisers for the real estate allocation, and this information is clearly presented in all fund communications. Thomas Nagle, a recognized sell-side research analyst and Papis's business school classmate, recently left the investment bank he worked for to start his own asset management firm, Accessible Real Estate. Nagle is trying to build his assets under management and contacts Papis about gaining some of the retirement fund's allocation. In the previous few years, the performance of the retirement fund's real estate investments was in line with the fund's benchmark but was not extraordinary. Papis decides to help out his old friend and also to seek better returns by moving the real estate allocation to Accessible. The only notice of the change in adviser appears in the next annual report in the listing of associated advisers.

> *Comment*: Papis has violated Standard VI(A) by not disclosing to his employer his personal relationship with Nagle. Disclosure of his past history with Nagle would allow his firm to determine whether the conflict may have impaired Papis's independence in deciding to change managers.
>
> See also Standard IV(C)—Responsibilities of Supervisors, Standard V(A)—Diligence and Reasonable Basis, and Standard V(B)—Communication with Clients and Prospective Clients.

Example 11 (Conflict of Interest and Business Relationships): Bob Wade, trust manager for Central Midas Bank, was approached by Western Funds about promoting its family of funds, with special interest in the service-fee class. To entice Central to promote this class, Western Funds offered to pay the bank a service fee of 0.25 percent. Without disclosing the fee being offered to the bank, Wade asked one of the investment managers to review the Western Funds family of funds to determine whether they were suitable for clients of Central. The manager completed the normal due diligence review and determined that the funds were fairly valued in the market with fee structures on a par with their competitors. Wade decided to accept Western's offer and instructed the team of portfolio managers to exclusively promote these funds and the service-fee class to clients seeking to invest new funds or transfer from their current investments. So as to not influence the investment managers, Wade did not disclose the fee offer and allowed that income to flow directly to the bank.

> *Comment*: Wade is violating Standard VI(A) by not disclosing the portion of the service fee being paid to Central. Although the investment managers may not be influenced by the fee, neither they nor the client have the proper information about Wade's decision to exclusively market this fund family and class of investments. Central may come to rely on the new fee as a component of the firm's profitability and may be unwilling to offer other products in the future that could affect the fees received.
>
> See also Standard I(B)—Independence and Objectivity.

B. Priority of Transactions

Investment transactions for clients and employers must have priority over investment transactions in which a Member or Candidate is the beneficial owner.

Guidance

Highlights:

- ▶ *Avoiding Potential Conflicts*
- ▶ *Personal Trading Secondary to Trading for Clients*
- ▶ *Standards for Nonpublic Information*
- ▶ *Impact on All Accounts with Beneficial Ownership*

Standard VI(B) reinforces the responsibility of members and candidates to give the interests of their clients and employers priority over their personal financial interests. This standard is designed to prevent any potential conflict of interest or the appearance of a conflict of interest with respect to personal transactions. Client interests have priority. Client transactions must take precedence over transactions made on behalf of the member's or candidate's firm or personal transactions.

Avoiding Potential Conflicts

Conflicts between the client's interest and an investment professional's personal interest may occur. Although conflicts of interest exist, nothing is inherently unethical about individual managers, advisers, or mutual fund employees making money from personal investments as long as 1) the client is not disadvantaged by the trade, 2) the investment professional does not benefit personally from trades undertaken for clients, and 3) the investment professional complies with applicable regulatory requirements.

Some situations occur where a member or candidate may need to enter a personal transaction that runs counter to current recommendations or what the portfolio manager is doing for client portfolios. For example, a member or candidate may be required at some point to sell an asset to make a college tuition payment or a down payment on a home, to meet a margin call, or so on. The sale may be contrary to the long-term advice the member or candidate is currently providing to clients. In these situations, the same three criteria given in the preceding paragraph should be applied in the transaction so as to not violate Standard VI(B).

Personal Trading Secondary to Trading for Clients

Standard VI(B) states that transactions for clients and employers must have priority over transactions in securities or other investments of which a member or candidate is the beneficial owner. The objective of the standard is to prevent personal transactions from adversely affecting the interests of clients or employers. A member or candidate having the same investment positions or being co-invested with clients does not always create a conflict. Some clients in certain investment situations require members or candidates to have aligned interests. Personal investment positions or transactions of members or candidates or their firm should never, however, adversely affect client investments.

Standards for Nonpublic Information

Standard VI(B) covers the activities of members and candidates who have knowledge of pending transactions that may be made on behalf of their clients or employers, who have access to nonpublic information during the normal preparation of research recommendations, or who take investment actions. Members and candidates are prohibited from conveying nonpublic information to any person whose relationship to the member or candidate makes the member or candidate a beneficial owner of the person's securities. Members and candidates must not convey this information to any other person if the nonpublic information can be deemed material.

Impact on All Accounts with Beneficial Ownership

Members or candidates may undertake transactions in accounts for which they are a beneficial owner only after their clients and employers have had adequate opportunity to act on a recommendation. Personal transactions include those made for the member's or candidate's own account, for family (including spouse, children, and other immediate family members) accounts, and for accounts in which the member or candidate has a direct or indirect pecuniary interest, such as a trust or retirement account. Family accounts that are client accounts should be treated like any other firm account and should neither be given special treatment nor be disadvantaged because of the family relationship. If a member or candidate has a beneficial ownership in the account, however, the member or candidate may be subject to preclearance or reporting requirements of the employer or applicable law.

Recommended Procedures for Compliance

Policies and procedures designed to prevent potential conflicts of interest, and even the appearance of a conflict of interest, with respect to personal transactions are critical to establishing investor confidence in the securities industry. Therefore, members and candidates should urge their firms to establish such policies and procedures. Because investment firms vary greatly in assets under management, types of clients, number of employees, and so on, each firm should have policies regarding personal investing that are best suited to the firm. Members and candidates should then prominently disclose these policies to clients and prospective clients.

The specific provisions of each firm's standards will vary, but all firms should adopt certain basic procedures to address the conflict areas created by personal investing. These procedures include the following:

▶ *Limited participation in equity IPOs*: Some eagerly awaited IPOs rise significantly in value shortly after the issue is brought to market. Because the new issue may be highly attractive and sought after, the opportunity to participate in the IPO may be limited. Therefore, purchases of IPOs by investment personnel create conflicts of interest in two principal ways. First, participation in an IPO may have the appearance of taking away an attractive investment opportunity from clients for personal gain—a clear breach of the duty of loyalty to clients. Second, personal purchases in IPOs may have the appearance that the investment opportunity is being bestowed as an incentive to make future investment decisions for the benefit of the party providing the opportunity. Members and candidates can avoid these conflicts or appearances of conflicts of interest by not participating in IPOs.

Reliable and systematic review procedures should be established to ensure that conflicts relating to IPOs are identified and appropriately dealt with by supervisors. Members and candidates should preclear their participation in IPOs, even in situations without any conflict of interest between a member's or candidate's participation in an IPO and the client's interests. Members and candidates should not benefit from the position that their clients occupy in the marketplace—through preferred trading, the allocation of limited offerings, and/or oversubscription.

▶ *Restrictions on private placements*: Strict limits should be placed on investment personnel acquiring securities in private placements, and appropriate supervisory and review procedures should be established to prevent noncompliance.

Firms do not routinely use private placements for clients (e.g., venture capital deals) because of the high risk associated with them. Conflicts related to private placements are more significant to members and candidates who manage large pools of assets or act as plan sponsors because these managers may be offered special opportunities, such as private placements, as a reward or an enticement for continuing to do business with a particular broker.

Participation in private placements raises conflict-of-interest issues that are similar to issues surrounding IPOs. Investment personnel should not be involved in transactions, including (but not limited to) private placements that could be perceived as favors or gifts that seem designed to influence future judgment or to reward past business deals.

Whether the venture eventually proves to be good or bad, managers have an immediate conflict concerning private placement opportunities. If and when the investments go public, participants in private placements have an incentive to recommend the investments to clients regardless of the suitability of the investments for their clients. Doing so increases the value of the participants' personal portfolios.

▶ *Establish blackout/restricted periods*: Investment personnel involved in the investment decision-making process should establish blackout periods prior to trades for clients so that managers cannot take advantage of their knowledge of client activity by "front-running" client trades (trading for one's personal account before trading for client accounts).

Individual firms must decide who within the firm should be required to comply with the trading restrictions. At a minimum, all individuals who are involved in the investment decision-making process should be subject to the same restricted period. Each firm must determine specific requirements related to blackout and restricted periods that are most relevant to the firm while ensuring that the procedures are governed by the guiding principles set forth in the Code and Standards. Size of firm and type of securities purchased are relevant factors. For example, in a large firm, a blackout requirement is, in effect, a total trading ban because the firm is continually trading in most securities. In a small firm, the blackout period is more likely to prevent the investment manager from front-running.

▶ *Reporting requirements*: Supervisors should establish reporting procedures for investment personnel, including disclosure of personal holdings/beneficial ownerships, confirmations of trades to the firm and the employee, and preclearance procedures. Once trading restrictions are in place, they must be enforced. The best method for monitoring and enforcing procedures to eliminate conflicts of interest in personal trading is through reporting requirements, including the following:

▶ **Disclosure of holdings in which the employee has a beneficial interest.** Disclosure by investment personnel to the firm should be made upon commencement of the employment relationship and at least annually thereafter. To address privacy considerations, disclosure of personal holdings should be handled in a confidential manner by the firm.

▶ **Providing duplicate confirmations of transactions.** Investment personnel should be required to direct their brokers to supply to firms duplicate copies or confirmations of all their personal securities transactions and copies of periodic statements for all securities accounts. The duplicate confirmation requirement has two purposes: 1) The requirement sends a message that there is independent verification, which reduces the likelihood of unethical behavior, and 2) it enables verification of the accounting of the flow of personal investments that cannot be determined from merely looking at holdings.

▶ **Preclearance procedures.** Investment personnel should examine all planned personal trades to identify possible conflicts prior to the execution of the trades. Preclearance procedures are designed to identify possible conflicts before a problem arises.

▶ *Disclosure of policies*: Upon request, members and candidates should fully disclose to investors their firm's policies regarding personal investing. The information about employees' personal investment activities and policies will foster an atmosphere of full and complete disclosure and calm the public's legitimate concerns about the conflicts of interest posed by investment personnel's personal trading. The disclosure must provide helpful information to investors; it should not be simply boilerplate language such as "investment personnel are subject to policies and procedures regarding their personal trading."

Application of the Standard

Example 1 (Personal Trading): Research analyst Marlon Long does not recommend purchase of a common stock for his employer's account because he wants to purchase the stock personally and does not want to wait until the recommendation is approved and the stock purchased by his employer.

> *Comment*: Long has violated Standard VI(B) by taking advantage of his knowledge of the stock's value before allowing his employer to benefit from that information.

Example 2 (Trading for Family Member Account): Carol Baker, the portfolio manager of an aggressive-growth mutual fund, maintains an account in her husband's name at several brokerage firms with which the fund and a number of Baker's other individual clients do a substantial amount of business. Whenever a hot issue becomes available, she instructs the brokers to buy it for her husband's account. Because such issues normally are scarce, Baker often acquires shares in hot issues but her clients are not able to participate in them.

> *Comment*: To avoid violating Standard VI(B), Baker must acquire shares for her mutual fund first and acquire them for her husband's account only after doing so, even though she might miss out on participating in new issues via her husband's account. She also must disclose the trading for her husband's

account to her employer because this activity creates a conflict between her personal interests and her employer's interests.

Example 3 (Family Accounts as Equals): Erin Toffler, a portfolio manager at Esposito Investments, manages the retirement account established with the firm by her parents. Whenever IPOs become available, she first allocates shares to all her other clients for whom the investment is appropriate; only then does she place any remaining portion in her parents' account, if the issue is appropriate for them. She has adopted this procedure so that no one can accuse her of favoring her parents.

> *Comment*: Toffler has violated Standard VI(B) by breaching her duty to her parents by treating them differently from her other accounts simply because of the family relationship. As fee-paying clients of Esposito Investments, Toffler's parents are entitled to the same treatment as any other client of the firm. If Toffler has beneficial ownership in the account, however, and Esposito Investments has preclearance and reporting requirements for personal transactions, she may have to preclear the trades and report the transactions to Esposito.

Example 4 (Personal Trading and Disclosure): Gary Michaels is an entry-level employee who holds a low-paying job serving both the research department and the investment management department of an active investment management firm. He purchases a sports car and begins to wear expensive clothes after only a year of employment with the firm. The director of the investment management department, who has responsibility for monitoring the personal stock transactions of all employees, investigates and discovers that Michaels has made substantial investment gains by purchasing stocks just before they were put on the firm's recommended "buy" list. Michaels was regularly given the firm's quarterly personal transaction form but declined to complete it.

> *Comment*: Michaels violated Standard VI(B) by placing personal transactions ahead of client transactions. In addition, his supervisor violated the Standard IV(C)—Responsibilities of Supervisors by permitting Michaels to continue to perform his assigned tasks without having signed the quarterly personal transaction form. Note also that if Michaels had communicated information about the firm's recommendations to a person who traded the security, that action would be a misappropriation of the information and a violation of Standard II(A)—Material Nonpublic Information.

Example 5 (Trading Prior to Report Dissemination): A brokerage's insurance analyst, Denise Wilson, makes a closed-circuit TV report to her firm's branches around the country. During the broadcast, she includes negative comments about a major company in the insurance industry. The following day, Wilson's report is printed and distributed to the sales force and public customers. The report recommends that both short-term traders and intermediate investors take profits by selling that insurance company's stock. Seven minutes after the broadcast, however, Ellen Riley, head of the firm's trading department, had closed out a long "call" position in the stock. Then, shortly thereafter, Riley established a sizable "put" position in the stock. When asked about her activities, Riley claimed she took the actions to facilitate anticipated sales by institutional clients.

> *Comment*: Riley did not give customers an opportunity to buy or sell in the options market before the firm itself did. By taking action before the report was disseminated, Riley's firm may have depressed the price of the calls and increased the price of the puts. The firm could have avoided a conflict of

interest if it had waited to trade for its own account until its clients had an opportunity to receive and assimilate Wilson's recommendations. As it is, Riley's actions violated Standard VI(B).

C. Referral Fees

Members and Candidates must disclose to their employer, clients, and prospective clients, as appropriate, any compensation, consideration, or benefit received from or paid to others for the recommendation of products or services.

Guidance

Standard VI(C) states the responsibility of members and candidates to inform their employer, clients, and prospective clients of any benefit received for referrals of customers and clients. Such disclosures allow clients or employers to evaluate 1) any partiality shown in any recommendation of services and 2) the full cost of the services. Members and candidates must disclose when they pay a fee or provide compensation to others who have referred prospective clients to the member or candidate.

Appropriate disclosure means that members and candidates must advise the client or prospective client, before entry into any formal agreement for services, of any benefit given or received for the recommendation of any services provided by the member or candidate. In addition, the member or candidate must disclose the nature of the consideration or benefit—for example, flat fee or percentage basis; one-time or continuing benefit; based on performance; benefit in the form of provision of research or other noncash benefit—together with the estimated dollar value. Consideration includes all fees, whether paid in cash, in soft dollars, or in kind.

Recommended Procedures for Compliance

Members and candidates should encourage their employers to develop procedures related to referral fees. The firm may completely restrict such fees. If the firm does not adopt a strict prohibition of such fees, the procedures should indicate the appropriate steps for requesting approval.

Employers should have investment professionals provide to the clients notification of approved referral fee programs and provide the employer regular (at least quarterly) updates on the amount and nature of compensation received.

Application of the Standard

Example 1 (Disclosure of Referral Arrangements and Outside Parties): Brady Securities, Inc., a broker/dealer, has established a referral arrangement with Lewis Brothers, Ltd., an investment counseling firm. In this arrangement, Brady Securities refers all prospective tax-exempt accounts, including pension, profit-sharing, and endowment accounts, to Lewis Brothers. In return, Lewis Brothers makes available to Brady Securities on a regular basis the security recommendations and reports of its research staff, which registered representatives of Brady Securities use in serving customers. In addition, Lewis Brothers conducts monthly economic and market reviews for Brady Securities personnel and directs all stock commission business generated by referral accounts to Brady Securities.

Willard White, a partner in Lewis Brothers, calculates that the incremental costs involved in functioning as the research department of Brady Securities are US$20,000 annually.

Referrals from Brady Securities last year resulted in fee income of US$200,000 for Brady Securities, and directing all stock trades through Brady Securities resulted in additional costs to Lewis Brothers' clients of US$10,000.

Diane Branch, the chief financial officer of Maxwell Inc., contacts White and says that she is seeking an investment manager for Maxwell's profit-sharing plan. She adds, "My friend Harold Hill at Brady Securities recommended your firm without qualification, and that's good enough for me. Do we have a deal?" White accepts the new account but does not disclose his firm's referral arrangement with Brady Securities.

> *Comment*: White has violated Standard VI(C) by failing to inform the prospective customer of the referral fee payable in services and commissions for an indefinite period to Brady Securities. Such disclosure could have caused Branch to reassess Hill's recommendation and make a more critical evaluation of Lewis Brothers' services.

Example 2 (Disclosure of Interdepartmental Referral Arrangements): James Handley works for the trust department of Central Trust Bank. He receives compensation for each referral he makes to Central Trust's brokerage department and personal financial management department that results in a sale. He refers several of his clients to the personal financial management department but does not disclose the arrangement within Central Trust to his clients.

> *Comment*: Handley has violated Standard VI(C) by not disclosing the referral arrangement at Central Trust Bank to his clients. Standard VI(C) does not distinguish between referral payments paid by a third party for referring clients to the third party and internal payments paid within the firm to attract new business to a subsidiary. Members and candidates must disclose all such referral fees. Therefore, Handley is required to disclose, at the time of referral, any referral fee agreement in place among Central Trust Bank's departments. The disclosure should include the nature and the value of the benefit and should be made in writing.

Example 3 (Disclosure of Referral Arrangements and Informing Firm): Katherine Roberts is a portfolio manager at Katama Investments, an advisory firm specializing in managing assets for high-net-worth individuals. Katama's trading desk uses a variety of brokerage houses to execute trades on behalf of its clients. Roberts asks the trading desk to direct a large portion of its commissions to Naushon, Inc., a small broker/dealer run by one of Roberts' business school classmates. Katama's traders have found that Naushon is not very competitive on pricing, and although Naushon generates some research for its trading clients, Katama's other analysts have found most of Naushon's research to be not especially useful. Nevertheless, the traders do as Roberts asks, and in return for receiving a large portion of Katama's business, Naushon recommends the investment services of Roberts and Katama to its wealthiest clients. This arrangement is not disclosed to either Katama or the clients referred by Naushon.

> *Comment*: Roberts is violating Standard VI(C) by failing to inform her employer of the referral arrangement.

Example 4 (Disclosure of Referral Arrangements and Employer Compensation): Yeshao Wen is a portfolio manager for a bank. He receives additional monetary compensation from his employer when he is successful in assisting in the sales process and generation of assets under management. The assets in question will be invested in proprietary products, such as affiliate company mutual funds.

> *Comment*: Standard VI(C) is meant to address instances where the investment advice provided by a member or candidate appears to be objective and independent but in fact is influenced by an unseen referral arrangement. It is not meant to cover compensation by employers to employees for generating new business when it would be obvious to potential clients that the employees are "referring" potential clients to the services of their employers.
>
> If Wen is selling the bank's investment management services in general, he does not need to disclose to potential clients that he will receive a bonus for finding new clients and acquiring new assets under management for the bank. Potential clients are probably aware that it would be financially beneficial both to the portfolio manager and the manager's firm for the portfolio manager to sell the services of the firm and attract new clients.
>
> In this example, however, the assets will be managed in "proprietary product offerings" of the manager's company (for example, an in-house mutual fund) and Wen will receive additional compensation for selling firm products. Some sophisticated investors may realize that it would be financially beneficial to the portfolio manager and the manager's firm if the investor were to buy the product offerings of the firm. Best practice dictates, however, that members or candidates acting as portfolio managers disclose to clients that they are compensated for selling firm products to clients. Such disclosure will meet the purpose of Standard VI(C), which is to allow investors to determine whether there is any partiality on the part of the portfolio manager making investment advice.

Example 5 (Disclosure of Referral Arrangements and Outside Organizations): Alex Burl is a portfolio manager at Helpful Investments, a local investment advisory firm. Burl is on the advisory board of his child's school, which is looking for ways to raise money to purchase new playground equipment for the school. Burl discusses a plan with his supervisor in which he will donate to the school a portion of his service fee from new clients referred by the parents of students at the school. Upon getting the approval from Helpful, Burl presents the idea to the school's advisory board and directors. The school agrees to announce the program at the next parent event and asks Burl to provide the appropriate written materials to be distributed. A week following the distribution of the flyers, Burl receives the first school-related referral. In establishing the client's investment policy statement, Burl clearly discusses the school's referral and outlines the plans for distributing the donation back to the school.

> *Comment*: Burl has not violated Standard VI(C) because he secured the permission of his employer, Helpful Investments, and the school prior to beginning the program and because he discussed the arrangement with the client at the time the investment policy statement was designed.

Example 6 (Disclosure of Referral Arrangements and Outside Parties): The sponsor of a state employee pension is seeking to hire a firm to manage the pension plan's emerging market allocation. To assist in the review process, the sponsor has hired Thomas Arrow as a consultant to solicit proposals from various advisers. Arrow is contracted by the sponsor to represent its best interest in selecting the most appropriate new manager. The process runs smoothly, and Overseas Investments is selected as the new manager.

The following year, news breaks that Arrow is under investigation by the local regulator for accepting kickbacks from investment managers after they are awarded new pension allocations. Overseas Investments is included in the list of firms allegedly making these payments. Although the sponsor is happy with the performance of Overseas since it has been managing the pension plan's emerging market funds, the sponsor still decides to have an independent review of the proposals and the selection process to ensure that Overseas was the appropriate firm for its needs. This review confirms that, even though Arrow was being paid by both parties, the recommendation of Overseas appeared to be objective and appropriate.

Comment: Arrow has violated Standard VI(C) because he did not disclose the fee being paid by Overseas. Withholding this information raises the question of a potential lack of objectivity in the recommendations Overseas is making; this aspect is in addition to questions about the legality of having firms pay to be considered for an allocation.

Regulators and governmental agencies may adopt requirements concerning allowable consultant activities. Local regulations sometimes include having a consultant register with the regulatory agency's ethics board. Regulator policies may include a prohibition on acceptance of payments from investment managers receiving allocations and require regular reporting of contributions made to political organizations and candidates. Arrow would have to adhere to these requirements as well as the Code and Standards.

STANDARD VII—RESPONSIBILITIES AS A CFA INSTITUTE MEMBER OR CFA CANDIDATE

A. Conduct as Members and Candidates in the CFA Program

Members and Candidates must not engage in any conduct that compromises the reputation or integrity of CFA Institute or the CFA designation or the integrity, validity, or security of the CFA examinations.

Guidance

Highlights:

► *Confidential Program Information*
► *Additional CFA Program Restrictions*
► *Expressing an Opinion*

Standard VII(A) covers the conduct of CFA Institute members and candidates involved with the CFA Program and prohibits any conduct that undermines the public's confidence that the CFA charter represents a level of achievement based on merit and ethical conduct. The standard's function is to hold members and candidates to a high ethical criterion while they are participating in or involved with the CFA Program. Conduct covered includes but is not limited to:

► cheating or assisting others on the CFA examination or any other CFA Institute examination;

▶ disregarding the rules and policies of the CFA Program related to exam administration;

▶ providing confidential program or exam information to candidates or the public;

▶ disregarding or attempting to circumvent security measures established by CFA Institute for the CFA exam;

▶ improperly using the CFA designation in any form of communication;

▶ improperly using an association with CFA Institute to further personal or professional goals;

▶ misrepresenting information on the Professional Conduct Statement or in the CFA Institute Continuing Education Program.

Confidential Program Information

CFA Institute is vigilant about protecting the integrity of the CFA Program content and examination process. The CFA Program prohibits candidates from disclosing confidential material gained during the exam process.

Examples of information that cannot be disclosed by candidates sitting for an exam include but are not limited to:

▶ specific details of questions appearing on the exam, and

▶ broad topical areas and formulas tested or not tested on the exam.

All aspects of the exam, including questions, broad topical areas, and formulas, tested or not tested, are considered confidential until such time as CFA Institute elects to release them publicly. This confidentiality requirement allows CFA Institute to maintain the integrity and rigor of the exam for future candidates. Standard VII(A) does not prohibit candidates from discussing nonconfidential information or curriculum material with others or in study groups in preparation for the exam.

Candidates increasingly use online forums and new technology as part of their exam preparations. CFA Institute actively polices blogs, forums, and related social networking groups for information considered confidential. The organization works with both individual candidates and the sponsors of online or offline services to promptly remove any and all violations. As noted in the discussion of Standard I(A)—Knowledge of the Law, candidates, members, and the public are encouraged to report suspected violations to CFA Institute.

Additional CFA Program Restrictions

The CFA Program examination administration policies define additional allowed and disallowed actions concerning the exams. Violating any of the testing policies, such as the calculator policy, personal belongings policy, or the Candidate Pledge, constitutes a violation of Standard VII(A). Candidates will find all of these policies on the CFA Program portion of the CFA Institute website (www.cfainstitute.org). Exhibit 2 provides the Candidate Pledge, which highlights the respect candidates must have for the integrity, validity, and security of the CFA exam.

Members may participate as volunteers in various aspects of the CFA Program. Standard VII(A) prohibits members from disclosing and/or soliciting confidential material gained prior to or during the exam and grading processes with those outside the CFA exam development process.

Examples of information that cannot be shared by members involved in developing, administering, or grading the exams include but are not limited to:

► questions appearing on the exam or under consideration;

► deliberation related to the exam process; and

► information related to the scoring of questions.

Expressing an Opinion

Standard VII(A) does *not* cover expressing opinions regarding the CFA Program or CFA Institute. Members and candidates are free to disagree and express their disagreement with CFA Institute on its policies, procedures, or any advocacy positions taken by the organization. When expressing a personal opinion, a candidate is prohibited from disclosing content-specific information, including any actual exam question and the information as to subject matter covered or not covered in the exam.

EXHIBIT 2	Sample of CFA Program Testing Policies
Candidate Pledge	As a candidate in the CFA Program, I am obligated to follow Standard VII(A) of the CFA Institute Standards of Professional Conduct, which states that members and candidates must not engage in any conduct that compromises the reputation or integrity of CFA Institute or the CFA designation or the integrity, validity, or security of the CFA exam.

► Prior to this exam, I have not given or received information regarding the content of this exam. During this exam, I will not give or receive any information regarding the content of this exam.

► After this exam, I will not **disclose any portion of this exam** and I will not remove **any exam materials** from the testing room in original or copied form. I understand that all exam materials, including my answers, are the property of CFA Institute and will not be returned to me in any form.

► I will follow **all** rules of the CFA Program as stated on the CFA Institute website and the back cover of the exam book. My violation of any rules of the CFA Program will result in CFA Institute voiding my exam results and may lead to suspension or termination of my candidacy in the CFA Program.

Application of the Standard

Example 1 (Sharing Exam Questions): Travis Nero serves as a proctor for the administration of the CFA examination in his city. In the course of his service, he reviews a copy of the Level II exam on the evening prior to the exam's administration and provides information concerning the exam questions to two candidates who use it to prepare for the exam.

Comment: Nero and the two candidates have violated Standard VII(A). By giving information about the exam questions to two candidates, Nero provided an unfair advantage to the two candidates and undermined the integrity and validity of the Level II exam as an accurate measure of the knowledge, skills, and abilities necessary to earn the right to use the CFA designation. By accepting the information, the candidates also compromised the integrity and validity of the Level II exam and undermined the ethical framework that is a key part of the designation.

Example 2 (Bringing Written Material into Exam Room): Loren Sullivan is enrolled to take the Level II CFA examination. He has been having difficulty remembering a particular formula, so prior to entering the exam room, he writes the formula on the palm of his hand. During the afternoon section of the exam, a proctor notices Sullivan looking at the palm of his hand. She asks to see his hand and finds the formula to be readable.

Comment: Because Sullivan wrote down information from the Candidate Body of Knowledge (CBOK) and took that written information into the exam room, his conduct compromised the validity of his exam performance and violated Standard VII(A). Sullivan's conduct was also in direct contradiction of the rules and regulations of the CFA Program, the Candidate Pledge, and the CFA Institute Code and Standards.

Example 3 (Writing after Exam Period End): At the conclusion of the morning section of the Level I CFA examination, the proctors announce that all candidates are to stop writing immediately. John Davis has not completed the exam, so he continues to randomly fill in ovals on his answer sheet. A proctor approaches Davis's desk and reminds him that he should stop writing immediately. Davis, however, continues to complete the answer sheet. After the proctor asks him to stop writing two additional times, Davis finally puts down his pencil.

Comment: By continuing to complete his exam after time was called, Davis has violated Standard VII(A). By continuing to write, Davis took unfair advantage of other candidates, and his conduct compromised the validity of his exam performance. Additionally, by not heeding the proctor's repeated instructions, Davis violated the rules and regulations of the CFA Program.

Example 4 (Sharing Exam Content): After completing Level II of the CFA Exam, Annabelle Rossi writes in her blog about her experience. She posts the following: "Level II is complete! I think I did fairly well on the exam. It was really difficult, but fair. I think I did especially well on the derivatives questions. And there were tons of them! I think I counted 18! The ethics questions were really hard. I'm glad I spent so much time on the Code and Standards. I was surprised to see there were no questions at all about IPO allocations. I expected there to be a couple. Well, off to celebrate getting through it. See you tonight?"

Comment: Rossi did not violate Standard VII(A) when she wrote about how difficult she found the exam or how well she thinks she may have done. By revealing portions of the CBOK covered on the exam and areas not covered, however, she did violate Standard VII(A) and the Candidate Pledge. Depending on the time frame in which the comments were posted, Rossi not only may have assisted future candidates but also may have provided an unfair advantage to candidates sitting for the same exam, thereby undermining the integrity and validity of the Level II exam.

Example 5 (Sharing Exam Content): Level I candidate Etienne Gagne has been a frequent visitor to an internet forum designed specifically for CFA Program candidates. The week after completing the Level I examination, Gagne and several others begin a discussion thread on the forum about the most challenging questions and attempt to determine the correct answers.

> *Comment*: Gagne has violated Standard VII(A) by providing and soliciting confidential exam information, which compromises the integrity of the exam process and violates the Candidate Pledge. In trying to determine correct answers to specific questions, the group's discussion included question-specific details considered to be confidential to the CFA Program. CFA Institute works with candidates and the sponsors of such online discussion boards and forums to remove information of this specific nature from these websites.

Example 6 (Sharing Exam Content): CFA4Sure is a company that produces test-preparation materials for CFA Program candidates. Many candidates register for and use the company's products. The day after the CFA examination, CFA4Sure sends an e-mail to all its customers asking them to share with the company the hardest questions from the exam so that CFA4Sure can better prepare its customers for the next exam administration. Marisol Pena e-mails a summary of the questions she found most difficult on the exam.

> *Comment*: Pena has violated Standard VII(A) by disclosing a portion of the exam questions. The information provided is considered confidential until publicly released by CFA Institute. CFA4Sure is likely to use such feedback to refine its review materials for future candidates. Pena's sharing of the specific questions undermines the integrity of the exam while potentially making the exam easier for future candidates.
>
> If the CFA4Sure employees who participated in the solicitation of confidential CFA Program information are CFA Institute members or candidates, they also have violated Standard VII(A).

Example 7 (Sharing Exam Questions): Ashlie Hocking is in London writing Level II of the CFA examination. After completing the exam, she immediately attempts to contact her friend in Sydney, Australia, to tip him off about specific questions on the exam.

> *Comment*: Hocking has violated Standard VII(A) by attempting to give her friend an unfair advantage, thereby compromising the integrity of the CFA exam process.

Example 8 (Discussion of Exam Grading Guidelines and Results): Prior to participating in grading CFA examinations, Wesley Whitcomb is required to sign a CFA Institute Grader Agreement. As part of the Grader Agreement, Whitcomb agrees not to reveal or discuss the exam materials with anyone except CFA Institute staff or other graders. Several weeks after the conclusion of the CFA exam grading, Whitcomb tells several colleagues who are candidates in the CFA Program which question he graded. He also discusses the guideline answer and adds that few candidates scored well on the question.

> *Comment*: Whitcomb violated Standard VII(A) by breaking the Grader Agreement and disclosing information related to a specific question on the exam, which compromised the integrity of the exam process.

Example 9 (Compromising CFA Institute Integrity as a Volunteer): Jose Ramirez is an investor-relations consultant for several small companies that are seeking greater exposure to investors. He is also the program chair for the CFA Institute society in the city where he works. Ramirez schedules only companies that are his clients to make presentations to the society and excludes other companies.

Comment: Ramirez, by using his volunteer position at CFA Institute to bene-fit himself and his clients, compromises the reputation and integrity of CFA Institute and thus violates Standard VII(A).

Example 10 (Compromising CFA Institute Integrity as a Volunteer): Mar-guerite Warrenski is a member of the CFA Institute GIPS Executive Committee, which oversees the creation, implementation, and revision of the GIPS stan-dards. As a member of the Executive Committee, she has advance knowledge of confidential information regarding the GIPS standards, including any new or revised standards the committee is considering. She tells her clients that her Executive Committee membership will allow her to better assist her clients in keeping up with changes to the Standards and facilitating their compliance with the changes.

Comment: Warrenski is using her association with the GIPS Executive Com-mittee to promote her firm's services to clients and potential clients. In defining her volunteer position at CFA Institute as a strategic business advantage over competing firms and implying to clients that she would use confidential information to further their interests, Warrenski is compromis-ing the reputation and integrity of CFA Institute and thus violating Stan-dard VII(A). She may factually state her involvement with the Executive Committee but cannot infer any special advantage to her clients from such participation.

B. Reference to CFA Institute, the CFA Designation, and the CFA Program

When referring to CFA Institute, CFA Institute membership, the CFA designation, or candidacy in the CFA Program, Members and Candi-dates must not misrepresent or exaggerate the meaning or implications of membership in CFA Institute, holding the CFA designation, or candi-dacy in the CFA Program.

Guidance

Highlights:

- ▶ *CFA Institute Membership*
- ▶ *Using the CFA Designation*
- ▶ *Referring to Candidacy in the CFA Program*
- ▶ *Proper Usage of the CFA Marks*

Standard VII(B) is intended to prevent promotional efforts that make prom-ises or guarantees that are tied to the CFA designation. Individuals may refer to their CFA designation, CFA Institute membership, or candidacy in the CFA Pro-gram but must not exaggerate the meaning or implications of membership in CFA Institute, holding the CFA designation, or candidacy in the CFA Program.

Standard VII(B) is not intended to prohibit factual statements related to the positive benefit of earning the CFA designation. However, statements referring to CFA Institute, the CFA designation, or the CFA Program that overstate the competency of an individual or imply, either directly or indirectly, that superior performance can be expected from someone with the CFA designation are not allowed under the standard.

Statements that highlight or emphasize the commitment of CFA Institute members, CFA charterholders, and CFA candidates to ethical and professional conduct or mention the thoroughness and rigor of the CFA Program are appropriate. Members and candidates may make claims about the relative merits of CFA Institute, the CFA Program, or the Code and Standards as long as those statements are implicitly or explicitly stated as the opinion of the speaker. Statements that do not express opinions have to be supported by facts.

Standard VII(B) applies to any form of communication, including but not limited to communications made in electronic or written form (such as on firm letterhead, business cards, professional biographies, directory listings, printed advertising, firm brochures, or personal resumes) and oral statements made to the public, clients, or prospects.

CFA Institute Membership

The term "CFA Institute member" refers to "regular" and "affiliate" members of CFA Institute who have met the membership requirements as defined in the CFA Institute Bylaws. Once accepted as a CFA Institute member, the member must satisfy the following requirements to maintain his or her status:

▶ remit annually to CFA Institute a completed Professional Conduct Statement, which renews the commitment to abide by the requirements of the Code and Standards and the CFA Institute Professional Conduct Program, and

▶ pay applicable CFA Institute membership dues on an annual basis.

If a CFA Institute member fails to meet any of these requirements, the individual is no longer considered an active member. Until membership is reactivated, individuals must not present themselves to others as active members. They may state, however, that they were CFA Institute members in the past or refer to the years when their membership was active.

Using the CFA Designation

Those who have earned the right to use the Chartered Financial Analyst designation may use the trademarks or registered marks "Chartered Financial Analyst" or "CFA" and are encouraged to do so but only in a manner that does not misrepresent or exaggerate the meaning or implications of the designation. The use of the designation may be accompanied by an accurate explanation of the requirements that have been met to earn the right to use the designation.

"CFA charterholders" are those individuals who have earned the right to use the CFA designation granted by CFA Institute. These people have satisfied certain requirements, including completion of the CFA Program and required years of acceptable work experience. Once granted the right to use the designation, individuals must also satisfy the CFA Institute membership requirements (see above) to maintain their right to use the designation.

If a CFA charterholder fails to meet any of the membership requirements, he or she forfeits the right to use the CFA designation. Until membership is reactivated, individuals must not present themselves to others as CFA charterholders. They may state, however, that they were charterholders in the past.

Referring to Candidacy in the CFA Program

Candidates in the CFA Program may refer to their participation in the CFA Program, but the reference must clearly state that an individual is a candidate in the CFA Program and must not imply that the candidate has achieved any type of partial designation. A person is a candidate in the CFA Program if:

▶ the person's application for registration in the CFA Program has been accepted by CFA Institute, as evidenced by issuance of a notice of acceptance, and the person is enrolled to sit for a specified examination; or

▶ the registered person has sat for a specified examination but exam results have not yet been received.

If an individual is registered for the CFA Program but declines to sit for an exam or otherwise does not meet the definition of a candidate as described in the CFA Institute Bylaws, then that individual is no longer considered an active candidate. Once the person is enrolled to sit for a future examination, his or her CFA candidacy resumes.

CFA candidates must never state or imply that they have a partial designation as a result of passing one or more levels or cite an expected completion date of any level of the CFA Program. Final award of the charter is subject to meeting the CFA Program requirements and approval by the CFA Institute Board of Governors.

If a candidate passes each level of the exam in consecutive years and wants to state that he or she did so, that is not a violation of Standard VII(B) because it is a statement of fact. If the candidate then goes on to claim or imply superior ability by obtaining the designation in only three years, however, he or she is in violation of Standard VII(B).

Exhibit 3 provides examples of proper and improper references to the CFA designation.

EXHIBIT 3	Proper and Improper References to the CFA Designation

Proper References	**Improper References**
"Completion of the CFA Program has enhanced my portfolio management skills."	"CFA charterholders achieve better performance results."
"John Smith passed all three CFA examinations in three consecutive years."	"John Smith is among the elite, having passed all three CFA examinations in three consecutive attempts."
"The CFA designation is globally recognized and attests to a charterholder's success in a rigorous and comprehensive study program in the field of investment management and research analysis."	"As a CFA charterholder, I am the most qualified to manage client investments."
"The credibility that the CFA designation affords and the skills the CFA Program cultivates are key assets for my future career development."	As a CFA charterholder, Jane White provides the "best value in trade execution."
"I enrolled in the CFA Program to obtain the highest set of credentials in the global investment management industry."	"Enrolling as a candidate in the CFA Program ensures one of becoming better at valuing debt securities."
"I passed Level I of the CFA exam."	"CFA, Level II"

(*Exhibit continued on next page . . .*)

EXHIBIT 3	(continued)

Proper References	Improper References
"I am a 2010 Level III CFA candidate." "I passed all three levels of the CFA Program and will be eligible for the CFA charter upon completion of the required work experience." "As a CFA charterholder, I am committed to the highest ethical standards."	"CFA, Expected 2011"

Proper Usage of the CFA Marks

Upon obtaining the CFA charter from CFA Institute, charterholders are given the right to use the CFA marks, including Chartered Financial Analyst®, CFA®, and the CFA Logo (a certification mark):

These marks are registered by CFA Institute in countries around the world.

The Chartered Financial Analyst and CFA marks must always be used either after a charterholder's name or as adjectives (never as nouns) in written documents or oral conversations. For example, to refer to oneself as "a CFA" or "a Chartered Financial Analyst" is improper.

The CFA Logo certification mark is used by charterholders as a distinctive visual symbol of the CFA designation that can be easily recognized by employers, colleagues, and clients. As a certification mark, it must be used only to directly refer to an individual charterholder or group of charterholders.

Exhibit 4 provides examples of correct and incorrect use of the marks. CFA charterholders should refer to the complete guidelines published by CFA Institute for additional and up-to-date information and examples illustrating proper and improper use of the CFA Logo, Chartered Financial Analyst mark, and CFA mark. These guidelines and the CFA logo are available on the CFA Institute website at www.cfainstitute.org.

EXHIBIT 4	Correct and Incorrect Use of the Chartered Financial Analyst and CFA Marks

Correct	Incorrect	Principle
He is one of two CFA charterholders in the company.	He is one of two CFAs in the company.	The CFA and Chartered Financial Analyst designations must always be used as adjectives, never as nouns or common names.
He earned the right to use the Chartered Financial Analyst designation.	He is a Chartered Financial Analyst.	

(Exhibit continued on next page . . .)

EXHIBIT 4   (continued)

Correct	Incorrect	Principle
Jane Smith, CFA	Jane Smith, C.F.A. John Doe, cfa	No periods. Always capitalize the letters "CFA".
John Jones, CFA	John, a CFA-type portfolio manager. The focus is on Chartered Financial Analysis. CFA-equivalent program. Swiss-CFA	Do not alter the designation to create new words or phrases.
John Jones, Chartered Financial Analyst	Jones Chartered Financial Analysts, Inc.	The designation must not be used as part of the name of a firm.
Jane Smith, CFA John Doe, Chartered Financial Analyst	Jane Smith, **CFA** John Doe, **Chartered Financial Analyst**	The CFA designation should not be given more prominence (e.g., larger, bold) than the charterholder's name.
Level I candidate in the CFA Program.	Chartered Financial Analyst (CFA), September 2011.	Candidates in the CFA Program must not cite the expected date of exam completion and award of charter.
Passed Level I of the CFA examination in 2010.	CFA Level I. CFA degree expected in 2011.	No designation exists for someone who has passed Level I, Level II, or Level III of the exam. The CFA designation should not be referred to as a degree.
I have passed all three levels of the CFA Program and may be eligible for the CFA charter upon completion of the required work experience.	CFA (Passed Finalist)	A candidate who has passed Level III but has not yet received his or her charter cannot use the CFA or Chartered Financial Analyst designation.
CFA, 2009, CFA Institute, (optional: Charlottesville, Virginia, USA)	CFA, 2009, CFA Society of the UK	In citing the designation in a resume, a charterholder should use the date that he or she received the designation and should cite CFA Institute as the conferring body.

Recommended Procedures for Compliance

Misuse of a member's CFA designation or CFA candidacy or improper reference to it is common by those in a member's or candidate's firm who do not possess knowledge of the requirements of Standard VII(B). As an appropriate step to reduce this risk, members and candidates should disseminate written information about Standard VII(B) and the accompanying guidance to their firm's legal, compliance, public relations, and marketing departments (see www.cfainstitute .org).

For materials that refer to employees' affiliation with CFA Institute, members and candidates should encourage their firms to create templates that are approved by a central authority (such as the compliance department) as being consistent with Standard VII(B). This practice promotes consistency and accuracy in the firm of references to CFA Institute membership, the CFA designation, and CFA candidacy.

Application of the Standard

Example 1 (Passing Exams in Consecutive Years): An advertisement for AZ Investment Advisors states that all the firm's principals are CFA charterholders and all passed the three examinations on their first attempt. The advertisement prominently links this fact to the notion that AZ's mutual funds have achieved superior performance.

> *Comment*: AZ may state that all principals passed the three examinations on the first try as long as this statement is true, but it must not be linked to performance or imply superior ability. Implying that 1) CFA charterholders achieve better investment results and 2) those who pass the exams on the first try may be more successful than those who do not violates Standard VII(B).

Example 2 (Right to Use CFA Designation): Five years after receiving his CFA charter, Louis Vasseur resigns his position as an investment analyst and spends the next two years traveling abroad. Because he is not actively engaged in the investment profession, he does not file a completed Professional Conduct Statement with CFA Institute and does not pay his CFA Institute membership dues. At the conclusion of his travels, Vasseur becomes a self-employed analyst accepting assignments as an independent contractor. Without reinstating his CFA Institute membership by filing his Professional Conduct Statement and paying his dues, he prints business cards that display "CFA" after his name.

> *Comment*: Vasseur has violated Standard VII(B) because his right to use the CFA designation was suspended when he failed to file his Professional Conduct Statement and stopped paying dues. Therefore, he no longer is able to state or imply that he is an active CFA charterholder. When Vasseur files his Professional Conduct Statement, resumes paying CFA Institute dues to activate his membership, and completes the CFA Institute reinstatement procedures he will be eligible to use the CFA designation.

Example 3 ("Retired" CFA Institute Membership Status): After a 25-year career, James Simpson retires from his firm. Because he is not actively engaged in the investment profession, he does not file a completed Professional Conduct Statement with CFA Institute and does not pay his CFA Institute membership dues. Simpson designs a plain business card (without a corporate logo) to hand out to friends with his new contact details, and he continues to put "CFA" after his name.

Comment: Simpson has violated Standard VII(B). Because he failed to file his Professional Conduct Statement and ceased paying dues, his membership has been suspended and he must give up the right to use the CFA designation. CFA Institute has procedures, however, for reclassifying a member and charterholder as "retired" and reducing the annual dues. If he wants to obtain retired status, he needs to file the appropriate paperwork with CFA Institute. When Simpson receives his notification from CFA Institute that his membership has been reclassified as retired and he resumes paying reduced dues, his membership will be reactivated and his right to use the CFA designation will be reinstated.

Example 4 (CFA Logo—Individual Use Only): Asia Futures Ltd is a small quantitative investment advisory firm. The firm takes great pride in the fact that all its employees are CFA charterholders. To underscore this fact, the firm's senior partner is proposing to change the firm's letterhead to include the following:

Asia Futures Ltd.

Comment: The CFA Logo is a certification mark intended to identify *individual* charterholders and must not be incorporated in a company name, confused with a company logo, or placed in such close proximity to a company name or logo as to give the reader the idea that the certification mark certifies the company. The only appropriate use of the CFA logo is on the business card or letterhead of each individual CFA charterholder.

Example 5 (Stating Facts about CFA Designation and Program): Rhonda Reese has been a CFA charterholder since 2000. In a conversation with a friend who is considering enrolling in the CFA Program, she states that she has learned a great deal from the CFA Program and that many firms require their employees to be CFA charterholders. She would recommend the CFA Program to anyone pursuing a career in investment management.

Comment: Reese's comments comply with Standard VII(B). Her statements refer to facts: The CFA Program enhanced her knowledge, and many firms require the CFA designation for their investment professionals.

Example 6 (Order of Professional and Academic Designations): Tatiana Prittima has earned both her CFA designation and a PhD in finance. She would like to cite both her accomplishments on her business card but is unsure of the proper method for doing so.

Comment: The order of designations cited on such items as resumes and business cards is a matter of personal preference. Prittima is free to cite the CFA designation either before or after citing her PhD.

PRACTICE PROBLEMS FOR READING 2

Unless otherwise stated in the question, all individuals in the following questions are CFA Institute members or candidates in the CFA Program and, therefore, are subject to the CFA Institute Code of Ethics and Standards of Professional Conduct.

1. Smith, a research analyst with a brokerage firm, decides to change his recommendation for the common stock of Green Company, Inc., from a "buy" to a "sell." He mails this change in investment advice to all the firm's clients on Wednesday. The day after the mailing, a client calls with a buy order for 500 shares of Green Company. In this circumstance, Smith should:

   A. accept the order.

   B. advise the customer of the change in recommendation before accepting the order.

   C. not accept the order because it is contrary to the firm's recommendation.

2. Which statement about a manager's use of client brokerage commissions violates the Code and Standards?

   A. A client may direct a manager to use that client's brokerage commissions to purchase goods and services for that client.

   B. Client brokerage commissions should be used to benefit the client and should be commensurate with the value of the brokerage and research services received.

   C. Client brokerage commissions may be directed to pay for the investment manager's operating expenses.

3. Jamison is a junior research analyst with Howard & Howard, a brokerage and investment banking firm. Howard & Howard's mergers and acquisitions department has represented the Britland Company in all of its acquisitions for the past 20 years. Two of Howard & Howard's senior officers are directors of various Britland subsidiaries. Jamison has been asked to write a research report on Britland. What is the best course of action for her to follow?

   A. Jamison may write the report but must refrain from expressing any opinions because of the special relationships between the two companies.

   B. Jamison should not write the report because the two Howard & Howard officers serve as directors for subsidiaries of Britland.

   C. Jamison may write the report if she discloses the special relationships with the company in the report.

4. Which of the following statements clearly *conflicts* with the recommended procedures for compliance presented in the CFA Institute *Standards of Practice Handbook?*

   A. Firms should disclose to clients the personal investing policies and procedures established for their employees.

   B. Prior approval must be obtained for the personal investment transactions of all employees.

   C. For confidentiality reasons, personal transactions and holdings should not be reported to employers unless mandated by regulatory organizations.

5. Bronson provides investment advice to the board of trustees of a private university endowment fund. The trustees have provided Bronson with the fund's financial information, including planned expenditures. Bronson receives a phone call on Friday afternoon from Murdock, a prominent alumnus, requesting that Bronson fax him comprehensive financial information about the fund. According to Murdock, he has a potential contributor but needs the information that day to close the deal and cannot contact any of the trustees. Based on the CFA Institute Standards, Bronson should:

   A. send Murdock the information because disclosure would benefit the client.

   B. not send Murdock the information to preserve confidentiality.

   C. send Murdock the information, provided Bronson promptly notifies the trustees.

6. Miller heads the research department of a large brokerage firm. The firm has many analysts, some of whom are subject to the Code and Standards. If Miller delegates some supervisory duties, which statement best describes her responsibilities under the Code and Standards?

   A. Miller's supervisory responsibilities do not apply to those subordinates who are not subject to the Code and Standards.

   B. Miller no longer has supervisory responsibility for those duties delegated to her subordinates.

   C. Miller retains supervisory responsibility for all subordinates despite her delegation of some duties.

7. Willier is the research analyst responsible for following Company X. All the information he has accumulated and documented suggests that the outlook for the company's new products is poor, so the stock should be rated a weak "hold." During lunch, however, Willier overhears a financial analyst from another firm whom he respects offer opinions that conflict with Willier's forecasts and expectations. Upon returning to his office, Willier releases a strong "buy" recommendation to the public. Willier:

   A. violated the Standards by failing to distinguish between facts and opinions in his recommendation.

   B. violated the Standards because he did not have a reasonable and adequate basis for his recommendation.

   C. was in full compliance with the Standards.

8. An investment management firm has been hired by ETV Corporation to work on an additional public offering for the company. The firm's brokerage unit now has a "sell" recommendation on ETV, but the head of the investment banking department has asked the head of the brokerage unit to change the recommendation from "sell" to "buy." According to the Standards, the head of the brokerage unit would be permitted to:

    A. increase the recommendation by no more than one increment (in this case, to a "hold" recommendation).

    B. place the company on a restricted list and give only factual information about the company.

    C. assign a new analyst to decide if the stock deserves a higher rating.

9. Albert and Tye, who recently started their own investment advisory business, have registered to take the Level III CFA examination. Albert's business card reads, "Judy Albert, CFA Level II." Tye has not put anything about the CFA designation on his business card, but promotional material that he designed for the business describes the CFA requirements and indicates that Tye participates in the CFA Program and has completed Levels I and II. According to the Standards:

    A. Albert has violated the Standards but Tye has not.

    B. Tye has violated the Standards but Albert has not.

    C. both Albert and Tye have violated the Standards.

10. Scott works for a regional brokerage firm. He estimates that Walkton Industries will increase its dividend by US$1.50 a share during the next year. He realizes that this increase is contingent on pending legislation that would, if enacted, give Walkton a substantial tax break. The U.S. representative for Walkton's home district has told Scott that, although she is lobbying hard for the bill and prospects for its passage are favorable, concern of the U.S. Congress over the federal deficit could cause the tax bill to be voted down. Walkton Industries has not made any statements about a change in dividend policy. Scott writes in his research report, "We expect Walkton's stock price to rise by at least US$8.00 a share by the end of the year because the dividend will increase by US$1.50 a share. Investors buying the stock at the current time should expect to realize a total return of at least 15 percent on the stock." According to the Standards:

    A. Scott violated the Standards because he used material inside information.

    B. Scott violated the Standards because he failed to separate opinion from fact.

    C. Scott violated the Standards by basing his research on uncertain predictions of future government action.

11. Which *one* of the following actions will help to ensure the fair treatment of brokerage firm clients when a new investment recommendation is made?

    A. Informing all people in the firm in advance that a recommendation is to be disseminated.

    B. Distributing recommendations to institutional clients prior to individual accounts.

    C. Minimizing the time between the decision and the dissemination of a recommendation.

12. The mosaic theory holds that an analyst:

    A. violates the Code and Standards if the analyst fails to have knowledge of and comply with applicable laws.

    B. can use material public information and nonmaterial nonpublic information in the analyst's analysis.

    C. should use all available and relevant information in support of an investment recommendation.

13. Jurgen is a portfolio manager. One of her firm's clients has told Jurgen that he will compensate her beyond the compensation provided by her firm on the basis of the capital appreciation of his portfolio each year. Jurgen should:

    A. turn down the additional compensation because it will result in conflicts with the interests of other clients' accounts.

    B. turn down the additional compensation because it will create undue pressure on her to achieve strong short-term performance.

    C. obtain permission from her employer prior to accepting the compensation arrangement.

14. One of the discretionary accounts managed by Farnsworth is the Jones Corporation employee profit-sharing plan. Jones, the company president, recently asked Farnsworth to vote the shares in the profit-sharing plan in favor of the slate of directors nominated by Jones Corporation and against the directors sponsored by a dissident stockholder group. Farnsworth does not want to lose this account because he directs all the account's trades to a brokerage firm that provides Farnsworth with useful information about tax-free investments. Although this information is not of value in managing the Jones Corporation account, it does help in managing several other accounts. The brokerage firm providing this information also offers the lowest commissions for trades and provides best execution. Farnsworth investigates the director issue, concludes that the management-nominated slate is better for the long-run performance of the company than the dissident group's slate, and votes accordingly. Farnsworth:

    A. violated the Standards in voting the shares in the manner requested by Jones but not in directing trades to the brokerage firm.

    B. did not violate the Standards in voting the shares in the manner requested by Jones or in directing trades to the brokerage firm.

    C. violated the Standards in directing trades to the brokerage firm but not in voting the shares as requested by Jones.

15. Brown works for an investment counseling firm. Green, a new client of the firm, is meeting with Brown for the first time. Green used another counseling firm for financial advice for years, but she has switched her account to Brown's firm. After spending a few minutes getting acquainted, Brown explains to Green that she has discovered a highly undervalued stock that offers large potential gains. She recommends that Green purchase the stock. Brown has committed a violation of the Standards. What should she have done differently?

- **A.** Brown should have determined Green's needs, objectives, and tolerance for risk before making a recommendation of any type of security.
- **B.** Brown should have thoroughly explained the characteristics of the company to Green, including the characteristics of the industry in which the company operates.
- **C.** Brown should have explained her qualifications, including her education, training, experience, and the meaning of the CFA designation.

16. Grey recommends the purchase of a mutual fund that invests solely in long-term U.S. Treasury bonds. He makes the following statements to his clients:

Statement 1: "The payment of the bonds is guaranteed by the U.S. government; therefore, the default risk of the bonds is virtually zero."

Statement 2: "If you invest in the mutual fund, you will earn a 10 percent rate of return each year for the next several years based on historical performance of the market."

Did Grey's statements violate the CFA Institute Code and Standards?

- **A.** Neither statement violated the Code and Standards.
- **B.** Only Statement 1 violated the Code and Standards.
- **C.** Only Statement 2 violated the Code and Standards.

17. Anderb, a portfolio manager for XYZ Investment Management Company—a registered investment organization that advises investment firms and private accounts—was promoted to that position three years ago. Bates, her supervisor, is responsible for reviewing Anderb's portfolio account transactions and her required monthly reports of personal stock transactions. Anderb has been using Jonelli, a broker, almost exclusively for brokerage transactions for the portfolio account. For securities in which Jonelli's firm makes a market, Jonelli has been giving Anderb lower prices for personal purchases and higher prices for personal sales than Jonelli gives to Anderb's portfolio accounts and other investors. Anderb has been filing monthly reports with Bates only for those months in which she has no personal transactions, which is about every fourth month. Which of the following is *most likely* to be a violation of the Code and Standards?

- **A.** Anderb failed to disclose to her employer her personal transactions.
- **B.** Anderb owned the same securities as those of her clients.
- **C.** Bates allowed Anderb to use Jonelli as her broker for personal trades.

18. Which of the following is a correct statement of a member's or candidate's duty under the Code and Standards?

  A. In the absence of specific applicable law or other regulatory requirements, the Code and Standards govern the member's or candidate's actions.

  B. A member or candidate is required to comply only with applicable local laws, rules, regulations, or customs, even though the Code and Standards may impose a higher degree of responsibility or a higher duty on the member or candidate.

  C. A member or candidate who trades securities in a securities market where no applicable local laws or stock exchange rules regulate the use of material nonpublic information may take investment action based on material nonpublic information.

19. Ward is scheduled to visit the corporate headquarters of Evans Industries. Ward expects to use the information he obtains there to complete his research report on Evans stock. Ward learns that Evans plans to pay all of Ward's expenses for the trip, including costs of meals, hotel room, and air transportation. Which of the following actions would be the *best* course for Ward to take under the Code and Standards?

  A. Accept the expense-paid trip and write an objective report.

  B. Pay for all travel expenses, including costs of meals and incidental items.

  C. Accept the expense-paid trip but disclose the value of the services accepted in the report.

20. Which of the following statements is *correct* under the Code and Standards?

  A. CFA Institute members and candidates are prohibited from undertaking independent practice in competition with their employer.

  B. Written consent from the employer is necessary to permit independent practice that could result in compensation or other benefits in competition with a member's or candidate's employer.

  C. Members and candidates are prohibited from making arrangements or preparations to go into a competitive business before terminating their relationship with their employer.

21. Smith is a financial analyst with XYZ Brokerage Firm. She is preparing a purchase recommendation on JNI Corporation. Which of the following situations is *most likely* to represent a conflict of interest for Smith that would have to be disclosed?

  A. Smith frequently purchases items produced by JNI.

  B. XYZ holds for its own account a substantial common stock position in JNI.

  C. Smith's brother-in-law is a supplier to JNI.

22. Michelieu tells a prospective client, "I may not have a long-term track record yet, but I'm sure that you'll be very pleased with my recommendations and service. In the three years that I've been in the business, my equity-oriented clients have averaged a total return of more than 26 percent a year." The statement is true, but Michelieu only has a few clients, and one of his clients took a large position in a penny stock (against Michelieu's advice) and realized a huge gain. This large return caused the average of all of Michelieu's clients to exceed 26 percent a year. Without this one investment, the average gain would have been 8 percent a year. Has Michelieu violated the Standards?

A. No.

B. Yes, because the statement misrepresents Michelieu's track record.

C. Yes, because the Standards prohibit members from guaranteeing future results.

23. An investment banking department of a brokerage firm often receives material nonpublic information that could have considerable value if used in advising the firm's brokerage clients. In order to conform to the Code and Standards, which one of the following is the best policy for the brokerage firm?

A. Permanently prohibit both "buy" and "sell" recommendations of the stocks of clients of the investment banking department.

B. Establish physical and informational barriers within the firm to prevent the exchange of information between the investment banking and brokerage operations.

C. Monitor the exchange of information between the investment banking department and the brokerage operation.

24. Stewart has been hired by Goodner Industries, Inc., to manage its pension fund. Stewart's duty of loyalty, prudence, and care is owed to:

A. the management of Goodner.

B. the participants and beneficiaries of Goodner's pension plan.

C. the shareholders of Goodner.

25. Which of the following statements is a stated purpose of disclosure in Standard VI(C)—Referral Fees?

A. Disclosure will allow the client to request discounted service fees.

B. Disclosure will help the client evaluate any possible partiality shown in the recommendation of services.

C. Disclosure means advising a prospective client about the referral arrangement once a formal client relationship has been established.

26. Rose, a portfolio manager for a local investment advisory firm, is planning to sell a portion of his personal investment portfolio to cover the costs of his child's academic tuition. Rose wants to sell a portion of his holdings in Household Products, but his firm recently upgraded the stock to "strong buy." Which of the following describes Rose's options under the Code and Standards?

   A. Based on his firm's "buy" recommendation, Rose cannot sell the shares because he would be improperly prospering from the inflated recommendation.

   B. Rose is free to sell his personal holdings once his firm is properly informed of his intentions.

   C. Rose can sell his personal holdings but only when a client of the firm places an order to buy shares of Household.

27. A former hedge fund manager, Jackman, has decided to launch a new private wealth management firm. From his prior experiences, he believes the new firm needs to achieve US$1 million in assets under management in the first year. Jackman offers a $10,000 incentive to any adviser who joins his firm with the minimum of $200,000 in committed investments. Jackman places notice of the opening on several industry web portals and career search sites. Which of the following is *correct* according to the Code and Standards?

   A. A member or candidate is eligible for the new position and incentive if he or she can arrange for enough current clients to switch to the new firm and if the member or candidate discloses the incentive fee.

   B. A member or candidate may not accept employment with the new firm because Jackman's incentive offer violates the Code and Standards.

   C. A member or candidate is not eligible for the new position unless he or she is currently unemployed because soliciting the clients of the member's or candidate's current employer is prohibited.

28. Carter works for Invest Today, a local asset management firm. A broker that provides Carter with proprietary research through client brokerage arrangements is offering a new trading service. The broker is offering low-fee, execution-only trades to complement its traditional full-service, execution-and-research trades. To entice Carter and other asset managers to send additional business its way, the broker will apply the commissions paid on the new service toward satisfying the brokerage commitment of the prior full-service arrangements. Carter has always been satisfied with the execution provided on the full-service trades, and the new low-fee trades are comparable to the fees of other brokers currently used for the accounts that prohibit soft dollar arrangements.

   A. Carter can trade for his accounts that prohibit soft dollar arrangements under the new low-fee trading scheme.

   B. Carter cannot use the new trading scheme because the commissions are prohibited by the soft dollar restrictions of the accounts.

   C. Carter should trade only through the new low-fee scheme and should increase his trading volume to meet his required commission commitment.

29. Rule has worked as a portfolio manager for a large investment management firm for the past 10 years. Rule earned his CFA charter last year and has decided to open his own investment management firm. After leaving his current employer, Rule creates some marketing material for his new firm. He states in the material, "In earning the CFA charter, a highly regarded credential in the investment management industry, I further enhanced the portfolio management skills learned during my professional career. While completing the examination process in three consecutive years, I consistently received the highest possible scores on the topics of Ethics, Alternative Investments, and Portfolio Management." Has Rule violated Standard VII(B)—Reference to CFA Institute, the CFA Designation, and the CFA Program in his marketing material?

  A. Rule violated Standard VII(B) in stating that he completed the exams in three consecutive years.

  B. Rule violated Standard VII(B) in stating that he received the highest scores in the topics of Ethics, Alternative Investments, and Portfolio Management.

  C. Rule did not violate Standard VII(B).

30. Stafford is a portfolio manager for a specialized real estate mutual fund. Her firm clearly describes in the fund's prospectus its soft dollar policies. Stafford decides that entering the CFA Program will enhance her investment decision-making skill and decides to use the fund's soft dollar account to pay the registration and exam fees for the CFA Program. Which of the following statements is *most likely* correct?

  A. Stafford did not violate the Code and Standards because the prospectus informed investors of the fund's soft dollar policies.

  B. Stafford violated the Code and Standards because improving her investment skills is not a reasonable use of the soft dollar account.

  C. Stafford violated the Code and Standards because the CFA Program does not meet the definition of research allowed to be purchased with brokerage commissions.

31. Long has been asked to be the keynote speaker at an upcoming investment conference. The event is being hosted by one of the third-party investment managers currently used by his pension fund. The manager offers to cover all conference and travel costs for Long and make the conference registrations free for three additional members of his investment management team. To ensure that the conference obtains the best speakers, the host firm has arranged for an exclusive golf outing for the day following the conference on a local championship-caliber course. Which of the following is *least likely* to violate Standard I(B)?

  A. Long may accept only the offer to have his conference-related expenses paid by the host firm.

  B. Long may accept the offer to have his conference-related expenses paid and may attend the exclusive golf outing at the expense of the hosting firm.

  C. Long may accept the entire package of incentives offered to speak at this conference.

32. Andrews, a private wealth manager, is conducting interviews for a new research analyst for his firm. One of the candidates is Wright, an analyst with a local investment bank. During the interview, while Wright is describing his analytical skills, he mentions a current merger in which his firm is acting as the adviser. Andrews has heard rumors of a possible merger between the two companies, but no releases have been made by the companies concerned. Which of the following actions by Andrews is *least likely* a violation of the Code and Standards?

  A. Waiting until the next day before trading on the information to allow time for it to become public.

  B. Notifying all investment managers in his firm of the new information so none of their clients are disadvantaged.

  C. Placing the securities mentioned as part of the merger on the firm's restricted trading list.

33. Pietro, president of Local Bank, has hired the bank's market maker, Vogt, to seek a merger partner. Local is currently not listed on a stock exchange and has not reported that it is seeking strategic alternatives. Vogt has discussed the possibility of a merger with several firms, but they have all decided to wait until after the next period's financial data are available. The potential buyers believe the results will be worse than the results of prior periods and will allow them to pay less for Local Bank.

  Pietro wants to increase the likelihood of structuring a merger deal quickly. Which of the following actions would *most likely* be a violation of the Code and Standards?

  A. Pietro could instruct Local Bank to issue a press release announcing that it has retained Vogt to find a merger partner.

  B. Pietro could place a buy order for 2,000 shares (or four times the average weekly volume) through Vogt for his personal account.

  C. After confirming with Local's chief financial officer, Pietro could instruct Local to issue a press release reaffirming the firm's prior announced earnings guidance for the full fiscal year.

34. ABC Investment Management acquires a new, very large account with two concentrated positions. The firm's current policy is to add new accounts for the purpose of performance calculation after the first full month of management. Cupp is responsible for calculating the firm's performance returns. Before the end of the initial month, Cupp notices that one of the significant holdings of the new accounts is acquired by another company, causing the value of the investment to double. Because of this holding, Cupp decides to account for the new portfolio as of the date of transfer, thereby allowing ABC Investment to reap the positive impact of that month's portfolio return.

  A. Cupp did not violate the Code and Standards because the GIPS standards allow composites to be updated on the date of large external cash flows.

  B. Cupp did not violate the Code and Standards because companies are allowed to determine when to incorporate new accounts into their composite calculation.

  C. Cupp violated the Code and Standards because the inclusion of the new account produces an inaccurate calculation of the monthly results according to the firm's stated policies.

35. Cannan has been working from home on weekends and occasionally saves correspondence with clients and completed work on her home computer. Because of worsening market conditions, Cannan is one of several employees released by her firm. While Cannan is looking for a new job, she uses the files she saved at home to request letters of recommendation from former clients. She also provides to prospective clients some of the reports as examples of her abilities.

A. Cannan is violating the Code and Standards because she did not receive permission from her former employer to keep or use the files after her employment ended.

B. Cannan did not violate the Code and Standards because the files were created and saved on her own time and computer.

C. Cannan violated the Code and Standards because she is prohibited from saving files on her home computer.

36. Quinn sat for the Level III CFA exam this past weekend. He updates his resume with the following statement:
"In finishing the CFA Program, I improved my skills related to researching investments and managing portfolios. I will be eligible for the CFA charter upon completion of the required work experience."

A. Quinn violated the Code and Standards by claiming he improved his skills through the CFA Program.

B. Quinn violated the Code and Standards by incorrectly stating that he is eligible for the CFA charter.

C. Quinn did not violate the Code and Standards with his resume update.

37. During a round of golf, Rodriguez, chief financial officer of Mega Retail, mentions to Hart, a local investment adviser and long-time personal friend, that Mega is having an exceptional sales quarter. Rodriguez expects the results to be almost 10 percent above the current estimates. The next day, Hart initiates the purchase of a large stake in the local exchange-traded retail fund for her personal account.

A. Hart violated the Code and Standards by investing in the exchange-traded fund that included Mega Retail.

B. Hart did not violate the Code and Standards because she did not invest directly in securities of Mega Retail.

C. Rodriguez did not violate the Code and Standards because the comments made to Hart were not intended to solicit an investment in Mega Retail.

38. Park is very frustrated after taking her Level II exam. While she was studying for the exam, to supplement the curriculum provided, she ordered and used study material from a third-party provider. Park believes the additional material focused her attention on specific topic areas that were not tested while ignoring other areas. She posts the following statement on the provider's discussion board: "I am very dissatisfied with your firm's CFA Program Level II material. I found the exam extremely difficult and myself unprepared for specific questions after using your product. How could your service provide such limited instructional resources on the analysis of inventories and taxes when the exam had multiple questions about them? I will not recommend your products to other candidates."

   A. Park violated the Code and Standards by purchasing third-party review material.

   B. Park violated the Code and Standards by providing her opinion on the difficulty of the exam.

   C. Park violated the Code and Standards by providing specific information on topics tested on the exam.

39. Paper was recently terminated as one of a team of five managers of an equity fund. The fund had two value-focused managers and terminated one of them to reduce costs. In a letter sent to prospective employers, Paper presents, with written permission of the firm, the performance history of the fund to demonstrate his past success.

   A. Paper did not violate the Code and Standards.

   B. Paper violated the Code and Standards by claiming the performance of the entire fund as his own.

   C. Paper violated the Code and Standards by including the historical results of his prior employer.

40. Townsend was recently appointed to the board of directors of a youth golf program that is the local chapter of a national not-for-profit organization. The program is beginning a new fund-raising campaign to expand the number of annual scholarships it provides. Townsend believes many of her clients make annual donations to charity. The next week in her regular newsletter to all clients, she includes a small section discussing the fund-raising campaign and her position on the organization's board.

   A. Townsend did not violate the Code and Standards.

   B. Townsend violated the Code and Standards by soliciting donations from her clients through the newsletter.

   C. Townsend violated the Code and Standards by not getting approval of the organization before soliciting her clients.

The following information relates to Questions 41–46

Elias Nano, a recent MBA graduate and a CFA Level II candidate, is an unpaid summer intern with Patriarch Investment Counsel and expects to be offered a full-time paid position in the fall. Through his efforts, he is able to convince some family members and friends to become clients of the firm, and he now assists with the management of their accounts. His supervisor congratulates him and states: "These clients are the foundation from which you will be able to build your career as an investment advisor." After working hard all summer, Nano is told that Patriarch will not be able to offer him a paid position.

Nano interviews with a number of firms, and tells each one about the accounts that he is managing and expects to be able to bring with him. Because he was merely an intern at Patriarch, he does not think he owes any particular loyalty to Patriarch. He gains further assurance that he can keep the clients from the fact that his former supervisor implied that these were Nano's clients.

Nano subsequently joins Markoe Advisors as an assistant director with supervisory responsibilities. Markoe Advisors is an investment management firm that advertises that it provides customized portfolio solutions for individual and institutional clients. As a matter of policy, Markoe does not reject as a client any individual meeting the account minimum size. Markoe has two strategies—aggressive growth equity and growth equity—and is always fully invested. Nano asks his family and friends to transfer their accounts from Patriarch to Markoe.

As the first CFA candidate to be employed by Markoe, Nano has been asked to head a team that is reviewing the firm's compliance policies and procedures, which Nano considers inadequate and incomplete. He states his concerns to President Markoe: "Although Markoe Advisors, as a firm, cannot adopt the CFA Institute Code of Ethics and Standards of Professional Conduct, the firm can adopt the CFA Institute Asset Manager Code of Professional Conduct." President Markoe tells Nano that the firm is considering acquiring another advisory firm that has similar compliance policies and procedures. Markoe says: "We are not going to consider any compliance changes at this time."

Nano decides to draft a model compliance document to guide discussions about compliance issues at the firm in the future. Nano's initial draft includes the following components of a compliance policy statement:

1. Performance Presentation

   Performance data must be documented for each of Markoe Advisors' active accounts, be disclosed upon request, and be compared with the firm's composite, which is composed of active accounts only. Performance data must be presented on a before-tax basis to all clients, with the disclosure that all performance data are presented gross of fees.

2. Suitability of Investments

   Markoe Advisors, to maintain consistency of performance, assigns each client to one of the firm's two portfolios. Both of these portfolios are sufficiently broadly diversified to meet the investment objectives of all of our clients.

3. Disclosures of Conflicts

   Markoe Advisors encourages its staff to be involved in the business and civic community. Only business or civic interests that relate to current portfolio holdings need to be reported to the firm.

4. Violations

   Any violation of the Markoe Advisors compliance policy statement will be reported to the president, and employees will receive an official warning.

5. Compensation

   All staff members of Markoe Advisors will discuss with their supervisor all outside compensation that they are receiving or may receive.

41. Does Nano comply with the CFA Institute Standards of Professional Conduct when he asks his clients to transfer their accounts to Markoe Advisors?

   A. No.

   B. Yes, because he contacted the clients after leaving Patriarch.

   C. Yes, because he was an intern and not a paid employee of Patriarch.

42. Is Nano's statement with respect to adoption of the CFA Institute Code of Ethics and Standards of Professional Conduct and the CFA Institute Asset Manager Code of Professional Conduct, respectively, correct?

	CFA Institute Code and Standards	CFA Institute Asset Manager Code of Professional Conduct
A.	No	No
B.	No	Yes
C.	Yes	No

43. According to the CFA Institute Code and Standards, what action should Nano take after discussing the firm's compliance policy with President Markoe? Nano should:

   A. resign from the firm.

   B. notify the board of directors.

   C. decline to accept supervisory responsibilities.

44. Does Nano's draft compliance policy statement conform to the CFA Institute Code and Standards with respect to performance presentation?

   A. No, because terminated accounts are excluded.

   B. No, because performance is reported to all clients gross of fees.

   C. No, because performance data are presented on a before-tax basis.

45. Does Nano's draft compliance policy statement conform to the CFA Institute Code and Standards with respect to:

	suitability of investments?	disclosures of conflicts?
A.	No	No
B.	No	Yes
C.	Yes	No

46. Does Nano's draft compliance policy statement conform to the CFA Institute Code and Standards with respect to:

	violations?	compensation?
A.	No	No
B.	No	Yes
C.	Yes	No

The following information relates to Questions 47–52

Patricia Jollie, CFA, is the fixed-income analyst and portfolio manager at Mahsud Financial Corporation, a small investment firm.

On 5 April, a friend who works for a bond-rating agency mentions to Jollie that a bond the agency is analyzing will experience a rating change. That bond also happens to be in Mahsud Financial's portfolios. Not wanting to trade ahead of the rating change announcement, Jollie decides to wait for distribution of the information through her friend's scheduled interview on a business television program the afternoon of 8 April. On the morning of 8 April, the information is released on a worldwide financial news service. Jollie immediately changes her mind about waiting for the interview and trades the bonds in Mahsud Financial's portfolios.

On 8 April, Jollie also trades a second bond to rebalance one of Mahsud Financial's portfolios. Jollie knows before executing her transaction that the bond is thinly traded. Although Jollie's trade will materially affect the bond's market price, it is not her intention to create price movement. A colleague witnesses the trade and large bond price change and says, "What a market overreaction; the bond price appears to be distorted now!" The colleague also points out to Jollie that Mahsud Financial's policy on market manipulation states: "Mahsud Financial employees must refrain from making transactions that distort security prices or volume with the intent to mislead market participants."

In conducting fixed-income research, Jollie believes that insight into prospective corporate bond returns can be derived from information that is also relevant to a company's stock. She spends several hours a week in equity investment chat rooms on the internet, and she pays particular attention to the research reports posted by Jill Dean, CFA, a self-employed analyst, on www.Jill_Dean_the_Independent_Analyst.com. Prior to writing each report, Dean is paid a flat fee by the companies whose stocks she researches, but she does not reveal this fact to readers of her reports. She produces reports only for those companies whose stocks she can legitimately give "buy" recommendations after conducting a thorough analysis. Otherwise, she returns the flat fee. Investors have come to recognize all her "buy" ratings as having a sound and reasonable basis.

Jollie considers Dean's summaries and forecasts to be very well-crafted. Dean has given Jollie written permission to use her summaries and forecasts, word for word and without attribution, in her own bond analysis reports. On occasion, Jollie has done so. In Dean's other internet postings, she reports the results of relevant academic finance studies. Once Jollie learns of a study by reading Dean's postings, she often reads the original study and mentions the results in her own reports. Jollie always cites the original study only and does not reveal that she learned of the study through Dean.

Mahsud Financial occasionally sponsors seminars on ethics. In the most recent seminar, the main speaker made statements about the relationship between ethics and the law, and also about potential sources of conflict of interest for research analysts. The seminar speaker's statements were:

Statement 1: An illegal action is unethical, and actions that are legal are ethically sound.

Statement 2: For analysts, a major source of conflict of interest is potential profit resulting from a weak barrier between the employer's research department and investment banking department.

Statement 3: For situations in which conflicts of interest cannot be avoided, Mahsud Financial's written compliance policy should include the following component: "For unavoidable conflicts of interest that the employee judges to be material, employees must disclose the conflicts of interest to clients prominently, and in plain language."

Statement 4: On the matter of gifts that might impair employees' objectivity, Mahsud Financial's written compliance policy should also include the following component: "Employees must disclose to Mahsud Financial all client gifts regardless of value."

47. Does Jollie violate the CFA Institute Standards of Professional Conduct by trading on the news of the bond rating change?

   A. No.

   B. Yes, only because she possessed material nonpublic information.

   C. Yes, only because she should have waited to trade until after her friend's television interview took place.

48. Are Jollie's 8 April trade of the second bond and Mahsud Financial's policy on market manipulation, respectively, consistent with CFA Institute Standards on market manipulation?

   A. Both Jollie's 8 April trade of the second bond and Mahsud Financial's policy on market manipulation are consistent with CFA Institute Standards.

   B. Jollie's 8 April trade of the second bond is inconsistent and Mahsud Financial's policy on market manipulation is consistent with CFA Institute Standards.

   C. Jollie's 8 April trade of the second bond is consistent and Mahsud Financial's policy on market manipulation is inconsistent with CFA Institute Standards.

49. Does Dean violate CFA Institute Standards in preparing and disseminating her equity reports?

   A. No.

   B. Yes, only by misrepresenting her recommendations as independent.

   C. Yes, only by accepting payment from the companies on which she produces reports.

50. In preparing investment reports, does Jollie violate the CFA Institute Standards with respect to her:

	use of Dean's summaries and forecasts?	citation of studies found in Dean's internet postings?
A.	No	Yes
B.	Yes	No
C.	Yes	Yes

51. Are the seminar speaker's Statements 1 and 2, respectively, correct?

	Statement 1	Statement 2
A.	No	No
B.	No	Yes
C.	Yes	No

52. Are the seminar speaker's Statements 3 and 4, respectively, sufficient to meet the requirements of related CFA Institute Standards?

	Statement 3	Statement 4
A.	No	No
B.	No	Yes
C.	Yes	No

The following information relates to Questions 53–58[1]

Stacia Finnegan, CFA, manages a regional office of Harvest Financial's brokerage business. Her responsibilities include training all personnel in compliance with the firm's standards, policies, procedures, and applicable laws and regulations.

Finnegan is currently providing training on the firm's new PlusAccount, a comprehensive fee-based brokerage account. "PlusAccounts," she tells the brokers, "are an excellent way to ensure that the financial advisor does not recommend trades for the purpose of generating commissions. The advisor and client's interests are aligned." She continues, "You will find that many clients will benefit from converting a traditional brokerage account to a PlusAccount. Be aware, however, that PlusAccounts are not appropriate for all categories of investors, including buy-and-hold clients and certain clients with assets less than $50,000." Finnegan distributes written compliance procedures for establishing and maintaining PlusAccounts. She carefully explains that regulatory rules "require that we have reasonable grounds for believing that the PlusAccount is appropriate for a particular customer. Additionally, we must review each account on an annual basis to determine whether PlusAccount status remains appropriate. The policies outlined in these documents are designed to ensure compliance with industry standards and regulatory requirements. You must follow these compliance procedures exactly."

---

[1] This case was written by Dorothy C. Kelly, CFA.

Finnegan then distributes and explains the sales and disclosure materials for clients. The materials include the following fee structure:

PlusAccount Annual Fee (as a Percent of Assets)*		
Account Asset Level	**Equity (%)**	**Mutual Fund/Fixed Income (%)**
From 0–$250,000	2.00	1.00
Next $250,000	1.50	1.00
Next $250,000	1.25	1.00
Next $250,000	1.00	1.00
More than $1 million	0.75	0.75

*Minimum annual fee of $1,000 billed quarterly.

Finnegan spends the rest of the afternoon training the staff on detailed procedures and answering their questions.

Chris Klein is a registered broker and financial advisor with Harvest. He is also a Level II Candidate in the CFA Program. Klein is excited about the new PlusAccounts and believes that they will be attractive for many clients.

One of Klein's clients is Elaine Vanderon, who contributes weekly to her brokerage account. Under Vanderon's directions, Klein invests the weekly contributions in actively managed mutual funds (unit trusts). The funds have below-average management fees and average returns. Commissions for Vanderon average $35 per transaction.

When Vanderon's account reaches $50,000 in assets, Klein recommends conversion to a PlusAccount. He carefully explains that in a PlusAccount, both the cost of investment advice and many implementation costs are wrapped into the management fee billed on a quarterly basis. Stock and bond commissions, he tells Vanderon, are discounted by 70%. Klein informs Vanderon that in a PlusAccount, she can buy or sell thousands of mutual funds or unit trusts (including those in which she invests) for no commissions or transaction charges. He explains that PlusAccounts are ideal for clients who trade often—or as part of a periodic investment program such as hers. Vanderon reads through the disclosure material provided by Klein and accepts his recommendation.

Klein routinely informs clients about the benefits of PlusAccount status and presents them with all the disclosure materials. Another client Klein encourages to open a PlusAccount is Lee Brown. Brown has accumulated stock holdings of $300,000 and trades equities almost daily. His annual commissions for the previous twelve months equal $9,100. His portfolio is well-diversified. He has a high risk tolerance and prefers growth stocks. After explaining the fee structure, Klein tells Brown "The PlusAccount is ideal for an active trader like you."

One year later, Finnegan is promoted. She delegates supervisory responsibility for Klein and 15 other brokers to her assistant branch manager.

The same month, Klein meets with Vanderon and Brown to review their portfolios and financial situations. Both clients are happy with their PlusAccounts. Vanderon's commission costs have declined to zero. Her account continues to grow in line with her plans and expectations. Brown is also happy with his account. His annual commission costs have declined 70% to $2,700.

Two months later, Vanderon receives a $1 million inheritance and places it in her PlusAccount. Although he conducted a full review two months earlier, Klein meets with Vanderon to review her financial situation and discuss potential changes to her investment policy. During their meeting, Klein mentions that he has completed Level III of the CFA examination. He informs Vanderon "Completion of the CFA Program has enhanced my portfolio management skills." He tells Vanderon "As a CFA charterholder, I am the best qualified to manage your investments." Vanderon congratulates Klein on his accomplishment and agrees to consider any changes he recommends to her PlusAccount.

The following month, Klein telephones Vanderon to recommend a highly-rated mutual fund. Klein states "The fund has an excellent performance history and is ranked in the top decile of comparable funds. For the past three- and five-year periods, its average annual return has exceeded the benchmark by 90 basis points. Of course, past performance is no guarantee of future returns, but several of my clients hold this fund and they are all very happy with it. One of them invested $50,000 five years ago. That investment is worth more than $100,000 today." When Vanderon asks about fees, Klein explains that the fund's management fees are 25 basis points higher than those of her existing investments. He adds "Because of your PlusAccount status, you won't incur a brokerage commission for this transaction even though I will receive a referral fee if you invest in the fund."

Six months later, Brown suffers serious medical and financial problems and stops trading. Klein telephones him to review his financial situation. Brown insists that he will make a full recovery and that he will be trading again shortly. During the next twelve months, Brown is too ill to trade. His growing expenses force him to withdraw large amounts from his PlusAccount. Within another 18 months, his PlusAccount value is less than $50,000.

53. When recommending Vanderon convert to a PlusAccount, does Klein violate any CFA Institute Standards of Professional Conduct?

   A. No.

   B. Yes, because he does not have a reasonable basis.

   C. Yes, because the account is unsuitable for Vanderon.

54. When recommending Brown convert to a PlusAccount, does Klein violate any CFA Institute Standards?

   A. No.

   B. Yes, relating to suitability.

   C. Yes, relating to reasonable basis.

55. When meeting with Vanderon, does Klein violate any CFA Standards?

   A. No.

   B. Yes, because he improperly references the CFA designation.

   C. Yes, because he claims enhanced portfolio management skills.

56. When recommending the mutual fund to Vanderon, does Klein violate any CFA Standards?

   A. No.

   B. Yes, relating to suitability.

   C. Yes, relating to referral fees.

57. In the eighteen months following Brown's change in financial situation, Klein is *least likely* to have violated the Standard relating to:

   A. loyalty, prudence, and care.

   B. diligence and reasonable basis.

   C. communication with clients and prospective clients.

58. In her supervisory duties, does Finnegan violate any CFA Standards?

   A. No.

   B. Yes, because she fails to ensure that compliance procedures are enforced.

   C. Yes, because she delegates supervisory authority to her assistant branch manager.

The following information relates to Questions 59–64[2]

A. J. Vinken, CFA, manages the Stonebridge Fund at Silk Road Capital Management. He develops a growth-stock selection model which produces highly favorable simulated performance results. He would like to employ the model in managing the Stonebridge Fund, a large-capitalization equity fund. He drafts a letter for distribution to all shareholders. In it, he discusses in detail his approach to equity selection using the model. He includes both the actual and simulated performance results of the Stonebridge Fund for the past three years as seen in Exhibit 1:

EXHIBIT 1	Stonebridge Fund Annual Returns	
Year	Stonebridge Fund (Simulated)	Stonebridge Fund (Actual)
1	10.71%	9.22%
2	2.83%	−4.13%
3	22.23%	22.23%
Average annual return	11.92%	9.11%

Vinken writes, "Using the proprietary selection model for the past three years, the Stonebridge Fund would have earned an average annual return of almost 300 basis points in excess of the fund's actual return. Based on these simulated results, I am confident that employing the model will yield better performance results in the future; however, Silk Road Capital Management can make no statement of assurances or guarantee regarding future investment returns."

D.S. Khadri, CFA, is also a portfolio manager at Silk Road. She recently assumed management of the small-cap Westlake Fund from Vinken.

Khadri implements an electronic record-retention policy when she becomes the Westlake manager. In accordance with her policy, all records for the fund, including investment analyses, transactions, and investment-related communications with clients and prospective clients, are scanned and electronically stored. Vinken maintained the same records in hard-copy format for the five years that he managed the Westlake Fund. Khadri has begun the process of scanning all of the past records of the Westlake Fund; however, Vinken complains that Khadri is wasting company resources by scanning old records. Vinken insists that he will continue to maintain only hard-copy records for the Stonebridge Fund for the five years required by regulators.

---

[2] This case was written by David S. Krause, PhD, and Dorothy C. Kelly, CFA.

Khadri writes a performance review of the Westlake Fund for its quarterly newsletter. She reports that Silk Road Capital Management is moving toward compliance with the Global Investment Performance Standards (GIPS). She states, "The Westlake Fund is already partially GIPS compliant. We expect to be fully compliant with the GIPS standards within the next 12 months."

In the quarterly newsletter, Khadri makes the following statements:

Statement 1: "China's pegging of the yuan to the U.S. dollar will end within the next 12 months which will lead to the yuan increasing in value by more than 40%, supporting our over-weighting of Chinese-related stocks in the Westlake Fund."

Statement 2: "Increased geo-political uncertainty around the globe should keep oil prices above 3-year levels and supports our recommendation for an over-weighting of equities in the small-cap energy sector."

Khadri also reports:

"The quarterly return of the Westlake Fund was 4.07%. The quarterly return exceeded the performance of its benchmark, the Russell 2000 Index by .16%. Investors should not expect this type of performance to continue into the foreseeable future.*

* Additional detailed information available upon request."

After the quarterly newsletter is distributed, a client contacts Khadri claiming that the Westlake Fund actually underperformed the benchmark during the quarter. After researching the issue, Khadri confirms that the client is correct and sends him a letter in which she provides the corrected results. In her letter to the client, she blames the discrepancy—which was the result of a human typographical error—on a computer programming error.

59. In his letter regarding the stock-selection model, does Vinken violate any CFA Institute Standards of Professional Conduct?

   A. No.

   B. Yes, because he uses simulated performance results.

   C. Yes, because he claims that the new model will yield better performance results.

60. Are the record-retention policies of both Khadri and Vinken consistent with CFA Institute Standards?

   A. Yes.

   B. No, Khadri's policy is not consistent.

   C. No, Vinken's policy is not consistent.

61. Are Khadri's statements regarding compliance with the Global Investment Performance Standards consistent with CFA Institute Standards?

   A. Yes.

   B. No, because Khadri may not claim partial compliance.

   C. No, because Khadri fails to disclose the areas of noncompliance.

62. Are Khadri's statements in the quarterly newsletter consistent with CFA Institute Standards?

   A. Yes.

   B. No, because Statement 1 is opinion, not fact.

   C. No, because Statement 2 is opinion, not fact.

63. Are Khadri's newsletter comments regarding returns consistent with CFA Institute Standards?

   A. Yes.

   B. No, because Khadri used an inappropriate benchmark.

   C. No, because Khadri did not disclose whether the performance results are before or after fees.

64. When responding to the client complaint regarding Westlake's performance, Khadri *least likely* violates the Standard relating to:

   A. misconduct.

   B. misrepresentation.

   C. performance presentation.

The following information relates to Questions 65–70[3]

Omega Financial, a large financial services firm, makes a market in more than 500 stocks. As a market-maker, the firm executes institutional orders as well as retail orders placed by its private wealth unit, its broker-dealer affiliate, and other third-party broker-dealers.

A page in Omega's compliance manual, which adheres to all legal and regulatory requirements, includes the following information:

OTC Stocks in Which Omega is a Market-Maker

Definitions:

Riskless principal transaction: an order in which a firm, after receiving a customer's order, executes the order on a principal basis from another market center.

Net Trade/Trade on a net basis: a principal transaction in which a market-maker, after having received an order, executes the order at one price with another broker-dealer or another customer and then sells to (buys from) the customer at a different price.

Compliance Policies:

Institutional Orders	Retail Orders
Riskless principal transactions may be traded on a net basis.	Riskless principal transactions may not be traded on a net basis. They receive the same execution price without mark-up, mark-down, commissions, or fees.

---

[3] This case was written by Dorothy C. Kelly, CFA.

Consistent with regulatory requirements, Omega discloses the information about riskless principal transactions to all clients and third-party broker-dealers. In addition, Omega informs third-party broker-dealers that it will seek best execution on retail orders.

Omega is developing an automated order-handling system to improve efficiencies in order flow. Anticipated benefits of the new system include much faster execution speeds. Additionally, the system design includes a trading mechanism that will execute portions of certain large orders to reduce market impact. The trading mechanism delays some orders to allow the firm to obtain a better overall price.

Xavier Brown, CFA, is responsible for overseeing the project to ensure its timely completion. Brown enlists the compliance department to review the programming during the initial development phase and identify any potential problems. The compliance department compares the order-handling function of the new system to the third-party software currently in use. They identify a number of potential problems including delays in execution of certain large market orders and embedded mark-ups and mark-downs on stocks in which the firm makes a market. According to the compliance department, changes are necessary to comply with regulatory requirements.

Brown directs the programmers to correct the problems and run tests and simulations. The programmers spend the next few months making changes to the system and adding comments throughout the code that clearly explain the purpose of particular functions. After several months, the programmers report that they have corrected all the identified problems and run the necessary tests and simulations. The following month, the firm switches to the automated order-handling system as planned.

Joy Chen, CFA, trades Xydeo stock for Omega. One month following the switch to the new order-handling system, Chen is able to execute a number of principal riskless transactions for both institutional and retail clients at $25.00 per share. When processing the customer buy orders totaling 500,000 shares, the new system automatically uses the best-publicized price of $25.01 and the firm issues client confirmations showing a purchase price of $25.01.

Stephen Smith, CFA, works across from Chen on the trading desk at Omega. His seat is close to a speaker for the company's squawk box, which is used to broadcast information about current analyst recommendations; news about market events; and information about pending block trades.

Smith's young brother-in-law, Adolfo Garcia, recently accepted a position as a broker at a third-party broker-dealer that trades with Omega. Garcia has a modest income and little savings. He is enthusiastic about investments and has enrolled as a CFA candidate. Smith calls Garcia early each morning to talk about the previous day's events. At the end of their conversation, Smith places the call on speakerphone and resumes his work.

In his office, Garcia can hear Omega's squawk box over the speakerphone. Garcia enjoys listening as Omega analysts discuss changes in ratings, economic forecasts, and capital market developments. He is careful not to trade in stocks mentioned explicitly on the squawk box. Rather, he sometimes researches competitors and other firms operating in the same industry. In one case, he immediately shorts the stock of Tefla Corporation after an Omega analyst downgrades a firm in the same industry.

Garcia frequently places large block orders for low-priced small-capitalization stocks at the market price. Once the new system is operational, Smith processes the orders through the new trading-system mechanism, which delays execution of portions of the orders and allows the firm to obtain a better price for Garcia.

65. For a CFA charterholder, would adhering to Omega's policies regarding riskless principal transactions result in a violation of the CFA Institute Standards of Professional Conduct?

   A. No.

   B. Yes, because Omega disadvantages institutional clients.

   C. Yes, because disclosure of the policy does not relieve Omega of its obligation to treat clients equally.

66. When overseeing the development of the automated-trading system, does Brown violate any CFA Institute Standards?

   A. No.

   B. Yes, because he accepted an assignment for which he was inadequately trained and skilled.

   C. Yes, because he did not ensure that the final system complied with regulatory requirements.

67. With regard to Chen's trades in Xydeo, do the institutional and retail trades both comply with CFA Institute Standards?

   A. Only the retail trades comply.

   B. Only the institutional trades comply.

   C. Neither the retail nor the institutional trades comply.

68. When placing the morning phone call on speakerphone, does Smith violate any CFA Institute Standards?

   A. No.

   B. Yes, his duty to Omega.

   C. Yes, his duty to clients and to Omega.

69. When listening to the Omega squawk box, does Garcia violate any CFA Institute Standards?

   A. No.

   B. Yes, the standard regarding professionalism.

   C. Yes, the standard regarding material nonpublic information.

70. When shorting Tefla stock, does Garcia violate any CFA Institute Standards?

   A. No.

   B. Yes, because he does not have a reasonable basis for the trade.

   C. Yes, because he is in possession of material nonpublic information.

The following information relates to Questions 71–76[4]

Sebastian Riser, CFA, works as a portfolio manager for Swibank, a small private bank in Switzerland. Riser manages the accounts of his clients according to best practices, keeping clients' interests before those of the bank and his own. He allocates investments in a fair manner when he deems them consistent with the stated objectives and constraints of clients.

Swibank has a Luxembourg subsidiary, which distributes fund-of-funds products. Riser recently received a request to serve on the board of directors for the subsidiary. In this role, Riser would advise management on business

---

[4] This case was written by Anne-Katrin Scherer, CFA.

strategies; market opportunities; potential clients; and current and prospective fund managers. For his role on the board, Riser would receive an annual payment directly from the subsidiary equivalent to 5% of his total portfolio manager salary in Switzerland.

The following month, Riser accepts the position on the board. The subsidiary registers each new fund-of-funds product with regulatory authorities in Luxembourg and discloses Riser's role as a board member in the required filings, which are public and readily available.

Riser serves as the contact person for the subsidiary's institutional clients in Switzerland and participates in the subsidiary's road shows in Switzerland. His role during these road shows varies. On some occasions, he simply attends the presentations while the operating management sells the products; on others he gives the actual presentation promoting the products. Riser's name does not appear in the promotional material distributed at the road shows.

Alexander Komm, a long-time colleague of Riser, is the founder of Komm Private Management, which provides asset management, advisory, and trust services to high-net-worth individuals. The firm has several well-managed proprietary funds. Komm offers Riser a position with the firm as managing partner. Riser is flattered, but declines the offer, explaining that he is very happy working at Swibank.

That same week, the subsidiary informs Riser that it needs an experienced fund manager to manage a new publicly-traded Japanese equity product. Riser is convinced that Komm Private Management would be qualified and recommends the firm for the new product. After a thorough search process, the subsidiary hires Komm Private Management for the new product.

Six months later, after numerous discussions, Komm finally convinces Riser to join Komm Private Management as a managing partner. The following week, Riser submits his resignation at the private bank. His position on the board of the subsidiary is not dependent on his employment at the bank, and he agrees to serve the remaining three years of his term.

After signing and submitting his employment contract to Komm, Riser takes three weeks of vacation before starting his new position. During this time he purchases 2,000 shares of the new Japanese equity product for his private account. When he begins working at Komm Private Management, he purchases a large block of shares in the Japanese equity product, which he allocates according to internal procedures to all accounts for which it is suitable.

71. According to the CFA Institute Standards of Professional Conduct, before accepting the position on the board of the subsidiary, Riser should:

    A. receive verbal consent from Swibank.

    B. receive verbal consent from his clients.

    C. disclose to his employer the financial compensation proposed by the subsidiary.

72. When participating in the road shows in Switzerland, Riser *least likely* violates the Standard relating to:

    A. Disclosure of Conflicts.

    B. Independence and Objectivity.

    C. Additional Compensation Arrangements.

73. When recommending Komm, does Riser violate any CFA Institute Standards?

   A. No.

   B. Yes, relating to duties to employer.

   C. Yes, relating to disclosure of conflicts.

74. When resigning from Swibank, does Riser violate any CFA Institute Standards?

   A. No.

   B. Yes, because he breaches his duty of loyalty to his employer.

   C. Yes, because he does not resign his position with the Luxembourg subsidiary.

75. In his original purchase of 2,000 shares of the Japanese equity product, Riser *least likely* violates the Standard relating to:

   A. Suitability.

   B. Priority of Transactions.

   C. Integrity of Capital Markets.

76. According to CFA Institute Standards, Riser is not required to disclose to clients his:

   A. holdings of the Japanese equity product.

   B. relationship with the Swibank subsidiary.

   C. compensation from the Swibank subsidiary.

The following information relates to Questions 77–82

Prudent Investment Associates (PIA) is a small-cap equity investment management company that uses fundamental equity analysis in its investment decision-making process. All portfolio managers at PIA manage both discretionary and non-discretionary accounts. Kevin Danko, CFA, is PIA's owner and chief investment officer and supervises May Chau, a recently hired portfolio manager. PIA has adopted the CFA Institute Code of Ethics and Standards of Professional Conduct.

Chau is enrolled to sit for the Level III CFA examination. In its marketing brochure, PIA states: "May Chau is a Level III candidate in the CFA Program." A colleague tells Chau this presentation may be incorrect according to the CFA Institute Code and Standards and suggests the following change: "May Chau has passed Level II of the CFA examination."

PIA has established a relationship with Fair Trading Incorporated (FTI), a regional investment bank and broker/dealer. FTI provides clients with access to research and analysts' recommendations via a user-registered website. This access is available on the condition that clients not forward any of the research and recommendations to any other parties. In exchange for this access and after concluding that FTI provides best execution, Danko directs to FTI most of his trade orders.

FTI also provides to a select group of brokerage clients, including PIA, information regarding several of its investment banking customers. This information includes the customers' own earnings projections. FTI instructs this select group of brokerage clients not to disseminate these earnings projections to the public until released by the investment banking customers.

On a regular basis, Danko reviews the list of "strong buys" on FTI's website to see if there have been any new "buy" recommendations. Danko quickly places orders for discretionary client accounts to purchase shares of any company for which the investment recommendation has been changed to a "strong buy." He takes this action so discretionary account clients do not miss any price appreciation. After each purchase, he instructs Chau to perform the appropriate fundamental analysis on these companies within five business days so the research file is adequately documented.

From time to time, PIA receives initial public offering (IPO) allocations from FTI. Danko allocates these IPOs to those discretionary accounts that normally participate in IPOs. If the IPO is oversubscribed, he excludes his wife's discretionary non-fee-paying account so that he is not accused of bias when allocating the oversubscribed IPOs.

During a recent presentation, Danko and Chau are asked what procedures PIA uses to ensure employees do not benefit from information prior to executing trades in client accounts. Danko responds that PIA has the following Trading Procedures:

Procedure 1:   Investment personnel are not permitted to trade securities for five business days prior to trades executed in discretionary client accounts.

Procedure 2:   Each quarter a randomly selected group of investment personnel must provide duplicate trade confirmations to the PIA compliance officer.

Procedure 3:   Investment personnel must receive prior approval for personal trades only for those trades greater than $5,000.

77. Does the reference to Chau's participation in the CFA Program, as presented in the marketing brochure, or in the suggested change, violate CFA Institute Standards of Professional Conduct?

   A. No.

   B. The marketing brochure is a violation, but the suggested change is not a violation.

   C. The suggested change is a violation, but the marketing brochure is not a violation.

78. Does Danko violate CFA Institute Standards when he directs trades to FTI?

   A. No.

   B. Yes, because by trading with FTI, Danko is putting PIA's interests ahead of his clients.

   C. Yes, because Danko has a duty to provide FTI's research to PIA's clients before executing trades.

79. According to CFA Institute Standards, which of the following actions is the *most* appropriate for Danko to take with respect to the use of the earnings projections? Danko should:

   A. disclose the information to the public.

   B. terminate PIA's relationship with FTI.

   C. keep the information confidential and not use it in his analysis.

80. Does Danko's decision to purchase shares that are recommended as a "strong buy" violate the CFA Institute Standards?

    A. No.

    B. Yes, because Danko must have a reasonable and adequate basis prior to purchasing the shares.

    C. Yes, because Danko must give non-discretionary accounts the opportunity to purchase equities at the same time he purchases equities in the discretionary accounts.

81. Does Danko violate the CFA Institute Standards when he allocates oversubscribed IPO issues?

    A. No.

    B. Yes, because he should allocate the oversubscribed IPOs across all discretionary accounts.

    C. Yes, because he should treat his wife's account the same as other discretionary accounts and include it in the oversubscribed IPO allocations.

82. Which of PIA's Trading Procedures is *most* consistent with the CFA Institute Standards?

    A. Procedure 1.

    B. Procedure 2.

    C. Procedure 3.

SOLUTIONS FOR READING 2

1. B is correct. This question involves Standard III(B)—Fair Dealing. Smith disseminated a change in the stock recommendation to his clients but then received a request contrary to that recommendation from a client who probably had not yet received the recommendation. Prior to executing the order, Smith should take additional steps to ensure that the customer has received the change of recommendation. Answer A is incorrect because the client placed the order prior to receiving the recommendation and, therefore, does not have the benefit of Smith's most recent recommendation. Answer C is also incorrect; simply because the client request is contrary to the firm's recommendation does not mean a member can override a direct request by a client. After Smith contacts the client to ensure that the client has received the changed recommendation, if the client still wants to place a buy order for the shares, Smith is obligated to comply with the client's directive.

2. C is correct. This question involves Standard III(A)—Loyalty, Prudence, and Care and the specific topic of soft dollars or soft commissions. Answer C is the correct choice because client brokerage commissions may not be directed to pay for the investment manager's operating expenses. Answer B describes how members and candidates should determine how to use brokerage commissions—that is, if the use is in the best interests of clients and is commensurate with the value of the services provided. Answer A describes a practice that is commonly referred to as "directed brokerage." Because brokerage is an asset of the client and is used to benefit the client, not the manager, such practice does not violate a duty of loyalty to the client. Members and candidates are obligated in all situations to disclose to clients their practices in the use of client brokerage commissions.

3. C is correct. This question involves Standard VI(A)—Disclosure of Conflicts. The question establishes a conflict of interest in which an analyst, Jamison, is asked to write a research report on a company that is a client of the analyst's employer. In addition, two directors of the company are senior officers of Jamison's employer. Both facts establish that there are conflicts of interest that must be disclosed by Jamison in her research report. Answer B is incorrect because an analyst is not prevented from writing a report simply because of the special relationship the analyst's employer has with the company as long as that relationship is disclosed. Answer A is incorrect because whether or not Jamison expresses any opinions in the report is irrelevant to her duty to disclose a conflict of interest. Not expressing opinions does not relieve the analyst of the responsibility to disclose the special relationships between the two companies.

4. C is correct. This question asks about compliance procedures relating to personal investments of members and candidates. The statement in answer C clearly conflicts with the recommended procedures in the *Standards of Practice Handbook*. Employers should compare personal transactions of employees with those of clients on a regular basis regardless of the existence of a requirement by any regulatory organization. Such comparisons ensure that employees' personal trades do not conflict with their duty to their clients, and the comparisons can be conducted in a confidential manner. The statement in answer A does not conflict with the procedures in the *Handbook*. Disclosure of such policies will give full information to clients regarding potential conflicts of interest on the part of those entrusted to manage their money. Answer B is incorrect because firms are encouraged to establish policies whereby employees clear their personal holdings and transactions with their employers.

5. B is correct. This question relates to Standard III(A)—Loyalty, Prudence, and Care and Standard III(E)—Preservation of Confidentiality. In this case, the member manages funds of a private endowment. Clients, who are, in this case, the trustees of the fund, must place some trust in members and candidates. Bronson cannot disclose confidential financial information to anyone without the permission of the fund, regardless of whether the disclosure may benefit the fund. Therefore, answer A is incorrect. Answer C is incorrect because Bronson must notify the fund and obtain the fund's permission before publicizing the information.

6. C is correct. Under Standard IV(C)—Responsibilities of Supervisors, members and candidates may delegate supervisory duties to subordinates but such delegation does not relieve members or candidates of their supervisory responsibilities. As a result, answer B is incorrect. Moreover, whether or not Miller's subordinates are subject to the Code and Standards is irrelevant to her supervisory responsibilities. Therefore, answer A is incorrect.

7. B is correct. This question relates to Standard V(A)—Diligence and Reasonable Basis. The opinion of another financial analyst is not an adequate basis for Willier's action in changing the recommendation. Answer C is thus incorrect. So is answer A because, although it is true that members and candidates must distinguish between facts and opinions in recommendations, the question does not illustrate a violation of that nature. If the opinion overheard by Willier had sparked him to conduct additional research and investigation that justified a change of opinion, then a changed recommendation would be appropriate.

8. B is correct. This question relates to Standard I(B)—Independence and Objectivity. When asked to change a recommendation on a company stock to gain business for the firm, the head of the brokerage unit must refuse in order to maintain his independence and objectivity in making recommendations. He must not yield to pressure by the firm's investment banking department. To avoid the appearance of a conflict of interest, the firm should discontinue issuing recommendations about the company. Answer A is incorrect; changing the recommendation in any manner that is contrary to the analyst's opinion violates the duty to maintain independence and objectivity. Answer C is incorrect because merely assigning a new analyst to decide whether the stock deserves a higher rating will not address the conflict of interest.

9. A is correct. Standard VII(B)—Reference to CFA Institute, the CFA Designation, and the CFA Program is the subject of this question. The reference on Albert's business card implies that there is a "CFA Level II" designation; Tye merely indicates in promotional material that he is participating in the CFA Program and has completed Levels I and II. Candidates may not imply that there is some sort of partial designation earned after passing a level of the CFA exam. Therefore, Albert has violated Standard VII(B). Candidates may communicate that they are participating in the CFA Program, however, and may state the levels that they have completed. Therefore, Tye has not violated Standard VII(B).

10. B is correct. This question relates to Standard V(B)—Communication with Clients and Prospective Clients. Scott has issued a research report stating that he expects the price of Walkton Industries stock to rise by US$8 a share "because the dividend will increase" by US$1.50 per share. He has made this statement knowing that the dividend will increase only if Congress enacts certain legislation, an uncertain prospect. By stating that the dividend will increase, Scott failed to separate fact from opinion.

The information regarding passage of legislation is not material nonpublic information because it is conjecture, and the question does not state whether the U.S. Representative gave Scott her opinion on the passage of the legislation in confidence. She could have been offering this opinion to anyone who asked. Therefore, statement A is incorrect. It may be acceptable to base a recommendation, in part, on an expectation of future events, even though they may be uncertain. Therefore, answer C is incorrect.

11. C is correct. This question, which relates to Standard III(B)—Fair Dealing, tests the knowledge of the procedures that will assist members and candidates in treating clients fairly when making investment recommendations. The steps listed in C will all help ensure the fair treatment of clients. Answer A may have negative effects on the fair treatment of clients. The more people who know about a pending change, the greater the chance that someone will inform some clients before the information's release. The firm should establish policies that limit the number of people who are aware in advance that a recommendation is to be disseminated. Answer B, distributing recommendations to institutional clients before distributing them to individual accounts, discriminates among clients on the basis of size and class of assets and is a violation of Standard III(B).

12. B is correct. This question deals with Standard II(A)—Material Nonpublic Information. The mosaic theory states that an analyst may use material public information and nonmaterial nonpublic information in creating a larger picture than shown by any individual piece of information and the conclusions the analyst reaches become material only after the pieces are assembled. Answers A and C are accurate statements relating to the Code and Standards but do not describe the mosaic theory.

13. C is correct. This question involves Standard IV(B)—Additional Compensation Arrangements. The arrangement described in the question—whereby Jurgen would be compensated beyond the compensation provided by her firm, on the basis of an account's performance—is not a violation of the Standards as long as Jurgen discloses the arrangement in writing to her employer and obtains permission from her employer prior to entering into the arrangement. Answers A and B are incorrect; although the private compensation arrangement could conflict with the interests of other clients and lead to short-term performance pressures, members and candidates may enter into such agreements as long as they have disclosed the arrangements to their employer and obtained permission for the arrangement from their employer.

14. B is correct. This question relates to Standard III(A)—Loyalty, Prudence, and Care—specifically, a member's or candidate's responsibility for voting proxies and the use of client brokerage. According to the facts stated in the question, Farnsworth did not violate Standard III(A). Although the company president asked Farnsworth to vote the shares of the Jones Corporation profit-sharing plan a certain way, Farnsworth investigated the issue and concluded, independently, the best way to vote. Therefore, even though his decision coincided with the wishes of the company president, Farnsworth is not in violation of his responsibility to be loyal and to provide care to his clients. In this case, the participants and the beneficiaries of the profit-sharing plan are the clients, not the company's management. Had Farnsworth not investigated the issue or had he yielded to the president's wishes and voted for a slate of directors that he had determined was not in the best interest of the company, Farnsworth would have violated his responsibilities to the beneficiaries of the plan. In addition, because the brokerage firm provides the lowest commissions and best execution for securities transactions, Farnsworth has met his obligations to the client in using this brokerage firm. It does not matter that the brokerage firm also provides research information that is not useful for the account generating the commission, because Farnsworth is not paying extra money of the client's for that information.

15. A is correct. In this question, Brown is providing investment recommendations before making inquiries about the client's financial situation, investment experience, or investment objectives. Brown is thus violating Standard III(C)—Suitability. Answers B and C provide examples of information members and candidates should discuss with their clients at the outset of the relationship, but these answers do not constitute a complete list of those factors. Answer A is the best answer.

16. C is correct. This question involves Standard I(C)—Misrepresentation. Statement 1 is a factual statement that discloses to clients and prospects accurate information about the terms of the investment instrument. Statement 2, which guarantees a specific rate of return for a mutual fund, is an opinion stated as a fact and, therefore, violates Standard I(C). If Statement 2 were rephrased to include a qualifying statement, such as "in my opinion, investors may earn. . .," it would not be in violation of the Standards.

17. A is correct. This question involves three of the Standards. Anderb, the portfolio manager, has been obtaining more favorable prices for her personal securities transactions than she gets for her clients, which is a breach of Standard III(A)—Loyalty, Prudence, and Care. In addition, she violated Standard I(D)—Misconduct by failing to adhere to company policy and by hiding her personal transactions from her firm. Anderb's supervisor, Bates, violated Standard IV(C)—Responsibilities of Supervisors; although the company had requirements for reporting personal trading, Bates failed to adequately enforce those requirements. Answer B does not represent a violation because Standard VI(B)—Priority of Transactions requires that personal trading in a security be conducted after the trading in that security of clients and the employer. The Code and Standards do not prohibit owning such investments, although firms may establish policies that limit the investment opportunities of members and candidates. Answer C does not represent a violation because the Code and Standards do not contain a prohibition against employees using the same broker they use for their personal accounts that they also use for their client accounts. This arrangement should be disclosed to the employer so that the employer may determine whether a conflict of interest exists.

18. A is correct. This question relates to Standard I(A)—Knowledge of the Law—specifically, global application of the Code and Standards. Members and candidates who practice in multiple jurisdictions may be subject to various securities laws and regulations. If applicable law is more strict than

the requirements of the Code and Standards, members and candidates must adhere to applicable law; otherwise, members and candidates must adhere to the Code and Standards. Therefore, answer A is correct. Answer B is incorrect because members and candidates must adhere to the higher standard set by the Code and Standards if local applicable law is less strict. Answer C is incorrect because when no applicable law exists, members and candidates are required to adhere to the Code and Standards, and the Code and Standards prohibit the use of material nonpublic information.

19. B is correct. The best course of action under Standard I(B)—Independence and Objectivity is to avoid a conflict of interest whenever possible. Therefore, for Ward to pay for all his expenses is the correct answer. Answer C details a course of action in which the conflict would be disclosed, but the solution is not as appropriate as avoiding the conflict of interest. Answer A would not be the best course because it would not remove the appearance of a conflict of interest; even though the report would not be affected by the reimbursement of expenses, it could appear to be.

20. B is correct. Under Standard IV(A)—Loyalty, members and candidates may undertake independent practice that may result in compensation or other benefit in competition with their employer as long as they obtain consent from their employer. Answer C is not consistent with the Standards because the Standards allow members and candidates to make arrangements or preparations to go into competitive business as long as those arrangements do not interfere with their duty to their current employer. Answer A is not consistent with the Standards because the Standards do not include a complete prohibition against undertaking independent practice.

21. B is correct. This question involves Standard VI(A)—Disclosure of Conflicts—specifically, the holdings of an analyst's employer in company stock. Answers A and C do not describe conflicts of interest that Smith would have to disclose. Answer A describes the use of a firm's products, which would not be a required disclosure. In answer C, the relationship between the analyst and the company through a relative is so tangential that it does not create a conflict of interest necessitating disclosure.

22. B is correct. This question relates to Standard I(C)—Misrepresentation. Although Michelieu's statement about the total return of his clients' accounts on average may be technically true, it is misleading because the majority of the gain resulted from one client's large position taken against Michelieu's advice. Therefore, this statement misrepresents the investment performance the member is responsible for. He has not taken steps to present a fair, accurate, and complete presentation of performance. Answer A is incorrect because Michelieu's statement is a misrepresentation of his performance history. Answer C is incorrect because Michelieu does not guarantee future results.

23. B is correct. The best policy to prevent violation of Standard II(A)—Material Nonpublic Information is the establishment of firewalls in a firm to prevent exchange of insider information. The physical and informational barrier of a firewall between the investment banking department and the brokerage operation prevents the investment banking department from providing information to analysts on the brokerage side who may be writing recommendations on a company stock. Prohibiting recommendations of the stock of companies that are clients of the investment banking department is an alternative, but answer A states that this prohibition would be permanent, which is not the best answer. Once an

offering is complete and the material nonpublic information obtained by the investment banking department becomes public, resuming publishing recommendations on the stock is not a violation of the Code and Standards because the information of the investment banking department no longer gives the brokerage operation an advantage in writing the report. Answer C is incorrect because no exchange of information should be occurring between the investment banking department and the brokerage operation, so monitoring of such exchanges is not an effective compliance procedure for preventing the use of material nonpublic information.

24. B is correct. Under Standard III(A)—Loyalty, Prudence, and Care, members and candidates who manage a company's pension fund owe these duties to the participants and beneficiaries of the pension plan, not the management of the company or the company's shareholders.

25. B is correct. Answer B gives one of the two primary reasons listed in the *Handbook* for disclosing referral fees to clients under Standard VI(C)—Referral Fees. (The other is to allow clients and employers to evaluate the full cost of the services.) Answer A is inconsistent because Standard VI(C) does not require members or candidates to discount their fees when they receive referral fees. Answer C is inconsistent with Standard VI(C) because disclosure of referral fees, to be effective, should be made to prospective clients before entering into a formal client relationship with them.

26. B is correct. Standard VI(B)—Priority of Transactions does not limit transactions of company employees that differ from current recommendations as long as the sale does not disadvantage current clients. Thus, answer A is incorrect. Answer C is incorrect because the Standard does not require the matching of personal and client trades.

27. C is correct. Standard IV(A)—Loyalty discusses activities permissible to members and candidates when they are leaving their current employer; soliciting clients is strictly prohibited. Thus, answer A is inconsistent with the Code and Standards even with the required disclosure. Answer B is incorrect because the offer does not directly violate the Code and Standards. There may be out-of-work members and candidates who can arrange the necessary commitments without violating the Code and Standards.

28. A is correct. The question relates to Standard III(A)—Loyalty, Prudence, and Care. Carter believes the broker offers effective execution at a fee that is comparable with those of other brokers, so he is free to use the broker for all accounts. Answer B is incorrect because the accounts that prohibit soft dollar arrangements do not want to fund the purchase of research by Carter. The new trading scheme does not incur additional commissions from clients, so it would not go against the prohibitions. Answer C is incorrect because Carter should not incur unnecessary or excessive "churning" of the portfolios (excessive trading) for the purpose of meeting the brokerage commitments of soft dollar arrangements.

29. B is correct. According to Standard VII(B)—Reference to CFA Institute, the CFA Designation, and the CFA Program, CFA Program candidates do not receive their actual scores on the exam. Topic and subtopic results are grouped into three broad categories, and the exam is graded only as "pass" or "fail." Although a candidate may have achieved a topical score of "above 70 percent," she or he cannot factually state that she or he received the highest possible score because that information is not reported. Thus, answer C is incorrect. Answer A is incorrect as long as the member or candidate actually completed the exams consecutively. Standard VII(B)

does not prohibit the communication of factual information about completing the CFA Program in three consecutive years.

30. C is correct. According to Standard III(A)—Loyalty, Prudence, and Care, the CFA Program would be considered a personal or firm expense and should not be paid for with the fund's brokerage commissions. Soft dollar accounts should be used only to purchase research services that directly assist the investment manager in the investment decision-making process, not to assist the management of the firm or to further education. Thus, answer A is incorrect. Answer B is incorrect because the reasonableness of how the money is used is not an issue; the issue is that educational expense is not research.

31. A is correct. Standard I(B)—Independence and Objectivity emphasizes the need for members and candidates to maintain their independence and objectivity. Best practices dictate that firms adopt a strict policy not to accept compensation for travel arrangements. At times, however, accepting paid travel would not compromise one's independence and objectivity. Answers B and C are incorrect because the added benefits—free conference admission for additional staff members and an exclusive golf retreat for the speaker—could be viewed as inducements related to the firm's working arrangements and not solely related to the speaking engagement. Should Long wish to bring other team members or participate in the golf outing, he or his firm should be responsible for the associated fees.

32. C is correct. The guidance to Standard II(A)—Material Nonpublic Information recommends adding securities to the firm's restricted list when the firm has or may have material nonpublic information. By adding these securities to this list, Andrews would uphold this standard. Because waiting until the next day will not ensure that news of the merger is made public, answer A is incorrect. Negotiations may take much longer between the two companies, and the merger may never happen. Andrews must wait until the information is disseminated to the market before he trades on that information. Answer B is incorrect because Andrews should not disclose the information to other managers; no trading is allowed on material nonpublic information.

33. B is correct. Through placing a personal purchase order that is significantly greater than the average volume, Pietro is violating Standard IIB—Market Manipulation. He is attempting to manipulate an increase in the share price and thus bring a buyer to the negotiating table. The news of a possible merger and confirmation of the firm's earnings guidance may also have positive effects on the price of Local Bank, but Pietro's action in instructing the release of the information does not represent a violation through market manipulation. Announcements of this nature are common and practical to keep investors informed. Thus, answers A and C are incorrect.

34. C is correct. Cupp violated Standard III(D)—Performance Presentations when he deviated from the firm's stated policies solely to capture the gain from the holding being acquired. Answer A is incorrect because the firm does not claim GIPS compliance and the GIPS standards require external cash flows to be treated in a consistent manner with the firm's documented policies. Answer B is incorrect because the firm does not state that it is updating its composite policies. If such a change were to occur, all cash flows for the month would have to be reviewed to ensure their consistent treatment under the new policy.

35. A is correct. According to Standard V(C)—Record Retention, Cannan needed the permission of her employer to maintain the files at home after her employment ended. Without that permission, she should have deleted the files. All files created as part of a member's or candidate's professional activity are the property of the firm, even those created outside normal work hours. Thus, answer B is incorrect. Answer C is incorrect because the Code and Standards do not prohibit using one's personal computer to complete work for one's employer.

36. B is correct. According to Standard VII(B)—Reference to CFA Institute, the CFA Designation, and the CFA Program, Quinn cannot claim to have finished the CFA Program or be eligible for the CFA charter until he officially learns that he has passed the Level III exam. Until the results for the most recent exam are released, those who sat for the exam should continue to refer to themselves as "candidates." Thus, answer C is incorrect. Answer A is incorrect because members and candidates may discuss areas of practice in which they believe the CFA Program improved their personal skills.

37. A is correct. Hart's decision to invest in the retail fund appears directly correlated with Rodriguez's statement about the successful quarter of Mega Retail and thus violates Standard II(A)—Material Nonpublic Information. Rodriguez's information would be considered material because it would influence the share price of Mega Retail and probably influence the price of the entire exchange-traded retail fund. Thus, answer B is incorrect. Answer C is also incorrect because Rodriguez shared information that was both material and nonpublic. Company officers regularly have such knowledge about their firms, which is not a violation. The sharing of such information, however, even in a conversation between friends, does violate Standard II(A).

38. C is correct. Standard VII(A)—Conduct as Members and Candidates in the CFA Program prohibits providing information to candidates or the public that is considered confidential to the CFA Program. In revealing that questions related to the analysis of inventories and analysis of taxes were on the exam, Park has violated this standard. Answer B is incorrect because the guidance for the standard explicitly acknowledges that members and candidates are allowed to offer their opinions about the CFA Program. Answer A is incorrect because candidates are not prohibited from using outside resources.

39. B is correct. Paper has violated Standard III(D)—Performance Presentation by not disclosing that he was part of a team of managers that achieved the results shown. If he had also included the return of the portion he directly managed, he would not have violated the standard. Thus, answer A is incorrect. Answer C is incorrect because Paper received written permission from his prior employer to include the results.

40. A is correct. Townsend has not provided any information about her clients to the leaders or managers of the golf program; thus, she has not violated Standard III(E)—Preservation of Confidentiality. Providing contact information about her clients for a direct-mail solicitation would have been a violation. Answer B is incorrect because the notice in the newsletter does not violate Standard III(E). Answer C is incorrect because the golf program's fund-raising campaign had already begun, so discussing the opportunity to donate was appropriate.

41. B is correct. Standard IV(A) prohibits employees from soliciting the clients of employers prior to, but not subsequent to, their departure.

42. B is correct. The CFA Code and Standards apply to individual members and candidates of CFA Institute, but firms are encouraged to adopt the Code and Standards as part of their firm code of ethics. The CFA Institute Asset Manager Code of Professional Conduct has been drafted specifically for firms.

43. C is correct. Standard IV(C) states that the member or candidate should decline in writing to accept supervisory responsibility until the firm adopts reasonable procedures to allow him to adequately exercise such responsibility.

44. A is correct. Standard III(D) states that both terminated and active accounts must be included as part of the performance history.

45. A is correct. By placing all clients in one of the two specialized portfolios it operates, Markoe Advisors is not giving adequate consideration to the individual needs, circumstances, and objectives of each client as required by the Standards. In addition, the Standards require that members and candidates disclose all actual and potential conflicts of interest, not just those that relate to current portfolio holdings.

46. A is correct. The Standards require that the supervisor promptly initiate an investigation to ascertain the extent of the violation and should take steps to ensure that violations will not be repeated by limiting or monitoring the employees' activities. The Standards also require that members and candidates obtain written permission from their employer before accepting any compensation or benefits from third parties that may create a conflict of interest.

47. A is correct. Jollie did not act on the material nonpublic information she possessed but waited until it became public. According to the *Standards of Practice Handbook,* "It is not necessary . . . to wait for the slowest methods of delivery."

48. A is correct. Jollie's transaction is a legitimate market order in a thinly-traded security, and Mahsud Financial's policy statement is consistent with CFA Institute Standards relating to the Integrity of Capital Markets.

49. B is correct. It is not a violation to accept compensation from an issuer in exchange for research but such arrangements must be disclosed prominently and in plain language.

50. B is correct. Receiving Dean's written permission does not absolve Jollie of her responsibility to provide attribution. Because Jollie uses the results of the research studies and does not use Dean's interpretation of the studies, it is appropriate to cite the original authors only.

51. B is correct. The first statement is incorrect and the second statement is correct. What is legal is not necessarily ethical. A weak barrier between the employer's research department and investment banking department is a potential source of conflicts.

52. B is correct. Statement 3 is incorrect. The disclosure of a conflict should be made—prominently and in plain language—regardless of whether the member views the conflict as material, so the client can determine the materiality of the conflict. Gifts (the $100 threshold is no longer applicable) from clients should be disclosed to the employer, which is responsible for determining whether the gift could affect the employee's independence and objectivity. Statement 4 is in compliance with CFA Institute Standards. The Mahsud Financial disclosure requirement exceeds, and therefore meets, CFA Institute Standards.

53. A is correct. Klein does not violate the CFA Standards of Professional Conduct when recommending a PlusAccount to Vanderon. His actions comply with Standard III(A)—Loyalty, Prudence, and Care; Standard III(C)—Suitability; and Standard V(A)—Diligence and Reasonable Basis. As required, Klein discloses the fee structure associated with the PlusAccount. Based on the fee structure and Vanderon's trading activity, the PlusAccount appears to be a suitable investment vehicle. By converting to PlusAccount status, Vanderon will incur an annual fee of $1,000 and eliminate approximately $1,800 in annual brokerage commissions. The potential savings of approximately $800 provides a reasonable basis for recommending PlusAccount status.

54. A is correct. Klein does not violate CFA Standards when recommending a PlusAccount to Brown. His actions comply with Standard III(A)—Loyalty, Prudence, and Care; Standard III(C)—Suitability; and Standard V(A)—Diligence and Reasonable Basis. As required, he discloses the fee structure. Based on the fee structure and Brown's annual commissions, the PlusAccount appears to be a suitable investment vehicle. By converting to PlusAccount status, Brown will incur an annual fee of $5,750 and save approximately $6,400 in annual brokerage commissions. The potential savings of approximately $650 provides a reasonable basis for recommending PlusAccount status.

55. B is correct. Klein improperly references the CFA designation when he states "As a CFA charterholder, I am the best qualified to manage your investments." He is in violation of Standard VII(B)—Reference to CFA Institute, the CFA Designation, and the CFA Program.

56. C is correct. Klein violates Standard VI(C) relating to Referral Fees because he fails to provide appropriate disclosure. The Standard states that members must disclose the nature of the consideration or benefit—for example, whether flat fee or percentage basis; one-time or continuing benefit; based on performance—together with the estimated dollar value. Although Klein acknowledges receipt of referral fees from the fund, he does not disclose an estimated dollar value or the nature of the consideration.

57. C is correct. In the months following Brown's change in financial status, Klein is least likely to violate Standard V(B) relating to communication with clients because he disclosed the basic format and other pertinent information regarding PlusAccounts and he distinguished between fact and opinions. During the time period, Klein does not make any new recommendations to Brown and thus is least likely to violate the Standard relating to Communication with Clients and Prospective Clients. During the period, Klein is in jeopardy of violating several other standards including those relating to Loyalty, Prudence, and Care; Suitability; and Diligence and Reasonable Basis. Because of the fee structure, PlusAccount status is not suitable for a client who trades infrequently. Klein neglects his duty of loyalty, prudence, and care by maintaining the PlusAccount Status for more than one year after Brown's change in trading activity. A diligent review of the account would indicate whether a client has a reasonable basis for maintaining PlusAccount status. Thus, Klein is most likely to violate Standards III(A), III(C), and V(A) during the period in question.

58. B is correct. Finnegan violates Standard IV(C)—Responsibilities of Supervisors by failing to ensure that compliance procedures are enforced. As she informed her staff, Harvest "must review each account on an annual

basis to determine whether PlusAccount status remains appropriate." Had Brown's account been reviewed annually in accordance with compliance procedures, it would have been clear that the PlusAccount was no longer suitable for Brown. Delegating supervisory authority to another individual does not violate the Standards.

59. A is correct. Vinken does not violate any CFA Standards of Professional Conduct in his letter. In accordance with Standard III(D)—Performance Presentation, he presents fair, accurate, and complete information when he identifies actual and simulated performance results. Also in accordance with the Standard, he does not guarantee superior future investment returns. In accordance with Standard V(B)—Communication with Clients and Prospective Clients, Vinken describes to his clients and prospective clients the process and logic of the new investment model. By providing the basic details of the model, Vinken provides his clients the basis for understanding the limitations or inherent risks of the investment strategy.

60. A is correct. The policies of both Khadri and Vinken are consistent with Standard V(C)—Record Retention, which states that members and candidates must develop and maintain appropriate records to support their investment analyses, recommendation, actions, performance and other communications with clients and prospective clients. The records required to support recommendations and/or investment actions depend on the role of the member or candidate in the investment decision-making process. Records can be maintained either in hard copy or electronic form. Even though they use different methods, Khadri and Vinken each maintain the appropriate records and have adequate systems of record control.

61. B is correct. Khadri is in violation of Standard III(D). When claiming compliance with GIPS, firms must meet all the requirements. GIPS standards, while voluntary, only apply on a firm-wide basis. Neither a firm nor a fund can claim partial compliance with GIPS standards.

62. B is correct. Standard V(B)—Communications with Clients and Prospective Clients requires the member or candidate to separate and distinguish "facts from opinions" in the presentation of analyses and investment recommendations. Statement 1 in the newsletter states that "China's pegging of the yuan to the U.S. dollar *will* end within the next 12 months which *will* lead to the yuan increasing in value by more than 40%, supporting our over-weighting of Chinese-related stocks in the portfolio." Khadri does not clearly differentiate between opinion and fact. The statement about the future of oil pricing is not as questionable because Khadri uses the term "should" which helps clients understand that this is an opinion and not a certainty. Members may communicate opinions, estimates, and assumptions about future values and possible events but they must take care to differentiate fact from opinion.

63. C is correct. Khadri violates the Standard relating to Performance Presentation because he does not disclose whether the performance results are before or after fees. Standard III(D) requires that members make reasonable efforts to ensure that investment performance information is "fair, accurate, and complete." According to the guidance provided in the *Standards of Practice Handbook*, members should include disclosures that fully explain the performance results (for example, whether the performance is gross of fees, net of fees, or after tax).

64. C is correct. As Khadri provides the corrected information in her letter to the client, she is least likely to violate the Standard relating to performance presentation. She is more likely to violate the Standards relating to

Misconduct and Misrepresentation because she knowingly misrepresents the cause of the error. Standard I(D)—Misconduct requires that members not engage in any professional conduct involving dishonesty. Standard I(C) prohibits members from knowingly making any misrepresentation relating to investment actions and professional activities.

65. A is correct. Mark-ups and mark-downs in net trades are considered fees paid by clients. Standard III(B)—Fair Dealing requires that members treat all clients fairly in light of their investment objectives and circumstances. Treating institutional and retail investors differently is not a violation. According to the Standards, members can differentiate their services to clients but different levels of service must be disclosed and should not negatively affect clients. Omega has made the appropriate disclosures to its clients in compliance with legal and regulatory requirements as well as the Standards.

66. C is correct. Brown is in violation of Standard IV(C)—Responsibilities of Supervisors because he did not ensure that the final system complied with regulatory requirements. According to the Standard, Brown has a responsibility to make reasonable efforts to detect and prevent violations of applicable laws, rules, and regulations. Alerted to potential problems by the compliance department, he had a responsibility to ensure that the modifications corrected the potential problems without introducing new problems.

67. B is correct. Only the institutional trades comply with CFA Institute Standards. All the trades were processed on a net basis. Because the firm disclosed that institutional orders may be executed on a net basis, the institutional trades did not result in a violation. The firm disclosed to clients that in riskless principal trades, retail clients will receive the same execution price without mark-up. Executing the retail orders on a net basis with a $.01 mark-up resulted in a violation of Standards I(C) and III(B) relating to misrepresentation and fair dealing.

68. C is correct. Smith violated his duties to both clients and Omega by not protecting confidential information. By providing Garcia access to confidential information such as changes in recommendations and information regarding block trades, Smith provided Garcia the opportunity to front-run, which could cause harm to both Omega and its clients. Thus, Smith's actions violate his duty of loyalty, prudence, and care to his clients and his duty of loyalty to his employer, Standards III(A) and IV(A), respectively.

69. B is correct. Garcia violated the Standard of Professionalism by engaging in eavesdropping on confidential information including changes in analyst recommendations and pending block trades. According to Standard I(D) members must not engage in professional conduct involving dishonesty, deceit, or fraud or commit any act that reflects adversely on their professional reputation, integrity, or competence. Garcia engages in deceitful conduct in obtaining information from the squawk box. His actions reflect adversely on his professional reputation and integrity and thus violate Standard I(D). Garcia is not in violation of Standard II(A)—Material Nonpublic Information, although he listens to the material nonpublic information on pending block trades. Possession of such material nonpublic information is not a violation of the Standard, which prohibits acting on the information.

70. C is correct. Garcia is in possession of material nonpublic information and acted on it in violation of Standard II(A). After the analyst's recommendation has been issued and/or distributed publicly, Garcia would be free to make the trade.

71. C is correct. According to Standard IV(B), members must not accept compensation that competes with their employers' interest unless they obtain written consent from all parties involved. Thus Riser must receive written, not verbal, consent from his employer before accepting the position on the subsidiary's board. According to the recommended procedures for compliance, Riser should make an immediate written report to his employer specifying the terms of the agreement; the nature of the compensation; the approximate amount of the compensation; and the duration of the agreement. The Standards do not require that members receive permission from clients before accepting board positions.

72. C is correct. Riser least likely violates Standard IV(B)—Additional Compensation Arrangements when participating in the road shows. The Standard provides guidance regarding the acceptance and disclosure of compensation that might conflict with an employer's interests. Participating in the road shows and receiving compensation from the subsidiary do not appear to conflict with his employer's interests.

When participating in the road shows, Riser may violate Standards I(B)—Independence and Objectivity and VI(A)—Disclosure of Conflicts. The Standard relating to Independence and Objectivity requires that members use reasonable care and judgment to achieve and maintain independence and objectivity in their professional activities. Riser's role as board member could jeopardize his objectivity and create a conflict of interest. Standard VI(A)—Disclosure of Conflicts requires that members make full and fair disclosure of all matters that could reasonably be expected to impair the independence and objectivity or interfere with respective duties to the clients, and prospective clients. Full disclosure allows clients to judge motives and possible biases for themselves. Riser does not appear to make adequate disclosure.

73. A is correct. No violation occurred. Riser's recommendation is based on his knowledge of Komm and the firm's "well-managed proprietary funds." He does not have a conflict when he makes the recommendation.

74. A is correct. No violation occurred. Riser is not required to resign his position with the subsidiary. Riser did not engage in any activities that would conflict with his employer's interest before his resignation became effective.

75. A is correct. Riser least likely violates Standard III(C) relating to suitability when purchasing shares for his own account. Riser may violate Standard II(A)—Material Nonpublic Information and possibly Standard VI(B)—Priority of Transactions when making the purchase. If, when trading for his own account, Riser knows that he will place a large block trade for Komm clients, he may be in possession of material nonpublic information. Standard VI(B) covers the activities of all members who have knowledge of pending transactions that may be made on behalf of their clients or employers. Riser has accepted the position of managing partner, has recommended the manager for the product, and knows, or should know, that he will purchase the product for at least some Komm clients once he begins work at Komm. His purchase ahead of Komm's clients might be front-running. Best practice would be to delay his private account purchase until after he purchases shares for clients.

76. C is correct. Standard VI(A)—Disclosure of Conflicts requires that members and candidates make full and fair disclosure of all matters that could reasonably be expected to impair their independence and objectivity or interfere with respective duties to their clients, prospective clients, and their employer. Riser's holdings of the Japanese equity product and his position on the board of the subsidiary could impair his objectivity and must be disclosed to clients. He need not disclose his compensation from the subsidiary because it is not a referral fee.

77. A is correct. Both the first and second presentations are consistent with the CFA Institute Code and Standards. According to the Standards, candidates may reference their participation in the CFA Program as long as they are active, but they cannot imply a partial designation. A statement about the level of the exam successfully passed or a level of the exam upcoming is appropriate, whereas indicating or implying a partial designation or citing a future date of expected completion of a level in the CFA Program is prohibited.

78. A is correct. Danko directs his trading with FTI only after taking into account FTI's ability to provide best execution. There is no indication that FTI requires a certain amount of trading for access to the website, only that access is provided in exchange for orders. This arrangement for trading in return for research services is discussed in the Guidance to the Standards under Standard III(A).

79. C is correct. The information that Danko received is material non-public information. Disclosing the information to the public is not his role; further, earning gains for his clients does not excuse the violation and is not a justifiable reason for taking action on the material non-public information. The only entities that should release the information are the corporations or another entity with their permission, perhaps FTI.

80. B is correct. Investment decision-making due to speed or based on third-party research alone is insufficient for meeting the standard set by Standard V(A).

81. A is correct. When an issue is oversubscribed, allocations cannot be made to accounts where members and candidates have beneficial interest; client orders must be filled first.

82. A is correct. A blackout period is appropriate for investment decision-making personnel so that managers do not take advantage of their knowledge of trading activity and 'front run' the trade. The actual detail of the blackout period is not specified in the Standards, only that one should exist.

STUDY SESSION 2
ETHICAL AND PROFESSIONAL STANDARDS IN PRACTICE

Using examples and case studies, the readings in this study session demonstrate the use of the CFA Institute Code of Ethics and Standards of Professional Conduct as a body of principles for ethical reasoning and decision making. The readings serve as effective aids in understanding and internalizing the values and standards presented in the CFA Institute *Standards of Practice Handbook*. By applying the Code and Standards to case study conflicts, the candidate will gain experience identifying and explaining fundamental principles of conduct that serve as the basis for dealing with real world challenges.

The Asset Manager Code of Professional Conduct uses the basic tenets of the CFA Institute Code of Ethics and Standards of Professional Conduct to establish ethical and professional standards for firms managing client assets. The Asset Manager Code of Professional Conduct also extends the Code and Standards to address investment management firm practices regarding trading, compliance, security pricing, and disclosure.

READING ASSIGNMENTS

Reading 3	Ethics in Practice	
	Ethics in Practice, by Philip Lawton, CFA	
Reading 4	The Consultant	
	Ethics Cases	
Reading 5	Pearl Investment Management (A), (B), and (C)	
	Ethics Cases	
Reading 6	Asset Manager Code of Professional Conduct	
	by Kurt Schacht, CFA, Jonathan J. Stokes, JD, and	
	Glenn Doggett, CFA	

ETHICS IN PRACTICE
by Philip Lawton, CFA

LEARNING OUTCOMES

The candidate should be able to:	Mastery
a. explain the ethical responsibilities required by each of the six provisions of the Code of Ethics and the seven Standards of Professional Conduct;	☐
b. interpret the Code of Ethics and Standards of Professional Conduct in situations involving issues of professional integrity and formulate corrective actions where appropriate.	☐

INTRODUCTION 1

Investment professionals often face unanticipated ethical dilemmas in their work. Training and practice can help them recognize issues, and sound, relevant principles of ethical conduct can help them make appropriate decisions. Written for investment professionals, this reading is an introduction and overview of the CFA Institute Code of Ethics and Standards of Professional Conduct (the Code and Standards), revised in 2005. Sections 2 through 4 provide a conceptual framework for reading, interpreting, and applying the Code and Standards: Section 2 discusses the criteria for a profession and the place of ethics in the investment profession; Section 3 treats the relationship between ethics and the law; and Section 4 outlines an approach to ethical reasoning, using the Code and Standards as a set of principles for ethically positive action in concrete situations. Sections 5 and 6 are devoted to the Preamble and the provisions of the Code. Section 7 introduces the Standards, and Sections 8 through 14 present and explain the provisions of the Standards with numerous practical examples. Section 15 sets up the case studies following the text as exercises in ethical reasoning. A summary is provided for review, and multiple-choice questions give readers an opportunity to test their comprehension of specific provisions of the Code and Standards. The reading is followed by an appendix of five short case studies, lifelike situations in which investment professionals encounter ethical challenges in their work.

2   ETHICS AND THE INVESTMENT PROFESSION

What makes investment analysis a profession as opposed to a business, a trade, or a craft? There is extensive philosophical literature on the criteria defining a profession. For the purpose of this discussion, however, there are two factors that, taken together, can be said to distinguish a profession from other forms of work:

1. an established body of knowledge
2. a commitment to a broader good than the practitioner's self-interest[1]

Investment analysis is clearly based upon a body of knowledge, including economic and financial theory, empirical findings, and analytical techniques. The rigorous curriculum of the CFA Program is accordingly designed to equip practitioners with the concepts and skills to meet the actual demands of their work. In addition to ethical and professional standards, the CFA body of knowledge includes quantitative methods; economics; financial statement analysis; corporate finance; the analysis of equity, debt, derivative, and alternative investment instruments; and portfolio management, including performance evaluation and presentation. There is, moreover, general agreement on the scope of this body of knowledge. With the likely exception of industry-specific ethical standards of practice, much the same list of technical topics would be covered in a graduate business school course of study centering on investments. Investment analysis patently satisfies the first criterion for a profession: It rests upon an established body of knowledge, one that continues to grow as new insights are published.

This is enough to characterize investment analysis as a trade or a craft (admittedly a highly advanced craft) but not yet as a profession; taken singly, the criteria mentioned above are necessary but not sufficient conditions.

The many ways in which the discipline of investment analysis may serve the practitioner's self-interest are readily apparent. A career in investment analysis offers extraordinary opportunities for intellectual development, creativity, and prestige. Qualified individuals can choose to work in small firms or large national or multinational corporations. Depending upon their interests and talents, they can (among many other alternatives) value securities, make deals, or manage portfolios. They can choose a specialization rewarding superior quantitative skills or a position requiring an exceptional ability to form relationships and to explain technical matters clearly; they can stay close to home or travel frequently to distant locations. A high level of income is also a potential benefit. But, beyond the practitioner's self-interest, what broader good does investment analysis advance in the same way, for example, that medicine promotes health and at its best the law champions justice and liberty?

---

[1] These criteria are adapted from Thomas Donaldson, "Are Business Managers 'Professionals'?", *Business Ethics Quarterly,* Vol. 10, No. 1 (January 2000), pp. 83–94.

In the most general terms, for a society as a whole, investment analysis may be said to foster the creation of wealth by attending to the efficient allocation of resources in a market economy. The fundamental task of investment analysis is pricing securities in view of their riskiness, that is, estimating their present worth or intrinsic value in light of current and prospective capital market, economic, and industry conditions and the issuer's credit quality, competitive strength, and earnings outlook. Collectively, security analysts contribute to market efficiency by attempting to identify the most attractive investment opportunities, and in so doing, they improve the likelihood that prices fairly reflect the best information publicly available. Their purchase and sale recommendations influence investors' decisions and, it may be hoped, tend over the long term to channel financial assets to their most economically productive uses. *A first greater good qualifying investment analysis as a profession is the promotion of fair and efficient capital markets.*

As a practical matter, however, investment analysis is for the most part conducted on behalf of clients, institutional or individual investors. Its direct purpose is not to nurture economic expansion but to achieve the investors' financial objectives. For the trustees of a pension plan, the primary investment objective is to earn returns enabling the sponsor to maintain sufficient plan assets to meet current and projected liabilities for the benefit of plan participants. For the officers of an endowment fund or a foundation, the overriding objective is to fund the spending program without loss of principal. For the individual investor, the objective might be to produce current income or to save for the future. *A second broader good served by investment analysis is the clients' financial well-being.* Along with the body of knowledge, it is a dual commitment to promoting fair and efficient capital markets and to protecting and furthering the investing clients' interests that makes investment analysis a profession.

Although they are not generally identified as criteria, there are other characteristics that professions typically exhibit. One of the most noteworthy is having a code of ethics endorsed by a professional association and designed to set forth shared values such as integrity and independence of judgment.[2] These values notably include the practitioner's commitment to maintaining his or her competence (the body of knowledge) and the primacy of the clients' interests (the broader good). A code of ethics articulates the ideals to which the profession adheres. If it is thoughtfully written by experienced leaders committed to furthering the profession, and especially if it is complemented by standards of practice, a code of ethics usefully offers practitioners principled guidance on the basis of which they can make ethically sound decisions. It additionally functions as an authoritative source to which they can refer in justifying a course of action to their colleagues and managers.

Ethical values are not incidental to the profession of investment analysis, nor for that matter to any other line of work that qualifies as professional. In effect, those who identify themselves as investment professionals are making a claim, not only about their expertise but also about their commitment to a broader good than their own self-interest. They are implicitly proclaiming (or "professing") their adherence to values like honesty and diligence and to principles such as respecting the priority of the client's interests and promoting the integrity of the capital markets. CFA charterholders and candidates can look to the CFA Institute Code of Ethics and Standards of Professional Conduct for practical direction in realizing these values and actualizing these principles in their work.

---

[2] Many professions are also licensed by regulatory authorities.

3   PROFESSIONAL ETHICS AND THE LAW

Why is it not enough just to obey the law?

Certainly investment professionals are ethically obligated to be familiar with applicable laws and regulations—the rules directly governing their work. They are expected to know and understand the legal and regulatory requirements that pertain to their professional activities. In the CFA Institute Standards of Professional Conduct, this fundamental expectation appears as the first item in the first standard, Professionalism, but it could also be considered a matter of competence to practice, and to supervise others, in a given area of specialization. Unless they are responsible for their firm's compliance, investment analysts generally need not be expert in legal and regulatory matters. They do have to know enough, however, to be able to conduct their routine work by the rules and to recognize when it is appropriate to seek authoritative guidance.

Investment professionals are, furthermore, ethically obligated to abide by applicable law and regulation. Thinkers have taken many positions on the philosophical foundations of positive law, but in many societies there is a tacit presumption that illegal actions are usually unethical. The CFA Institute Standards of Professional Conduct hold that investment professionals must not only know but also comply with the laws, rules, and regulations governing their work. In general, if an action is illegal, it is also deemed unethical.

This is not to suggest that there is no such thing as an unjust law. Investment professionals are not *ethically* bound to comply with unjust laws. Nor, clearly, does the presupposition that illegal activity is unethical mean that legal action is necessarily ethical. For example, it may not be against the law to overstate one's expertise in order to win a job or a client, but it certainly conflicts with the fundamental ethical principles of honesty and integrity. There are significant ethical obligations beyond what is required by law, and it is therefore possible to be legally unassailable but ethically in the wrong, to the certain detriment of one's reputation and the possible disadvantage of others who merit honest and equitable treatment. This is why it is not enough, in striving for the ethical excellence legitimately expected of investment professionals, simply to obey the law.

4   INTERPRETING AND APPLYING THE CFA INSTITUTE CODE AND STANDARDS

Ethical reasoning is logical but not mathematically precise. The imperatives of the Code of Ethics and Standards of Professional Conduct have the general form, "Members of CFA Institute and candidates for the CFA designation must do *X*," for instance, "act with integrity." These are general orders based upon abstract concepts. Although apparently uncomplicated, words and expressions like "integrity" and "respect" and "in a professional and ethical manner" are not technical terms susceptible to clear-cut and unequivocal definition. They remain words used in ordinary language with all its ambiguity. This is not at all to suggest that they cannot be understood or that a consensus cannot be reached on their meaning. But it does mean that interpreting them may take some effort.

Consider Standard V(B.2), discussed later in this reading. It requires individuals to use "reasonable judgment" in identifying the factors that are important to their investment analysis, recommendations, or actions and to address those factors in their communications to clients and prospective clients. "Reasonable judgment" is a variant of phrases encountered elsewhere in the Code of Ethics and Standards of Professional Conduct. For example, the Code calls upon those people who are governed by its provisions to "use reasonable care and exercise independent professional judgment"; Standard I(B)—Independence and Objectivity refers to "reasonable care and judgment"; and Standard III(A)—Loyalty, Prudence, and Care requires covered persons to "act with reasonable care and exercise prudent judgment."

Let us make two observations. First, the term "judgment" is associated with "care" in the Code and Standards. Second, whether an investment professional is using "reasonable judgment" in identifying and communicating pertinent factors is itself a matter of judgment. This is not an impasse, but it is a challenge. Judgment is acquired with education and experience (and education may be seen as a means of gaining experience more systematically and rapidly than personally witnessing events would permit). The "reasonable judgment" required by the Code and Standards is the practical wisdom displayed by mature experts, competent investment professionals qualified by training and practice not only to identify relevant factors but also to evaluate their significance and to weigh their relative importance.

It is not only the words that may, despite their apparent simplicity and straightforwardness, be open to interpretation. It is, above all, the circumstances in which we find ourselves that may prove complicated and ambiguous. It is impossible, however, to anticipate every case, much less to capture the nuances of each situation. The idea of a code of ethics is to have a concise set of general principles which one can bear in mind as specific questions arise. Aristotle wrote, "The whole theory of [right] conduct is bound to be an outline only and not an exact system. . . . And if this is true of the general theory of ethics, still less is exact precision possible in dealing with particular cases of conduct, for these come under no science or professional tradition, but the agents themselves have to consider what is suited to the circumstances on each occasion, just as is the case with the art of medicine or navigation."[3] The CFA Institute Code and Standards articulate general principles and shared values to guide investment analysts, but one of the basic practical issues for ethical decision making is how to apply them correctly to complicated situations.

In any specific case, the initial and easiest step is to determine which provisions of the Code and Standards are pertinent. Consider, for example, having to explain the risks of a private equity investment opportunity to a client. The issuer, a manufacturer of capital goods, has an exciting new product but will face substantial challenges in winning acceptance in the marketplace, where competitors are entrenched and there are significant switching costs for potential buyers. How does the analyst choose the right words to characterize the risk? A relevant section of the Standards of Professional Conduct is Section I(C)—Misrepresentation: "Members and candidates must not knowingly make any misrepresentations relating to investment analysis, recommendations, actions, or other professional activities." Other sections may also apply—for example, the requirements to have a reasonable and adequate basis for investment analyses and recommendations and to include the pertinent factors in client communications—but this one, prohibiting misrepresentation, is unquestionably germane.

Of course, that doesn't directly help answer the analyst's question, how to convey the riskiness of a deal when the financial projections are necessarily based upon assumptions about such matters as the future state of the economy, industrial purchasing managers' behavior, and competitors' responses. But it

---

[3] Aristotle, *Nichomachean Ethics*, II.ii.3–5. Translated by H. Rackham. Loeb Classical Library, Vol. XIX. Harvard University Press (1968), pp. 75–77.

does offer some direction. For example, characterizing the issuer's early-stage business risk as "slight" could be adjudged misrepresentation by objective, experienced investment analysts.

Interpreting the Code and Standards and applying them to actual situations, often involving real money, complex investment strategies, and several parties at interest, requires ethical wisdom. Even with a code of ethics and a set of professional standards written specifically to guide investment analysts, there aren't cookbook solutions for many concrete ethical problems. It takes training to recognize when there are ethical as opposed to "merely" technical matters to be addressed, and it takes practice to discern the principles and values at stake, to formulate the alternatives, and to decide upon the most suitable course of action in a particular situation.

Nonetheless, some general ideas, or at least some helpful questions, may be suggested. First, having identified the pertinent sections of the Code and Standards, the analyst must consider whether a course of action under consideration is consistent with their intent. Does the proposed action conform to the Code and Standards, or would another resolution be more in line with the principles and values they advance?

Second, when evaluating an alternative in view of the Code and Standards, it is useful to consider what the client would be likely to think if he were told all the circumstances. Would the client then agree that you had done the right thing? Or would the client conclude that you are untrustworthy?

Third, if your decision and the full circumstances surrounding it came to light, would your own or your firm's reputation for fair dealing be enhanced or compromised? How would it read in the press? Of course, not all journalists have the training to describe complex financial instruments and strategies correctly, but they themselves are generally subject to their own publishers' codes stressing integrity, independence, and accuracy. Assume for the present purpose that an article setting forth your action was comprehensive and factually correct. How would it sound?

Finally, is your decision commendable? Is it consistent with what one would expect of a leader? Does it set a good example for others? In a broader context, practicing the profession in an ethical manner means not merely following the rules but trying to become a person who knows and does the right thing.

Let us now turn to a survey of the Code of Ethics.

5   PREAMBLE TO THE CODE OF ETHICS

The Preamble to the CFA Institute Code of Ethics makes three points. It places the Code in the context of CFA Institute's educational mission, specifies who is bound by it, and mentions the sanctions to which violators are subject.

Throughout its long history, CFA Institute and its predecessors[4] have been dedicated to serving investors and members as a global leader in educating and examining investment managers and analysts and in sustaining high standards of professional conduct. CFA Institute's stated mission is "to lead the investment profession globally by setting the highest standards of ethics, education, and pro-

---

[4] CFA Institute is the name given the former Association for Investment Management and Research (AIMR) by vote of the membership in 2004. AIMR was founded in January 1990, when the Financial Analysts Federation (FAF) merged with the Institute of Chartered Financial Analysts (ICFA). The FAF was originally established in 1947 as a service organization for investment professionals in its societies and chapters. The ICFA was founded in 1959 to examine candidates and award the Chartered Financial Analyst (CFA) designation.

fessional excellence." It carries forward this goal not only through the CFA Program but also through conferences, publications, and the activities of its affiliated societies around the world.

Clearly, the Code of Ethics and the Standards of Professional Conduct are central to the mission of CFA Institute as a professional standard-setting association. As the Preamble mentions, the Code and the Standards were originally formulated in the 1960s. The Financial Analysts Federation first adopted a code of ethics in 1962, and the Institute of Chartered Financial Analysts adapted the FAF code in 1964.[5] The ethical standards have been expanded and clarified over time, but they have consistently emphasized certain core values such as the priority of client transactions over personal transactions. The version of the Code and Standards currently in force was revised by the members of the Standards of Practice Council in the period 2003–05.

The Code and Standards apply to all CFA Institute members, including CFA charterholders, and to candidates for the CFA designation. Upon joining CFA Institute as a member or entering the CFA program, individuals agree to be bound by the ethical standards.

The Preamble indicates that disciplinary sanctions may be imposed for violations of the Code and Standards. This position reflects the longstanding conviction of CFA Institute that breaches of ethical standards are serious matters; even the first version of the ethical guidelines, published over forty years ago, provided for terminating a violator's right to use the CFA designation. CFA Institute has developed carefully defined protocols for dealing with alleged infractions.

To remain in good standing, members of CFA Institute must submit an annual Professional Conduct Statement. Failure to file a Professional Conduct Statement can result in suspension of one's membership in CFA Institute, one's right to use the CFA designation, or both. By filing the Professional Conduct Statement, members disclose whether they have been the subject of any written complaints involving their professional conduct or of certain types of legal or regulatory action. Members additionally certify that they agree to comply with CFA Institute's Code of Ethics, Standards of Professional Conduct, Bylaws, and Rules of Procedure for Proceedings Related to Professional Conduct and to cooperate with CFA Institute in any investigation of their conduct. The current form of the Professional Conduct Statement is available on the CFA Institute website.

CFA Institute also accepts complaints from others about its members' professional conduct. Information about how to make a complaint appears on the CFA Institute website.

Investigations of alleged violations of the Code and Standards and subsequent actions including hearing panels, review panels, and the imposition of disciplinary sanctions are governed by the CFA Institute Rules of Procedure for Proceedings Related to Professional Conduct. Disciplinary sanctions may be imposed if a candidate is found to have violated the Code and Standards. Possible sanctions can include private censure, public censure, prohibition from future participation in the CFA Program, revocation of CFA Institute membership, and revocation of the right to use the CFA designation. Complete information about disciplinary procedures, including provisions for dealing with candidate misconduct during the CFA examination administration process, is available on the CFA Institute website.

---

[5] Nancy Regan, *The Institute of Chartered Financial Analysts: A Twenty-Five Year History,* The Institute of Chartered Financial Analysts (1987), pp. 50–52. The original (1964) version of the ICFA's ethical guidelines is reprinted as an appendix to Regan's history (p. 169).

THE CODE OF ETHICS

The Code of Ethics applies to members of CFA Institute, including CFA charterholders, and candidates for the CFA designation. In the Code, they are collectively referred to as "members and candidates." (We will use the phrase "covered persons" to refer to the individuals to whom the Code and Standards apply.) Note that the Code and Standards apply to individuals, not to investment organizations.

The Code stipulates that covered persons must adhere to six provisions.

I. First, they must "act with integrity, competence, diligence, respect, and in an ethical manner" in their professional dealings. "Integrity" is a key word throughout the Code and the accompanying Standards of Professional Conduct. It means "honesty," but it further connotes wholeness, consistency, or being uncompromised and unflawed. Integrity is, of course, a word sometimes used in contexts other than ethics. For example, architects and engineers speak of a building's "structural integrity," referring to its stability, and quantitative analysts speak of "data integrity," signifying the reliability of statistical information. People of integrity can be relied upon to be trustworthy and truthful.

In this context, "competence" may be seen as an ethical requirement for individuals of integrity who hold themselves out as having expertise in a certain area. Investment professionals claim to have special qualifications, acquired through training and experience, equipping them to offer others sound advice about securities, whether or not they are financially compensated for their service. Individuals who identify themselves as professionals imply that they have mastered the relevant body of knowledge. But to assert something one knows to be false—to claim to have expertise or competence one actually lacks—would bespeak a lack of integrity.

"Diligence" and "respect" are also required of covered persons under the Code of Ethics. Diligence—conscientious attention to the task at hand, whether valuing a security, managing a portfolio, conducting an asset/liability study, carrying out a manager search, recommending an investment strategy, analyzing performance, or engaging in any other professional activity—naturally accompanies technical competence, on the one hand, and respect for oneself, one's employer, and the investor, on the other.

Finally, the first point of the Code adds the requirement that covered persons conduct themselves "in an ethical manner." Those to whom integrity, competence, diligence, respect, and ethical treatment are due include the public, clients and prospective clients, employers and employees, colleagues in the investment profession, and "other participants in the global capital markets." In short, covered persons are called upon with the hardness of the ethical "must" to practice the profession of investment analysis in accordance with high moral principles, even when they are not face-to-face or in a direct interpersonal relationship with other individuals, as they are with their clients and coworkers.

II. The second provision of the Code requires covered persons to place the integrity of the investment profession and the interests of clients above their own personal interests. Covered persons are called upon not to damage or compromise the profession, the community of experts serving a greater good than its members' self-interest. One of the greater goods advanced by the investment profession is the clients' financial well-being. In this key provision of the Code, covered persons are specifically directed to place their clients' interests above their own. The primacy of the clients' interests will be a consistent theme in the Standards of Professional Conduct.

III. The third requirement is to use "reasonable care" and "independent professional judgment" in professional practice. Presupposing competence and diligence, exercising reasonable care means identifying and taking into account all the factors that materially affect the investment characteristics of a security or a strategy. For example, competent, diligent analysts using reasonable care in evaluating a fixed income private placement will consider not only the security issuer's capital structure, competitive position, and earnings potential, but also such factors as the quality of its management, the dependability and relative power of its suppliers and customers, and the strength of the restrictive covenants intended to reduce the lender's risk, among many other things. If they are deciding whether to recommend the deal to a client, they will also think about its suitability in view of the investors' financial objectives and risk tolerance.

Exercising independent professional judgment is an absolutely fundamental requirement of the Code of Ethics as well as the Standards of Professional Conduct examined below. It means thinking for oneself and evaluating investment alternatives dispassionately in order to determine what course of action is best for the client, the investor. Analysts must reach their own conclusions, no matter what answer their management or colleagues might favor. They must, moreover, conduct investment analysis objectively, with the good of the investor in mind and, above all, without regard to their own personal financial or other interests.

Occasionally, conflicts of interest are manifest. For instance, a large financial services organization may offer incentives motivating its employees with direct client contact to sell additional products and services. Other cases in which there is no overt pecuniary conflict of interest may be more subtle. For example, investment consultants may find it attractive to channel client assets to a particular advisor, not in exchange for direct financial compensation but simply to demonstrate their influence or to gain power.

Under the Code, however, investment professionals must first and always consider the client's best interest, and place the client's interest ahead of their own. In the examples cited above, it may well be the case that an additional product offered by the investment professional's employer is entirely appropriate to meet a real client need and the investment advisor under consideration may in fact be the best choice, but the professional must think critically and proceed with great care before making these recommendations. The importance of exercising independent professional judgment cannot be overstated.

IV. The fourth proviso of the Code of Ethics holds that covered persons must "practice and encourage others to practice in a professional and ethical manner that will reflect credit on themselves and the profession." Essential here is the admonition to promote ethical and creditable behavior on the part of others—not only one's peers but also one's subordinates (toward whom the investment professional has special responsibilities) and one's managers. It is incumbent upon those subject to the Code to foster a culture in which ethical ideals are valued, not merely in name but in daily practice.

With one's peers, it may be possible to lead only by personal example, although occasions may arise in the ordinary course of business to counsel colleagues on the applicability of the Code and Standards to specific situations. Some firms additionally have the policy of submitting their employees' work to peer review. For instance, a pension or asset consulting firm may expect its professionals periodically to make formal presentations and to respond to their colleagues' questions about each client's entire investment program, in order to ensure that suboptimal structures or strategies do not go unexamined or unaddressed with the passage of time.

The greatest opportunity to encourage others to practice the investment profession ethically is undoubtedly to be found in a supervisory role, both informally in the day-to-day conduct of business and formally in staff training and performance reviews. Supervisors are not only accountable for their staff's actions, in a professional setting, they are also coaches, and they can have a lasting effect on their employees' professional development. However, employees should also take the initiative to bring up pertinent ethical issues with their managers, who might not otherwise be alert to potential missteps.

V. The fifth requirement of the Code of Ethics is to "promote the integrity of, and uphold the rules governing, global capital markets." Contributing to the fair and efficient functioning of the capital markets is one of the "greater goods" that make investment analysis a profession. Under the Code, there is a positive ethical obligation not only to respect and comply with applicable laws, rules, and regulations but to act in such a way as to foster and justify investors' trust in the equitability of the markets. Securities markets are based upon the fair pricing of risky assets and vitally dependent upon investors' confidence. In addition to causing possible economic damages to specific parties, actions intended to manipulate capital markets to the unjust advantage of certain participants undermine public trust in the fairness of market-based asset pricing. Obvious examples include unduly promoting or "hyping" stocks to trigger short-term price increases for a quick sale and circulating unfounded or exaggerated rumors to drive down the price of a stock in which one has a short position. The Code of Ethics prohibits such actions.

VI. Finally, the Code re-emphasizes the importance of professional competence by requiring covered persons to "maintain and improve their own competence and strive to maintain and improve the competence of other investment professionals." Staying intellectually fit and keeping up with advances in the field of investment analysis as well as with new investment products and strategies is mandatory if one is to make sound decisions and well-informed recommendations. The CFA curriculum and examination program are designed for generalists who are expected to be conversant with a wide range of topics. In addition, in the course of their careers members and charterholders often specialize in highly technical domains such as evaluating mortgage-backed securities or negotiating private placements, to name just a few of the possibilities. In order to maintain and enhance their expertise, investment professionals employed in these fields have to stay current with such matters as deal structures, legal developments, and market trends as well as new analytic techniques. One could make similar observations about other specialized areas of professional practice.

As noted, covered persons are further called upon to endeavor to maintain and improve other investment professionals' competence. Supervisors, of course, have particularly relevant opportunities to foster their professional staff members' continuing development through some combination of on-the-job coaching, internal educational programs, and, if possible, outside seminars or conferences. However, even "individual contributors" without managerial responsibilities can routinely share what they learn about the state of the art with their colleagues. This practice fosters excellence in the firm and contributes, however modestly and indirectly, to the repute of the investment profession.

INTRODUCTION TO THE STANDARDS OF PROFESSIONAL CONDUCT

The Standards of Professional Conduct are composed of seven sets of norms identified as:

  I Professionalism;

 II Integrity of Capital Markets;

III Duties to Clients;

IV Duties to Employers;

 V Investment Analysis, Recommendations, and Actions;

VI Conflicts of Interest; and

VII Responsibilities as a CFA Member or CFA Candidate.

The Standards complement the broad imperatives of the Code by addressing topics of concern more explicitly. We will give an overview of the Standards here, with particular attention to their rationale—the values and ideals they reflect and advance. However, we refer the reader to the Guidance for Standards I–VII reading for the most authoritative and detailed direction in interpreting and applying them correctly in specific professional situations.

STANDARD I—PROFESSIONALISM   8

Under the heading of Professionalism, the first set of Standards sets forth members' and candidates' responsibilities with regard to knowledge of the law, independence and objectivity, misrepresentation, and misconduct.

Standard I(A)—Knowledge of the Law advances three ideas. First, covered persons must understand and comply with all applicable laws, rules, and regulations, including the Code and Standards themselves. Not all investment professionals are expected to have the scope and level of expertise achieved by compliance officers and attorneys specializing in securities law and regulatory matters. However, covered persons are required to have sufficient familiarity with the laws, rules, and regulations directly affecting their work to recognize covered situations and to avoid violations.

Second, in the event of a conflict between the requirements of different rule-making bodies, covered persons must comply with the more strict law, rule, or regulation. With increasing globalization, investment professionals working across borders are often subject to more than one legal system. It would not be in the spirit of meeting the highest standards to use compliance with the more liberal conventions of one country as a dodge to avoid or evade the more stringent laws and regulations of another. In addition, there may be instances when the ethical obligations imposed by the Code and Standards are more exacting than the applicable legal and regulatory requirements. In such cases, the provisions of the Code and Standards prevail.

Third, covered persons must not knowingly participate or assist in, and must dissociate themselves from, any violation of the laws, rules, or regulations governing their professional activities. "Knowingly participating or assisting" in a breach of the rules means 1) knowing the law, as required by this standard, 2) being aware of the factual situation, and 3) nonetheless playing an active or facilitating role in the commission of a violation. Covered persons must not only decline to play such a part but also take positive steps to "dissociate" or distance themselves from a transgression.

The specific steps to be taken depend upon situational factors. For example, it may suffice for investment professionals to call an actual or contemplated breach to the attention of their colleagues or manager who simply might not be aware of both the law and the facts. If the investment professionals are supervisors, however, and members of their staff engage in illegal or unethical activity, it is their responsibility to put a stop to it and to initiate corrective or disciplinary action. There may be cases when it is appropriate to contact the firm's compliance officer. There may also be cases when it becomes necessary to resign from the firm or to report the matter to the authorities. Generally, progressive escalation is a sound approach. It is prudent, moreover, to document one's efforts to correct a transgression. What is not acceptable is to allow oneself to be compromised by going along with improper practices.

Standard I(B)—Independence and Objectivity goes to the heart of the investment professional's ethical responsibilities because it requires that the clients' best interests be evaluated and served impartially. In other words, the only part investment professionals should take is the client's, and their only interest should be the client's best interest, the client's financial welfare. The standard sets forth two mandates, one positive and the other negative. First, covered persons *must* "use reasonable care and judgment to achieve and maintain independence and objectivity in their professional activities." Second, they *must not* offer or accept any sort of consideration that could be "reasonably expected" to impair their own or another's independence and objectivity.

Interestingly, observing these mandates necessarily presupposes mature professional judgment and independent thinking. For example, because the standard does not specify a monetary amount as a guideline for determining that offering or accepting a gift is improper, it is up to investment professionals to make their own decisions about a questionable exchange, with due attention to firm-specific guidelines for employee conduct. The only rule of thumb suggested in the standard is that if a consideration could sensibly be perceived as unfitting by others, notably including the client and other investment professionals committed to the value of uncompromised objectivity, then it is to be rejected. In general, ethical decision-making means not only knowing the rules but also discerning the most fitting course of action, and ethical discernment requires, in turn, a willingness and ability to think for oneself.

Security and credit analysts may be subject to pressure to conform their opinions to the desires of interested parties, usually for favorable coverage. For example, the firm that employs them may have extraneous commercial lending or investment banking relationships with issuers of publicly traded securities covered by the analyst group. The companies whose security prices are influenced by analysts' appraisals certainly prefer positive reports and recommendations, as do portfolio managers who are holding the securities. A great deal of money may ride on the analysts' opinions, and in the recent past, interested parties have been found to exert direct or indirect pressure in an attempt to influence analysts' conclusions. A well-managed firm whose organizational culture values objectivity will take steps to protect the analysts' independence, but it nonetheless remains the analysts' responsibility to be vigilant in maintaining impartiality.[6]

It is not security and credit analysts alone, of course, who are susceptible to outside influences. For instance, investment professionals working on behalf of institutional investors are no less required to uphold their independence in decision-making. Investment officers of pension plans, endowments, and foundations are often approached by service providers such as custodians, securities lending organizations, and transition managers as well as long-term investment managers seeking to win business. The influential consultants to whom plan sponsors look for sound, objective advice in structuring, implementing, and monitoring their investment program effectively serve as gatekeepers to the same service providers. Plan sponsors and investment consultants subject to the Code and Standards must take care to ensure that their actions promote the best interests of those who have a legitimate claim on their professionalism, without regard

---

[6] See the CFA Institute Research Objectivity Standards (2003) on the CFA Institute website.

to their own personal advantage and the desires of other parties. In the cases mentioned here, pension plan assets must be invested for the benefit of the plan participants, and endowment and foundation assets must be managed to support current and future spending in furtherance of the institution's stated objectives. Investment bankers and dealmakers are likewise required to act in the client's interest without, of course, undermining the integrity of the capital markets.

Standard I(C)—Misrepresentation holds that covered persons must not knowingly misstate facts relating to investment analysis, recommendations, actions, or "other professional activities." Misrepresentation is not merely outright falsification but also includes misleading a client or decision-maker. For instance, slanting a proposal by selectively omitting or downplaying certain factors and unduly emphasizing others so as to persuade the client to approve a preferred course of action would likely constitute misrepresentation. A key word is "knowingly." In this context, if investment professionals know *or should know under the duties of competence and diligence* that an analysis is biased and nonetheless proceed to recommend or to take inadequately supported investment action, they are in breach of the Standard. They may not have consciously and deliberately intended to mislead, although they may have acted in bad faith by not taking care to present all the facts that affect the investment characteristics to be taken into account in making an objectively defensible recommendation or decision.

Several kinds of misrepresentation merit special attention. The prohibition of misrepresentation implicitly bars covered persons from making or implying any guarantees or assurances about any investment. In other words, it is impermissible to tell clients or prospective clients that an investment cannot fail, that a positive return is assured, or that there is no possibility of an unfavorable outcome. In fact, there are no risk-free assets.[7] Nor are there risk-free strategies; even well-designed hedges structured to lock in returns regardless of interim market movements are subject to unexpected outcomes due to faulty assumptions or extraordinary events. It is a most serious violation of professional ethics to mislead a client into believing that a proposed investment is guaranteed. By extension, it is improper to understate the riskiness of a recommended course of action.

It is, however, permissible and indeed desirable to communicate accurate factual information about the characteristics, terms, and issuer's obligations under a particular instrument or type of security. For example, fixed income instruments known as Guaranteed Investment Contracts (GICs) are a form of "stable value investments." GICs are obligations of insurance companies providing a fixed interest rate and a fixed maturity. They are typically accorded amortized cost or book value accounting treatment that exempts the investor from reporting changes in market value due to fluctuations in the level of interest rates.[8] Investment advisors suggesting the use of a GIC or similar stable value instrument should clearly explain its contractual terms. They should also clarify that, despite the appearance of the word "guaranteed" in the very name of the instrument, there is credit risk, and the quality of the "guarantee" depends upon the creditworthiness of the issuer.

---

[7] Capital market theory assumes the existence of a risk-free asset (an asset with zero variance) and the ability of investors to borrow and lend at a risk-free rate of return. However, even default-free short-term securities are subject to changes in the supply and demand of capital and the expected rate of inflation. See Frank K. Reilly, CFA and Keith C. Brown, CFA, *Investment Analysis and Portfolio Management,* 7th ed., South-Western (2003), pp. 17–19.

[8] For a more complete description, see Kenneth L. Walker, "Stable Value Investments," in Frank J. Fabozzi, CFA, Ed., *The Handbook of Fixed Income Securities,* 6th ed., McGraw-Hill (2001), pp. 399–400.

Plagiarism—copying material prepared by another, or using such material with minor changes but in substantially the same form, without acknowledging the source of the material and identifying the author or publisher—is another form of misrepresentation. Investment analysis is heavily dependent upon others' original work. It is imperative for covered persons to cite the sources of ideas, facts, and opinions taken substantially unchanged from others and, when appropriate, to secure the owners' permission to use their work. Tacitly giving the reader or listener to believe that somebody else's work is one's own constitutes misrepresentation because it may lead others to infer that an investment professional has greater credibility than he or she actually does. Plagiarists misrepresent themselves as having more originality, superior expertise, better resources, or more sophisticated analytical capabilities than they truly possess.

Misrepresentation in this context also applies to one's own and one's organization's experience, credentials, and qualifications to engage in specific professional activities. For example, enrolling in the CFA program and earning the right to use the CFA designation are certainly important and meritorious steps, but their significance must not be overstated by suggesting that CFA candidates or charterholders have technical expertise unavailable to other investment analysts nor to imply that they have superior competence in any particular area of specialization. [See also Standard VII(B).]

It should be observed that the prohibition of misrepresentation is central to the Standards of Professional Conduct. In practice, many violations of other provisions of the Standards also involve misrepresentation. For example, recommending that a particular client engage in an inappropriate strategy in violation of Standard III(C) might also constitute misrepresentation if the investment professional implies that the strategy is suitable for the client. Communicating incomplete or misleading performance information in contravention of Standard III(D) also amounts to misrepresentation. Failing to distinguish between facts and opinions in violation of Standard V(B)3 may lead to misrepresenting the analyst's outlook or projections as reality. Misrepresentation flouts integrity, a core ethical value in the Code and Standards, and is inconsistent with the investment analyst's professional responsibilities in general and in detail.

Standard I(D)—Misconduct stipulates first that covered persons "must not engage in any professional conduct involving dishonesty, fraud, [or] deceit. . . ." Actions taken in the course of one's work as an investment professional that show individuals to be lacking in integrity and trustworthiness damage not only their own reputation but also the good name of their firm and the ethical standing of the entire profession. Dishonesty and deceit abuse the trust upon which professional relationships are based, and fraud undercuts the investor confidence upon which the capital markets rely. Professional misconduct is a grave transgression of the Code and Standards.

Standard I(D) further enjoins covered persons not to "commit *any* act that reflects adversely on their professional reputation, integrity, or competence." (Emphasis added.) While the primary thrust of this Standard is to ban deceitful professional conduct, deeds, and habits that are unrelated to work but affect or call into question an individual's professionalism may constitute breaches of this Standard.

Finally, actions that raise questions about a practitioner's professional competence may be seen as a violation of trust. Professionals hold themselves out as having expertise, and their clients and employers have a right to expect competent performance. Presenting substandard work products, making haphazard investment recommendations, and acting on ill-considered decisions are an abuse of confidence and may be deemed a violation of the first Standard.

STANDARD II—INTEGRITY OF CAPITAL MARKETS

Standard II—Integrity of Capital Markets has two parts. The first addresses the use of material nonpublic information, and the second, the broad issue of market manipulation.

Standard II(A)—Material Nonpublic Information holds that covered persons in possession of material nonpublic information, defined in context as "information that could affect the value of an investment," must not act or cause others to act on it. For the purpose of this discussion, information is material if it is apt to change the price of a security or if it reflects advance market knowledge or security-specific intelligence that a reasonable investor would take into account when making an investment decision. Information is nonpublic if it has not been disseminated to the marketplace in general so that all investors have a fair chance to act on it.

Material nonpublic information may take many forms, but examples include learning that a pharmaceutical company has been granted or denied regulatory approval to bring a new medication to market, or hearing of an imminent event of default on an issuer's fixed income securities, or becoming apprised of a planned but as yet unannounced tender offer. Similarly, awareness of a large volume of unexecuted transactions in specific securities would place a person in possession of material nonpublic knowledge and position that person to engage in "front-running," trading ahead of the impending transactions. In addition to company-specific news, material nonpublic information can also take (and, indeed, has taken) the form of advance knowledge of economic news prior to its official release, for example, by agencies of the federal government. For instance, inflation data or the results of an unemployment survey may be leaked, despite the government's efforts to protect the confidentiality of official economic reports. If the early figures are at variance with the market's expectations, the person with advance knowledge can anticipate a market movement with predictable effects on the direction of security prices in affected sectors.

The ethical rationale for prohibiting the use of material nonpublic information is twofold. First, trading on significant knowledge restricted to a select few enables them to make profits unfairly at the expense of uninformed market participants; second, it erodes public confidence in the capital markets, which may come to be seen as biased to the advantage of insiders.

The investment profession rests upon analysts' abilities to derive insights from the study of information about security issuers and the industries in which they compete. Much of that information is publicly available, but some may come directly from the issuing entity, for example, in the course of routine interviews with financial officers or investor relations personnel. If the information derived from inside sources is not material, analysts may use it in combination with material public information to confirm their perceptions of the issuer's prospects and the security's inherent value. This is metaphorically known as the "mosaic theory" of financial analysis because astute analysts piece facts together to form a pattern or a picture. The Standard does not by any means preclude such analysis, which contributes to the fair and efficient pricing of securities.

In the event investment professionals inadvertently come into possession of material nonpublic information, they must not only forebear acting on it or divulging it to others who might take action, they must additionally take steps to rectify the situation. They should, for example, encourage the issuer to make the information public, and they should inform their manager or their firm's compliance department so that the security can be placed on a restricted list until the information has been publicly disseminated or has become immaterial. It is also prudent for professionals to document their internal and external communications on the subject, just in case their actions should come under scrutiny.

Standard II(B)—Market Manipulation prohibits engaging in "practices that distort prices or artificially inflate trading volume with the intent to mislead market participants." In this case, the practitioner's intention or purpose is the critical element for distinguishing between legitimate trading strategies and duplicitous ploys. It is permissible, for example, to sell and repurchase a holding in order to realize a gain or loss in accordance with the provisions of a tax code or to rebalance positions in different portfolios, but it is impermissible to buy and sell a security among various accounts under one's control for the purpose of running up the bid price. It would be similarly improper for a commodity trading company to enter a large volume of related-party transactions disguised as arm's-length open market trades to enhance its perceived market power or to influence the price of derivative instruments tied to the traded product.

Acceptable trading strategies with fitting and explainable business purposes may exploit asymmetrical information but are not intended to deceive counterparties or other market participants. While determining the intent of the person initiating a transaction or a series of transactions may seem to be a matter of dubious psychological inference, investment professionals who know the markets and the instruments can reliably tell the difference when all the facts are disclosed.

The twofold ethical basis for outlawing market manipulation is by now familiar. Engaging in deceptive practices in order to gain an edge over others may cause them to suffer undue financial damages and impedes the fair and efficient operation of the capital markets.

10   STANDARD III—DUTIES TO CLIENTS

Standard III addresses five areas of ethical concern. They are the loyalty, prudence, and care due to clients; fair dealing; the suitability of investments; performance presentation; and the preservation of confidentiality.

Standard III(A)—Loyalty, Prudence, and Care stresses that covered persons must not only act for the benefit of their clients but also place their clients' interests before their firm's and their own. There can be no "utilitarian calculus" where an action which is very good for the firm or the professional and "not too bad" for the client is acceptable. Under the Standard, investment professionals are obligated to act in the best interest of the client without regard to their employer's potentially divergent interests or their own advantage.

Moreover, covered persons have a "duty of loyalty" to their clients. Professional relationships are generally governed by legal contracts under which one person, the professional, consents to give another, the client, the benefit of his or her special competence in exchange for compensation during the term of the agreement. Accordingly, professional relationships are not, as a rule, personal in the sense of friendships or family ties. However, neither are they merely commercial. Investors place trust in professionals to whom they look for judicious, expert advice, and investment professionals are obligated by the nature of this relationship of trust to keep faith with their clients. They must not merely refrain from deceiving or defrauding the clients; they must ensure that the investment recommendations they offer are sound and the actions they take are well-considered.

In practical terms, this duty of loyalty to the client means using "reasonable care" and applying "prudent judgment." Acting with reasonable care implies identifying and taking into account all the factors that materially affect the investment characteristics of a security or a strategy. In the context of professional investment analysis, exercising prudent judgment reflects a high standard of care because it signifies the caution of an expert in evaluating the risk and reward characteristics of a security or a strategy. The investment professional serves the client's interests by proceeding with reasonable care and exercising prudent judgment when making recommendations and taking action.

In the language of some legal systems, the word "fiduciary" is used as a noun to identify the role and as an adjective to describe the obligations of a person to whom property or decision-making authority are entrusted on behalf of another. Fiduciaries are legally bound to act solely in the interest of the person for whose benefit they manage assets under the terms of the governing agreement. It is vitally important for investment professionals acting in a fiduciary capacity to determine to whom the duty of loyalty is owed. For example, in general corporate pension assets must be managed exclusively for the benefit of the plan's participants and beneficiaries, even though it is the plan sponsor who has the authority to hire and fire investment managers. Of course, the plan sponsor also has fiduciary obligations toward the participants and beneficiaries.

While the legal concept of fiduciary obligations is not universally applicable, under the Code and Standards, covered persons have comparable ethical responsibilities when assets are entrusted to their care. It should be observed that loyalty is owed by investment managers of a mutual fund to the shareholders of that fund just as it is owed by managers to their separate account clients.

Standard III(B)—Fair Dealing requires fair and objective treatment for all clients and prospective clients in the conduct of one's professional activities. For example, in the absence of specific client-initiated constraints, attractively priced securities must be proportionately allocated among accounts managed in the same style so as not to give preference to some clients over others. Similarly, securities held in multiple accounts should be liquidated in an orderly and equitable manner so that one client, or one group of clients, does not receive more favorable treatment than another.

Fair dealing is an area requiring particular attention, both because there have been serious abuses (for instance, in the allocation of initial public offerings) and because it may sometimes seem natural in the course of business to offer special rewards to valued clients or inducements to desirable prospects. It is improper to do so at the expense of others. In economic terms, the opportunity cost to a client denied fair access to an undervalued security is no less material than a loss unfairly apportioned. Individuals must take care to see that clients are treated fairly in all their dealings. Moreover, with regard to the examples cited above, their firms' trading processes must be designed and monitored to uphold the objective equitability of transactions. While directed primarily to the issue of "best execution," the CFA Institute Trade Management Guidelines include ensuring that all clients are treated fairly in the execution of orders and allocation of trades. It is remarked there, "The term 'fairly' implies that Firms should take care not to discriminate against clients or place the interests of some clients over those of others."[9]

Standard III(B) refers to existing clients. However, it is desirable for professionals to disclose their firm's policies and procedures for disseminating investment advice and allocating trades to prospective as well as existing clients. In addition, professionals should communicate the availability, nature, and cost of any premium services such as in-depth investment analysis. Such premium services should be designed in such a way that, while beneficial to those who are in

---

[9] CFA Institute, "Trade Management Guidelines" (2002), 1.D, p. 9.

a position to take advantage of them, they are not unfairly disadvantageous to other classes of clients.

Standard III(C)—Suitability addresses two distinct situations. In the first, professionals are providing investment advice to clients and prospective clients (typically clients whose assets are held in actively managed separate accounts); in the second, they may not have direct contact with specific clients but are responsible for managing a portfolio such as a commingled fund or a mutual fund in accordance with a stated mandate, strategy, or style. In both cases, it is the professionals' duty to ensure that investment recommendations and decisions are fitting, but the particular requirements differ.

When providing advice, covered persons are first directed to inquire about the client's investment experience, objectives, and constraints before they make any recommendations or take any action. [See Standard III(C.1.a).] A primary purpose served by asking about the client's investment experience is to determine how to communicate investment ideas most clearly and effectively. For example, an inexperienced investor with modest savings will undoubtedly need more basic education about financial instruments and strategies than a seasoned investor with extensive, diversified holdings. It might be considered questionable to place the assets of a client unfamiliar with the investment industry at risk in complex, highly leveraged derivative instruments that surpass the client's understanding.

The advisor must also ascertain the client's or prospective client's return objectives and risk tolerance. A financial planner interviewing a retail client may use a questionnaire to determine the individual's orientation toward current income or asset appreciation and to assess the client's attitudes toward financial risk-taking. A consultant advising the officers of a university's endowment fund will consider such factors as the significance of the endowment in relation to the institution's overall budget, the fund's annual spending plan, and pertinent inflation projections such as estimated tuition increases affecting future scholarship needs. The advisor must additionally establish whether there are special constraints or considerations of any sort to be taken into account in formulating an investment plan.

With this background, the advisor is further directed to determine that an investment is suitable to the client's financial situation. [See Standard III(C.1.b).] Making such a determination always requires critical thinking and often calls for superior judgment. For example, the trustees of a currently underfunded public pension plan with an aggressive, legislatively mandated timetable for achieving fully funded status might ask an investment professional for advice about investing a significant portion of the plan's assets in alternative asset classes offering high expected returns. Although it is difficult to assess the riskiness of illiquid securities, the advisor might conclude that under prevailing market conditions the return premiums appear to be in line with their perceived quality. Nonetheless, the investment professional must seriously consider if the possibility of loss is unacceptably high, potentially necessitating substantial cash infusions to sustain the plan's viability. In such a situation, it may be imprudent to attempt to achieve the target level of return, and the proposed investment program might in fact be unsuitable to the client's financial condition. This example illustrates the need not only for sound judgment but also, in some instances, for political courage. The investment advisor's best course might be to urge the trustees to seek legislative relief rather than to risk far greater financial setbacks in the pursuit of excess return.

Under the same section, covered persons must further determine that an investment under consideration is consistent with the client's objectives, mandates, and constraints.

Written investment policy statements are widely used by institutional investors such as pension plan sponsors, endowment and foundation officers, and insurance companies. Among other elements, policy statements typically set forth the investor's financial objectives, including return expectations, sensitivity to risk, and the fund's time horizon. They also identify permitted asset classes and investment vehicles and articulate portfolio constraints intended to control risk. Charles Ellis wrote, "The principal reason for articulating long-term investment policy explicitly and *in writing* is to enable the client and portfolio manager to protect the portfolio from ad hoc revisions of sound long-term policy, and to help them hold to long-term policy when short-term exigencies are most distressing and the policy is most in doubt."[10]

Investment professionals working on behalf of the institution, whether as employees or advisors, must make recommendations and decisions with the policy statement in view. Portfolio managers must not only attend to the general spirit of the policy statement, notably with regard to risk tolerance, but must also comply with its detailed provisions. For example, the policy statement may limit an individual equity portfolio's economic sector exposure to a certain percentage of portfolio assets or of the comparable benchmark weight. A fixed income portfolio may be constrained to hold no securities rated below investment grade and to maintain the portfolio's weighted average duration within a specified range, often expressed as a percentage of the benchmark duration. Such restrictions are intended to preserve the fund from a loss in value due to inadequate sector diversification, excessive credit quality risk, or unacceptable levels of interest rate risk.

It is at present less common for individuals to have written investment policy statements. Nonetheless, investment professionals are obligated under the Standards to determine that an investment is consistent with the client's objectives, mandates, and constraints before making a recommendation or taking action. The best practice is to document the client's guidelines and to follow them when offering advice and making decisions.

When providing advice to clients and prospective clients, there is a third and final directive for determining the appropriateness of an investment recommendation or action. [See Standard III(C.1.c).] Covered persons are instructed to judge the suitability of investments in the context of the client's "total portfolio," that is, the client's entire set of personal, real, and financial assets.

The principle of portfolio optimization through diversification is well established in investment theory. Given reasonable assumptions about prospective asset class returns, volatilities, and covariance, portfolio returns can be maximized for a specified level of risk, or alternately risk can be minimized for a specified target return, by aptly weighting holdings in various asset classes which do not move in concert. The Standard applies the same logic to the client's overall financial situation, with the objective of avoiding an excessive concentration of assets, and correlatively of risk, in any domain. For instance, if the client's major assets are residential real estate and the stock of a closely held specialty chemical company where the client is also employed, the client's investment program might well emphasize marketable securities issued predominately by corporations engaged in other lines of business.

To protect their privacy, some clients may refuse to disclose all their holdings to an investment advisor. In that case, it remains the advisor's responsibility to explain the importance of diversification and the nature of the investments under consideration.

---

[10] Charles D. Ellis, *Investment Policy; How to Win the Loser's Game*, Dow Jones-Irwin (1985), p. 53. Ellis's emphasis.

A difficult situation arises when clients specifically request transactions that the investment analyst considers inappropriate. For instance, the client might ask for a reallocation of portfolio assets that would result in an imprudent concentration of risk. In this event, it is incumbent upon the investment professional to inform the client, in plain language, that the proposed course of action is unwise and can be implemented only against the investment professional's advice.

As noted, many investment professionals are engaged in managing asset pools like mutual funds on behalf of investors whose acquaintance they never make and whose financial circumstances are unknowable. Clearly, covered persons who do not provide investment advice are not expected to judge the suitability of investment vehicles, mandates, strategies, or styles for the individuals and institutions who choose them. However, under Standard III(C.2), they are obligated to adhere to the declared mandate, strategy, or style by making recommendations and decisions that are consistent with the portfolio's stated objectives and constraints. Investors select mutual funds and other commingled vehicles to meet certain financial needs within their total portfolios, and they expect the fund manager to invest accordingly. For example, it would be unethical for a portfolio manager with a pure value mandate to include stocks with growth characteristics such as high price-earnings multiples, high price-book ratios, and low dividend yields in the portfolio in order to improve performance when value stocks are out of favor in the marketplace.

Standard III(D)—Performance Presentation requires covered persons to make reasonable efforts to ensure that investment performance information they communicate is "fair, accurate, and complete." Investors and investment consultants take the pertinent performance record of asset management organizations into account along with other factors when selecting firms to implement their investment program. They also monitor their investment managers' results and evaluate them in comparison with agreed-upon performance measures such as absolute target returns, selected capital market index returns, or peer group returns. They rely upon investment professionals to provide performance information that is fair, accurate, and complete, and those covered by the Code and Standards are obligated to "make reasonable efforts" to meet these expectations.

It is important to clarify the relationship between Standard III(D) and the Global Investment Performance Standards (GIPS®), which were developed and promulgated with the objective of achieving "fair representation and full disclosure" of performance information. The GIPS standards require compliant firms to use accurate input data and approved calculation methods, to present the performance record in accordance with a prescribed format, and to make certain disclosures. The GIPS standards apply on a firm-wide basis, and a firm's compliance is voluntary. (To be clear, a firm that voluntarily claims to be in compliance with the GIPS standards must conform to the Global Investment Performance Standards in all particulars; the firm cannot choose to satisfy some requirements of the GIPS standards but not others.) [11]

The GIPS standards then, apply only to investment management firms, and the firms' compliance is voluntary. Standard III(D) applies to individual covered persons, and compliance is mandatory. This does not mean that covered persons cannot work for firms that are not GIPS-compliant, although they should encourage their firms to comply with the GIPS standards. It does mean, however, that when they communicate investment performance they must endeavor to

---

[11] The CFA Institute website provides extensive information about the Global Investment Performance Standards (GIPS).

provide information that represents the historical record fairly, accurately, and completely. Moreover, it is not permissible to pass along performance information that one knows to be materially incorrect or misleading. If the performance information in question has been prepared by another department, the individual should attempt to explain its deficiencies to those responsible for preparing it so that they can make it acceptable for use in communicating with clients and prospective clients.

Finally, **Standard III(E)**—Preservation of Confidentiality directs members to keep information about current, former, and prospective clients confidential. The only exceptions enumerated in the Standard are when the information concerns illegal activities, disclosure is required by law, or the client permits the practitioner to disclose the information. Investment professionals often come into possession of highly sensitive information about their clients' and prospective clients' financial affairs. Indeed, as we saw in our discussion of suitability, advisors are duty-bound to make reasonable inquiries into their clients' and prospective clients' financial situation so that they can make appropriate investment recommendations and decisions. Former, existing, and prospective clients have a right to expect personal information divulged in the course of a professional relationship to be held in confidence, and under the Standards covered persons are obligated to respect and protect their privacy.

STANDARD IV—DUTIES TO EMPLOYERS   11

Having addressed members' and candidates' duties to clients, the Standards take up their responsibilities toward employers. Standard IV has three sections, focusing on loyalty, additional compensation arrangements, and the responsibilities of supervisors.

Standard IV(A)—Loyalty maintains that in matters related to their employment covered persons must "act for the benefit of their employer." The Standard goes on to clarify the nature of the loyalty expected here by specifying that individuals must not "deprive their employer of the advantage of their skills and abilities, divulge confidential information, or otherwise cause harm to their employer."

Employee loyalty and the firm's reciprocity raise extremely complex ethical issues.[12] Businesses are established to provide goods and services at a profit, not to promote their employees' social development, but the workplace can nonetheless satisfy important human needs for affiliation, and identifying with an organization can contribute significantly to a person's sense of self. Moreover, working absorbs much of our time and energy. Depending upon one's view of human nature, being loyal to colleagues and to the firm itself may almost seem to be as much an innate propensity as a moral choice. (One can be loyal not only to other persons but also to organizations, including corporations no less than, say, colleges and sports teams.) If loyalty is in some sense a natural tendency, then the ethical questions are not only, "What does loyalty to the firm legitimately require of us?" but also, "What are the limits of loyalty?"

As noted, the Standard stipulates that covered persons must not deprive the employer of their skills and abilities, for example, by shirking assignments, doing careless work, using business hours and resources for outside interests, or

---

[12] See Brian Schrag's paper, "The Moral Significance of Employee Loyalty," *Business Ethics Quarterly,* Vol. 11, No. 1 (January 2001), pp. 41–66.

engaging in professional activities "on the side" in competition with one's employer. The Standard also states that confidential information is not to be disclosed. Confidential information would include, for example, client contacts, proprietary analytic techniques, and product strategies, among other things. The Standard further asserts that covered persons "must not otherwise cause harm to their employer." How is this provision to be interpreted and applied in particular situations?

Identifying so exclusively with the firm and working so single-mindedly to further the firm's interests that one neglects one's health or family is certainly not expected. When personal matters may interfere with their work on a regular or significant basis, members and candidates should enter into a dialogue with their employers about balancing personal and professional obligations.

In addition, covered persons are not expected to consent to firm policies and practices that are contrary to ethical standards. "Whistleblowers"—individuals who disclose their firm's misdeeds—are often accused of disloyalty to their colleagues and their employers, but such reactions to an individual's difficult decision to report an uncorrected wrong reflect a serious misunderstanding of the duty of loyalty. On the contrary, it may be the case that going public, or going to regulatory authorities, bespeaks the employee's commitment to the identity, culture, and values of a firm whose reputation for excellence is in jeopardy due to others' poor judgment or ethical failures.

Although their leaving might be harmful to the firm, covered persons are neither required nor expected by the Standard to remain in the firm's employ when other opportunities are more attractive. Best practice is to give advance notice of their departure and assist the firm in effecting a smooth transition. In some cases, a directly competing organization may extend an offer of employment to an individual or even to an entire team; in other cases, employees may decide to start their own business. The departing employees may attempt to rationalize clandestinely removing or copying the firm's property as the products of their own creativity, but without permission it is wrong for them to take the firm's client list, software, files, or other assets with the intention of entering into competition with their former employer.

Global competition has made attaining ever greater operational efficiency a matter of corporate survival in many industries, including financial services. Business combinations are often initiated to achieve productivity improvements through economies of scale or better cost control. "Downsizing" and "outsourcing" have entered the business vocabulary, and the nature of the relationship between employers and employees has changed. Broker/dealers have long engaged in boom-and-bust cycles of staff recruitment and termination, but traditionally stable organizations like banks and insurance companies no longer offer the job security their long-term personnel once took for granted. Employment is increasingly seen as a temporary economic arrangement for the mutual benefit of the company and the worker, and it lasts only as long as both parties find it advantageous. Examining the employer's responsibilities to employees goes beyond the scope of the present discussion. However, the employer/employee relationship imposes duties and responsibilities on both parties. If they expect to have committed and productive employees, employers should refrain from exploiting their workers' natural proclivity to identify with the firm and should reward their loyalty by recognizing their contributions and treating them with honesty and respect.

Standard IV(B)—Additional Compensation Arrangements is clear-cut. Covered persons must not accept any form of inducement or recompense—the Standard mentions "gifts, benefits, compensation, or consideration"—that competes with their employer's interest or that might reasonably be expected to produce a conflict between their own and their employer's interest, *unless* they obtain written consent from all parties involved. For example, employees must not accept a consulting assignment, an appointment to a board of directors, or a publishing contract without clearly and realistically explaining the terms of the commitment to their employer or manager and getting approval to proceed *in writing*. Similarly, they should make the other organization aware of the nature and the demands of their regular employment, and they should have written evidence that the other organization understands any limits on their ability to work on its behalf. The Standard applies to situations in which the investment professionals' compensated outside interests might interfere with their concentrating as fully as expected on their regular work as well as to situations in which they plan to engage in an activity directly competing with their firm's business. Many corporations have formal procedures for approving their staff's outside engagements.

Finally, **Standard IV(C)**—Responsibilities of Supervisors explicitly states that covered persons in managerial positions "must make reasonable efforts to *detect and prevent* violations of applicable laws, rules, [and] regulations," as well as breaches of the Code and Standards, by persons subject to their supervision or authority. (Emphasis added.) Reasonable prevention and detection measures would include defining and documenting policies and procedures, training staff members, designing and implementing controls, and monitoring the unit's activities with an eye to spotting unethical or illegal conduct. Staff training should cover not only the firm's standards but also the applicable laws, rules, and regulations in sufficient depth to equip employees to perform their routine functions and to raise questions in doubtful cases.

It is also advisable to inform staff members about the provisions of the Code and Standards. Although they themselves may not be members or candidates, managers who are subject to the Code and Standards can be found in violation for failing to supervise the activities of those under their authority in the event of a contravention. In addition, it should be acknowledged that managers set expectations and lead by example. Along with senior management, the group or unit supervisor is responsible for establishing a culture in which ethically sound decisions are expected and rewarded.

STANDARD V—INVESTMENT ANALYSIS, RECOMMENDATIONS, AND ACTIONS

12

Standard V lies at the heart of ethical Standards for investment professionals. The Standard has three sections, addressing the requirement that investment analysis, recommendations, and decisions be based upon reasonable and adequate grounds; the norms for clear and informative client communications; and the need to retain supporting documentation.

Standard V(A)—Diligence and Reasonable Basis first reiterates the requirement that covered persons exercise diligence, independence, and thoroughness in their professional work. Diligence and the exercise of independent professional judgment figure prominently in the Code of Ethics, and independence and objectivity were addressed in connection with Standard I(B). We focus attention here on the second provision of Standard V(A). Covered persons are required to have "a reasonable and adequate basis, supported by appropriate research and investigation, for any investment analysis, recommendation, [or] action."

In investment analysis as in any other discipline, a rational, well-founded conclusion will be based upon theoretically and logically sound premises, plausibly argued, and above all supported by factual evidence.

The idea of "theoretically and logically sound premises" is not intended to preclude original work by requiring hypotheses to be consistent with conventional ideas about risk, return, or the capital markets. For example, style-based investment strategies, now widely accepted, emerged from research on stock market anomalies indicating that price/book ratios and company size were promising alternatives to beta in accounting for security returns.[13] In one view of scientific discovery, knowledge advances through what the philosopher Karl Popper called "conjectures and refutations," as individuals and groups seek to determine whether suppositions about empirical relationships withstand tests designed to disprove them.[14] Nor does the expectation that analyses be theoretically grounded and logically developed necessarily rule out approaches which do not assert causal connections between conditions or patterns and outcomes. ("Technical analysis" may be broadly characterized as such an approach.) However, when clients' assets are put at risk, there is a practical demand that investment analysis, and the recommendations and decisions to which it leads, must be explainable and defensible rather than merely reflecting an analyst's hunch. In this context, it is imperative to offer a plausible explanation of observed phenomena.

Most important—indeed, indispensable—is factual research. Analyses, recommendations, and actions *must* be predicated upon reliable, up-to-date data. The capital markets have a way of disproving hypotheses most convincingly, and the analyst's rigorously logical reasoning is no defense when he or she has misconstrued or ignored available facts that should have been taken into consideration.

This is not by any means to suggest that analysts cannot accept others' research as the basis for a conclusion. A great deal of investment analysis is dependent upon other researchers' papers, secondary sources, and commercially developed databases. In the vast majority of cases, conducting unassisted research would be inefficient to the point of impracticality. It is necessary, however, for analysts to make a reasonable inquiry into the reliability of their sources. They should be tolerably assured that the analytical techniques are solid, the quality controls are dependable, and the data are timely and accurate.

At most investment management organizations, research and analysis are conducted in a group setting. There are frequently occasions when the consensus is at variance with an individual analyst's considered position. In such cases, investment professionals must weigh the requirements for independent thinking and for well-founded decisions. If the group's decision process is rational, pertinent facts have been ascertained and evaluated, the analyst has been given a fair opportunity to express contrary views, and the conclusions are not unreasonable (although arguably incorrect), then investment professionals may justifiably acquiesce and consent to have their names associated with the group's view. Reasonable people can disagree, for example, on the timing and magnitude of a correction in the general level of interest rates or the attractiveness of an economic sector.

If, on the other hand, the process is flawed, important and undeniable facts have been disregarded, or extraneous business considerations have improperly influenced the debate, then the analysts may have to conclude that the group

[13] The original research by Eugene F. Fama and Kenneth R. French (1992) and others leading to the development of style-based equity investment strategies is recalled in Louis K. C. Chan and Josef Lakonishok, "Value and Growth Investing: Review and Update," *Financial Analysts Journal*, Vol. 60, No. 1 (January/February 2004), p. 71.

[14] See Karl Popper, *Conjectures and Refutations: The Growth of Scientific Knowledge*, Harper & Row (1968).

does not have a reasonable and adequate basis for its conclusions and that endorsing the outcome would compromise their integrity. In this event, the analysts are faced with a difficult decision about the best course of action. They may elect to hold their fire for a more consequential issue or to submit a dissenting opinion or to request that their name be removed from a published report. If the firm's management routinely misuses the research and analysis process to validate foregone conclusions, then the analysts will have to decide whether they can continue to meet their professional obligations in that organization.

With **Standard V(B)**—Communication with Clients and Prospective Clients, we proceed from conducting investment analysis to conveying the results of analysis to the clients and potential clients whom it may benefit.

Standard V(B.1) requires covered persons to describe their investment decision-making process. For example, one firm engaged in active equity management may conduct fundamental "economic-industry-company" analysis, while another favors enhanced indexing and focuses on the development and application of quantitative portfolio optimization techniques. These two organizations will differ substantially in the investment principles, research resources, screening techniques, decision rules, and process controls they employ. The nature of the risks to which the investor is exposed will also differ with two such dissimilar approaches. By clearly explaining the basic format and the general principles of the firm's approach to portfolio construction, the investment professional enables clients and prospective clients to determine whether the firm is well matched to their preferences for the mandate under consideration. Similarly, by promptly communicating significant modifications in the way the firm conducts research, selects securities for purchase and sale, and constructs and trims portfolios, the investment professional equips clients and prospective clients to monitor the impact of changes and to make informed decisions about their asset mix and roster of managers on the basis of up-to-date information.

Standard V(B.2) requires covered persons to use reasonable judgment in identifying the factors that are important to their investment analysis, recommendation, or actions, and to address those factors in their communications to clients and prospective clients. As we saw earlier, the "reasonable judgment" expected here is that of a knowledgeable and experienced practitioner.

Note that the factors to be communicated are the factors that were significant in conducting the analysis, formulating the recommendation, or reaching the decision. If a projection of the future course of interest rates, for example, or an appraisal of the attractiveness of an industry was an important piece of the work, then its contribution to the analyst's reasoning must be made clear. The communication should, in short, convey the "reasonable and adequate basis" or the factual and logical grounds for the conclusion. If the report includes an investment recommendation, then it is best practice for the professional explicitly to address the risks, along with any mitigating factors, so that the clients or prospective clients can make an informed decision.

The pertinence of the factors to be considered and communicated further depends, of course, upon the context. For example, an introductory discussion of the investment characteristics of an asset class, such as convertible bonds, will be broader and more general than an evaluation of the terms and pricing of a specific convertible issue. In the former case, the analyst will help the investor understand how convertibles are structured, how they respond to different equity and fixed income market conditions, how their valuation is related to the volatility of a particular stock as well as the credit-worthiness of the issuer, what role they can play in an overall investment program, what tradeoffs and generic risks they represent, and how they are valued in the marketplace. In the latter case, the analyst will focus on security-specific valuation issues, considering among other things the prevailing and prospective equity and fixed income market conditions; the particular issue's bond characteristics, such as coupon and current yield; the price and the historical price variability of the related common stock; and the issuer's earnings outlook.

Accordingly, in deciding what topics to cover, investment professionals must not only review their own thought processes in reaching a conclusion but also think about the context and purpose of the communication. In the case of a one-on-one presentation or a memorandum written for a specific client or group of clients, investment professionals should consider the recipient's preparedness to understand the material. An investor who has not previously been exposed to convertibles may need to be given more background information about the asset class than someone who already grasps the opportunities, risks, and valuation techniques. When writing for a mass audience, it is not as easy to decide what "goes without saying," but the professional should take pains to be as clear as possible in communicating technical material.

Standard V(B.3) requires covered persons to distinguish between "facts" and "opinions" in the presentation of investment analysis and recommendations. For instance, it may be a fact that the general level of interest rates in a certain country is relatively low by post–World War II historical standards, but it is the analyst's opinion that resurgent inflation will cause rates to rise, or that the central bank will raise the short-term target rate by 25 basis points at its next meeting, or that the yield on five-year federal debt issues will increase by 50 basis points in the second half, or that residential mortgage refinancings will slow next year. The Standard requires investment professionals to differentiate facts and opinions in their communications, so that clients do not mistake a possibility for a certainty or an estimate for a guarantee.

Standard V(C)—Record Retention stipulates that covered persons must develop and maintain appropriate records to support their analysis, recommendations, actions, performance, and other investment-related communications with clients and prospective clients. The objective is to allow for subsequent review in the event that questions arise, for example, about the reasonability and adequacy of the research on which a recommendation or decision was based, or about the authorship of a report, or about the firm's investment results. Consulting firms and investment management organizations generally formulate record retention guidelines or policies for their staff, but whether or not individual members and candidates are subject to compliance audits, it remains their own professional responsibility to ensure that appropriate records are available for review.

13   STANDARD VI—CONFLICTS OF INTEREST

As we have seen, under the Code and Standards, covered persons must place the client's and their employer's interests before their own and exercise independent professional judgment. These mandates cannot be broken. Nonetheless, there are conflict-of-interest situations in which what is most beneficial for the client may or may not coincide with what is most advantageous to the investment professional. In other words, there may be incentives for the professional to make certain recommendations or decisions whether or not they are entirely suitable for the client. Even though the member or candidate scrupulously acts in the client's best interest, the very existence of a conflict may raise questions about the investment professional's independence and objectivity. Standard VI tacitly reaffirms the principle of the priority of client transactions and describes the disclosures required when there are conflicts of interest.

Standard VI(A) states that covered persons "must make *full and fair disclosure* of all matters that could *reasonably be expected to impair their independence and objectivity* or interfere with their respective duties to their employer, clients, and prospective clients." (Emphasis added.) For example, clients should be told if investment professionals own stock in a company they recommend. By giving clients information about situations or arrangements that might influence their reasoning, investment professionals alert them to the need for critical thinking. The clients are then well advised to judge for themselves whether there is a sound basis for the professionals' recommendations and they are indeed acting in the clients' best interest.

Take as an example the "bundled services" some financial services companies offer pension plan sponsors. The provider may conduct an asset allocation study and recommend an asset mix optimized on the basis of the provider's assumptions about asset class returns, volatilities, and correlations. The provider may additionally implement the recommended investment program by accepting the client's assets into commingled funds managed in accordance with the specified strategies. Although intended primarily to assist the sponsors of small to midsize pension plans lacking the expertise or the time to conduct manager searches, bundled services of the sort described here may have built-in conflicts of interest. For instance, the advisory fees for certain recommended strategies may be substantially greater than they are for others. If members or candidates are involved in the sale or management of bundled pension investment services, they are obligated by Standard VI(A) to ensure that the client or prospective client is fully aware that the fees for some alternatives are higher than for others.

The Standard goes on to specify that disclosures of conflicts of interest must be prominent and delivered in plain language, and they must "communicate the relevant information effectively." Ambiguous or excessively legalistic "disclosures" tucked away unnoticeably in a presentation would not suffice to satisfy the requirement.

It should be stressed that, whenever possible, conflicts of interest are to be avoided in the interest of independence and objectivity. Where conflicts exist, they must be fully and clearly disclosed, but disclosure is not a substitute for impartiality. The investment professional is in every case ethically obligated to make recommendations and decisions in the best interest of the client.

Standard VI(B)—Priority of Transactions states that investment transactions for clients and employers must have priority over investment transactions in which a covered person has a personal interest. Members and candidates cannot act on behalf of themselves or members of their household before clients and employers have been given a fair opportunity to act on a recommendation. If investment advisors have discretionary authority over a client's account, and the transaction is suitable, then the advisors cannot initiate the transaction for themselves before entering an order on behalf of the client. This requirement is consistent with a fundamental provision of the Code of Ethics, namely, that covered persons place the interests of clients and the interests of their employer above their own personal interests.

Standard VI(C)—Referral Fees specifically requires the disclosure of any compensation received by the member or candidate for recommending products or services. It additionally requires members and candidates to disclose if they have compensated others for recommending their own or their firms' products or services. It is not up to the client to ask about referral arrangements, and failure to inform them of compensation agreements might leave them with the misimpression that an endorsement was offered without inducement. Referral fees constitute the sort of arrangement that must be divulged under Standard VI(A) above, but they are of such importance and so frequently used that they warrant separate and explicit treatment. Indeed, not to disclose the existence, nature, and estimated value of referral fees is an abuse of the investor's trust.

14

STANDARD VII—RESPONSIBILITIES AS A CFA INSTITUTE MEMBER OR CFA CANDIDATE

Standard VII, the last of the Standards of Professional Conduct, treats the ethical obligations of members and candidates in their very capacity as members of CFA Institute or candidates for the CFA designation. The standard has two provisions, covering the individual's conduct in the CFA program and the need for accuracy in references to CFA Institute, the CFA designation, and the CFA program.

Standard VII(A) holds that covered persons must not engage in any conduct that compromises the reputation or integrity of CFA Institute, the CFA designation, or the integrity, validity, or security of the CFA examinations. The intent of the Standard is to prohibit any actions that discredit the CFA designation as an achievement based strictly upon merit and ethical conduct or that might disparage the reputation of CFA Institute as an organization with high standards of professional excellence. For example, cheating on an examination undermines the validity and integrity of the credential program, and lying on a Professional Conduct Statement impairs CFA Institute enforcement efforts.

Finally, **Standard VII(B)** prohibits covered persons from misrepresenting or exaggerating the meaning or implications of membership in CFA Institute, holding the CFA designation, or candidacy in the CFA program. For instance, it is entirely permissible to express one's opinions about the thoroughness and rigor of the CFA program, but suggesting that clients or prospective clients will enjoy superior investment results if they hire CFA charterholders to manage their assets would constitute a serious violation of the Standard. The Guidance presents useful information about correct ways to describe and use the CFA designation and to refer to one's candidacy in the CFA program.

15

ETHICAL PROBLEM-SOLVING

This reading has given an overview of the CFA Institute Code of Ethics and Standards of Professional Conduct. However, Adam Smith wrote, "it is in particular instances only that the propriety or impropriety, the merit or demerit of actions is very obvious and discernible."[15] The case studies that follow are designed as practical exercises in ethical reasoning. The "case facts" present situations, and the "case discussions" frame the primary ethical issues with explicit reference to pertinent provisions of the Code and Standards. The "suggested actions" following the case discussions may not be the only ways in which the individuals can address and resolve the ethical issues confronting them in conformity with the Code and Standards. In addition, there might be other actions the individuals could take to improve the working environment in such a way as to reduce or eliminate the ethical challenges they face. We encourage readers to think critically about the situations described in the case facts, to evaluate the wording and the intent of applicable provisions of the Code and Standards, and to reach their own conclusions about the proper course of action.

---

[15] Adam Smith, *The Theory of Moral Sentiments*, Part IV, Chapter II. Oxford: Clarendon Press (1976), pp. 187–188.

SUMMARY

- Investment analysis meets the two criteria for a profession: 1) It rests upon an established body of knowledge, and 2) it serves a broader good than the practitioner's self-interest. One such broader good is promoting fair and efficient capital markets, and a second is serving the client's financial well-being. Another characteristic of a profession is having a code of ethics.

- Individuals are not ethically bound to comply with unjust laws. It is presupposed that illegal activity is unethical, but legally compliant actions are not necessarily ethical.

- Ethical reasoning is logical but not mathematically precise. The CFA Institute Code of Ethics and Standards of Professional Conduct articulate general principles and shared values to guide investment analysts. A practical approach to ethical decision-making in a given case is to ask if a proposed course of action is consistent with the pertinent provisions of the Code and Standards, if the client would approve, if the action would enhance or compromise the individual's and the firm's reputations, and if the action exemplifies ethical leadership.

- Disciplinary sanctions may be imposed for violations of the Code and Standards. They range from private censure to revocation of participation in the CFA Program, membership in CFA Institute, or the right to use the CFA designation.

- The Code of Ethics has six provisions. They are to act with integrity, competence, diligence, respect, and in an ethical manner; to place the integrity of the investment profession and the interests of clients above one's own interests; to use reasonable care and exercise independent professional judgment; to practice and encourage others to practice in a professional and ethical manner; to promote the integrity of, and uphold the rules governing, capital markets; and to maintain and improve one's professional competence and to strive to maintain the competence of other investment professionals. Please refer to the Code of Ethics for the exact wording of these provisions.

- The Standards of Professional Conduct have seven major sections. They are Professionalism; Integrity of Capital Markets; Duties to Clients; Duties to Employers; Investment Analysis, Recommendations, and Actions; Conflicts of Interest; and Responsibilities as a CFA Institute Member or CFA Candidate. They are summarized below. Please refer to the Standards of Professional Conduct for the exact wording of all provisions.

- Standard I—Professionalism requires covered persons to understand and comply with applicable laws, rules, and regulations; to achieve and maintain independence and objectivity; not to misrepresent facts; and not to engage in any professional conduct involving dishonesty, fraud, or deceit, nor to commit any act that reflects adversely on their professional reputation, integrity, or competence.

- Standard II—Integrity of Capital Markets prohibits covered persons from acting or causing others to act on material nonpublic information that could affect the value of an investment and from engaging in practices that distort prices or artificially inflate trading volume with the intent to mislead market participants.

- Standard III—Duties to Clients stipulates that covered persons must act for the benefit of their clients, use reasonable care, exercise prudent judgment, and comply with applicable fiduciary duty. Covered persons must deal fairly and objectively with all clients. When in an advisory relationship, they must determine that an investment is suitable for the client, and when managing a portfolio to a specific mandate, they must only make recommendations and take actions that are consistent with the stated objectives and constraints of the portfolio. When covered persons communicate investment performance information, they must make reasonable efforts to ensure that it is fair, accurate, and complete. They must keep information about current, former, and prospective clients confidential unless the information concerns illegal activities, disclosure is required by law, or the client provides permission to disclose the information.

▶ Standard IV—Duties to Employers obligates covered persons to act for the benefit of their employer and not to deprive their employer of the advantage of their skills and abilities, divulge confidential information, or otherwise cause harm to their employer. They must not accept gifts, benefits, compensation, or consideration that competes with or might reasonably be expected to create a conflict of interest with their employer unless they obtain written consent from all parties involved. Supervisors must make reasonable efforts to detect and prevent violations of applicable laws, rules, regulations, and the Code and Standards by anyone subject to their supervision or authority.

▶ Standard V—Investment Analysis, Recommendations, and Actions requires covered persons to exercise diligence, independence, and thoroughness and to have a reasonable and adequate basis for any investment analysis, recommendation, and action. Covered persons must disclose the basic format and general principles of the investment process and promptly disclose any material process changes; include the factors important to their analyses, recommendations, or actions in client communications; and distinguish between fact and opinion. Covered persons must develop and maintain appropriate records to support their investment analysis, recommendations, actions, and other investment-related communications with clients and prospective clients.

▶ Standard VI—Conflicts of Interest requires covered persons to make full and fair disclosure, in plain language, of all matters that could reasonably be expected to impair their independence and objectivity or interfere with their respective duties to their employer, clients, and prospective clients. Investment transactions for clients and employers must have priority over transactions in which the covered person is the beneficial owner. Covered persons must disclose to their employer, clients, and prospective clients, as appropriate, any compensation, consideration, or benefit received by or paid to others for the recommendation of products or services (referral fees).

▶ Standard VII—Responsibilities as a CFA Institute Member or CFA Candidate requires members and candidates not to engage in any conduct that compromises the reputation or integrity of CFA Institute or the CFA designation or the integrity, validity, or security of the CFA examinations. Members and candidates must not misrepresent or exaggerate the meaning or implications of membership in CFA Institute, holding the CFA designation, or candidacy in the CFA program.

APPENDIX 3: CASE STUDIES

CASE STUDY 1: ARGENT CAPITAL MANAGEMENT

Case Facts

Françoise Vandezande, CFA, is a senior relationship manager in the New York office of Argent Capital Management, a French investment management firm. Her responsibilities include explaining the performance of separately managed global portfolios to institutional investors. One of her clients is the defined benefit pension plan sponsored by a U.S. subsidiary of Chimie Industrielle, a French manufacturer and distributor of specialty chemicals. The members of Chimie Industrielle's U.S. Investment Committee are highly sophisticated in the areas of international economics and finance, and Vandezande usually looks forward to interesting discussions at their quarterly meetings.

As the next quarterly meeting approached, however, she was worried. A performance attribution report prepared by Argent's performance analytics group showed that the Chimie Industrielle portfolio's disappointing results for the most recent quarter were due primarily to substantial losses incurred on foreign currency transactions. Moreover, Vandezande was aware that the client's investment policy statement imposed certain restrictions on active foreign currency management, and she suspected that Argent might have violated the constraints. She picked up her telephone to call Aidan McNamara, CFA, the portfolio manager for the Chimie Industrielle account.

Reputedly one of the leading managers of international mutual funds and separate accounts, Argent Capital Management is organized to capitalize on its strengths in economic forecasting. The global markets research team analyzes national economies and forecasts foreign exchange rates among major currencies, while the global industries group evaluates the relative attractiveness of industrial and commercial sectors in various regions of the world. Argent has always considered currency decisions to be distinct from asset allocation decisions.

After hearing the quarterly reports of the two research areas, the firm's investment council decides upon target weights both for industries within regions and for currency exposures. Although it is not always possible to find the requisite volume of fairly priced stocks in each category, Argent has generally been able to make this complex top-down investment decision process work by virtue of the firm's extensive cross-border network.

The two-day investment council meetings in Argent's headquarters are characterized by vigorous debate leading to a consensus view of near- and intermediate-term investment threats and opportunities across industries, regions, and currencies. The investment council accordingly defines tactical positions for the next quarter and communicates guidelines to the portfolio managers, securities analysts, and foreign exchange traders for execution. Guided by the target regional industry weights, the global securities analysis group recommends stock purchases and sales to the portfolio managers, and the foreign exchange desk enters forward and futures contracts to implement the currency strategy. The portfolio managers are responsible for monitoring positions for compliance with the clients' investment policies.

When Vandezande called him, McNamara sounded tense. "All the portfolios took a currency hit," the portfolio manager complained. "Global markets made a bad call on the Euro–yen exchange rate, but because they were so convinced they were right they maneuvered the Investment Council into approving a huge long position on the Euro and an equally short position on the yen. The markets moved against them." When Vandezande asked if these exposures were consistent with her client's investment policy statement, McNamara fell silent. "Off the top of my head, I don't know," he admitted. "I have a lot of portfolios to keep track of. I'll have to look into it."

Vandezande pulled Chimie Industrielle's investment policy statement from her filing cabinet. Three provisions leapt out at her:

1. Investment mandate: The international equity portfolio is benchmarked to the MSCI EAFE® Index.

5. The investment manager has explicit approval to manage currency risk but may not engage in currency speculation. The investment manager may enter currency forward and futures contracts to hedge currency risk back to U.S. dollars only up to 100% of the portfolio's underlying exposure.

9. The portfolio as a whole should be managed keeping in mind the original mandate under which the manager was hired. No extreme position should be taken which would alter the character of the portfolio that could produce results inconsistent with this mandate.

With Chimie Industrielle's U.S. Investment Committee meeting coming up in three days, Vandezande started to compose a high-priority e-mail message to the head of her department, the portfolio manager, the chief investment officer, and the director of compliance. The subject line read, "Foreign Exchange Losses in the Chimie Industrielle Portfolio."

Case Discussion

The portfolio manager appears to be unfamiliar with the client's mandate and constraints, and he has evidently violated the client's investment policies. His action is not in compliance with Standard III(C.1.b), which requires covered persons to "determine that an investment is suitable to the client's financial situation and consistent with the client's objectives, mandates, and constraints before making an investment recommendation or taking investment action."

In this case, Chimie Industrielle's written investment policy statement identifies the portfolio's investment mandate in terms of its benchmark, the MSCI EAFE® Index, and specifies that the advisor should not take any extreme position altering the character of the portfolio in such a way as to produce results inconsistent with the mandate. The benchmark does not hold short positions in currencies. In addition, the client's investment policy statement clearly states that the investment manager may not engage in currency speculation. By allowing Argent Capital Management's tactical currency management position to affect the risk profile of the Chimie Industrielle portfolio, the portfolio manager violated both these constraints.

Suggested Actions

Françoise Vandezande should:

▶ communicate to Chimie Industrielle a complete explanation of the events, including a review of the investment decision process and a statement of the Global Markets Research team's rationale in recommending atypical foreign exchange exposures; and

▶ explain how the firm will avoid similar situations in the future.

In order to improve internal controls, senior management should:

- ► modify the investment decision process to enable portfolio managers to exclude specific portfolios from firm-wide investment actions;
- ► re-educate the portfolio managers on the necessity of monitoring transactions for compliance with investment policy statements; and
- ► institute a policy of periodically auditing portfolios for compliance with client guidelines.

CASE STUDY 2: RIVER CITY PENSION FUND

Case Facts

Jack Aldred, CFA, was reviewing his notes in preparation for an Investment Commission meeting when his manager, River City treasurer, Barbara Castel, stepped into his office. "The meeting is in two hours," she said. "I want to know what you're planning to say about Northwest Capital."

Aldred is the chief investment officer of the River City Pension Fund, a mature defined benefit pension plan for municipal employees. He accepted this appointment six months ago after taking early retirement when his previous employer, an insurance company, was reorganized. While he worried that he was still a novice in navigating city politics, Aldred had already initiated significant improvements in the management of the city's pension assets. In particular, he recommended changes to the investment policy statement, designed more informative performance reports for the Investment Commission, and gained the commission's approval to engage in securities lending through the plan's custodian. Although he has only one person on his staff, Aldred sees further opportunities to improve the investment program. For example, he believes that the pension plan has more active managers than it needs, that their mandates overlap, and that the plan is consequently paying higher investment advisory fees than the investment program requires. His immediate problem, however, is deciding what to do about one of the pension plan's external managers in particular.

Northwest Capital Advisors has managed a small-cap value equity portfolio for the River City Pension Fund since the firm was founded eleven years ago. Under the leadership of the president and CEO, Roger Gray, a CFA charterholder, Northwest has emerged as one of the area's foremost small businesses. Among many other highly visible contributions to the community, Northwest donated financial expertise to a low-income housing program developed by the River City Interfaith Coalition, and the firm was credited with winning the Coalition a substantial grant from the state government. Northwest's employees also contributed large amounts in their own names to the election campaigns of local politicians with progressive policies, including the treasurer, as Aldred unintentionally discovered when he noticed some personal checks on her assistant's desk. Aldred was aware that the state legislature had enacted a law several years ago making it illegal for officers of firms doing business with municipalities to make campaign contributions to elected officials or candidates who might be in a position to influence the selection of vendors.

Although Northwest Capital Advisors is well regarded in the community, in the last three years the firm's always mediocre investment performance has declined substantially. Aldred looked at the results as reported by the manager and the custodial bank's performance measurement group:

River City Pension Fund

	Most Recent Quarter (%)	Year-to-Date (%)	1 Year (%)	3 Years (%)
Northwest Capital Advisors (Manager's Returns)	−0.89	1.51	3.29	10.11
Northwest Capital Advisors (Custodian's Returns)	−1.28	0.99	2.71	9.42
Benchmark Returns	−0.73	2.64	4.64	12.79

When he asked Roger Gray about the discrepancies between the returns calculated by Northwest and by the custodian, Gray explained that the custodian's standard asset pricing sources did not properly value the portfolio's small-cap holdings. "Those pricing services are geared to highly liquid, frequently traded stocks with large market capitalizations," he said. "We're the experts in the small-cap market. We're out there transacting every day!" However, the custodian stood by its valuations after reaffirming the prices of some of the securities specifically challenged by Northwest.

No less troubling was preliminary evidence that Northwest had strayed from its small-cap value mandate. Value investing had fallen out of favor in the marketplace, with growth stocks achieving substantially better rates of return for five of the last six quarters. Aldred wondered if Northwest was tactically introducing a growth tilt in an attempt to improve reported results in comparison with the benchmark and other small-cap value managers. At Aldred's request, the custodian had provided the holdings-based portfolio characteristics shown below. They were computed as of the end of the most recent quarter and as of the same time a year ago.

River City Pension Fund

	Current		One Year Ago	
	Northwest Capital Advisors	Benchmark	Northwest Capital Advisors	Benchmark
Market Capitalization ($ Billions)	6.54	9.12	8.57	8.93
Price/Earnings Ratio	27	19	18	17
Dividend Yield	0.05	0.08	0.09	0.08
Price/Book Ratio	6.2	3.4	4.5	3.9
Earnings Growth Rate %	14.3	8.2	7.6	7.4

Finally, Aldred was concerned by the fact that Northwest's small-cap value portfolio manager, one of the three original principals, had suddenly left the firm. When Aldred learned of this from an acquaintance, he called Gray, who declared that the portfolio manager had left amicably to accept a better-paying position at a larger corporation. Northwest was actively recruiting a replacement, but in the meantime Gray himself had assumed responsibility for the pension plan's portfolio. "And don't forget," he said, "we have a whole team of experienced people here."

Aldred looked at his boss. "I think the Investment Commission has to take some action," he said, "and I have a few ideas about how to proceed. But you understand the politics, and I'll do whatever you say. What are your instructions?"

Case Discussion—Jack Aldred, CFA

By indicating that he will do whatever his supervisor directs him to do, Aldred is at risk of violating Standard III(A) by disregarding his obligation to act for the benefit of the client and comply with applicable fiduciary duty. He may also fail to exercise independent professional judgment in violation of the Code and Standard I(B).

Aldred is an investment professional employed by a municipal pension plan sponsor, River City, with a fiduciary obligation to act on behalf of the plan participants and beneficiaries. He must monitor the performance of the system's external managers and take appropriate corrective action when their investment results are unfavorable. This primary responsibility overrides any other concerns, however worthy, such as supporting a local small business with a strong record of community involvement.

In addition, Aldred is obligated under the Code and Standards to exercise independent professional judgment. In this case, rather than simply assuring his supervisor that he will do whatever she tells him to do, he should set forth the alternative courses of action and give the treasurer his specific recommendations.

Suggested Actions

Jack Aldred should:

▶ determine which set of performance figures to use;

▶ determine whether the portfolio is being managed in conformity with its mandate;

▶ determine whether the departure of the portfolio manager adversely affects the firm's ability to produce acceptable investment results; and

▶ advise the treasurer how he thinks they should proceed with an evaluation of Northwest Capital Advisors' continuing eligibility to manage assets on behalf of the pension plan participants and beneficiaries.

Case Discussion—Roger Gray, CFA

Roger Gray, CFA, may be in violation of Standard III(D), which requires the fair, accurate, and complete presentation of investment performance, and Standard III(C.2), which requires investment managers to make recommendations and take actions that are consistent with the portfolio mandate. He may also be in violation of Standard I(A)—Knowledge of the Law and/or Standard IV(C)—Responsibilities of Supervisors.

There is disturbing evidence in the case facts that Gray may be overstating asset values in order to improve the firm's reported performance. If so, this would constitute a violation of Standard III(D), which obligates members and candidates to make reasonable efforts to ensure that investment performance information is fair, accurate, and complete.

Standard III(C.2) reads, "When Members and Candidates are responsible for managing a portfolio to a specific mandate, strategy, or style, they must only make investment recommendations or take investment actions that are consistent with the stated objectives and constraints of the portfolio." If it is the case that Gray is introducing growth securities to a value portfolio, he is taking investment actions at variance with the portfolio's mandate in breach of the Standard.

Officers of Northwest Capital Advisors appear to be making illegal campaign contributions. If Gray himself is making such contributions, he is personally in violation of Standard I(A), which requires covered persons to understand and comply with all applicable laws, rules, and regulations. In any event, as president and CEO of the firm, he has supervisory responsibility under Standard IV(C) to make reasonable efforts to detect and prevent violations of applicable laws, rules, and regulations by those subject to his supervision or authority.

Suggested Actions

Roger Gray should:

▶ critically review the firm's pricing sources and practices to ensure that portfolio valuations are fair and accurate;

▶ re-examine portfolio holdings to ensure that they are consistent with the mandate to invest in small-cap value securities; and

▶ discontinue, and instruct his employees to discontinue, the practice of making illegal campaign contributions.

CASE STUDY 3: MACROECONOMIC ASSET MANAGEMENT

Case Facts

Alice Chapman, CFA, director of marketing for Macroeconomic Asset Management, was reading a letter from Arlington Verification Service, a verification firm, when she received an e-mail from Jack Storrs. Jack, who reports to Alice, heads the RFP unit for Macroeconomic Asset Management. Alice set aside the letter and opened the e-mail. The subject was "Leeds Request for Proposal (RFP)." She read:

> Alice:
>
> James River Consulting is conducting a manager search for Leeds Machine Tool Corporation. The deadline for responding to the RFP is the end of next week.
>
> I have two questions:
>
> 1. The RFP asks if our compliance with the GIPS standards has been verified. What is the status of the verification project?
> 2. The RFP asks for a GIPS-compliant performance presentation with year-to-date results through the most recent measurement period. Has the performance group released the third quarter returns?
>
> Thanks! Regards, Jack

Alice closed the e-mail and picked up the letter from Arlington Verification Service. The manager of the verification project had written:

> We regret to inform you that we cannot issue a verification report for Macroeconomic Asset Management. Our review of the firm's policies and processes and our examination of sample portfolios and composites revealed significant deficiencies in the following areas:
>
> ► missing or inadequate documentation (e.g., client agreements and composite definitions);
> ► actual, fee-paying, discretionary portfolios not included in at least one composite;
> ► inconsistent application of the firm's policies regarding asset valuations and the treatment of external cash flows, affecting the accuracy of reported composite returns; and
> ► missing or incorrect elements of performance presentations (e.g., certain composites did not include dispersion measures).
>
> The attached memorandum provides further details, along with our recommendations on how to correct the noncompliant conditions. . . .

Alice knew that James River Consulting was an influential organization and that Leeds Machine Tool Corporation would be a significant addition to Macroeconomic Asset Management's client list. She thought the consultants would accept the firm's not having been verified, but they would likely consider compliance with the GIPS standards a requirement for winning the mandate. She started to consider how Macroeconomic Asset Management could respond most advantageously to the RFP. Perhaps, she thought, they could gain time by continuing to claim compliance while challenging the verifier's conclusions. Alice picked up the telephone to call Terry Larson, CFA, the firm's director of performance measurement.

Case Discussion

Alice Chapman is subject to the CFA Institute Code of Ethics and Standards of Professional Conduct. The Code pertinently requires her to "act with integrity, competence, diligence, respect, and in an ethical manner with . . . prospective clients. . . ." The Standards prohibit covered persons from participating or assisting in any violation of applicable laws, rules, or regulations, including the Code and Standards themselves; prohibit misrepresentation; and obligate covered persons to "make reasonable efforts to ensure that [investment performance information] is fair, accurate, and complete."

Standard I(A) stipulates that covered persons "must understand and comply with all applicable laws, rules, and regulations (including CFA Institute's Code of Ethics and Standards of Professional Conduct) of any government, governmental agency, regulatory organization, licensing agency, or professional association governing professional activities. . . . Members and candidates must not knowingly participate or assist in and must dissociate from any violation of such laws, rules, or regulations." Standard I(C) prohibits covered persons from making "any statement that misrepresents facts relating to investment analysis, recommendations, actions, or other professional activities." It is Macroeconomic Asset Management as a firm that claims compliance with the GIPS standards, but Alice is responsible for communications with prospective clients, and she is in a position to determine if the claim of compliance is valid. It is unclear whether Alice has the authority to withdraw the claim of compliance, but it is certainly within her power to determine the facts, inform senior management of her conclusions, and recommend, if appropriate, that the claim be omitted from the firm's performance presentations. Arlington's refusal to issue a verification report constitutes strong evidence that Macroeconomic Asset Management is not justified in claiming to comply with the GIPS standards. If the verifier's findings are correct and Alice does not take appropriate action, she would appear to be in violation of Standard I(A) by knowingly helping the firm persist in making a false claim, and she herself would arguably be guilty of misrepresentation under Standard I(C).

Alice Chapman is not responsible for preparing performance presentations for Macroeconomic Asset Management; that assignment appears to fall to Terry Larson, CFA. However, she does communicate investment performance information to prospective clients. Moreover, she is aware of the seriousness of Arlington's allegations about "significant deficiencies" in the firm's performance-related policies and processes. Standard III(D) does not require firms to comply with the GIPS standards, but it does require covered persons to make "reasonable efforts" to ensure that performance information they communicate is "fair, accurate, and complete." Especially troubling in this regard are Arlington's assertions that not all actual, fee-paying, discretionary portfolios are included in at least one composite and that the accuracy of reported composite returns is questionable. Standard III(D) obliges Alice not to include performance data in the Leeds Machine Tool RFP without first attempting to ascertain whether it is a fair, accurate, and complete representation of Macroeconomic Asset Management's investment results for the strategy sought by the prospective client.

Suggested Actions

Alice Chapman should:

▶ determine whether Arlington Verification Service's conclusions about Macroeconomic Asset Management's performance policies and processes are justified;

▶ avoid making any statement that claims or implies that the firm complies with the GIPS standards unless and until the firm does in fact meet all the requirements for GIPS compliance; and

▶ make reasonable efforts to ensure that performance information provided by Macroeconomic Asset Management reflects the firm's investment results fairly, accurately, and completely.

CASE STUDY 4: BOB EHRLICH

Case Facts

"How was the luncheon, Bob?"

"Very interesting!"

"Good! When you get a chance, write a memorandum summarizing the discussion and circulate it to analytic group."

"I will. Probably not today, though—I have a deadline to meet for the McGregor Foundation."

Bob Ehrlich watched his supervisor go into a conference room, where a meeting was already in progress. Ehrlich, a performance analyst in the U.K. custodial division of a large international bank, had just returned from a luncheon sponsored by an investment consulting firm. A panel of speakers had discussed benchmark selection for fixed income portfolios, but Ehrlich found the informal talk at his table more stimulating.

One person seated at Ehrlich's table had been especially engaging. He introduced himself as Peter Neustadt and said that he had recently started his own firm to assist investment management boutiques in gathering assets. Neustadt seemed extremely interested in Ehrlich's work at the bank. Ehrlich was flattered by the attention, and he readily agreed with Neustadt's suggestion that they meet in a pub at the end of the day to continue their conversation.

"Bob," Neustadt confided, "I have many contacts in the money management business, and the future is promising, but right now I have a small firm without much technological support. I'm hoping that, with your analytical talent and your access to information, you might be willing to join me as a part-time consultant. The work would be light, and you might find the extra income very attractive. Over the long term, as my business grows, I may be able to offer you a full-time position with equity in the firm. What do you think?"

"Well," Ehrlich said, "I'd certainly like to hear more!"

Neustadt explained that he represented newly organized investment management firms—he called them "emerging firms"—in search of institutional investors. Neustadt's clients typically had portfolio management and trading experience but lacked marketing skills and sophisticated performance analytics. "I can put together a first-rate marketing presentation," Neustadt concluded, "but I need the performance data—benchmark returns, attributions, style analyses, economic commentaries—all the things that you, and your bank, do so well."

The two men talked about Ehrlich's family and his career path at the bank until it was time for Ehrlich to head home for dinner. He promised to think about Neustadt's offer and to call him the next day.

Case Discussion

Neustadt is proposing an inappropriate arrangement. Even if Ehrlich were to do the work on his own time, it is clear that Neustadt expects him to make use of his employer's facilities for personal benefit in violation of the Code and Standards. The Code requires covered persons to "place the integrity of the investment profession . . . and the interests of their employer above their own personal interests" and to "practice in a professional and ethical manner that will reflect credit on themselves and the profession." Under Standard I(D)—Misconduct, covered persons "must not engage in any professional conduct involving dishonesty, fraud, or deceit or commit any act that reflects adversely on their integrity, good reputation, [or] trustworthiness. . . ." If Ehrlich were to make unauthorized use of the bank's performance measurement and related systems in service to Neustadt, he would be engaging in professional misconduct.

Especially pertinent are provisions of Standard IV—Duties to Employers. Standard IV(A) addresses Loyalty, and Standard IV(B) addresses Additional Compensation Arrangements. In addition, Standard VI(A)—Disclosure of Conflicts might apply in this case.

Standard IV(A) reads, "In matters related to their employment, Members and Candidates must act for the benefit of their employer and not deprive their employer of the advantage of their skills and abilities, divulge confidential information, or otherwise cause harm to their employer." The course of action Neustadt is urging is potentially harmful to the bank that employs Ehrlich. If Ehrlich were to utilize the bank's computer, analytic, and information resources without management approval (see Standard IV(B) below), he would not only be exploiting a position of trust for personal gain but also misusing his employer's physical and intellectual property. (The bank may also have an employee code of conduct addressing this point.) In addition, he might be divulging confidential information and exposing the bank to financial and reputational risk. For example, capital market index data is costly, and the providers generally impose legally binding restrictions intended to prevent subscribers from disseminating data to nonsubscribers. Were Ehrlich to give Neustadt benchmark returns, and to use benchmark constituent data in performance attribution analyses prepared for Neustadt's clients, he would almost certainly be redistributing index data illicitly. Neustadt also mentions economic commentaries among the items he would like to receive. His intentions are unclear, but he might plan to portray proprietary work done by bank employees for bank clients as originating with the investment management firms he represents in the marketplace. Ehrlich's accepting Neustadt's invitation would reflect disloyalty to his employer.

Standard IV(B) reads, "Members and Candidates must not accept gifts, benefits, compensation, or consideration that competes with, or might reasonably be expected to create a conflict of interest with, their employer's interest unless they obtain written consent from all parties involved." Neustadt has offered to pay Ehrlich for his work, and accordingly Ehrlich would be required by the Standards of Professional Conduct to secure, in writing, his management's approval of the arrangement. In fairness, Ehrlich would have to disclose his understanding with Neustadt in full, including Neustadt's expectation that Ehrlich will use information and analytical resources available to him only because he is a bank employee. While the bank's management may not disapprove Ehrlich's accepting outside employment on his own time, it is unlikely they would agree to his use of corporate assets. Nonetheless, Ehrlich is not free under the Standards of Professional Conduct to accept the consulting position from Neustadt without his employer's approval.

Standard VI(A) stipulates that covered persons "must make full and fair disclosure of all matters that could reasonably be expected to . . . interfere with their respective duties to their employer, clients, and prospective clients." Such disclosures must "communicate the relevant information effectively." As previously observed, the arrangement Neustadt is proposing appears to conflict with Ehrlich's duties to his employer, for example, his responsibility to safeguard intellectual property belonging to the bank and its vendors. In addition, it is possible that the bank would consider providing performance measurement services to Neustadt's clients. If so, Ehrlich would be working in competition with his employer. Unless he disclosed the conflict, Ehrlich would be in violation of the Standards.

Suggested Action

▶ Ehrlich should reject Neustadt's offer.

CASE STUDY 5: ALEX KAYE

Case Facts

Alex Kaye has a production problem. Kaye, a member of CFA Institute, is the head of performance measurement advisory services for a regional office of a large consulting organization headquartered overseas. The market demand for verifications that investment management firms are in compliance with the Global Investment Performance Standards has increased sharply, and, mindful of the firm's challenging profitability goals, Kaye has accepted a number of investment management firms as new clients. At the same time, however, his staff has a backlog of unfinished verification assignments. In addition, he recently lost an experienced project manager and a capable analyst, both of whom indicated in their exit interviews that they could no longer meet the strains of the workload. Senior management has approved hiring replacements, and the recruitment process is underway, but Kaye knows it will take time to find, hire, and train new employees. In the meantime, Kaye promoted Derek Nelson to the vacant project manager's position. Nelson has about nine months' experience as a verification analyst.

With the new clients impatient to get started, Kaye decided that he had to engage in "triage" to regain control of the verification practice in his region. He instructed his four team leaders to submit status reports and expedited timeframes for completing their current assignments. In reply Nelson, who was out of town on assignment, wrote the e-mail shown below. Kaye needed Nelson to finish his work and move on to a new project, and he wondered if he had made a mistake in promoting him.

Tuesday, 11 November, 23:15

Subject: Argent Asset Management Verification

Alex:

Before I can respond to your request for a revised schedule to complete the Argent Asset Management verification, I need your guidance on two areas of concern. The project initially fell behind because the client was unprepared and had to spend a great deal of time gathering information and then of course my predecessor quit, but now that we are on-site and the work is underway we have encountered some difficulties. How fast we can wrap up the engagement and get back to the office will depend upon how we resolve these issues.

1. We learned that documentation for about two-thirds of the accounts we sampled was recently turned over to an external records management company for archiving and will not be available for inspection until it has all been catalogued. The documentation in question includes investment management agreements and client-directed policy guidelines upon which we base our determination that the accounts are discretionary as Argent Asset Management defines that term. The documentation we have been able to examine is in order, and the client maintains that all the accounts are properly classified as discretionary. Should we wait until the remaining documentation is available, select other accounts whose files are known to be here, or simply accept the client's representation?

> **2.** We found several instances where the treatment of large external cash flows was inconsistent with Argent Asset Management's composite-specific policies. The process generally appears to be well controlled, but in these apparently isolated cases there was a material impact on portfolio returns for the periods in which the cash flows occurred. The return impact was random; some returns would have been higher and others lower if the cash flows had been handled properly. However, in my opinion the exceptions were significant enough to raise questions about the validity of composite returns. Should we do more testing, or is it acceptable to conclude that any errors are likely to be offsetting and on average the composite returns are reasonably accurate?
>
> I think we can move ahead fairly quickly with the rest of the engagement, but I'd like to discuss these items with you. Please call me when you can.
>
> Regards, Derek

Case Discussion

Despite the business pressures in their verification practice, Kaye and Nelson are obligated under the Code to act with competence and diligence, to use reasonable care, to exercise independent judgment in the conduct of their professional activities, and to maintain and improve their professional competence. Standard I(A) requires covered persons to understand and comply with all applicable laws, rules, and regulations, including those of any professional association governing professional activities; in the present case, this requirement may be taken to apply to the GIPS provisions for verification. Standard III(A) requires covered persons to "act for the benefit of their clients and place their clients' interests before their employer's or [their] own interests" and to "act with reasonable care and exercise prudent judgment." Under Standard IV(C), Kaye is also accountable for taking reasonable measures to detect and prevent violations of applicable laws, rules, regulations, and the Code and Standards by those subject to his supervision or authority.

Kaye and Nelson are obligated by the Code to act with competence and by the Standards to know and comply with applicable laws, rules, and regulations. By holding themselves out as verifiers, they are additionally obligated to understand all the requirements and recommendations of the GIPS standards, which are themselves ethical standards. Accordingly, they are required to be familiar with and to adhere to the required verification procedures set forth in the Global Investment Performance Standards.

For background, two provisions of the GIPS standard are pertinent to Nelson's question about the missing documentation: First, verifiers must be satisfied that all of the firm's actual discretionary fee-paying portfolios are included in a composite and that the firm's definition of discretion has been consistently applied over time. Second, verifiers must obtain a listing of all firm portfolios and determine on a sampling basis whether the manager's classification of the account as discretionary or nondiscretionary is appropriate by referring to the account's agreement and the firm's written guidelines for determining investment discretion.

Although it is entirely possible that poor planning made pertinent documentation temporarily unavailable, it is also conceivable that Argent Asset Management has deliberately contrived to withhold or conceal client agreements and investment policy statements that would not support its claim of compliance with the GIPS standards. In this situation, selecting additional accounts among those Argent Asset Management is making readily available would not appear to be conclusive, and accepting the client's representations that all the accounts selected for sampling are properly classified as discretionary or nondiscretionary would not reflect the exercise of due care and independent professional judgment.

With regard to the inconsistent treatment of large external cash flows, the GIPS standards for verification advise that the presence of errors may warrant selecting a larger sample or applying additional verification procedures.

Standard III(A) of the CFA Institute Standards of Professional Conduct reads in pertinent part, "Members and Candidates must act for the benefit of their clients and place their clients' interests before their employer's or their own interests. Members and Candidates have a duty of loyalty to their clients and must act with reasonable care and exercise prudent judgment. . . ." In the present case, Kaye is in danger of signaling to his staff members that they should take shortcuts in order to complete their assignments as quickly as possible. Kaye risks placing his employer's interest in profitability and his own interest in compensation and advancement within the consulting organization ahead of the clients' interests in having their compliance with the GIPS standards properly verified.

Finally, Standard IV(C) requires covered persons to make "reasonable efforts to detect and prevent violations of applicable laws, rules, regulations, and the Code and Standards by anyone subject to their supervision or authority." It is Kaye's responsibility as Nelson's supervisor to prevent Nelson from violating the Code of Ethics, the Standards of Professional Conduct, and the GIPS standards as they apply to verification.

Suggested Actions

Alex Kaye should:

- ► cease taking on new business until his office has capacity to handle it professionally;
- ► ensure that his staff members are adequately trained in required and recommended verification procedures in accordance with the GIPS standards;
- ► communicate to his staff that all assignments are to be completed with due care; and
- ► provide Nelson appropriate guidance in response to the issues raised in Nelson's e-mail.

PRACTICE PROBLEMS FOR READING 3

1. The Code of Ethics explicitly requires covered persons to:
   A. uphold the rules governing capital markets.
   B. report suspected violations to CFA Institute.
   C. report suspected violations to regulatory authorities.

2. Members and candidates must:
   A. endorse the principles of sound corporate governance.
   B. foster the expansion of regulatory oversight in the investment industry.
   C. strive to maintain and improve the competence of other investment Professionals.

3. In the event that the Code and Standards are stricter than applicable law, covered persons must understand and comply with:
   A. applicable law.
   B. the Code and Standards.

4. A covered person might be excused for assisting in a violation of applicable regulations if she:
   A. did not know the regulations.
   B. knew the regulations but did not believe they applied.
   C. knew the regulations but was unaware a violation was taking place.

5. The most accurate statement about gifts is that members and candidates must not solicit or accept any gift that could reasonably be expected to:
   A. exceed customary business practice.
   B. radically change their standard of living.
   C. compromise their independence and objectivity.

6. Under the provision of the Standards governing misconduct, covered persons must not commit any act that reflects adversely on their:
   A. investment performance.
   B. loyalty to their employer.
   C. professional reputation, integrity, or competence.

7. Non-public information is material if it:
   A. violates client confidentiality.
   B. would affect the price of a security.
   C. has not been fully disclosed to all market participants.

8. Members and candidates must not engage in practices that:
   A. exploit asymmetrical information.
   B. achieve gains at the expense of other market participants.
   C. distort prices with the intent to mislead market participants.

9. The duty of loyalty, prudence, and care requires:
   A. developing and maintaining appropriate records.
   B. acting with reasonable care and exercising prudent judgment.
   C. giving an employer the advantage of one's skills and abilities.

10. Fair dealing does *not* require covered persons to:
- **A.** provide the same level of service to all clients.
- **B.** monitor the objective equitability of trading processes.
- **C.** proportionally allocate securities among discretionary accounts managed in the same investment strategy or style.

11. A covered person in an advisory relationship should inquire about the client's total portfolio in order to:
- **A.** determine the client's level of investment experience.
- **B.** estimate the client's needs for current income over the planning horizon.
- **C.** avoid contributing to an undue concentration of risk in the client's assets.

12. When covered persons communicate investment performance information, they must make reasonable efforts to ensure that it:
- **A.** applies on a firm-wide basis.
- **B.** is fair, accurate, and complete.
- **C.** complies with the Global Investment Performance Standards (GIPS®).

13. The requirement to keep client information confidential does not apply when it:
- **A.** concerns illegal activity.
- **B.** has been reported in public media.
- **C.** concerns a former rather than an existing client.

14. The most accurate statement about accepting additional compensation from external sources is that members and candidates:
- **A.** must not directly compete with their employer.
- **B.** must obtain written consent from all parties involved.
- **C.** must not allow their outside work to interfere with their regular work.

15. Supervisors who are CFA charterholders must:
- **A.** inform their employees of the Code and Standards.
- **B.** conduct regular evaluations of employees' performance.
- **C.** make reasonable efforts to detect and prevent regulatory violations by their employees.

16. Investment analyses and recommendations must be based upon:
- **A.** certainty, not scenarios or projections.
- **B.** original research, not secondary sources.
- **C.** reliable, up-to-date evidence, not prejudgments.

17. Members and candidates must disclose to clients and prospective clients:
- **A.** proprietary models for screening and selecting investments.
- **B.** the basic format and general principles of the investment process.
- **C.** the firm's history of regulatory violations, including current investigations.

18. Investment professionals cannot initiate transactions for themselves unless:
- **A.** the investment is unsuitable for their clients.
- **B.** clients and employers have had a fair chance to invest.
- **C.** the professionals are the beneficial owner of the account.

19. The most accurate statement about referral fees is that they must be disclosed:

    A. only to prospective clients.

    B. if the client asks about them.

    C. to employers, clients, and prospective clients.

20. Earning the CFA designation signifies:

    A. superior investment insight.

    B. completion of a rigorous program.

    C. a commitment to active portfolio management.

SOLUTIONS FOR READING 3

1. A is correct.

2. C is correct.

3. B is correct.

4. C is correct.

5. C is correct.

6. C is correct.

7. B is correct.

8. C is correct.

9. B is correct.

10. A is correct.

11. C is correct.

12. B is correct.

13. A is correct.

14. B is correct.

15. C is correct.

16. C is correct.

17. B is correct.

18. B is correct.

19. C is correct.

20. B is correct.

THE CONSULTANT
by Jules A. Huot, CFA

LEARNING OUTCOMES

The candidate should be able to:	Mastery
a. evaluate professional conduct and formulate an appropriate response to actions that violate the Code of Ethics and Standards of Professional Conduct;	☐
b. prepare appropriate policy and procedural changes needed to assure compliance with the Code of Ethics and Standards of Professional Conduct.	☐

CASE FACTS   1

Mark Vernley, CFA, is quite disturbed by Plains Pipeline Systems' recent allegation that he has, in essence, acted unethically—the first such accusation in Vernley's career. Although Vernley was exonerated of any allegation of wrongdoing by the authorities, he is worried that his personal reputation and integrity and those of his engineering consulting firm have been damaged. He has decided to make some changes in his personal portfolio and the procedures of the firm to prevent unethical conduct, breaches of the law, or the appearance of improprieties.

Mark Vernley

Vernley, a petroleum engineer with a doctorate in engineering and 30 years' business experience, began his career as a reservoir engineer with Deepwell Explorations. After 15 years with Deepwell, he joined a major brokerage firm as a securities analyst specializing in energy issues. During that time, he acquired his CFA charter and became a member of CFA Institute. Some eight years later, he set up his own consulting firm, Energetics, Inc., which currently employs 10 professional engineers. Energetics consults on a broad array of projects, including asset and project valuations.

During his years in the investment industry, Vernley invested actively in the stock market (with a concentration in energy stocks). When he worked for Deepwell Explorations, however, he had participated in the employee stock purchase plan and had exercised the stock options granted to him. As a result, a sizable portion of his wealth is now in the shares of Deepwell Explorations.

The market value and composition of his current portfolio is as follows:

Deepwell Explorations	$250,000
National Marketing and Refining	50,000
Integrated Energy Resources	45,000
Highridge Oil Pipeline	50,000
Interplains Gas Pipeline	75,000
Logline Well Service	35,000
Subtotal	$505,000
Shares in other industries	475,000
Total portfolio	$980,000

Vernley's practice during the past seven years has been quite profitable, and business is brisk. His peers generally consider him very successful. He has kept up his membership in CFA Institute and has taken an active part in energy industry affairs. He is a long-standing member of his local and national professional engineers society. He has served as president of the local engineers society for several terms and as a member of the society's professional standards committee on the national level. Although he has never written down the professional standards he expects of the company's employees, all of the engineers belong to the professional engineers society, and he has made clear in personal communications that he expects them to meet high standards in honesty, fairness, and avoiding conflicts of interest. Vernley himself is known for his professionalism, expertise, and integrity.

The Consulting Contract

Energetics recently won a contract, for which Vernley wrote the proposal, from Highridge Oil Pipeline to devise a plan to resolve conflicts with Highridge's clients. Highridge has a long history of disputes with the users of its pipeline—the shippers of oil—over the tolls charged. Highridge wants to recover increases in its operating costs; the shippers want regulations that reflect the market-driven, competitive conditions of the industry. They believe such regulations will force Highridge to increase efficiency in its operations. Both parties have engaged in expensive and acrimonious hearings before the regulatory agency. Vernley's plan for Highridge consists of an incentive-based method to set pipeline tolls, which would give Highridge a financial incentive to operate its pipeline more economically than at present. Under the plan, Highridge will share with the oil companies, including Deepwell Explorations and Integrated Energy Resources, any increase in earnings that results from reduced costs. The result should lower pipeline tolls, eliminate contentious rate hearings, and increase Highridge's profits.

After lengthy hearings, the regulatory agency ratified this plan. But Plains Pipeline Systems, a consistently more efficient and profitable carrier than

Highridge, filed an objection with the regulatory agency to the effect that Vernley's plan is flawed because he has a conflict of interest arising from his personal portfolio positions. At a subsequent hearing, the regulatory agency rejected Plains Pipeline Systems' objection and confirmed its prior decision.

> *Discuss the actions that Vernley could have taken to avoid any allegations of conflict of interest based on his holdings of energy company shares. Create a plan that will enable Vernley to shield his company from unethical acts that his employees might commit.*

CASE DISCUSSION   2

In this case, a professional engineer has been charged with having a conflict of interest that prevented him from offering objective advice to his client. The engineer/owner has spent his entire career in the oil industry and enjoyed an excellent reputation and strong financial success. This allegation is the first of any kind made against him or his firm. It has been dismissed, and he is confident that all his employees are honest and that he can rely on them to act in an ethical and professional manner, something he took for granted until now. He is disturbed, however, about the effect of the allegations on his and his firm's reputation, and he wants to avoid any further allegations in the future.

Conflicts of Interest in a Personal Portfolio

Vernley can deal with conflicts of interest in two ways. The ideal is to avoid all conflicts of interest, real or perceived. If a conflict of interest cannot be avoided, however, then full disclosure must be made to the interested parties. Each approach entails various options.

Avoidance

Vernley can avoid any conflict between the interests of his clients and his personal investments if he refrains from investing in any energy-related securities. Because he already holds a portfolio heavily invested in such stock, the next logical step if he follows this course is divestiture. Selling his investments is a drastic option, however, that Vernley might find unreasonable. After all, he built up his portfolio gradually over the course of his long career when he could not foresee his current situation.

Another option is to establish a "blind trust," in which the account is fully discretionary and the trust beneficiary is not aware of the holdings until they are reported by the manager to the extent required by law, usually on a quarterly basis. To retain his current holdings, Vernley's investment policy might specify that his account hold a certain percentage of energy-related issues. Under this arrangement, Vernley would still know what his holdings are, however, if only after the fact. Although he would not know the exact nature of future transactions in his portfolio, he could reasonably anticipate their general direction (because of the account policies and guidelines). In any event, he could still be perceived as having a conflict, which would require that he disclose it to his clients.

An option that would keep Vernley at arm's length would be to make his oil and gas investments by way of a mutual fund specializing in energy-related issues, which would be managed by a third party over which Vernley would have no influence. In this way, he would share in a portfolio that is likely to be much more diversified than his current portfolio, thereby removing any question of the materiality of any one holding. He would also not take part in any investment decision making.

Disclosure

Whenever Vernley has a real or perceived conflict of interest because he holds shares whose prices may change if his clients adopt his recommendations, he must disclose such conflicts to his clients. Disclosure can take many forms, which depend on the circumstances. At a minimum, Vernley must disclose to clients of Energetics the existence and the nature of any conflict of interest surrounding a consulting assignment. Vernley must ensure that such disclosures are prominent, are delivered in plain language, and communicate the relevant information effectively. Then, it is up to the client to evaluate the materiality of Vernley's beneficial ownership of shares and whether the conflict of interest is significant enough to affect Vernley's ability to give advice or make recommendations that are unbiased and objective. If, in order to keep his personal matters private, Vernley decides to disclose conflicts to clients only when they are material, he is flirting with danger. Establishing what is material is difficult in any context because of the judgment required. Many people will perceive a conflict of interest no matter what the materiality.

Some of Energetics's consulting assignments may entail the preparation of a submission to the regulatory agency. In certain circumstances, Energetics would need to disclose in the submission a detailed list of Vernley's holdings. Because these documents are usually in the public domain, such declarations generally constitute public disclosure.

A Plan for Energetics

Nothing in this case suggests that any member of Energetics acted unethically. On the contrary, the description of Vernley's activities, the engineers' affiliations, and the overall reputation of Vernley and his firm lead to the conclusion that ethical values permeate the company, infusing the organization and its operating systems with a self-sustaining ethical culture. Energetics operates in an environment, however, in which the absence of a formal compliance program could expose it to costly liabilities in the event of a mishap. At a minimum, the perception of a potential conflict of interest could place the firm in an unfavorable light in the eyes of its clients.

Vernley needs to establish a comprehensive formal compliance system. The main objectives of the program will be to deter unethical or illegal acts and to provide an "affirmative defense" in the event of employee violations. The fear of being caught and of being punished are prominent enforcement characteristics of compliance systems.

For proper implementation, a compliance program must have a number of features: communication, education, and compliance procedures.

Communication

The company must inform employees of the standards to which they must conform and must deliver to employees copies of these standards—whether statutes, codes of conduct, or standards of practice. In this case, Vernley could use the CFA Institute Code of Ethics and Standards of Professional Conduct as the basis for a formal compliance manual.

Education

The company must educate employees about the main features of the adopted standards and some of their intricacies through workshops and training sessions. Attendance at these sessions should be compulsory, and the sessions should include case studies to illustrate practical applications of the standards.

Procedures for Compliance

Companies should have written documents that spell out their compliance procedures. A company can document several measures that are aids in managing its compliance program effectively, including:

- ▶ annual certification by employees that they have maintained familiarity with the standards and agree to abide by them;
- ▶ for the purpose of detecting conflicts of interest or insider trading, required reporting by employees, at least quarterly, of all securities transactions for their own personal accounts or those in which they have a beneficial interest;
- ▶ disclosing to management the existence and nature of any possible or actual compensation from sources other than the employer;
- ▶ certification by employees that they have not entered into an independent business activity in competition with their employer. The purpose of this measure is to protect the firm from, for example, misappropriation of trade secrets, misuse of confidential information, solicitation of customers prior to cessation of employment, or self-dealing; and
- ▶ employee memberships in organizations that maintain standards required for the practice of their professions—for example, continued affiliation by Energetics's engineers with the association of professional engineers.

Culture and Leadership

Finally, Vernley should continue instilling an ethical culture in Energetics by developing a corporate credo and moral system based on his and his colleagues' professional standards, self-interest, values, and ideals. The intention is for the system to become a social arrangement among interdependent peers that is grounded in responsible conduct and self-governance according to the chosen values. The essential characteristic of this approach is that the culture be based on the collective integrity of the organization, with its members sharing a set of guiding principles and agreeing to joint accountability.

This approach recommended for Vernley is leader driven. Leaders gain credibility when they develop and communicate their guiding values, integrate them in their operations, and imbue the company's decision-making processes with them.

PEARL INVESTMENT MANAGEMENT (A), (B), AND (C)

by Glen A. Holden, Jr., CFA

LEARNING OUTCOMES

The candidate should be able to:	Mastery
a. evaluate professional conduct and formulate an appropriate response to actions that violate the Code of Ethics and Standards of Professional Conduct;	☐
b. prepare appropriate policy and procedural changes needed to assure compliance with the Code of Ethics and Standards of Professional Conduct.	☐

PEARL INVESTMENT MANAGEMENT (A)   1

Case Facts

After obtaining an M.B.A. in finance, Peter Sherman is offered a position as an account manager with Pearl Investment Management, an investment counseling firm specializing in equity portfolio management for pension and profit-sharing funds, endowment funds, and high-net-worth individuals' accounts. Sherman begins work in the firm's back office, handling administrative tasks for his assigned accounts, settling transactions, balancing the accounts to bank records, and ensuring that client guidelines are followed.

Pearl is a large firm with a number of different departments, including account administration, research, and portfolio management. Having its own research staff allows Pearl to temper its reliance on brokerage firm research, to weigh its conclusions against the opinions of others, and to perform security analysis on companies that are not well followed for Pearl's proprietary use in client portfolio recommendations.

Many of the portfolio managers and analysts at Pearl are CFA charterholders, and as a result, the firm has adopted the CFA Institute Code of Ethics and Standards of Professional Conduct as part of its policy for internal compliance.

The firm policy manual also contains excerpts from laws and regulations that govern investment advisors such as Pearl (and its employees), including sections from the U.S. Securities Act of 1933, the U.S. Securities Exchange Act of 1934, the Investment Advisers Act of 1940, and the National Association of Securities Dealers manual. All employees must read and sign a statement when they join the firm that they have read Pearl's policies and must repeat this procedure at the beginning of each subsequent year as a reminder of their compliance responsibilities.

On Sherman's first day on the job, his department head gives him the policy manual as part of his orientation program, requests that he read it during the day before signing the compliance statement, and advises him that the firm's compliance department will answer any questions he may have. Sherman reads through the manual quickly and then signs the company's personnel policies statement.

After a few months, Sherman feels comfortable handling the administrative tasks related to the client accounts he manages at Pearl and ensuring that client investment guidelines are being followed. He enjoys the challenges of being the account manager for his (and Pearl's) clients, the close access to investment information and strategies, and the opportunity to invest his savings with greater insight and understanding than he had before this job. Previously, his personal investments had been in no-load mutual funds, but in his new position, he sees that he can achieve greater reward by building a portfolio of his own.

To further this goal, Sherman reads books about investments and portfolio strategy, as well as the company summaries generated by the firm's research department, and he follows the daily price changes of the firm's major holdings. He enjoys discussing his new-found knowledge with family and friends. To put his new knowledge to work in his own portfolio, Sherman decides to open an account with a national discount broker and purchase a few of the stocks that are Pearl's largest equity positions.

Identify violations or possible violations of the CFA Institute Code and Standards in this case; state what actions are required by Sherman and/or his supervisor to correct the potential violations, and make a short policy statement a firm could use to prevent the violations.

Case Discussion

This case illustrates how easily a young, unwary analyst can slip into questionable actions. The potential violations evident in this case relate to the responsibilities of supervisors, the obligation to obey all laws and regulations, the standards for trading for personal accounts, and the prohibition against conveying confidential client information.

Knowledge of the Law

Under the Code and Standards, the basis for Pearl's policy manual, Peter Sherman, his supervisor, and all employees at Pearl have certain fundamental responsibilities.

Governing Laws and Regulations   Standard I(A)—Knowledge of the Law requires Sherman to know about the laws and regulations governing his behavior and that of the firm. Allusions in the case to Sherman's use of information gained through employment at Pearl indicate that Sherman is not aware of all the regulations governing his behavior. Sherman is in a junior position, however, and the responsibility for educating junior employees generally lies with their supervisors. In a large firm such as Pearl, the compliance department, in addition to the supervisor's training, should offer instruction and education in this critical area.

Legal and Ethical Violations   For supervisors, top managers, or any employees, to knowingly participate in or assist in a violation of the Code and Standards gives rise to a violation of Standard I(A). The requirement "knowingly" is important: Although members are presumed to know all applicable laws, rules, and regulations, they may not recognize violations if they are not aware of all the facts giving rise to the violations.

Actions Required   Sherman's supervisor should monitor the activities of Sherman for any violations of the securities laws, the Code and Standards, or other firm policies and procedures.

Policy Statement for a Firm   "Supervisors shall exercise reasonable supervision over those employees subject to their control and shall monitor all actions of employees in their charge to determine that the firm's policies are being followed and to prevent any violation by such persons of applicable statutes, regulations, or provisions of the Code of Ethics and Standards of Professional Conduct. Supervisors shall review the contents of the compliance manual with all direct charges when they are hired and answer any questions or concerns the employees may have."

Responsibilities of Supervisors

Under Standard IV(C)—Responsibilities of Supervisors, those in a supervisory position must make reasonable efforts to detect and prevent violations of applicable laws, rules, regulations, and the Code and Standards by anyone subject to their supervision or authority. CFA Institute members who act in supervisory roles should understand what constitutes an adequate compliance system for the firm and make reasonable efforts to see that appropriate procedures are established, documented, and communicated to covered personnel and to the legal, compliance, and auditing departments. The facts that Pearl has a compliance manual as part of the employee handbook and that compliance is monitored by the compliance department do not release Sherman's department head from his supervisory duty. A supervisor must take steps to ensure that the compliance procedures are adequate and followed by the employees they supervise. Sherman's supervisor should have reviewed the contents of the compliance manual with Sherman when he was hired and answered any of Sherman's questions or concerns. The supervisor should have also monitored all Sherman's actions to ensure that he was following the firm's policies.

Trading in Client Securities for Personal Accounts

Sherman may be trading in securities that the portfolio managers are purchasing (or selling) for the firm's client accounts and, in doing so, may be violating Standard III(B)—Fair Dealing and Standard VI(B)—Priority of Transactions. (Members also must not engage in trading ahead of the dissemination of research reports or investment recommendations to clients—a practice that creates a conflict with members' duties to clients.) The mutual funds that Sherman used previously would not violate these provisions because Sherman would not be privy to the mutual fund managers' investment actions or security selections. Now, any change in Sherman's investment strategy may well be a result of gaining proprietary information. Under the Code and Standards, Sherman may not invest in the same or related securities for his personal account using proprietary information communicated to him in the course of his job in advance of such information being given to all the firm's clients or in advance of client trades. This restriction includes both Sherman's personal account and any other related account in which Sherman has a beneficial ownership (e.g., a direct or indirect pecuniary interest). Personal trades under the Code and Standards must not come before those for client portfolios, whether or not the employee is restricted from purchase for some specified period of time.

Actions Required   Before placing orders related to individual securities for his own account, Sherman should submit these plans to the compliance department for confirmation that his actions will not interfere with or take priority over client transactions.

Policy Statement for a Firm   "Employees shall submit personal trades to the compliance department for approval in advance of any personal investment action in order to clear the trades against client transactions. In the event that an employee wishes to transact in securities that are being traded for clients, the employee will be allowed to trade only after all client transactions have been processed, the compliance department has approved the request, and a 24-hour moratorium has expired. On a monthly basis, all personal trades (as shown on brokerage statements of account) must be submitted to the compliance department for review."

Conveying Confidential Client Information

Sherman has a duty to see that the proprietary nature of Pearl's investment strategy is maintained and not communicated in the course of his investment activities. The fact that Sherman enjoys discussing his "new-found knowledge" with friends and family suggests a potential violation under Standard IV(A)—Duties to Employers: Loyalty and Standard III(A)—Loyalty, Prudence, and Care. Because of his relationship of special trust, Sherman is obligated to take care that he communicates no information that would breach this trust. This obligation is in force whether or not he acts on the information himself.

Actions Required   Sherman must take care not to divulge specific investment actions or information exclusive to client relationships that breach his fiduciary responsibility to the firm and its clients. When in doubt, Sherman should request guidance from the compliance department.

Policy Statement for a Firm   "Proprietary information shall not be communicated outside the firm. 'Proprietary' includes information about client portfolios, investment strategies, and portfolio actions and recommendations. Furthermore, employees should be mindful of the special relationship with Pearl's clients and ensure that the highest degree of care is preserved when investment action is taken on their behalf."

PEARL INVESTMENT MANAGEMENT (B)

Case Facts

Competition for the infrequent job openings at Pearl Investment Management is extensive, both from within the firm and from the outside. After a year in Pearl's back office as one of the account managers, Peter Sherman is told that obtaining a CFA charter would greatly enhance his chances of moving into the firm's research area. Sherman studies at length and passes Level I of the CFA exam.

In the next year, Sherman is helpful in clearing up problems related to the allocation of block trades among certain large client accounts. The most difficult problem is a misallocation related to an initial public offering (IPO) of Gene Alteration Research Corporation. Sherman was assigned this project because of his accounting experience and because none of his client portfolios was involved, although most of his institutional accounts and a few of his larger individual accounts are "total rate of return" portfolios.

Because his review is a rush project, Sherman does not have time to consult the clients' investment policy statements, but he feels certain that the portfolio managers would direct only trades suitable to their client accounts. Furthermore, he believes the trading desk would have acted as a second review for client investment guidelines. Sherman reconciles the transactions related to the block trades across all the portfolios in question. As a result, certain securities are shifted among accounts. Sherman believes that with the adjustments and with the transactions reversed and reallocated at the IPO price for the Gene Alteration issue, all clients have been treated fairly, but he wonders how the problems arose in the first place.

Several activities at Pearl are or could be in violation of the Code of Ethics and Standards of Professional Conduct. Identify violations and possible violations; state what actions are required by Sherman and/or the firm to correct the potential violations, and make a short policy statement a firm could use to prevent the violations.

Case Discussion

The pressure of a rush project assigned by one's bosses and faulty assumptions can lead to inappropriate shortcuts even when intentions are good. This case involves violations or potential violations of the CFA candidate's compliance responsibility, fair dealing with clients, fiduciary duty to clients, appropriateness or suitability of investment recommendations or investment action, and correction of trading errors in client accounts.

Responsibility of Candidates to Comply with the Code and Standards

As an employee, Sherman was bound only by Pearl's own personnel policies. As a CFA candidate, he is subject to the Code and Standards, and he must rely more on his own knowledge of the Code and Standards to maintain compliance, with assistance from Pearl's compliance department, than on company explanations of the Code and Standards. As a CFA candidate, Sherman is now subject to disciplinary action by CFA Institute for violations of the Code and Standards, whether or not Pearl takes action.

Actions Required   Sherman should reacquaint himself with Pearl's personnel policies and read through the CFA Institute *Standards of Practice Handbook* to increase his familiarity with the Code and Standards and the subtleties of implementing the Standards on a day-to-day basis. The detailed discussion of Standards and examples in the *Handbook* provide explanations and add depth to the meanings of the various standards. Finally, Sherman should document for his supervisor that, as a CFA candidate, he is obligated to comply with CFA Institute's Code and Standards and that he is subject to disciplinary sanctions for violations thereof.

Dealing with Clients

The case presents evidence of failure by Pearl Investment Management and its employees to carry out their fiduciary duties and their obligation to treat all clients equitably.

Responsibilities to Clients   Standard III(A)—Loyalty, Prudence, and Care requires members to take investment actions for the sole benefit of the client and in the best interest of the client *given the known facts and circumstances*. In other words, members must manage any pool of assets in their control in accordance with the needs and circumstances of clients. The case notes that Sherman did not consult the clients' investment policy statements, however, when reallocating the IPO trades. He assumed the portfolio managers and/or the trading desk would have done so. Therefore, Sherman violated his responsibilities to his clients by not making sure that the reallocations were in the best interests of all clients and suitable to each client.

Fair Dealing   In allocating or reallocating block trades, a member must ensure that Standard III(B)—Fair Dealing is upheld. The case notes that among the problems Sherman was asked to review was allocation of an IPO "among certain large client accounts." By favoring their large client accounts over others with similar investment objectives, the portfolio managers, the trading desk, and the account managers involved violated CFA Institute's and Pearl's standards on fair dealing.

Members have a duty to treat all clients *fairly* so that no one client is advantaged or disadvantaged—no matter what the size of the portfolio or other qualifications. Clients' investment guidelines often differ significantly, however, so portfolio managers and the trading desk must determine, in advance, which accounts have similar investment objectives and should receive similar allocations when new purchases are made. Even if clients have identical investment objectives, the accounts may have different cash reserves, dissimilar inclinations toward leverage through the use of margin, and distinct minimums for transaction size. All these factors must be taken into account in the decision-making process.

Ultimately, however, Pearl should treat portfolios with similar investment objectives and constraints similarly regardless of the size of the portfolios or the fees that they convey to Pearl. In making new securities purchases, firms should allocate the purchase for all suitable accounts, using a pro rata or similar system of distribution when less than the full order is received.

Actions Required   Sherman must reinvestigate the investment objectives for all affected client portfolios to make certain that orders were not entered in violation of client guidelines. He must also ensure that the allocation of block trades is made on an equitable basis for *all* client portfolios of similar objectives; in carrying out this assignment, he must keep in mind minimum transaction size but include all accounts that have similar investment criteria.

Policy Statement for a Firm   "Employees owe a duty of loyalty, prudence and care to clients, and in all instances, the interests of clients shall come first. Action contrary to this policy is expressly prohibited. Allocation of trades shall be on a fair and equitable basis for all portfolios with similar investment objectives and constraints."

Bearing the Financial Risk of Errors in Client Accounts

When trades are made in error or are misallocated, under no circumstance should client portfolios bear the risk of an inappropriate transaction; nor should the firm shift the burden to another portfolio or client account. The burden or financial risk must be absorbed by the firm, not by the client (either directly or indirectly).

The reversal of trades described in the case and the reallocation of securities at the IPO price comes close to being a complete resolution of the problem Sherman was asked to solve, but Pearl should have credited short-term interest to those accounts from which transactions were removed because the clients' cash accounts were used to cover the trades.

In some instances, investment management firms shift financial risk to a client (or clients) indirectly by using such techniques as letting soft-dollar trades "cover" the financial aspects of a reversal, canceling an order through a "sale" from one account and a coincident "repurchase" in another account, or other transactions to compensate the firm for any loss it incurred by transacting at levels different from the market. Many client portfolios may be involved in order to spread the financial effects over a broad number of portfolios, which complicates the firm's or the manager's efforts to discern this ethical infraction. Any activity of this sort is a violation of the CFA Institute Code and Standards related to fair dealing and fiduciary duty.

Actions Required   Pearl should see that no client bears a financial loss by the misallocation of transaction by any Pearl employee. As compensation for the use of the clients' funds, Pearl should credit short-term interest to all accounts for which trades were reversed, with Pearl bearing the loss. Short-term interest should *not* be charged against accounts that received shares.

Policy Statement for a Firm   "The firm will take all steps necessary to ensure the integrity of its client accounts. When errors do occur, the clients' portfolios will be restored with no loss of value to the client. To the extent that such losses occur, Pearl will indemnify its clients and make the appropriate restitution."

PEARL INVESTMENT MANAGEMENT (C)   3

Case Facts

After Peter Sherman passed Level II of the CFA exam, Tomas Champa, Pearl Investment Management's director of research, requested that Sherman be transferred to the research department with the understanding that his apprenticeship in the department as a junior analyst would last at least until he was awarded the CFA charter. Sherman was thrilled at the prospect of moving into research, and he accepted the transfer.

Champa came to Pearl when he decided to remain in the United States after completing a five-year U.S. tour of duty for a major international bank with which he had served for 20 years. His background in international banking has made him particularly well suited to be the research director at Pearl. Champa has seven analysts in his department—five senior analysts and two junior analysts. Sherman is one junior analyst, and the other is a Level III CFA candidate. Champa is anxious to lead the firm's research efforts into international securities and wants to begin with companies in the developing countries whose markets have experienced spectacular performance in recent years. He tells the analysts that Pearl must come up with research recommendations in emerging market equities quickly or the department will face criticism from senior management and the firm's clients. He also wants to be able to attract prospective clients by demonstrating the firm's expertise in this area.

Although Sherman is new to the department, Champa gives him difficult assignments because he believes Sherman's lack of preconceived notions about emerging market companies makes him an ideal analyst for this area. Sherman is to concentrate on Central and South America, areas where Champa believes he has special insight and can direct Sherman.

Sherman reads several brokerage reports on Latin American markets, spends time with Champa and other members of the research department discussing trends in these markets, and browses through the statistical section of Standard & Poor's *International Stock Guide*. For a briefing by someone with actual experience, Champa refers Sherman to one of his old banking contacts, Gonzalo Alves, who is well connected in Mexico and on the board of directors of a number of important Mexican corporations.

Sherman spends several hours speaking with Alves about the Mexican economy and the companies for which Alves serves as a director. Alves tells Sherman about the strategic direction of each company, some potential acquisition targets, and how changes in the Mexican economy will affect each company directly. Sherman now feels comfortable using this information in writing his research reports.

Champa asks Sherman to produce a research report on several Mexican telecommunications and cable companies. Because of the deadline Champa gives Sherman for the report, Sherman cannot develop the research easily on his own, so he plans to incorporate information from his reading of the brokerage firm reports, his conversation with Alves, and other sources. Sherman hastily finishes his two-page report, "Telecommunications Companies in Mexico," which includes excerpts from the brokerage reports, general trends and ratios from the S&P *International Stock Guide*, and paraphrased opinions from Alves. It concludes with an internal recommendation that stock in the Mexican telecommunications companies be bought for Pearl clients for which such stock is suitable. Sherman does not cite the brokerage reports as sources because they are so widely distributed in the investment community.

Pearl's upper managers applaud Champa and his staff for their quick response to the market demand for emerging market research, and the portfolio managers ask the research department for more recommendations. Jill Grant, however, the other junior research analyst, asks Sherman why his report did not include specific details about the Mexican economy or the historical exchange rate fluctuations between the Mexican peso and the U.S. dollar. She questions the comparability of Mexican securities with U.S. securities and notes that the diversification available from investing in global markets is achieved only if the correlation between the specific non-U.S. market and the U.S. market is low. Sherman's response, supported by Champa, is, "Our clients are sophisticated investors; they know these things already."

The case reveals several activities at Pearl that are or could be in violation of the CFA Institute Code of Ethics and Standards of Professional Conduct. Identify violations and possible violations; state what actions are required by Sherman or his supervisor to correct the potential violations, and make a short policy statement a firm could use to prevent the violations.

Case Discussion

The pressures to succeed that come from one's self and one's boss can lead to noncompliance in perfectly ordinary business activities. The violations or potential violations in this case relate to using proper care and independent judgment, use of insider information (particularly under international applications of the Code and Standards and the obligation of members to comply with governing laws and regulations), several aspects of research and research reports, and representation of services.

Proper Care and Independent Judgment

A requirement stipulated in the CFA Institute Code of Ethics is to use reasonable care and exercise independent professional judgment when conducting investment analysis. When Sherman succumbed to the time pressures exerted by Tomas Champa, he was thus violating a basic provision of the Code and Standard V(A)—Diligence and Reasonable Basis.

Actions Required   Sherman must keep in mind the necessary steps in the research and portfolio decision-making process and resist attempts to rush his analysis.

Policy Statement for a Firm   "Analysts shall use proper care and exercise independent professional judgment in the preparation of research reports to ensure that reports are thorough, accurate, and include all relevant factors."

Use of Insider Information

Sherman must base any investment recommendations on his research alone, without incorporating material nonpublic information and without engaging in illegal or unethical actions. The situation in which Sherman found himself discussing a number of important corporations with Alves was compromising at best. Based on the local laws and customs with which they were most familiar, Champa and Alves may have found a candid discussion about the corporations where Alves served in a close relationship to be perfectly acceptable. In the course of conversation, however, Alves could have conveyed material nonpublic information to Sherman. If Sherman used such material nonpublic information in his report, which contained recommendations for investment actions, he violated Standard II(A)—Material Nonpublic Information.

One of the more difficult aspects for members is reconciling their obligations under the Code and Standards with the different laws, rules, regulations, and customs of various countries. CFA charterholders, CFA candidates, and CFA Institute members are held to the highest standards. Therefore, regardless of local laws, they are obligated by the Code and the Standards to refrain from using confidential information to their advantage or the advantage of their clients. Being compelled to hold to a higher standard than the local norm can be disadvantageous to CFA charterholders and, sometimes, their clients and customers. The higher standard, however, is what sets CFA charterholders apart in terms of the integrity of the investment profession.

Champa's referral of Sherman to Alves can aid Sherman in his research, but Sherman must use the information in an ethical manner. A consideration of the "mosaic theory" can add a useful perspective to judging proper and improper use of information. The mosaic theory states that a compilation of information that is *not material* or is *public* is not a violation of the Standards; it is the result of good analytical work. For example, if Sherman is doing a thorough review and analysis of all companies within a specific sector or industry, he may well develop a greater sense of the interrelationships among companies than if he were studying only one or a few of them. In that case, Sherman may be able, based on public information gathered from a variety of sources *and* his unique understanding, to form conclusions about a particular company that may appear to be based on nonpublic information but are not.

Actions Required   If Sherman has come into possession of material nonpublic information in his contact with Alves, he must disclose this fact to Pearl's compliance department or compliance officer. If Sherman has used such information in his reports, either directly or indirectly, in order to use it on behalf of his clients, he has violated the Code and Standards.

Policy Statement for a Firm   "Analysts and portfolio managers are prohibited from using material nonpublic information in any form in making investment recommendations or taking investment action. Any employees who have come into possession of material nonpublic information (or who believe they have) shall contact the compliance department or compliance officer for guidance. If the information is determined to be material nonpublic information, the employee must refrain from acting on it and should take steps to disseminate the information publicly."

Using the Research of Others

Sherman's research reports must acknowledge and give credit to the research of others unless the information is of a statistical nature and widely held to be in the public domain. The case says that Sherman did "not cite the brokerage reports as sources because they are so widely distributed in the investment community." To use the proprietary research of others—brokerage reports, for example—without giving them due credit is a violation of Standard I(C)—Misrepresentation.

Actions Required   In order to avoid an ethical violation, Sherman must acknowledge the use of someone else's information and identify its author or publisher. In particular, Sherman must give credit to the author(s) of any brokerage reports he uses extensively in the preparation of internal recommendations.

Policy Statement for a Firm   "Analysts are prohibited from using the work of others without reference and are prohibited from plagiarizing the work of others by not giving due credit to the author, whether or not the author is employed by the firm."

Reasonable Basis for a Research Opinion

Standard V(A)—Diligence and Reasonable Basis requires Sherman to "exercise diligence, independence, and thoroughness in analyzing investments, making investment recommendations, and taking investment actions . . . [and] have a reasonable and adequate basis, supported by appropriate research and investigation, for any investment analysis." Sherman's lack of care and independent research in the preparation of his report is a violation of Standard V(A).

Sherman was essentially taking over the recommendations of others, which may or may not have had a reasonable basis. The research he used may have incorporated material misrepresentations that he did not identify or correct. By copying the work and ideas of others, Sherman may have been copying serious deficiencies and attaching his name and approval to them.

Because of the time pressure from Champa, Sherman did not adequately review the entire industry in the context of the overall economy and global markets (as evidenced by Jill Grant's questions). His reliance on a few brokerage firm reports and other sources is not sufficient to be considered, in the words of Standard V(A), "appropriate research and investigation." Furthermore, his report lacks documentation, not only in detail but also in substance.

Relevant Factors and Fact versus Opinion in Research Reports

Grant was right to question the exclusion of relevant and basic risk factors in Sherman's report. Sherman has an obligation under Standard V(B.2)—Communication with Clients and Prospective Clients to use reasonable judgment in identifying which factors are important to his investment analyses, recommendations, or actions and include those factors in communications with his clients and prospective clients. By excluding important factors, he shirked his responsibility to the firm's clients and violated Standard V(B.2). Champa's contention that the firm's clients are sophisticated investors who are aware of the characteristics of markets and particular investments does not relieve Sherman of his duty to include relevant factors in his research report.

Actions Required   Sherman's reports should be as thorough as possible. When dealing with markets and economies that are significantly different from domestic markets and economies, Sherman should provide a full explanation. The research reports should provide a reasonable basis for decisions, include all relevant factors that reasonably come into play in an investment recommendation, and avoid material misrepresentation of investment characteristics so that the appropriateness of investments for various clients can be judged. Sherman also must maintain records to support his research reports.

Policy Statement for a Firm   "All relevant factors, including the basic characteristics involved in the investment, are to be included in a research report, with a corresponding discussion of the potential risks involved."

Misrepresentation of Services and Performance Presentation

The case raises the issue of potential violations of Standard I(C)—Misrepresentation. Whether violations are actual would depend, of course, on how the firm's current and prospective clients are made aware of the qualifications of the firm and the research department's experience in emerging markets. If Pearl's research is represented as a reaction to a changing marketplace and the increased globalization of securities markets, no violation has occurred. If Pearl is actively soliciting new and existing clients based on its "expertise" in the research and management of emerging market portfolios, however, then a violation of Standard I(C) has occurred.

The presentation of performance—that is, actual investment returns for its emerging market strategy—will be problematic for Pearl in the beginning. Pearl will not be able to report actual performance until it begins to manage portfolios made up of emerging market securities or portfolios that include some meaningful concentration of securities from emerging markets.

Actions Required   Pearl must not hold itself out as having experience or any "track record" in the management of emerging market portfolios until it actually manages assets in this area. It can suggest to clients, however, that the qualifications of the firm as demonstrated by its current efforts *might* produce returns that are comparable in a different environment because of the use of a similar methodology.

Policy Statement for a Firm   "Employees shall make only those statements, either verbally or in writing, about the firm and its qualifications that represent the firm properly and with the integrity it has tried to achieve. The firm shall not solicit clients, new or existing, for a new investment style without full disclosure of the firm's qualifications and expectations for both risk and potential return. Performance results for a new investment style will be in compliance with Standard III(D)—Performance Presentation, as discussed in the CFA Institute *Standards of Practice Handbook.*"

The following information relates to Questions 1–6 and is based on "Guidance for Standards I–VII," "Ethics in Practice," and this reading

Jason Locke, CFA, has recently been hired as the Chief Investment Officer of the Escarpment Regional Government Employees' Pension Fund (the Fund). Currently, he is conducting evaluations of all external managers employed by the Fund to ensure that they are providing the highest possible returns for their mandates, while complying with all applicable laws and regulations.

Locke is evaluating the activity of Niagara Growth Managers (NGM), a local money manager allocated 10 percent of the Fund's assets. He realizes that any reduction in the allocation to this local manager will be met with considerable political pressure. The investment policy statement (IPS) for NGM's portion of the Fund's assets states that NGM is to actively manage an equity portfolio of local small-cap, high-tech companies.

Upon his review of NGM's activity, Locke is concerned about two items that he would like explained. At a meeting with NGM's portfolio manager, Emma Black, CFA, Locke asks her to comment on each item:

Commodities Positions

Locke: "Over the last year, several large positions in commodities have been taken by the Fund's portfolio. This is inconsistent with the IPS."

Black: "Commodities have significantly outperformed high-tech equities recently. I added commodities to larger clients' portfolios on a temporary basis. Clients were not informed because the positions will be sold once market sentiment shifts. I have not managed commodities before, but I am getting good returns."

Locke: "I am uncomfortable with these investments in this portfolio."

IPO Share Allocation

Locke: "The Fund's portfolio received 50,000 shares of an initial public offering (IPO) on 1 April. On 15 May, 30,000 shares were removed at the current market price."

Black: "There was a problem with NGM's IPO allocation algorithm. Initially, you were over-allocated and when we discovered the error, your account was adjusted."

Locke: "Short-term interest should have been credited to the Fund for use of its cash to cover the trade. In any case, this was an IPO of a large international high-tech company. It was not an appropriate investment for the portfolio."

After the meeting, Locke is not satisfied with Black's comments and decides that further action is required. He also decides that he will allow NGM to continue to manage Fund assets until he finishes his evaluation. This decision is based on the superior returns of the NGM-managed assets, the significant diversification this portfolio adds to the Fund, and also the political implications of firing the local money manager.

The next week, Locke calls Black and outlines several conditions that must be fulfilled for NGM to continue as a manager for the Fund. One of the conditions outlined relates to trade allocations.

Trade Allocation

Locke: "Provide written trade allocation procedures consistent with the CFA Institute Standards of Professional Conduct."

Black: "I will mail you a copy of our new procedures stating that trade allocations must be reviewed at the end of each month against clients' IPS. It also says that interest will be credited to accounts that have been incorrectly allocated shares and debited from those accounts that should have received shares."

With his evaluation complete, Locke must now consider whether to retain NGM as one of the Fund's asset managers.

1. According to the CFA Institute Standards of Professional Conduct, Locke owes his primary duty of loyalty in managing the Fund to:
   A. the plan trustees.
   B. all of the pension plan beneficiaries.
   C. the Escarpment Regional Government.

2. With respect to the commodities positions, which of the following actions *best* describes Black's violation of the CFA Institute Standards of Professional Conduct? Black violated CFA Institute Standards by:
   A. buying an asset class in which she has no prior management experience.
   B. buying assets that are inconsistent with the portfolio's Investment Policy Statement.
   C. failing to notify the client that she would temporarily deviate from the client's Investment Policy Statement.

3. With regard to the IPO share allocation, are both NGM's method of trade correction on 15 May and Locke's demand for a short-term interest credit, respectively, consistent with the CFA Institute Standards of Professional Conduct?
   A. Yes.
   B. No, only the method of trade correction is consistent.
   C. No, only the demand for a short-term interest credit is consistent.

4. After his initial meeting with Black, does Locke's decision to allow NGM to continue managing the portfolio violate the CFA Institute Standards of Professional Conduct?
   A. No.
   B. Yes, because he allowed political factors to influence his decision.
   C. Yes, because he is obligated to immediately suspend NGM until he finishes his evaluation.

5. With regard to Locke's condition regarding trade allocation, does Black's response violate the CFA Institute Standards of Professional Conduct with respect to allocation reviews *and* interest adjustments, respectively?

   A. Yes.

   B. No, it violates the standards only with respect to allocation reviews.

   C. No, it violates the standards only with respect to interest adjustments.

6. Based on his complete evaluation, what is Locke's *best* course of action with respect to NGM's management of the Fund's assets?

   A. Reduce NGM's allocation of the Fund's assets until NGM has demonstrated its compliance with Locke's conditions.

   B. Eliminate NGM as a manager since Locke cannot be sure that NGM will act fairly and in accordance with the Fund's IPS.

   C. Maintain NGM's allocation of the Fund's assets and concentrate on evaluating managers with larger proportions of the Fund's assets or with sub-standard performance.

$$\left(\frac{D_0}{r-g_c}\right)\left[\left(1-g_c\right)+\left(\frac{N}{2}\right)\left(g_s-g_c\right)\right]$$

$$-(1-B)t_{cg}$$

$$r^* = r\left(1 - p t - p t - p t\right)$$

$$T^* = \frac{t_{cg}(1-p-p-p)}{(1-pt-pt-pt)}$$

$$FVIF = \left(1+r^*\right)^N\left(1-T^*\right)+T^* - (1-B)$$

SOLUTIONS FOR READING 5

1. B is correct. Locke's primary duty is to his clients. In the case of a pension plan, the clients are all of the ultimate beneficiaries.

2. B is correct. Under no circumstances should a manager take investment action that is inconsistent with the client's IPS.

3. C is correct. Locke's interest claim is legitimate since the Fund's cash was employed to purchase equities that were later removed from the account. Therefore, the Fund is owed interest for the period in question.

4. A is correct. Until Locke's investigation is complete, he has no obligation to suspend the manager or take any other action. He believes the manager can and does add value through superior returns and diversification, and therefore it may be reasonable to retain NGM if Locke can be satisfied that the manager can act within the constraints of the IPS and CFA Institute Standards. Until the analysis is complete, it would not be practical, and Locke would be violating his fiduciary duty, to suspend the manager and leave the assets unmanaged or to temporarily move them to another manager for safe-keeping.

5. A is correct. Client suitability for an investment must be reviewed prior to allocation, not afterward. With respect to interest adjustments, clients who were incorrectly allocated shares must be paid for the use of their cash; however, in no instance should clients suffer a loss because of an allocation error by the manager (that is, have interest removed from their portfolio even though shares are put in their account on a back-dated basis).

6. B is correct. Locke has a fiduciary duty to the pension plan beneficiaries. He would be violating that trust if he continues to employ a manager who does not manage its mandate or demonstrate that it is aware of and complies with its own fiduciary and regulatory duties to clients. He must demonstrate his own professional competence by firing the manager.

ASSET MANAGER CODE OF PROFESSIONAL CONDUCT

by Kurt Schacht, CFA, Jonathan J. Stokes, JD, and
Glenn Doggett, CFA

The candidate should be able to:	Mastery
a. explain the ethical responsibilities required by the six components of the Asset Manager Code;	☐
b. interpret the Asset Manager Code in situations that present issues of compliance, disclosure, or professional conduct;	☐
c. recommend practices and procedures designed to prevent violations of the Asset Manager Code.	☐

INTRODUCTION

Asset managers hold a unique place of trust in the lives of millions of investors. Investment professionals and firms that undertake and perform their responsibilities with honesty and integrity are critical to maintaining investors' trust and confidence and to upholding the client covenant of trust, loyalty, prudence, and care. CFA Institute and its members are committed to reinforcing those principles. The CFA Institute mission is to lead the investment profession globally by setting the highest standards of ethics, education, and professional excellence. To foster this culture of ethics and professionalism, CFA Institute offers this voluntary code of conduct. It is designed to be broadly adopted within the industry as a template and guidepost for investors seeking managers who adhere to sound ethical practice.

The Asset Manager Code of Professional Conduct outlines the ethical and professional responsibilities of firms that manage assets on behalf of clients. Whereas the CFA Institute Code of Ethics and Standards of Professional Conduct address individual conduct, this Code is meant to apply, on a global basis, to firms that manage client assets as separate accounts or pooled funds (including collective investment schemes, mutual funds, and fund of funds organizations); we refer to such firms as "Managers." In part, this document responds to requests from Managers to extend the scope of the Code and Standards to the firm level. Although many institutional asset managers, particularly those in well-regulated jurisdictions, already have such a code in place, they should use this Code to evaluate their own code and ensure that all of this Code's principles have been included. This Code also has been developed for use by asset managers, including hedge fund managers, who may not already have such a code in place. This second edition of the Code includes provisions relating to risk management as well as guidance for Managers seeking to claim compliance.

Ethical leadership begins at the highest level of an organization; therefore, the Code should be adopted by the Manager's senior management, board of directors, and similar oversight bodies. Such adoption sends a strong message regarding the importance of ethical behavior at the firm. Rather than creating rules that apply only to certain people or groups, this Code is intended to cover all employees of the firm. Although not every employee is actively involved in conduct covered in the Code, a code that is broadly applied reinforces the need for all employees to understand the ethical issues involved in the asset management business. By adopting and enforcing a code of conduct for their organizations, Managers demonstrate their commitment to ethical behavior and the protection of investors' interests. In doing so, the Managers also protect and enhance the reputation of their organizations.

The Code sets forth minimum ethical standards for providing asset management services for clients. It is meant to be general in nature and allows flexibility for asset managers of various sizes and structures to develop the particular policies and procedures necessary to implement the Code. The goal of this Code is to set forth a useful framework for all asset managers to provide services in a fair and professional manner and to fully disclose key elements of those services to clients, regardless of whether individual Managers are required to register or comply with applicable securities laws or regulations. Unregistered hedge fund managers, in particular, are encouraged to adopt the Code and implement its provisions to ensure fair dealing and integrity and to promote self-regulation in this dynamic sector.

We recognize that in the highly regulated and complex business of investment management, the adoption of a code of ethics by itself is not sufficient to ensure ethical conduct. To be implemented effectively, the principles and standards embodied in the Code must be supported by appropriate compliance procedures. The specific procedures that translate principle into practice will depend on a variety of factors, including the business of the Manager, the type of clients, the size of the Manager (based on assets under management and on number of employees), the regulatory régime with which the Manager must comply, and other factors.

Managers must adhere to all applicable laws and regulations governing their activities. Thus, the provisions of this Code may need to be supplemented with additional provisions to meet the requirements of applicable security regulation in markets around the world. Inevitably, in some markets, the Code will closely reflect or be aligned with existing regulation or accepted best practice and in other markets, the Code will expand on the existing work of regulatory authorities or may even break new ground. Furthermore, Managers operate in different types of market structures, which may affect the manner in which the Code can be applied. Despite these differences, the Code provides a universal set of principles and standards relevant to all asset managers.

Clients have a responsibility to be aware of, understand, and monitor how their assets are invested. Yet, to fulfill this responsibility, clients must be able to count on full and fair disclosure from their Managers. Providing clients with a code of ethics that sets a framework for how the Manager conducts business is an important step toward developing the trust and confidence necessary for a successful investment management relationship.

Adopting the Code and Claiming Compliance

Adoption of or compliance with the Asset Manager Code of Professional Conduct requires firms to adhere to all the principles of conduct and provisions set forth in the Code (pages 268–271). Many asset management firms already have codes of ethics and other policies and procedures that address or go beyond the principles and provisions of the Code. Adoption of or compliance with the Code does not require a firm to amend its existing code of ethics or other policies and procedures as long as they are at least consistent with the principles and provisions set forth in the Code. Managers are strongly encouraged to review and consider the material in the Appendix when developing and reviewing their codes and other policies and procedures, although because of the many variables in size and complexity among asset management firms, compliance with the Code does not require strict adherence to this guidance.

If the Manager has not complied with each of the principles of conduct and provisions of the Code, the Manager cannot represent that it is in compliance with the Code. Statements referring to partial or incomplete compliance (e.g., "the firm complies with the Asset Manager Code *except for* . . ." or "the firm complies with parts A, B, and C of the Asset Manager Code") are prohibited.

Once a Manager has met each of the required elements of the Code, the firm must make the following statement whenever the firm claims compliance with the Code:

"[Insert name of Firm] claims compliance with the CFA Institute Asset Manager Code of Professional Conduct. This claim has not been verified by CFA Institute."

Acknowledgement of Claim of Compliance to CFA Institute

Managers also must notify CFA Institute of their claim of compliance with the Asset Manager Code of Professional Conduct through the CFA Institute online notification process at www.cfainstitute.org/assetcode. This acknowledgement form is for communication and information-gathering purposes only and does not represent that CFA Institute engages in enforcement or quality control of an organization's claim of compliance. CFA Institute does not verify either the Manager's claim of compliance or actual compliance with the Code.

GENERAL PRINCIPLES OF CONDUCT

Managers have the following responsibilities to their clients. Managers must:

1. Act in a professional and ethical manner at all times.
2. Act for the benefit of clients.
3. Act with independence and objectivity.
4. Act with skill, competence, and diligence.
5. Communicate with clients in a timely and accurate manner.
6. Uphold the applicable rules governing capital markets.

ASSET MANAGER CODE OF PROFESSIONAL CONDUCT

A. Loyalty to Clients

Managers must:

1. Place client interests before their own.
2. Preserve the confidentiality of information communicated by clients within the scope of the Manager–client relationship.
3. Refuse to participate in any business relationship or accept any gift that could reasonably be expected to affect their independence, objectivity, or loyalty to clients.

B. Investment Process and Actions

Managers must:

1. Use reasonable care and prudent judgment when managing client assets.
2. Not engage in practices designed to distort prices or artificially inflate trading volume with the intent to mislead market participants.
3. Deal fairly and objectively with all clients when providing investment information, making investment recommendations, or taking investment action.

4. Have a reasonable and adequate basis for investment decisions.

5. When managing a portfolio or pooled fund according to a specific mandate, strategy, or style:

   a. Take only investment actions that are consistent with the stated objectives and constraints of that portfolio or fund.

   b. Provide adequate disclosures and information so investors can consider whether any proposed changes in the investment style or strategy meet their investment needs.

6. When managing separate accounts and before providing investment advice or taking investment action on behalf of the client:

   a. Evaluate and understand the client's investment objectives, tolerance for risk, time horizon, liquidity needs, financial constraints, any unique circumstances (including tax considerations, legal or regulatory constraints, etc.) and any other relevant information that would affect investment policy.

   b. Determine that an investment is suitable to a client's financial situation.

C. Trading

Managers must:

1. Not act or cause others to act on material nonpublic information that could affect the value of a publicly traded investment.

2. Give priority to investments made on behalf of the client over those that benefit the Managers' own interests.

3. Use commissions generated from client trades to pay for only investment-related products or services that directly assist the Manager in its investment decision making process, and not in the management of the firm.

4. Maximize client portfolio value by seeking best execution for all client transactions.

5. Establish policies to ensure fair and equitable trade allocation among client accounts.

D. Risk Management, Compliance, and Support

Managers must:

1. Develop and maintain policies and procedures to ensure that their activities comply with the provisions of this Code and all applicable legal and regulatory requirements.

2. Appoint a compliance officer responsible for administering the policies and procedures and for investigating complaints regarding the conduct of the Manager or its personnel.

3. Ensure that portfolio information provided to clients by the Manager is accurate and complete and arrange for independent third-party confirmation or review of such information.

4. Maintain records for an appropriate period of time in an easily accessible format.

5. Employ qualified staff and sufficient human and technological resources to thoroughly investigate, analyze, implement, and monitor investment decisions and actions.

6. Establish a business-continuity plan to address disaster recovery or periodic disruptions of the financial markets.

7. Establish a firmwide risk management process that identifies, measures, and manages the risk position of the Manager and its investments, including the sources, nature, and degree of risk exposure.

E. Performance and Valuation

Managers must:

1. Present performance information that is fair, accurate, relevant, timely, and complete. Managers must not misrepresent the performance of individual portfolios or of their firm.

2. Use fair-market prices to value client holdings and apply, in good faith, methods to determine the fair value of any securities for which no independent, third-party market quotation is readily available.

F. Disclosures

Managers must:

1. Communicate with clients on an ongoing and timely basis.

2. Ensure that disclosures are truthful, accurate, complete, and understandable and are presented in a format that communicates the information effectively.

3. Include any material facts when making disclosures or providing information to clients regarding themselves, their personnel, investments, or the investment process.

4. Disclose the following:

    a. Conflicts of interests generated by any relationships with brokers or other entities, other client accounts, fee structures, or other matters.

    b. Regulatory or disciplinary action taken against the Manager or its personnel related to professional conduct.

    c. The investment process, including information regarding lock-up periods, strategies, risk factors, and use of derivatives and leverage.

    d. Management fees and other investment costs charged to investors, including what costs are included in the fees and the methodologies for determining fees and costs.

    e. The amount of any soft or bundled commissions, the goods and/or services received in return, and how those goods and/or services benefit the client.

    f. The performance of clients' investments on a regular and timely basis.

    g. Valuation methods used to make investment decisions and value client holdings.

    h.   Shareholder voting policies.

    i.   Trade allocation policies.

    j.   Results of the review or audit of the fund or account.

    k.   Significant personnel or organizational changes that have occurred at the Manager.

    l.   Risk management processes.

APPENDIX 6— RECOMMENDATIONS AND GUIDANCE

Adoption of the Code is insufficient by itself for a Manager to meet its ethical and regulatory responsibilities. Managers must adopt detailed policies and procedures to effectively implement the Code. This section provides guidance explaining the Code and includes recommendations and illustrative examples to assist Managers that are seeking to implement the Code. These examples are not meant to be exhaustive, and the policies and procedures needed to support the Code will depend on the particular circumstances of each organization and the legal and regulatory environment in which the Manager operates.

    The following guidance highlights particular issues that Managers should consider when developing their internal policies and procedures that accompany the Code. The guidance is not intended to cover all issues or aspects of a Manager's operations that would have to be included in such policies and procedures to fully implement and support the Code.

A. Loyalty to Clients

Managers must:

1. Place client interests before their own.

Client interests are paramount. Managers should institute policies and procedures to ensure that client interests supersede Manager interests in all aspects of the Manager–client relationship, including (but not limited to) investment selection, transactions, monitoring, and custody. Managers should take reasonable steps to avoid situations in which the Manager's interests and client interests conflict and should institute operational safeguards to protect client interests. Managers should implement compensation arrangements that align the financial interests of clients and Managers and avoid incentives that could result in Managers taking action in conflict with client interests.

2. Preserve the confidentiality of information communicated by clients within the scope of the Manager–client relationship.

As part of their ethical duties, Managers must hold information communicated to them by clients or other sources within the context of the Manager–client relationship strictly confidential and must take all reasonable measures to preserve that confidentiality. This duty applies when Managers obtain information on the basis of their confidential relationship with the client or their special ability to conduct a portion of the client's business or personal affairs. Managers should create a privacy policy that addresses how confidential client information will be collected, stored, protected, and used.

The duty to maintain confidentiality does not supersede a duty (and in some cases the legal requirement) to report suspected illegal activities involving client accounts to the appropriate authorities. Where appropriate, Managers should consider creating and implementing a written anti-money-laundering policy to prevent their organizations from being used for money laundering or the financing of any illegal activities.

3. Refuse to participate in any business relationship or accept any gift that could reasonably be expected to affect their independence, objectivity, or loyalty to clients.

As part of holding clients' interests paramount, Managers must establish policies for accepting gifts or entertainment in a variety of contexts. To avoid the appearance of a conflict, Managers must refuse to accept gifts or entertainment from service providers, potential investment targets, or other business partners of more than a minimal value. Managers should define what the minimum value is and should confer with local regulations which may also establish limits.

Managers should establish a written policy limiting the acceptance of gifts and entertainment to items of minimal value. Managers should consider creating specific limits for accepting gifts (e.g., amount per time period per vendor) and prohibit the acceptance of any cash gifts. Employees should be required to document and disclose to the Manager, through their supervisor, the firm's compliance office, or senior management, the acceptance of any gift or entertainment.

This provision is not meant to preclude Managers from maintaining multiple business relationships with a client as long as potential conflicts of interest are managed and disclosed.

B. Investment Process and Actions

Managers must:

1. Use reasonable care and prudent judgment when managing client assets.

Managers must exhibit the care and prudence necessary to meet their obligations to clients. Prudence requires caution and discretion. The exercise of prudence requires acting with the care, skill, and diligence that a person acting in a like capacity and familiar with such matters would use under the same circumstances. In the context of managing a client's portfolio, prudence requires following the investment parameters set forth by the client and balancing risk and return. Acting with care requires Managers to act in a prudent and judicious manner in avoiding harm to clients.

2. Not engage in practices designed to distort prices or artificially inflate trading volume with the intent to mislead market participants.

Market manipulation is illegal in most jurisdictions and damages the interests of all investors by disrupting the efficient functioning of financial markets and causing deterioration in investor confidence.

Market manipulation includes practices that distort security prices or values or artificially inflate trading volumes with the intent to deceive persons or entities that rely on information in the market. Such practices may involve, for example, transactions that deceive market participants by distorting the price-setting mechanism of financial instruments and the dissemination of false or misleading information. Transaction-based manipulation includes, but is not limited to, transactions that artificially distort prices or volume to give the impression of activity or price movement in a financial instrument (e.g., trading in illiquid stocks at the end of a measurement period to drive up the price and improve Manager performance) and securing a large position with the intent to exploit and manipulate the price of an asset and/or a related derivative. Information-based manipulation includes, but is not limited to, spreading knowingly false rumors to induce trading by others and pressuring sell-side analysts to rate or recommend a security in such a way that benefits the Manager or the Manager's clients.

3. **Deal fairly and objectively with all clients when providing investment information, making investment recommendations, or taking investment action.**

To maintain the trust that clients place in them, Managers must deal with all clients in a fair and objective manner. Managers must not give preferential treatment to favored clients to the detriment of other clients. In some cases, clients may pay for a higher level of service or certain services and certain products may only be made available to certain qualifying clients (e.g., certain funds may be open only to clients with assets above a certain level). These practices are permitted as long as they are disclosed and made available to all clients.

This provision is not intended to prevent Managers from engaging in secondary investment opportunities—referred to in some jurisdictions as "side-letter," "sidecar," or "tag-along" arrangements—with certain clients as long as such opportunities are fairly allocated among similarly situated clients for whom the opportunity is suitable.

4. **Have a reasonable and adequate basis for investment decisions.**

Managers must act with prudence and make sure their decisions have a reasonable and adequate basis. Prior to taking action on behalf of their clients, Managers must analyze the investment opportunities in question and should act only after undertaking due diligence to ensure there is sufficient knowledge about specific investments or strategies. Such analysis will depend on the style and strategy being used. For example, a Manager implementing a passive strategy will have a very different basis for investment actions from that of a Manager that uses an active strategy.

Managers can rely on external third-party research as long as Managers have made reasonable and diligent efforts to determine that such research has a reasonable basis. When evaluating investment research, Managers should consider the assumptions used, the thoroughness of the analysis performed, the timeliness of the information, and the objectivity and independence of the source.

Managers should have a thorough understanding of the securities in which they invest and the strategies they use on behalf of clients. Managers should understand the structure and function of the securities, how they are traded, their liquidity, and any other risks (including counterparty risk).

Managers who implement complex and sophisticated investment strategies should understand the structure and potential vulnerabilities of such strategies and communicate these in an understandable manner to their clients. For example, when implementing complex derivative strategies, Managers should understand the various risks and conduct statistical analysis (i.e., stress testing) to determine how the strategy will perform under different conditions. By undertaking adequate due diligence, Managers can better judge the suitability of investments for their clients.

5. **When managing a portfolio or pooled fund according to a specific mandate, strategy, or style:**

   a. **Take only investment actions that are consistent with the stated objectives and constraints of that portfolio or fund.**

   When Managers are given a specific mandate by clients or offer a product, such as a pooled fund for which the Managers do not know the specific financial situation of each client, the Managers must manage the funds or portfolios within the stated mandates or strategies. Clients need to be able to evaluate the suitability of the investment funds or strategies for themselves. Subsequently, they must be able to trust that Managers will not diverge from the stated or agreed-on mandates or strategies. When market events or opportunities change to such a degree that Managers wish to have flexibility to take advantage of those occurrences, such flexibility is not improper but should be expressly understood and agreed to by Managers and clients. Best practice is for Managers to disclose such events to clients when they occur or, at the very least, in the course of normal client reporting.

   b. **Provide adequate disclosures and information so investors can consider whether any proposed changes in the investment style or strategy meet their investment needs.**

   To give clients an opportunity to evaluate the suitability of investments, Managers need to provide adequate information to them about any proposed material changes to their investment strategies or styles. They must provide this information well in advance of such changes. Clients should be given enough time to consider the proposed changes and take any actions that may be necessary. If the Manager decides to make a material change in the investment strategy or style, clients should be permitted to redeem their investment, if desired, without incurring any undue penalties.

6. **When managing separate accounts and before providing investment advice or taking investment action on behalf of the client:**

   a. **Evaluate and understand the client's investment objectives, tolerance for risk, time horizon, liquidity needs, financial constraints, any unique circumstances (including tax considerations, legal or regulatory constraints, etc.) and any other relevant information that would affect investment policy.**

   Prior to taking any investment actions for clients, Managers must take the necessary steps to understand and evaluate the client's financial situation, constraints, and other relevant factors. Without understanding the client's situation, the Manager cannot select and implement an appropriate investment strategy. Ideally, each client will have an investment policy statement (IPS) that includes a discussion of risk tolerances (both the ability and willingness of the client to bear risk), return objectives, time horizon, liquidity requirements, liabilities, tax considerations, and any legal, regulatory, or other unique circumstances.

The purpose of the IPS is to provide Managers with written strategic plans to direct investment decisions for each client. The Manager should take an opportunity to review the IPS for each client, offer any suggestions on clarifying the IPS, and discuss with the client the various techniques and strategies to be used to meet the client's investment goals. Managers should review each client's IPS with the client at least annually and whenever circumstances suggest changes may be needed.

The information contained in an IPS allows Managers to assess whether a particular strategy or security is suitable for a client (in the context of the rest of the client's portfolio), and the IPS serves as the basis for establishing the client's strategic asset allocation. (Note: In some cases, the client will determine the strategic asset allocation; in other cases, that duty will be delegated to the Manager). The IPS should also specify the Manager's role and responsibilities in managing the client's assets and establish schedules for review and evaluation. The Manager should reach agreement with the client as to an appropriate benchmark or benchmarks by which the Manager's performance will be measured and any other details of the performance evaluation process (e.g., when performance measurement should begin).

b. Determine that an investment is suitable to a client's financial situation.

Managers must evaluate investment actions and strategies in light of each client's circumstances. Not all investments are suitable for every client, and Managers have a responsibility to ensure that only appropriate investments and investment strategies are included in a client's portfolio. Ideally, individual investments should be evaluated in the context of clients' total assets and liabilities, which may include assets held outside of the Manager's account, to the extent that such information is made available to the Manager and is explicitly included in the context of the client's IPS.

C. Trading

Managers must:

1. Not act or cause others to act on material nonpublic information that could affect the value of a publicly traded investment.

Trading on material nonpublic information, which is illegal in most jurisdictions, erodes confidence in capital markets, institutions, and investment professionals and promotes the perception that those with inside and special access can take unfair advantage of the general investing public. Although trading on such information may lead to short-term profitability, over time, individuals and the profession as a whole suffer if investors avoid capital markets because they perceive them to be unfair by favoring the knowledgeable insider.

Different jurisdictions and regulatory regimes may define materiality differently, but in general, information is "material" if it is likely that a reasonable investor would consider it important and if it would be viewed as significantly altering the total mix of information available. Information is "nonpublic" until it has been widely disseminated to the marketplace (as opposed to a select group of investors).

Managers must adopt compliance procedures, such as establishing information barriers (e.g., fire walls), to prevent the disclosure and misuse of material nonpublic information. In many cases, pending trades or client or fund holdings may be considered material nonpublic information, and Managers must be sure to keep such information confidential. In addition, merger and acquisition information, prior to its public disclosure, is generally considered material nonpublic information. Managers should evaluate company-specific information that they may receive and determine whether it meets the definition of material nonpublic information.

This provision is not meant to prevent Managers from using the mosaic theory to draw conclusions—that is, combine pieces of material public information with pieces of nonmaterial nonpublic information to draw conclusions that are actionable.

2. Give priority to investments made on behalf of the client over those that benefit the Managers' own interests.

Managers must not execute their own trades in a security prior to client transactions in the same security. Investment activities that benefit the Manager must not adversely affect client interests. Managers must not engage in trading activities that work to the disadvantage of clients (e.g., front-running client trades).

In some investment arrangements, such as limited partnerships or pooled funds, Managers put their own capital at risk alongside that of their clients to align their interests with the interests of their clients. These arrangements are permissible only if clients are not disadvantaged.

Managers should develop policies and procedures to monitor and, where appropriate, limit the personal trading of their employees. In particular, Managers should require employees to receive approval prior to any personal investments in initial public offerings or private placements. Managers should develop policies and processes designed to ensure that client transactions take precedence over employee or firm transactions. One method is to create a restricted list and/or watch list of securities that are owned in client accounts or may be bought or sold on behalf of clients in the near future; prior to trading securities on such a list, employees would be required to seek approval. In addition, Managers could require employees to provide the compliance officer with copies of trade confirmations each quarter and annual statements of personal holdings.

3. Use commissions generated from client trades to pay for only investment-related products or services that directly assist the Manager in its investment decision-making process, and not in the management of the firm.

Managers must recognize that commissions paid (and any benefits received in return for commissions paid) are the property of the client. Consequently, any benefits offered in return for commissions must benefit the Manager's clients.

To determine whether a benefit generated from client commissions is appropriate, Managers must determine whether it will directly assist in the Manager's investment decision-making process. The investment decision-making process can be considered the qualitative and quantitative process and the related tools used by the Manager in rendering investment advice to clients. The process includes financial analysis, trading and risk analysis, securities selection, broker selection, asset allocation, and suitability analysis.

Some Managers have chosen to eliminate the use of soft commissions (also known as soft dollars) to avoid any conflicts of interest that may exist. Managers should disclose their policy on how benefits are evaluated and used for the client's benefit. If Managers choose to use a soft commission or bundled brokerage arrangement, they should disclose this use to their clients. Managers should consider complying with industry best practices regarding the use and reporting of such an arrangement, which can be found in the CFA Institute Soft Dollar Standards.

4. Maximize client portfolio value by seeking best execution for all client transactions.

When placing client trades, Managers have a duty to seek terms that secure best execution for and maximize the value of each client's portfolio (i.e., ensure the best possible result overall). Managers must seek the most favorable terms for client trades within each trades' particular circumstances (such as transaction size, market characteristics, liquidity of security, and security type). Managers also must decide which brokers or venues provide best execution while considering, among other things, commission rates, timeliness of trade executions, and the ability to maintain anonymity, minimize incomplete trades, and minimize market impact.

When a client directs the Manager to place trades through a specific broker or through a particular type of broker, Managers should alert the client that by limiting the Manager's ability to select the broker, the client may not be receiving best execution. The Manager should seek written acknowledgment from the client of receiving this information.

5. Establish policies to ensure fair and equitable trade allocation among client accounts.

When placing trades for client accounts, Managers must allocate trades fairly so that some client accounts are not routinely traded first or receive preferential treatment. Where possible, Managers should use block trades and allocate shares on a pro-rata basis by using an average price or some other method that ensures fair and equitable allocations. When allocating shares of an initial or secondary offering, Managers should strive to ensure that all clients for whom the security is suitable are given opportunities to participate. When Managers do not receive a large enough allocation to allow all eligible clients to participate fully in a particular offering, they must ensure that certain clients are not given preferential treatment and should establish a system to ensure that new issues are allocated fairly (e.g., pro rata). Manager's trade allocation policies should specifically address how initial public offerings and private placements are to be handled.

D. Risk Management, Compliance, and Support

Managers must:

1. **Develop and maintain policies and procedures to ensure that their activities comply with the provisions of this Code and all applicable legal and regulatory requirements.**

Detailed and firmwide compliance policies and procedures are critical tools to ensure that Managers meet their legal requirements when managing client assets. In addition, the fundamental, principle-based, ethical concepts embodied in the Code should be put into operation by the implementation of specific policies and procedures.

Documented compliance procedures assist Managers in fulfilling the responsibilities enumerated in the Code and ensure that the standards expressed in the Code are adhered to in the day-to-day operation of the firms. The appropriate compliance programs, internal controls, and self-assessment tools for each Manager will depend on such factors as the size of the firm and the nature of its investment management business.

2. **Appoint a compliance officer responsible for administering the policies and procedures and for investigating complaints regarding the conduct of the Manager or its personnel.**

Effective compliance programs require Managers to appoint a compliance officer who is competent, knowledgeable, and credible and is empowered to carry out his or her duties. Depending on the size and complexity of the Manager's operations, Managers may designate an existing employee to also serve as the compliance officer, may hire a separate individual for that role, or may establish an entire compliance department. Where possible, the compliance officer should be independent from the investment and operations personnel and should report directly to the CEO or board of directors.

The compliance officer and senior management should regularly make clear to all employees that adherence to compliance policies and procedures is crucial and that anyone who violates them will be held liable. Managers should consider requiring all employees to acknowledge that they have received a copy of the Code (as well as any subsequent material amendments), that they understand and agree to comply with it, and that they will report any suspected violations of the Code to the designated compliance officer. Compliance officers should take steps to implement appropriate employee training and conduct continuing self-evaluation of the Manager's compliance practices to assess the effectiveness of the practices.

Among other things, the compliance officer should be charged with reviewing firm and employee transactions to ensure the priority of client interests. Because personnel, regulations, business practices, and products constantly change, the role of the compliance officer (particularly the role of keeping the firm up to date on such matters) is particularly important.

The compliance officer should document and act expeditiously to address any compliance breaches and work with management to take appropriate disciplinary action.

3. **Ensure that portfolio information provided to clients by the Manager is accurate and complete and arrange for independent third-party confirmation or review of such information.**

Managers have a responsibility to ensure that the information they provide to clients is accurate and complete. By receiving an independent third-party confirmation or review of that information, clients have an additional level of confidence that the information is correct, which may enhance the Manager's credibility. Such verification is also good business practice because it may serve as a risk management tool to help the Manager identify potential problems. The confirmation of portfolio information may take the form of an audit or review, as is the case with most pooled vehicles, or may take the form of copies of account statements and trade confirmations from the custodian bank where the client assets are held.

4. Maintain records for an appropriate period of time in an easily accessible format.

Managers must retain records that substantiate their investment activities, the scope of their research, the basis for their conclusions, and the reasons for actions taken on behalf of their clients. Managers should also retain copies of other compliance-related records that support and substantiate the implementation of the Code and related policies and procedures, as well as records of any violations and resulting actions taken. Records can be maintained either in hard copy or electronic form.

Regulators often impose requirements related to record retention. In the absence of such regulation, Managers must determine the appropriate minimum time frame for keeping the organization's records. Unless otherwise required by local law or regulation Managers should keep records for at least seven years.

5. Employ qualified staff and sufficient human and technological resources to thoroughly investigate, analyze, implement, and monitor investment decisions and actions.

To safeguard the Manager–client relationship, Managers need to allocate all the resources necessary to ensure that client interests are not compromised. Clients pay significant sums to Managers for professional asset management services, and client assets should be handled with the greatest possible care.

Managers of all sizes and investment styles struggle with issues of cost and efficiency and tend to be cautious about adding staff in important operational areas. Nevertheless, adequate protection of client assets requires appropriate administrative, back-office, and compliance support. Managers should ensure that adequate internal controls are in place to prevent fraudulent behavior.

A critical consideration is employing only *qualified* staff. Managers must ensure that client assets are invested, administered, and protected by qualified and experienced staff. Employing qualified staff reflects a client-first attitude and helps ensure that Managers are applying the care and prudence necessary to meet their obligations to clients. This provision is not meant to prohibit the outsourcing of certain functions, but the Manager retains the liability and responsibility for any outsourced work.

Managers have a responsibility to clients to deliver the actual services they claim to offer. Managers must use adequate resources to carry out the necessary research and analysis to implement their investment strategies with due diligence and care. Also, Managers must have adequate resources to monitor the portfolio holdings and investment strategies. As investment strategies and instruments become increasingly sophisticated, the need for sufficient resources to analyze and monitor them becomes ever more important.

6. Establish a business-continuity plan to address disaster recovery or periodic disruptions of the financial markets.

Part of safeguarding client interests is establishing procedures for handling client accounts and inquiries in situations of national, regional, or local emergency or market disruption. Commonly referred to as business-continuity or disaster-recovery planning, such preparation is increasingly important in an industry and world highly susceptible to a wide variety of disasters and disruptions.

The level and complexity of business-continuity planning depends on the size, nature, and complexity of the organization. At a minimum, Managers should consider having the following:

▶ adequate backup, preferably off-site, for all account information;

▶ alternative plans for monitoring, analyzing, and trading investments if primary systems become unavailable;

▶ plans for communicating with critical vendors and suppliers;

▶ plans for employee communication and coverage of critical business functions in the event of a facility or communication disruption; and

▶ plans for contacting and communicating with clients during a period of extended disruption.

Numerous other factors may need to be considered when creating the plan. According to the needs of the organization, these factors may include establishing backup office and operational space in the event of an extended disruption and dealing with key employee deaths or departures.

As with any important business planning, Managers should ensure that employees and staff are knowledgeable about the plan and are specifically trained in areas of responsibility. Plans should be tested on a firmwide basis at intervals to promote employee understanding and identify any needed adjustments.

7. Establish a firmwide risk management process that identifies, measures, and manages the risk position of the Manager and its investments, including the sources, nature, and degree of risk exposure.

Many investors, including those investing in hedge funds and alternative investments or leveraged strategies, invest specifically to increase their risk-adjusted returns. Assuming some risk is a necessary part of that process. The key to sound risk management by Managers is seeking to ensure that the risk profile desired by clients matches the risk profile of their investments. Risk management should complement rather than compete with the investment management process. Investment managers must implement risk management techniques that are consistent with their investment style and philosophy.

The types of risks faced by Managers include, but are not limited to, market risk, credit risk, liquidity risk, counterparty risk, concentration risk, and various types of operational risk. Such types of risks should be analyzed by Managers as part of a comprehensive risk management process for portfolios, investment strategies, and the firm. These examples are illustrative only and may not be applicable to all investment organizations.

Although portfolio managers consider risk issues as part of formulating an investment strategy, the firm's risk management process must be objective, independent, and insulated from influence of portfolio managers. Managers may wish to describe to clients how the risk management framework complements the portfolio management process while remaining separate from that process. Managers should consider outsourcing risk management activities if a separate risk management function is not appropriate or feasible because of the size of the organization.

An effective risk management process will identify risk factors for individual portfolios as well as for the Manager's activities as whole. It will often be appropriate for managers to perform stress tests, scenario tests, and backtests as part of developing risk models that comprehensively capture the full range of their actual and contingent risk exposures. The goal of such models is to determine how various changes in market and investment conditions could affect investments. The risk models should be continuously evaluated and challenged, and Managers should be prepared to describe the models to clients. Despite the importance of risk models, however, effective risk management ultimately depends on the experience, judgment, and ability of the Managers in analyzing their risk metrics.

E. Performance and Valuation

Managers must:

1. **Present performance information that is fair, accurate, relevant, timely, and complete. Managers must not misrepresent the performance of individual portfolios or of their firm.**

Although past performance is not necessarily indicative of future performance, historical performance records are often used by prospective clients as part of the evaluation process when hiring asset managers. Managers have a duty to present performance information that is a fair representation of their record and includes all relevant factors. In particular, Managers should be certain not to misrepresent their track records by taking credit for performance that is not their own (i.e., when they were not managing a particular portfolio or product) or by selectively presenting certain time periods or investments (i.e., cherry picking). Any hypothetical or backtested performance must be clearly identified as such. Managers should provide as much additional portfolio transparency as feasibly possible. Any forward-looking information provided to clients must also be fair, accurate, and complete.

A model for fair, accurate, and complete performance reporting is embodied in the Global Investment Performance Standards (GIPS®), which are based on the principles of fair representation and full disclosure and are designed to meet the needs of a broad range of global markets. By adhering to these standards for reporting investment performance, Managers help assure investors that the performance information being provided is both complete and fairly presented. When Managers comply with the GIPS standards, both prospective and existing clients benefit because they can have a high degree of confidence in the reliability of the performance numbers the Managers are presenting. This confidence may, in turn, enhance clients' sense of trust in their Managers.

2. **Use fair-market prices to value client holdings and apply, in good faith, methods to determine the fair value of any securities for which no independent, third-party market quotation is readily available.**

In general, fund Managers' fees are calculated as a percentage of assets under management. In some cases, an additional fee is calculated as a percentage of the annual returns earned on the assets. Consequently, a conflict of interest may arise where the portfolio Manager has the additional responsibility of determining end-of-period valuations and returns on the assets.

These conflicts may be overcome by transferring responsibility for the valuation of assets (including foreign currencies) to an independent third party. For pooled funds that have boards of directors comprising independent members, the independent members should have the responsibility of approving the asset valuation policies and procedures and reviewing the valuations. For pooled funds without independent directors, we recommend that this function be undertaken by independent third parties who are expert in providing such valuations.

Managers should use widely accepted valuation methods and techniques to appraise portfolio holdings of securities and other investments and should apply these methods on a consistent basis.

F. Disclosures

Managers must:

1. Communicate with clients on an ongoing and timely basis.

Developing and maintaining clear, frequent, and thorough communication practices is critical to providing high-quality financial services to clients. Understanding the information communicated to them allows clients to know how Managers are acting on their behalf and gives clients the opportunity to make well-informed decisions regarding their investments. Managers must determine how best to establish lines of communication that fit their circumstances and that enable clients to evaluate their financial status.

2. Ensure that disclosures are truthful, accurate, complete, and understandable and are presented in a format that communicates the information effectively.

Managers must not misrepresent any aspect of their services or activities, including (but not limited to) their qualifications or credentials, the services they provide, their performance records, and characteristics of the investments or strategies they use. A misrepresentation is any untrue statement or omission of fact or any statement that is otherwise false or misleading. Managers must ensure that misrepresentation does not occur in oral representations, marketing (whether through mass media or printed brochures), electronic communications, or written materials (whether publicly disseminated or not).

To be effective, disclosures must be made in plain language and in a manner designed to effectively communicate the information to clients and prospective clients. Managers must determine how often, in what manner, and under what particular circumstances disclosures must be made.

3. Include any material facts when making disclosures or providing information to clients regarding themselves, their personnel, investments, or the investment process.

Clients must have full and complete information to judge the abilities of Managers and their actions in investing client assets. "Material" information is information that reasonable investors would want to know relative to whether or not they would choose to use or continue to use the Manager.

4. Disclose the following:

a. Conflicts of interests generated by any relationships with brokers or other entities, other client accounts, fee structures, or other matters.

Conflicts of interests often arise in the investment management profession and can take many forms. Best practice is to avoid such conflicts if possible. When

Managers cannot reasonably avoid conflicts, they must carefully manage them and disclose them to clients. Disclosure of conflicts of interests protects investors by providing them with the information they need to evaluate the objectivity of their Managers' investment advice and actions taken on behalf of clients and by giving them the information to judge the circumstances, motives, and possible Manager bias for themselves. Examples of some of the types of activities that can constitute actual or potential conflicts of interest are the use of soft dollars or bundled commissions, referral and placement fees, trailing commissions, sales incentives, directed brokerage arrangements, allocation of investment opportunities among similar portfolios, Manager or employee holdings in the same securities as clients, whether the Manager co-invests alongside clients, and use of affiliated brokers.

b. Regulatory or disciplinary action taken against the Manager or its personnel related to professional conduct.

Past professional conduct records are an important factor in an investor's selection of a Manager. Such records include actions taken against a Manager by any regulator or other organization. Managers must fully disclose any significant instances in which the Manager or an employee was found to have violated standards of conduct or other standards in such a way that reflects badly on the integrity, ethics, or competence of the organization or the individual.

c. The investment process, including information regarding lock-up periods, strategies, risk factors, and use of derivatives and leverage.

Managers must disclose to clients and prospects the manner in which investment decisions are made and implemented. Such disclosures should address the overall investment strategy and should include a discussion of the specific risk factors inherent in such a strategy.

Understanding the basic characteristics of an investment is an important factor in judging the suitability of each investment on a stand-alone basis, but it is especially important in determining the effect each investment will have on the characteristics of the client's portfolio. Only by thoroughly understanding the nature of the investment product or service can a client determine whether changes to that product or service could materially affect his or her investment objectives.

d. Management fees and other investment costs charged to investors, including what costs are included in the fees and the methodologies for determining fees and costs.

Investors are entitled to full and fair disclosures of costs associated with the investment management services provided. Material that should be disclosed includes information relating to any fees to be paid to the Managers on an ongoing basis and periodic costs that are known to the Managers and that will affect investors' overall investment expenses. At a minimum, Managers should provide clients with gross- and net-of-fees returns and disclose any unusual expenses.

A general statement that certain fees and other costs will be assessed to investors may not adequately communicate the total amount of expenses that investors may incur as a result of investing. Therefore, Managers must not only use plain language in presenting this information but must clearly explain the methods for determining all fixed and contingent fees and costs that will be borne by investors and also must explain the transactions that will trigger the imposition of these expenses.

Managers should also retrospectively disclose to each client the actual fees and other costs charged to the clients, together with itemizations of such charges when requested by clients. This disclosure should include the specific management fee, any incentive fee, and the amount of commissions Managers paid on behalf of clients during the period. In addition, Managers must disclose to prospective clients the average or expected expenses or fees clients are likely to incur.

e. The amount of any soft or bundled commissions, the goods and/or services received in return, and how those goods and/or services benefit the client.

Commissions belong to the client and should be used in their best interests. Any soft or bundled commissions should be used only to benefit the client. Clients deserve to know how their commissions are spent, what is received in return for them, and how those goods and/or services benefit them.

f. The performance of clients' investments on a regular and timely basis.

Clients may reasonably expect to receive regular performance reporting about their accounts. Without such performance information, even for investment vehicles with lock-up periods, clients cannot evaluate their overall asset allocations (i.e., including assets not held or managed by the Managers) and determine whether rebalancing is necessary. Accordingly, unless otherwise specified by the client, Managers must provide regular, ongoing performance reporting. Managers should report to clients at least quarterly, and when possible, such reporting should be provided within 30 days after the end of the quarter.

g. Valuation methods used to make investment decisions and value client holdings.

Clients deserve to know whether the assets in their portfolios are valued on the basis of closing market values, third-party valuations, internal valuation models, or other methods. This type of disclosure allows clients to compare performance results and determine whether different valuation sources and methods may explain differences in performance results. This disclosure should be made by asset class and must be meaningful (i.e., not general or boilerplate) so that clients can understand how the securities are valued.

h. Shareholder voting policies.

As part of their fiduciary duties, Managers that exercise voting authority over client shares must vote them in an informed and responsible manner. This obligation includes the paramount duty to vote shares in the best interests of clients.

To fulfill their duties, Managers must adopt policies and procedures for the voting of shares and disclose those policies and procedures to clients. These disclosures should specify, among other things, guidelines for instituting regular reviews for new or controversial issues, mechanisms for reviewing unusual proposals, guidance in deciding whether additional actions are warranted when votes are against corporate management, and systems to monitor any delegation of share-voting responsibilities to others. Managers also must disclose to clients how to obtain information on the manner in which their shares were voted.

i. Trade allocation policies.

By disclosing their trade allocation policies, Managers give clients a clear understanding of how trades are allocated and provide realistic expectations of what priority they will receive in the investment allocation process. Managers must disclose to clients any changes in the trade allocation policies.

By establishing and disclosing trade allocation policies that treat clients fairly, Managers foster an atmosphere of openness and trust with their clients.

j.   Results of the review or audit of the fund or account.

If a Manager submits its funds or accounts (generally pooled or mutual funds) for an annual review or audit, it must disclose the results to clients. Such disclosure enables clients to hold Managers accountable and alerts them to any potential problems.

k.   Significant personnel or organizational changes that have occurred at the Manager.

Clients should be made aware of significant changes at the Manager in a timely manner. "Significant" changes would include personnel turnover, merger and acquisition activities of the Manager, and similar actions.

l.   Risk management processes.

Managers must disclose their risk management processes to clients. Material changes to the risk management process also must be disclosed. Managers should further consider regularly disclosing specific risk information and specific information regarding investment strategies related to each client. Managers must provide clients information detailing what relevant risk metrics they can expect to receive at the individual product/portfolio level.

PRACTICE PROBLEMS FOR READING 6

The following information relates to Questions 1–6[1]

Bornelli Asset Management offers traditional long-only funds as well as a variety of hedge funds for both private and institutional clients. Bornelli is a well-managed firm of more than 100 employees. Its board of directors has voted to adopt the Asset Manager Code of Professional Conduct (the Code).

Bornelli has hired Ava Campanelli as chief compliance officer with responsibility for implementing the Code. Campanelli develops a plan to evaluate the firm's current policies and procedures for compliance with the Code. Campanelli begins by reviewing three of the firm's compliance procedures:

Portfolio review	Portfolio information provided to clients is reviewed by an independent third-party.
Record retention	The firm retains records to substantiate all investment decisions for six years. In compliance with regulatory requirements, the firm also retains copies of all emails for the same period. The firm retains its records in a combination of both hard-copy and electronic formats.
Investigation of complaints	The chief compliance officer (CCO) is responsible for investigating and documenting all complaints. The CCO reports to the chief investment officer and works with management to take appropriate disciplinary action in cases of compliance breaches.

Campanelli then evaluates the firm's business-continuity plan. Under the current plan, the technology division backs up all of the firm's computer systems and client records twice daily. The back-ups are stored in a fireproof storage facility offsite. Bornelli outsources certain emergency plans to a disaster recovery firm. The disaster recovery firm is responsible for developing and implementing plans to communicate with employees and mission-critical vendors and suppliers in the event of a facility or communication disruption. The same firm also provides plans for contacting and communicating with clients in event of an extended disruption.

For her next project, Campanelli reviews the disclosures provided to both prospective and current clients. The disclosures regarding management fees state:

> Bornelli charges a 2% asset-based management fee. In addition to the management fee, clients may pay an incentive fee at the end of each year. The incentive fee is equal to 20% of the account's net investment income and net realized and unrealized capital gains for the year.
>
> No incentive fee will be paid unless the Fund has offset all prior net realized capital losses and net investment losses with realized capital gains, unrealized appreciation, and net investment income from all securities held by the Fund.

---

[1] This case was written by Dorothy C. Kelly, CFA, and Anne-Katrin Scherer, CFA.

Campanelli's evaluation of the management fee disclosures is interrupted by a more urgent matter involving a client. The client has requested monthly performance reporting of his investment in a long-short equity hedge fund. The fund's administrator argues "Our procedures call for us to provide clients with both gross- and net-of-fees returns within 30 days of the end of the quarter." He adds "Quarterly reporting is the industry standard."

The administrator complains "This client, Rossi, is overly demanding. He telephoned yesterday and requested an itemization of the fees and other costs charged to him for the past three years. He wants to know the specific management fee, the incentive fee, and the amount of commissions paid. The more time we spend answering his requests, the less time we have to research investments." Campanelli promises to look into the matter for the administrator.

The following week, Campanelli meets with Lee Bruno, manager of the firm's alternative assets fund. Bruno informs Campanelli, "The fund has a three-year lock-up period. We disclosed to all the prospective clients in writing before they invested that this is a long-term investment and that they should not focus on short-term performance results. During the lock-up period, we provide semi-annual reporting. After the lock-up, we report quarterly."

Bruno informs Campanelli that whenever possible, the firm uses fair market prices to value client holdings. He adds "Of course, our fund invests in alternative assets—some of which are very difficult to value. They aren't like public equities with independent, third-party market quotations available, so we use an internal model to value client holdings." He continues, "We disclose the use of internal models for valuation purposes on all our reports."

Following her conversation with Bruno, Campanelli researches a complaint from a new client regarding the valuations of his fund's holdings. The client complains that another management firm reported much lower valuations on similar instruments. Campanelli researches the methodologies Bornelli uses for valuing fund holdings. She determines the following:

▶ All publicly traded U.S. and foreign equities, including large-, mid-, small-, and micro-cap shares are valued at the last available closing price.

▶ The value of certain securities such as swaps are based on quotes collected from broker-dealers.

▶ When prices are not available from either of the above sources, valuations are based on internal models.

1. Are the three compliance procedures reviewed by Campanelli consistent with both the required and recommended standards of the CFA Institute Asset Manager Code of Professional Conduct?

    A. No, the procedures regarding record retention are inconsistent.

    B. No, the procedures regarding portfolio review are inconsistent.

    C. No, the procedures regarding investigation of complaints are inconsistent.

2. Is Bornelli's disaster recovery plan consistent with both the required and recommended standards of the Asset Manager Code?

    A. Yes.

    B. No, because the plan lacks a backup plan for monitoring, analyzing, and trading investments.

    C. No, because the plan only provides for contacting and communicating with clients during periods of extended disruption.

3. Are the firm's disclosures regarding management fees consistent with the required and recommended standards of the Asset Manager Code?

   A. Yes.

   B. No, because they do not use plain language.

   C. No, because they do not include the average or expected expenses or fees clients are likely to incur.

4. Are the performance reporting procedures described by the fund's administrator consistent with the required disclosure standards of the Asset Manager Code?

   A. Yes.

   B. No, because the AMC requires firms to report performance to all clients on a monthly basis.

   C. No, because the AMC requires firms to provide performance on a monthly basis when requested by clients.

5. To comply with both the required and recommended standards of the Asset Manager Code, must Bornelli honor Rossi's telephone request regarding an itemization of fees?

   A. Yes.

   B. No, because the firm is not required to disclose the amount of incentive fee charged to an individual client.

   C. No, because unless the firm claims compliance with the Soft Dollar Standards, it is not required to disclose the amount of commissions paid on clients' behalf.

6. Are the policies of the alternative assets fund consistent with the required and recommended standards of the Asset Manager Code?

   A. Yes.

   B. No, the frequency of reporting is inconsistent with the AMC.

   C. No, the use of internal valuation models is inconsistent with the AMC.

The following information relates to Questions 7–12

Henry Schmidt, David Zane, and Andrew Ronoldo founded SZR LLC (SZR), an investment advisory firm managing portfolios for individuals. Although none of the founders hold the CFA charter, SZR has adopted the CFA Institute Asset Manager Code of Professional Conduct.

SZR's client portfolios average $50,000 and are entirely invested in SZR's commingled fund, managed by Ronoldo. Ronoldo implements a quantitative enhanced index process in SZR's fund and has consistently added moderate performance (alpha) over the fund's mid-cap benchmark index. After five years of strong performance, Ronoldo worries that the mid-cap fund will lag broad market indices, so he decides to broaden the fund's strategy. After doing research, he adds micro-cap, foreign, and convertible preferred stocks to the fund and doubles some holdings so that their weights are much larger than they are in the benchmark index. Since the fund achieves even stronger performance, both against the benchmark mid-cap index and major market indices, Ronoldo plans to describe the new strategy in the company's next annual newsletter, due to be sent to clients in three months.

As a prominent member of the community, Schmidt has just joined the board of a local company, Trezeguet Baking Company, which recently went public. Trezeguet's shares are in most micro-capitalization (cap) indices. As a board member, Schmidt receives a small annual stipend of $2,000; however, he is granted several thousand stock options, which he can exercise after 24 months' board service. Since his stipend is insignificant and he will not exercise his options for at least 24 months, Schmidt does not disclose his Trezeguet board service to SZR clients.

One of SZR's clients is president of Sastre International. Because of SZR's success, this client hires SZR to manage $800 million of Sastre International's corporate cash in a separate account, but asks that its hiring of SZR not be made public. Sastre's board asks Ronoldo to direct all of the Sastre account trades through a local financial advisor, to thank the advisor for selecting SZR. Ronoldo is concerned that this direction may limit SZR's ability to achieve best execution, but after Sastre acknowledges in writing that this is their preference, Ronoldo agrees to follow Sastre's direction.

As head of operations, Zane wishes to simplify trading and implements a new trade policy: first place trades for the Sastre account through the local financial advisor and then submit the commingled fund's trades through national brokerage houses and electronic networks. The local financial advisor is pleased with this arrangement, as he is able to buy securities before other clients; he informs Zane that he'll recommend SZR to additional clients.

Schmidt, SZR's sales director, sends the commingled fund's stellar performance track record to several investment consultants, who serve as "gatekeepers" for large institutional clients, but he is told that SZR is too small to be considered by their clients. After Schmidt reveals that Sastre has recently hired SZR, and offers to negotiate the same special fee discount that has been given to Sastre, one consultant agrees to consider SZR for its clients. The consultant indicates that if SZR agrees to sponsor the consulting firm's annual conference, Schmidt will meet many potential clients. Schmidt considers this conference sponsorship, but decides that it is too costly for SZR's budget, so he declines the offer.

As SZR grows, Zane hires his brother-in-law, John Karna (top salesman for a local auto parts company) as Compliance Officer. Karna is tasked with writing SZR's Code of Ethics and its Investment Policies and Procedures Manual. Karna is also put in charge of the firm's Business Continuity Plan. The plan consists of his taking home, each evening, the computer records of SZR's daily trades.

7. Does Ronoldo violate the CFA Institute Asset Manager Code of Professional Conduct with respect to his broader investment strategy?

    A. No.

    B. Yes, with respect to client disclosure only.

    C. Yes, with respect to reasonable and adequate basis only.

8. Does Schmidt violate the CFA Institute Asset Manager Code of Professional Conduct with respect to his current Trezeguet board service?

    A. No.

    B. Yes, with respect to priority of client interests only.

    C. Yes, with respect to priority of client interests and participation in business relationships.

9. By agreeing to Sastre's direction, does Ronoldo violate the CFA Institute Asset Manager Code of Professional Conduct?

    A. No.

    B. Yes, only with respect to best execution.

    C. Yes, only with respect to fair and equitable trade allocation.

10. Does Zane's revision of SZR's trading process violate the CFA Institute Asset Manager Code of Professional Conduct?

    A. No.

    B. Yes, only with respect to best execution.

    C. Yes, with respect to best execution and fair, equitable trade allocation.

11. Does Schmidt violate the CFA Institute Asset Manager Code of Professional Conduct in his interaction with consultants?

    A. No.

    B. Yes, only with respect to confidentiality.

    C. Yes, only with respect to business relationships that could affect independence.

12. Does Karna's role as Chief Compliance Officer, and the process of SZR's Business Continuity Plan, respectively, conform to the requirements and recommendations of the CFA Institute Asset Manager Code of Professional Conduct?

    A. Neither Karna's role nor the Business Continuity Plan conforms.

    B. Karna's role conforms, but the Business Continuity Plan does not conform.

    C. Karna's role does not conform, but the Business Continuity Plan does conform.

SOLUTIONS FOR READING 6

1. C is correct. According to the recommendations of Section D(2) of the Asset Manager Code, where possible, the CCO should be independent from the investment and operations personnel and should report directly to the CEO or the board of directors.

2. B is correct. According to the guidance provided in Section D(6) of the Asset Manager Code, the level and complexity of business-continuity planning depends on the size, nature, and complexity of the organization involved. Bornelli is a large firm with hedge fund investments and it should have alternative plans for monitoring, analyzing, and trading investments if primary systems become unavailable.

3. C is correct. According to the recommendations and guidance of Section F(4d) of the Asset Manager Code, managers must disclose to prospective clients the average or expected expenses or fees clients are likely to incur, and to existing clients the actual fees and other costs charged to them.

4. A is correct. The performance reporting procedures described by the administrator are consistent with the Asset Manager Code (AMC) which requires disclosing the "performance of clients' investments on a regular and timely basis." The AMC recommends that "managers should report to clients at least quarterly, and when possible, such reporting should be provided within 30 days after the end of the quarter." The AMC also states that "at a minimum, Managers should provide clients with gross- and net-of-fees returns." Because quarterly reporting is the recommended minimum, managers may choose to provide more timely performance to clients.

5. A is correct. According to the recommendations of Section F(4d) of the Asset Manager Code, managers should disclose to each client the actual fees and other costs charged to them, together with itemizations of such charges, when requested by clients. The disclosure should include the specific management fee, incentive fee, and the amount of commissions paid on clients' behalf during the period.

6. B is correct. Clients must have regular performance information to evaluate their overall asset allocations and to determine whether rebalancing is necessary. This concept applies even to investment vehicles with lock-up periods. According to the Asset Manager Code, unless otherwise specified by the client, managers should report to clients at least quarterly, and when possible, within 30 days of the end of the period.

7. B is correct. Ronoldo should have disclosed his change in investment strategy to clients, allowing them to move their accounts if not in agreement. Until he disclosed a planned change in strategy, he should have continued to manage in the manner for which clients had hired him.

8. C is correct. Schmidt is on the board of a company whose stock is in micro-cap indices. This is a conflict of interest, as Ronoldo's widened investment guidelines allow purchase of Trezeguet stock for the fund. As Schmidt is an insider for the company and received options that can be sold (after 24 months), this relationship should be terminated.

9. A is correct. The Sastre board requests directed trading for its discretionary account and acknowledges, in writing, that trading through the local financial advisor may limit best execution. As this is a discretionary (not pension) account, the client has the right to direct to a less-than-optimal trading venue.

10. C is correct. Zane should have pursued best execution for all clients in the fund (which is not accomplished by placing trades with the local financial advisor first versus with national brokers or electronic networks), and fairly traded for all clients. While Sastre is welcome to direct trades, Zane's change in procedures harms other clients.

11. B is correct. Schmidt violated Code A-2 by revealing Sastre's hiring of SZR and its special fee discount.

12. A is correct. Schmidt's qualification as compliance officer is inadequate (D-2, D-5), and taking tapes home each night is inadequate business continuity for a firm of $1.5 billion (D-6).

GLOSSARY

10-year moving average price/earnings A price-to-earnings ratio in which the numerator (in a U.S. context) is defined as the real S&P 500 price index and the denominator as the moving average of the preceding 10 years of real reported earnings on the S&P 500.

Absolute return objective A return objective that is independent of a reference or benchmark level of return.

Absolute-return vehicles Investments that have no direct benchmark portfolios.

Accounting risk The risk associated with accounting standards that vary from country to country or with any uncertainty about how certain transactions should be recorded.

Accreting swap A swap where the notional amount increases over the life of the swap.

Accrual equivalent after-tax return The tax-free return that, if accrued annually, produces the same after-tax accumulation as the taxable portfolio.

Accrual equivalent tax rate A method of measuring tax drag that finds the annual accrual tax rate that would produce the same after-tax accumulation as a tax system based in whole or in part on deferred realized gains.

Accrual taxes Taxes that are levied and paid on a periodic basis, usually annually.

Accumulated benefit obligation (ABO) The present value of pension benefits, assuming the pension plan terminated immediately such that it had to provide retirement income to all beneficiaries for their years of service up to that date.

Accumulated service Years of service of a pension plan participant as of a specified date.

Active investment approach An approach to portfolio construction in which portfolio composition responds to changes in the portfolio manager's expectations concerning asset returns.

Active management An approach to investing in which the portfolio manager seeks to outperform a given benchmark portfolio.

Active return The portfolio's return in excess of the return on the portfolio's benchmark.

Active risk A synonym for tracking risk.

Active/immunization combination A portfolio with two component portfolios: an immunized portfolio which provides an assured return over the planning horizon and a second portfolio that uses an active high-return/high-risk strategy.

Active/passive combination Allocation of the core component of a portfolio to a passive strategy and the balance to an active component.

Active-lives The portion of a pension fund's liabilities associated with active workers.

Actual extreme events A type of scenario analysis used in stress testing. It involves evaluating how a portfolio would have performed given movements in interest rates, exchange rates, stock prices, or commodity prices at magnitudes such as occurred during past extreme market events (e.g., the stock market crash of October 1987).

Adaptive markets hypothesis (AMH) A hypothesis that applies principles of evolution—such as competition, adaptation, and natural selection—to financial markets in an attempt to reconcile efficient market theories with behavioral alternatives.

Ad valorem fees Fees that are calculated by multiplying a percentage by the value of assets managed; also called assets under management (AUM) fees.

Add-on interest A procedure for determining the interest on a bond or loan in which the interest is added onto the face value of a contract.

Adverse selection risk The risk associated with information asymmetry; in the context of trading, the risk of trading with a more informed trader.

After-tax asset allocation The distribution of asset classes in a portfolio measured on an after-tax basis.

Algorithmic trading Automated electronic trading subject to quantitative rules and user-specified benchmarks and constraints.

Allocation/selection interaction return A measure of the joint effect of weights assigned to both sectors and individual securities; the difference between the weight of the portfolio in a given sector and the portfolio's benchmark for that sector, times the difference between the portfolio's and the benchmark's returns in that sector, summed across all sectors.

Alpha Excess risk-adjusted return.

Alpha and beta separation An approach to portfolio construction that views investing to earn alpha and investing to establish systematic risk exposures as tasks that can and should be pursued separately.

Alpha research Research related to capturing excess risk-adjusted returns by a particular strategy; a way investment research is organized in some investment management firms.

Alternative investments Groups of investments with risk and return characteristics that differ markedly from those of traditional stock and bond investments.

American option An option that can be exercised on any day through the expiration day. Also referred to as *American-style exercise*.

Amortizing and **accreting swaps** A swap in which the notional principal changes according to a formula related to changes in the underlying.

Amortizing swap A swap where the notional amount declines over the life of the swap.

Anchoring and adjustment bias An information-processing bias in which the use of a psychological heuristic influences the way people estimate probabilities.

Anchoring trap The tendency of the mind to give disproportionate weight to the first information it receives on a topic.

Angel investor An accredited individual investing chiefly in seed and early-stage companies.

Anomalies Apparent deviations from market efficiency.

Appraisal data Valuation data based on appraised rather than market values.

Arbitrage The condition in a financial market in which equivalent assets or combinations of assets sell for two different prices, creating an opportunity to profit at no risk with no commitment of money. In a well-functioning financial market, few arbitrage opportunities are possible. Equivalent to the *law of one price*.

Arrears swap A type of interest rate swap in which the floating payment is set at the end of the period and the interest is paid at that same time.

Ask price (or ask, offer price, offer) The price at which a dealer will sell a specified quantity of a security.

Ask size The quantity associated with the ask price.

Asset allocation reviews A periodic review of the appropriateness of a portfolio's asset allocation.

Asset covariance matrix The covariance matrix for the asset classes or markets under consideration.

Asset location The choice of accounts in which specific assets are placed.

Asset swap A swap, typically involving a bond, in which fixed bond payments are swapped for payments based on a floating rate.

Asset/liability management The management of financial risks created by the interaction of assets and liabilities.

Asset/liability management approach In the context of determining a strategic asset allocation, an asset/liability management approach involves explicitly modeling liabilities and adopting the allocation of assets that is optimal in relationship to funding liabilities.

Asset-only approach In the context of determining a strategic asset allocation, an approach that focuses on the characteristics of the assets without explicitly modeling the liabilities.

Assurity of completion In the context of trading, confidence that trades will settle without problems under all market conditions.

Assurity of the contract In the context of trading, confidence that the parties to trades will be held to fulfilling their obligations.

Asynchronism A discrepancy in the dating of observations that occurs because stale (out-of-date) data may be used in the absence of current data.

At the money An option in which the underlying value equals the exercise price.

AUM fee A fee based on assets under management; an ad valorem fee.

Automated trading Any form of trading that is not manual, including trading based on algorithms.

Availability bias An information-processing bias in which people take a heuristic approach to estimating the probability of an outcome based on how easily the outcome comes to mind.

Average effective spread A measure of the liquidity of a security's market. The mean effective spread (sometimes dollar weighted) over all transactions in the stock in the period under study.

Back office Administrative functions at an investment firm such as those pertaining to transaction processing, record keeping, and regulatory compliance.

Backtesting A method for gaining information about a model using past data. As used in reference to VAR, it is the process of comparing the number of violations of VAR thresholds over a time period with the figure implied by the user-selected probability level.

Back-to-back transaction A transaction where a dealer enters into offsetting transactions with different parties, effectively serving as a go-between.

Backwardation A condition in the futures markets in which the benefits of holding an asset exceed the costs, leaving the futures price less than the spot price.

Balance of payments An accounting of all cash flows between residents and nonresidents of a country.

Bancassurance The sale of insurance by banks.

Barbell portfolio A portfolio made up of short and long maturities relative to the investment horizon date and interim coupon payments.

Base-rate neglect A type of representativeness bias in which the base rate or probability of the categorization is not adequately considered.

Basis The difference between the cash price and the futures price.

Basis point value (BPV) Also called *present value of a basis point* or *price value of a basis point* (PVBP), the change in the bond price for a 1 basis point change in yield.

Basis risk The risk that the basis will change in an unpredictable way.

Basis swap A swap in which both parties pay a floating rate.

Bayes' formula A mathematical rule explaining how existing probability beliefs should be changed given new information; it is essentially an application of conditional probabilities.

Bear spread An option strategy that involves selling a put with a lower exercise price and buying a put with a higher exercise price. It can also be executed with calls.

Behavioral finance An approach to finance based on the observation that psychological variables affect and often distort individuals' investment decision making.

Behavioral finance macro A focus on market level behavior that considers market anomalies that distinguish markets from the efficient markets of traditional finance.

Behavioral finance micro A focus on individual level behavior that examines the behavioral biases that distinguish individual investors from the rational decision makers of traditional finance.

Benchmark Something taken as a standard of comparison; a comparison portfolio; a collection of securities or risk factors and associated weights that represents the persistent and prominent investment characteristics of an asset category or manager's investment process.

Best efforts order A type of order that gives the trader's agent discretion to execute the order only when the agent judges market conditions to be favorable.

Beta A measure of the sensitivity of a given investment or portfolio to movements in the overall market.

Beta research Research related to systematic (market) risk and return; a way investment research is organized in some investment management firms.

Bid price (or bid) The price at which a dealer will buy a specified quantity of a security.

Bid size The quantity associated with the bid price.

Bid–ask spread The difference between the current bid price and the current ask price of a security.

Binary credit options Options that provide payoffs contingent on the occurrence of a specified negative credit event.

Binomial model A model for pricing options in which the underlying price can move to only one of two possible new prices.

Binomial tree A diagram representing price movements of the underlying in a binomial model.

Block order An order to sell or buy in a quantity that is large relative to the liquidity ordinarily available from dealers in the security or in other markets.

Bond option An option in which the underlying is a bond; primarily traded in over-the-counter markets.

Bond-yield-plus-risk-premium method An approach to estimating the required return on equity which specifies that required return as a bond yield plus a risk premium.

Bottom-up Focusing on company-specific fundamentals or factors such as revenues, earnings, cash flow, or new product development.

Bounded rationality The notion that people have informational and cognitive limitations when making decisions and do not necessarily optimize when arriving at their decisions.

Box spread An option strategy that combines a bull spread and a bear spread having two different exercise prices, which produces a risk-free payoff of the difference in the exercise prices.

Broad market indexes An index that is intended to measure the performance of an entire asset class. For example, the S&P 500 Index, Wilshire 5000, and Russell 3000 indexes for U.S. common stocks.

Broker An agent of a trader in executing trades.

Brokered markets Markets in which transactions are largely effected through a search-brokerage mechanism away from public markets.

Brokers   See *Futures commission merchants.*

Bubbles   Episodes in which asset market prices move to extremely high levels in relation to estimated intrinsic value.

Buffering   With respect to style index construction, rules for maintaining the style assignment of a stock consistent with a previous assignment when the stock has not clearly moved to a new style.

Build-up approach   Synonym for the risk premium approach.

Bull spread   An option strategy that involves buying a call with a lower exercise price and selling a call with a higher exercise price. It can also be executed with puts.

Bullet portfolio   A portfolio made up of maturities that are very close to the investment horizon.

Business cycle   Fluctuations in GDP in relation to long-term trend growth, usually lasting 9–11 years.

Business risk   The equity risk that comes from the nature of the firm's operating activities.

Butterfly spread   An option strategy that combines two bull or bear spreads and has three exercise prices.

Buy side   Investment management companies and other investors that use the services of brokerages.

Buy-side analysts   Analysts employed by an investment manager or institutional investor.

Buy-side traders   Professional traders that are employed by investment managers and institutional investors.

Calendar rebalancing   Rebalancing a portfolio to target weights on a periodic basis; for example, monthly, quarterly, semiannually, or annually.

Calendar-and-percentage-of-portfolio rebalancing   Monitoring a portfolio at regular frequencies, such as quarterly. Rebalancing decisions are then made based upon percentage-of-portfolio principles.

Call   An option that gives the holder the right to buy an underlying asset from another party at a fixed price over a specific period of time.

Calmar ratio   The compound annualized rate of return over a specified time period divided by the absolute value of maximum drawdown over the same time period.

Cap   A combination of interest rate call options designed to hedge a borrower against rate increases on a floating-rate loan.

Cap rate   With respect to options, the exercise interest rate for a cap.

Capital adequacy ratio   A measure of the adequacy of capital in relation to assets.

Capital allocation line   A graph line that describes the combinations of expected return and standard deviation of return available to an investor from combining an optimal portfolio of risky assets with a risk-free asset.

Capital flows forecasting approach   An exchange rate forecasting approach that focuses on expected capital flows, particularly long-term flows such as equity investment and foreign direct investment.

Capital market expectations (CME)   Expectations concerning the risk and return prospects of asset classes.

Caplet   Each component call option in a cap.

Capped swap   A swap in which the floating payments have an upper limit.

Carried interest   A private equity fund manager's incentive fee; the share of the private equity fund's profits that the fund manager is due once the fund has returned the outside investors' capital.

Carry   Another term for owning an asset, typically used to refer to commodities. (See also *carry market.*)

Carry market   A situation where the forward price is such that the return on a cash-and-carry is the risk-free rate.

Cash balance plan   A defined-benefit plan whose benefits are displayed in individual recordkeeping accounts.

Cash flow at risk   A variation of VAR that measures the risk to a company's cash flow, instead of its market value; the minimum cash flow loss expected to be exceeded with a given probability over a specified time period.

Cash flow matching   An asset/liability management approach that provides the future funding of a liability stream from the coupon and matured principal payments of the portfolio. A type of dedication strategy.

Cash price or **spot price**   The price for immediate purchase of the underlying asset.

Cash settlement   A procedure used in certain derivative transactions that specifies that the long and short parties engage in the equivalent cash value of a delivery transaction.

Cause-and-effect relationship   A relationship in which the occurrence of one event brings about the occurrence of another event.

Cautious investors   Investors who are generally averse to potential losses.

Cell-matching technique   (stratified sampling) A portfolio construction technique used in indexing that divides the benchmark index into cells related to the risk factors affecting the index and samples from index securities belonging to those cells.

Centralized risk management or **companywide risk management**   When a company has a single risk management group that monitors and controls all of the risk-taking activities of the organization. Centralization permits economies of scale and allows a company to use some of its risks to offset other risks. (See also *enterprise risk management.*)

Certainty equivalent   The maximum sum of money a person would pay to participate or the minimum sum of money a person would accept to not participate in an opportunity.

Chain-linking   A process for combining periodic returns to produce an overall time-weighted rate of return.

Cheapest to deliver   A bond in which the amount received for delivering the bond is largest compared with the amount paid in the market for the bond.

Cherry-picking   When a bankrupt company is allowed to enforce contracts that are favorable to it while walking away from contracts that are unfavorable to it.

Civil law   A legal system derived from Roman law, in which judges apply general, abstract rules or concepts to particular cases. In civil systems, law is developed primarily through legislative statutes or executive action.

Claw-back provision   With respect to the compensation of private equity fund managers, a provision that specifies that money from the fund manager be returned to investors if, at the end of a fund's life, investors have not received back their capital contributions and contractual share of profits.

Clearinghouse   An entity associated with a futures market that acts as middleman between the contracting parties and guarantees to each party the performance of the other.

Closed-book markets   Markets in which a trader does not have real-time access to all quotes in a security.

Closeout netting   In a bankruptcy, a process by which multiple obligations between two counterparties are consolidated into a single overall value owed by one of the counterparties to the other.

Cobb-Douglas production function (Cobb-Douglas model)   A production function (model for economic output) based on factors of labor and capital that exhibits constant returns to scale.

Cognitive dissonance The mental discomfort that occurs when new information conflicts with previously held beliefs or cognitions.

Cognitive errors Behavioral biases resulting from faulty reasoning; cognitive errors stem from basic statistical, information processing, or memory errors.

Coincident economic indicators A set of economic variables whose values correlate with current economic activity.

Collar An option strategy involving the purchase of a put and sale of a call in which the holder of an asset gains protection below a certain level, the exercise price of the put, and pays for it by giving up gains above a certain level, the exercise price of the call. Collars also can be used to provide protection against rising interest rates on a floating-rate loan by giving up gains from lower interest rates.

Collateral return (or collateral yield) The component of the return on a commodity futures contract that comes from the assumption that the full value of the underlying futures contract is invested to earn the risk-free interest rate.

Collateralized debt obligation A securitized pool of fixed-income assets.

Combination matching (or horizon matching) A cash flow matching technique; a portfolio is duration-matched with a set of liabilities with the added constraint that it also be cash-flow matched in the first few years, usually the first five years.

Commingled real estate funds (CREFs) Professionally managed vehicles for substantial commingled (i.e., pooled) investment in real estate properties.

Commitment period The period of time over which committed funds are advanced to a private equity fund.

Commodities Articles of commerce such as agricultural goods, metals, and petroleum; tangible assets that are typically relatively homogeneous in nature.

Commodity forward A contract in which the underlying asset is oil, a precious metal, or some other commodity.

Commodity futures Futures contracts in which the underlying is a traditional agricultural, metal, or petroleum product.

Commodity option An option in which the asset underlying the futures is a commodity, such as oil, gold, wheat, or soybeans.

Commodity spread Offsetting long and short positions in closely related commodities. (See also *crack spread* and *crush spread*.)

Commodity swap A swap in which the underlying is a commodity such as oil, gold, or an agricultural product.

Commodity trading advisors Registered advisors to managed futures funds.

Common law A legal system which draws abstract rules from specific cases. In common law systems, law is developed primarily through decisions of the courts.

Community property regime A marital property regime under which each spouse has an indivisible one-half interest in property received during marriage.

Completeness fund A portfolio that, when added to active managers' positions, establishes an overall portfolio with approximately the same risk exposures as the investor's overall equity benchmark.

Confidence band With reference to a quality control chart for performance evaluation, a range in which the manager's value-added returns are anticipated to fall a specified percentage of the time.

Confidence interval An interval that has a given probability of containing the parameter it is intended to estimate.

Confirmation bias A belief perseverance bias in which people tend to look for and notice what confirms their beliefs, to ignore or undervalue what contradicts their beliefs, and to misinterpret information as support for their beliefs.

Confirming evidence trap The bias that leads individuals to give greater weight to information that supports an existing or preferred point of view than to evidence that contradicts it.

Conjunction fallacy An inappropriate combining of probabilities of independent events to support a belief. In fact, the probability of two independent events occurring in conjunction is never greater than the probability of either event occurring alone; the probability of two independent events occurring together is equal to the multiplication of the probabilities of the independent events.

Conservatism bias A belief perseverance bias in which people maintain their prior views or forecasts by inadequately incorporating new information.

Consistent growth A growth investment substyle that focuses on companies with consistent growth having a long history of unit-sales growth, superior profitability, and predictable earnings.

Constant maturity swap or **CMT swap** A swap in which the floating rate is the rate on a security known as a constant maturity treasury or CMT security.

Constant maturity treasury or **CMT** A hypothetical U.S. Treasury note with a constant maturity. A CMT exists for various years in the range of 2 to 10.

Constant returns to scale A characteristic of a production function such that a given percentage increase in capital stock and labor input results in an equal percentage increase in output.

Constraints 1) Restricting conditions; 2) Relating to an investment policy statement, limitations on the investor's ability to take full or partial advantage of particular investments. Such constraints are either internal (such as a client's specific liquidity needs, time horizon, and unique circumstances) or external (such as tax issues and legal and regulatory requirements).

Contango A condition in the futures markets in which the costs of holding an asset exceed the benefits, leaving the futures price more than the spot price.

Contingent claims Derivatives in which the payoffs occur if a specific event occurs; generally referred to as options.

Contingent immunization A fixed-income strategy in which immunization serves as a fall-back strategy if the actively managed portfolio does not grow at a certain rate.

Continuous auction markets Auction markets where orders can be executed at any time during the trading day.

Continuous time Time thought of as advancing in extremely small increments.

Contrarian A value investment substyle focusing on stocks that have been beset by problems.

Controlled foreign corporation A company located outside a taxpayer's home country and in which the taxpayer has a controlling interest as defined under the home country law.

Convenience yield The nonmonetary return offered by an asset when the asset is in short supply, often associated with assets with seasonal production processes.

Conversion factor An adjustment used to facilitate delivery on bond futures contracts in which any of a number of bonds with different characteristics are eligible for delivery.

Convexity A measure of how interest rate sensitivity changes with a change in interest rates.

Convexity adjustment An estimate of the change in price that is not explained by duration.

Cooling degree day The greater of i) the average daily temperature minus 65 degrees Fahrenheit, and ii) zero.

Core capital The amount of capital required to fund spending to maintain a given lifestyle, fund goals, and provide adequate reserves for unexpected commitments.

Core-plus A fixed-income mandate that permits the portfolio manager to add instruments with relatively high return potential to core holdings of investment-grade debt.

Core-satellite A way of thinking about allocating money that seeks to define each investment's place in the portfolio in relation to specific investment goals or roles.

Core-satellite portfolio A portfolio in which certain investments (often indexed or semiactive) are viewed as the core and the balance are viewed as satellite investments fulfilling specific roles.

Corner portfolio Adjacent corner portfolios define a segment of the minimum-variance frontier within which portfolios hold identical assets and the rate of change of asset weights in moving from one portfolio to another is constant.

Corner portfolio theorem In a sign-constrained mean–variance optimization, the result that the asset weights of any minimum-variance portfolio are a positive linear combination of the corresponding weights in the two adjacent corner portfolios that bracket it in terms of expected return (or standard deviation of return).

Corporate governance The system of internal controls and procedures used to define and protect the rights and responsibilities of various stakeholders.

Corporate venturing Investments by companies in promising young companies in the same or a related industry.

Cost basis The amount paid to acquire an asset.

Cost of carry The costs of holding an asset.

Cost of carry model A model for pricing futures contracts in which the futures price is determined by adding the cost of carry to the spot price.

Country beta A measure of the sensitivity of a specified variable (e.g., yield) to a change in the comparable variable in another country.

Covariance A measure of the extent to which the returns on two assets move together.

Coverage Benchmark coverage is defined as the proportion of a portfolio's market value that is contained in the benchmark.

Covered call An option strategy involving the holding of an asset and sale of a call on the asset.

Covered interest arbitrage A transaction executed in the foreign exchange market in which a currency is purchased (sold) and a forward contract is sold (purchased) to lock in the exchange rate for future delivery of the currency. This transaction should earn the risk-free rate of the investor's home country.

Crack spread The difference between the price of crude oil futures and that of equivalent amounts of heating oil and gasoline.

Credit default swap A swap used to transfer credit risk to another party. A protection buyer pays the protection seller in return for the right to receive a payment from the seller in the event of a specified credit event.

Credit derivative A contract in which one party has the right to claim a payment from another party in the event that a specific credit event occurs over the life of the contract.

Credit event An event affecting the credit risk of a security or counterparty.

Credit forwards A type of credit derivative with payoffs based on bond values or credit spreads.

Credit method When the residence country reduces its taxpayers' domestic tax liability by the amount of taxes paid to a foreign country that exercises source jurisdiction.

Credit protection seller With respect to a credit derivative, the party that accepts the credit risk of the underlying financial asset.

Credit risk or **default risk** The risk of loss caused by a counterparty's or debtor's failure to make a timely payment or by the change in value of a financial instrument based on changes in default risk.

Credit spread forward A forward contract used to transfer credit risk to another party; a forward contract on a yield spread.

Credit spread option An option based on the yield spread between two securities that is used to transfer credit risk.

Credit spread risk The risk that the spread between the rate for a risky bond and the rate for a default risk-free bond may vary after the purchase of the risky bond.

Credit swap A type of swap transaction used as a credit derivative in which one party makes periodic payments to the other and receives the promise of a payoff if a third party defaults.

Credit VAR A variation of VAR related to credit risk; it reflects the minimum loss due to credit exposure with a given probability during a period of time.

Credited rates Rates of interest credited to a policyholder's reserve account.

Credit-linked notes Fixed-income securities in which the holder of the security has the right to withhold payment of the full amount due at maturity if a credit event occurs.

Cross hedging With respect to hedging bond investments using futures, hedging when the bond to be hedged is not identical to the bond underlying the futures contract. With respect to currency hedging, a hedging technique that uses two currencies other than the home currency.

Cross-default provision A provision stipulating that if a borrower defaults on any outstanding credit obligations, the borrower is considered to be in default on all obligations.

Cross-product netting Netting the market values of all contracts, not just derivatives, between parties.

Crush spread The difference between the price of a quantity of soybeans and that of the soybean meal and oil that can be produced by those soybeans.

Currency forward A forward contract in which the underlying is a foreign currency.

Currency option An option that allows the holder to buy (if a call) or sell (if a put) an underlying currency at a fixed exercise rate, expressed as an exchange rate.

Currency return The percentage change in the spot exchange rate stated in terms of home currency per unit of foreign currency.

Currency risk The risk associated with the uncertainty about the exchange rate at which proceeds in the foreign currency can be converted into the investor's home currency.

Currency swap A swap in which the parties make payments based on the difference in debt payments in different currencies.

Currency-hedged instruments Investment in nondomestic assets in which currency exposures are neutralized.

Current credit risk (or jump-to-default risk) The risk of credit-related events happening in the immediate future; it relates to the risk that a payment currently due will not be paid.

Cushion spread The difference between the minimum acceptable return and the higher possible immunized rate.

Custom security-based benchmark A custom benchmark created by weighting a manager's research universe using the manager's unique weighting approach.

Cyclical stocks The shares of companies whose earnings have above-average sensitivity to the business cycle.

Daily settlement See *Marking to market*.

Data-mining bias Bias that results from repeatedly "drilling" or searching a dataset until some statistically significant pattern is found.

Day traders Traders that rapidly buy and sell stocks in the hope that the stocks will continue to rise or fall in value for the seconds or minutes they are prepared to hold a position. Day traders hold a position open somewhat longer than a scalper but closing all positions at the end of the day.

Dealer (or market maker)   A business entity that is ready to buy an asset for inventory or sell an asset from inventory to provide the other side of an order.

Decentralized risk management   A system that allows individual units within an organization to manage risk. Decentralization results in duplication of effort but has the advantage of having people closer to the risk be more directly involved in its management.

Decision price (also called arrival price or strike price)   The prevailing price when the decision to trade is made.

Decision risk   The risk of changing strategies at the point of maximum loss.

Dedication strategies   Specialized fixed-income strategies designed to accommodate specific funding needs of the investor.

Deduction method   When the residence country allows taxpayers to reduce their taxable income by the amount of taxes paid to foreign governments in respect of foreign-source income.

Deemed dispositions   Tax treatment that assumes property is sold. It is sometimes seen as an alternative to estate or inheritance tax.

Deemed distribution   When shareholders of a controlled foreign corporation are taxed as if the earnings were distributed to shareholders, even though no distribution has been made.

Deep in the money   Options that are far in-the-money.

Deep out of the money   Options that are far out-of-the-money.

Default risk   The risk of loss if an issuer or counterparty does not fulfill its contractual obligations.

Default risk premium   Compensation for the possibility that the issue of a debt instrument will fail to make a promised payment at the contracted time and in the contracted amount.

Default swap   A contract in which the swap buyer pays a regular premium; in exchange, if a default in a specified bond occurs, the swap seller pays the buyer the loss due to the default.

Defaultable debt   Debt with some meaningful amount of credit risk.

Deferred swap   A swap with terms specified today, but for which swap payments begin at a later date than for an ordinary swap.

Deferred taxes   Taxes that are postponed until some future date.

Defined-benefit plan   A pension plan that specifies the plan sponsor's obligations in terms of the benefit to plan participants.

Defined-contribution plan   A pension plan that specifies the sponsor's obligations in terms of contributions to the pension fund rather than benefits to plan participants.

Deflation   A decrease in the general level of prices; an increase in the purchasing power of a unit of currency.

Delay costs (or slippage)   Implicit trading costs that arise from the inability to complete desired trades immediately due to order size or market liquidity.

Delivery   A process used in a deliverable forward contract in which the long pays the agreed-upon price to the short, which in turn delivers the underlying asset to the long.

Delivery option   The feature of a futures contract giving the short the right to make decisions about what, when, and where to deliver.

Delta   The relationship between the option price and the underlying price, which reflects the sensitivity of the price of the option to changes in the price of the underlying.

Delta hedge   An option strategy in which a position in an asset is converted to a risk-free position with a position in a specific number of options. The number of options per unit of the underlying changes through time, and the position must be revised to maintain the hedge.

Delta-normal method   A measure of VAR equivalent to the analytical method but that refers to the use of delta to estimate the option's price sensitivity.

Demand deposit   A deposit that can be drawn upon without prior notice, such as a checking account.

Demutualizing   The process of converting an insurance company from mutual form to stock.

Derivative   A financial instrument that offers a return based on the return of some other underlying asset.

Derivatives dealers   The commercial and investment banks that make markets in derivatives. Also referred to as market makers.

Descriptive statistics   Methods for effectively summarizing data to describe important aspects of a dataset.

Deteriorating fundamentals sell discipline   A sell discipline involving ongoing review of holdings in which a share issue is sold or reduced if the portfolio manager believes that the company's business prospects will deteriorate.

Diff swap   A swap in which payments are based on the difference in floating interest rates on a given notional amount denominated in a single currency.

Differential returns   Returns that deviate from a manager's benchmark.

Diffusion index   An index that measures how many indicators are pointing up and how many are pointing down.

Direct commodity investment   Commodity investment that involves cash market purchase of physical commodities or exposure to changes in spot market values via derivatives, such as futures.

Direct market access   Platforms sponsored by brokers that permit buy-side traders to directly access equities, fixed income, futures, and foreign exchange markets, clearing via the broker.

Direct quotation   Quotation in terms of domestic currency/foreign currency.

Discount interest   A procedure for determining the interest on a loan or bond in which the interest is deducted from the face value in advance.

Discounted cash flow (DCF) models   Valuation models that express the idea that an asset's value is the present value of its (expected) cash flows.

Discrete time   Time thought of as advancing in distinct finite increments.

Discretionary trust   A trust structure in which the trustee determines whether and how much to distribute in the sole discretion of the trustee.

Disintermediation   To withdraw funds from financial intermediaries for placement with other financial intermediaries offering a higher return or yield. Or, to withdraw funds from a financial intermediary for the purposes of direct investment, such as withdrawing from a mutual fund to make direct stock investments.

Disposition effect   As a result of loss aversion, an emotional bias whereby investors are reluctant to dispose of losers. This results in an inefficient and gradual adjustment to deterioration in fundamental value.

Distressed debt arbitrage   A distressed securities investment discipline that involves purchasing the traded bonds of bankrupt companies and selling the common equity short.

Distressed securities   Securities of companies that are in financial distress or near bankruptcy; the name given to various investment disciplines employing securities of companies in distress.

Diversification effect   In reference to VAR across several portfolios (for example, across an entire firm), this effect equals the difference between the sum of the individual VARs and total VAR.

Dividend recapitalization   A method by which a buyout fund can realize the value of a holding; involves the issuance of debt by the holding to finance a special dividend to owners.

Dollar duration A measure of the change in portfolio value for a 100 bps change in market yields.

Double inflection utility function A utility function that changes based on levels of wealth.

Downgrade risk The risk that one of the major rating agencies will lower its rating for an issuer, based on its specified rating criteria.

Downside deviation A measure of volatility using only rate of return data points below the investor's minimum acceptable return.

Downside risk Risk of loss or negative return.

Due diligence Investigation and analysis in support of an investment action or recommendation, such as the scrutiny of operations and management and the verification of material facts.

Duration A measure of the approximate sensitivity of a security to a change in interest rates (i.e., a measure of interest rate risk).

Dynamic approach With respect to strategic asset allocation, an approach that accounts for links between optimal decisions at different points in time.

Dynamic hedging A strategy in which a position is hedged by making frequent adjustments to the quantity of the instrument used for hedging in relation to the instrument being hedged.

Earnings at risk (EAR) A variation of VAR that reflects the risk of a company's earnings instead of its market value.

Earnings momentum A growth investment substyle that focuses on companies with earnings momentum (high quarterly year-over-year earnings growth).

Econometrics The application of quantitative modeling and analysis grounded in economic theory to the analysis of economic data.

Economic exposure The risk associated with changes in the relative attractiveness of products and services offered for sale, arising out of the competitive effects of changes in exchange rates.

Economic indicators Economic statistics provided by government and established private organizations that contain information on an economy's recent past activity or its current or future position in the business cycle.

Economic surplus The market value of assets minus the present value of liabilities.

Effective capital gain tax rate A rate that adjusts the capital gains tax rate to reflect previously taxed dividends, income, or realized capital gains.

Effective duration Duration adjusted to account for embedded options.

Effective spread Two times the distance between the actual execution price and the midpoint of the market quote at the time an order is entered; a measure of execution costs that captures the effects of price improvement and market impact.

Efficient frontier The graph of the set of portfolios that maximize expected return for their level of risk (standard deviation of return); the part of the minimum-variance frontier beginning with the global minimum-variance portfolio and continuing above it.

Electronic communications networks (ECNs) Computer-based auctions that operate continuously within the day using a specified set of rules to execute orders.

Emerging market debt The sovereign debt of nondeveloped countries.

Emotional biases Behavioral biases resulting from reasoning influenced by feelings; emotional biases stem from impulse or intuition.

Endogenous variable A variable whose values are determined within the system.

Endowment bias An emotional bias in which people value an asset more when they hold rights to it than when they do not.

Endowments Long-term funds generally owned by operating non-profit institutions such as universities and colleges, museums, hospitals, and other organizations involved in charitable activities.

Enhanced derivatives products companies (or special purpose vehicles) A type of subsidiary separate from an entity's other activities and not liable for the parent's debts. They are often used by derivatives dealers to control exposure to ratings downgrades.

Enterprise risk management An overall assessment of a company's risk position. A centralized approach to risk management sometimes called firmwide risk management.

Equal probability rebalancing Rebalancing in which the manager specifies a corridor for each asset class as a common multiple of the standard deviation of the asset class's returns. Rebalancing to the target proportions occurs when any asset class weight moves outside its corridor.

Equal weighted In an equal-weighted index, each stock in the index is weighted equally.

Equitized Given equity market systematic risk exposure.

Equitizing cash A strategy used to replicate an index. It is also used to take a given amount of cash and turn it into an equity position while maintaining the liquidity provided by the cash.

Equity forward A contract calling for the purchase of an individual stock, a stock portfolio, or a stock index at a later date at an agreed-upon price.

Equity-indexed annuity A type of life annuity that provides a guarantee of a minimum fixed payment plus some participation in stock market gains, if any.

Equity options Options on individual stocks; also known as stock options.

Equity q The ratio of a company's equity market capitalization divided by net worth measured at replacement cost.

Equity risk premium Compensation for the additional risk of equity compared with debt.

Equity swap A swap in which the rate is the return on a stock or stock index.

ESG risk The risk to a company's market valuation resulting from environmental, social, and governance factors.

Estate All of the property a person owns or controls; may consist of financial assets, tangible personal assets, immovable property, or intellectual property.

Estate planning The process of preparing for the disposition of one's estate (e.g., the transfer of property) upon death and during one's lifetime.

Eurodollar A dollar deposited outside the United States.

European option An option that can be exercised only at expiration. Also referred to as *European-style exercise*.

Eurozone The region of countries using the euro as a currency.

Ex post alpha (or Jensen's alpha) The average return achieved in a portfolio in excess of what would have been predicted by CAPM given the portfolio's risk level; an after-the-fact measure of excess risk-adjusted return.

Excess capital An investor's capital over and above that which is necessary to fund their lifestyle and reserves.

Excess currency return The expected currency return in excess of the forward premium or discount.

Exchange A regulated venue for the trading of investment instruments.

Exchange fund A fund into which several investors place their different share holdings in exchange for shares in the diversified fund itself.

Exchange for physicals (EFP) A permissible delivery procedure used by futures market participants, in which the long and short arrange a delivery procedure other than the normal procedures stipulated by the futures exchange.

Execution uncertainty Uncertainty pertaining to the timing of execution, or if execution will even occur at all.

Exemption method When the residence country imposes no tax on foreign-source income by providing taxpayers with an exemption, in effect having only one jurisdiction impose tax.

Exercise or **exercising the option** The process of using an option to buy or sell the underlying.

Exercise rate or **strike rate** The fixed rate at which the holder of an interest rate option can buy or sell the underlying.

Exogenous shocks Events from outside the economic system that affect its course. These could be short-lived political events, changes in government policy, or natural disasters, for example.

Exogenous variable A variable whose values are determined outside the system.

Expiration date The date on which a derivative contract expires.

Explicit transaction costs The direct costs of trading such as broker commission costs, taxes, stamp duties, and fees paid to exchanges; costs for which the trader could be given a receipt.

Externality Those consequences of a transaction (or process) that do not fall on the parties to the transaction (or process).

Factor covariance matrix The covariance matrix of factors.

Factor push A simple stress test that involves pushing prices and risk factors of an underlying model in the most disadvantageous way to estimate the impact of factor extremes on the portfolio's value.

Factor sensitivities (also called factor betas or factor loadings) In a multifactor model, the responsiveness of the dependent variable to factor movements.

Factor-model-based benchmark A benchmark that is created by relating one or more systematic sources of returns (factors or exposures) to returns of the benchmark.

Fallen angels Debt that has crossed the threshold from investment grade to high yield.

Family offices Entities, typically organized and owned by a family for its benefit, that assume responsibility for services such as financial planning, estate planning, and asset management.

Fed model An equity valuation model that relates the earnings yield on the S&P 500 to the yield to maturity on 10-year U.S. Treasury bonds.

Federal funds rate The interest rate on overnight loans of reserves (deposits) between U.S. Federal Reserve System member banks.

Fee cap A limit on the total fee paid regardless of performance.

Fiduciary A person or entity standing in a special relation of trust and responsibility with respect to other parties.

Fiduciary call A combination of a European call and a risk-free bond that matures on the option expiration day and has a face value equal to the exercise price of the call.

Financial capital As used in the text, an individual investor's investable wealth; total wealth minus human capital. Consists of assets that can be traded such as cash, stocks, bonds, and real estate.

Financial equilibrium models Models describing relationships between expected return and risk in which supply and demand are in balance.

Financial futures Futures contracts in which the underlying is a stock, bond, or currency.

Financial risk Risks derived from events in the external financial markets, such as changes in equity prices, interest rates, or currency exchange rates.

Fiscal policy Government activity concerning taxation and governmental spending.

Fixed annuity A type of life annuity in which periodic payments are fixed in amount.

Fixed trust A trust structure in which distributions to beneficiaries are prescribed in the trust document to occur at certain times or in certain amounts.

Fixed-income forward A forward contract in which the underlying is a bond.

Fixed-rate payer The party to an interest rate swap that is obligated to make periodic payments at a fixed rate.

Floating supply of shares (or free float) The number of shares outstanding that are actually available to investors.

Floating-rate loan A loan in which the interest rate is reset at least once after the starting date.

Floating-rate payer The party to an interest rate swap that is obligated to make periodic payments based on a benchmark floating rate.

Floor A combination of interest rate options designed to provide protection against interest rate decreases.

Floor broker An agent of the broker who, for certain exchanges, physically represents the trade on the exchange floor.

Floor traders or **locals** Market makers that buy and sell by quoting a bid and an ask price. They are the primary providers of liquidity to the market.

Floored swap A swap in which the floating payments have a lower limit.

Floorlet Each component put option in a floor.

Forced heirship rules Legal ownership principles whereby children have the right to a fixed share of a parent's estate.

Formal tools Established research methods amenable to precise definition and independent replication of results.

Forward contract An agreement between two parties in which one party, the buyer, agrees to buy from the other party, the seller, an underlying asset at a later date for a price established at the start of the contract.

Forward curve The set of forward or futures prices with different expiration dates on a given date for a given asset.

Forward discount (or forward premium) The forward rate less the spot rate, divided by the spot rate; called the forward discount if negative, and forward premium if positive.

Forward hedging Hedging that involves the use of a forward contract between the foreign asset's currency and the home currency.

Forward price or **forward rate** The fixed price or rate at which the transaction scheduled to occur at the expiration of a forward contract will take place. This price is agreed on at the initiation date of the contract.

Forward rate agreement (FRA) A forward contract calling for one party to make a fixed interest payment and the other to make an interest payment at a rate to be determined at the contract expiration.

Forward strip Another name for the *forward curve.*

Forward swap A forward contract to enter into a swap.

Foundations Typically, grant-making institutions funded by gifts and investment assets.

Fourth market A term occasionally used for direct trading of securities between institutional investors; the fourth market would include trading on electronic crossing networks.

Framing bias An information-processing bias in which a person answers a question differently based on the way in which it is asked (framed).

Front office The revenue generating functions at an investment firm such as those pertaining to trading and sales.

Front-run To trade ahead of the initiator, exploiting privileged information about the initiator's trading intentions.

Full replication When every issue in an index is represented in the portfolio, and each portfolio position has approximately the same weight in the fund as in the index.

Fully funded plan A pension plan in which the ratio of the value of plan assets to the present value of plan liabilities is 100 percent or greater.

Functional (or multifunctional) **duration** The key rate duration.

Fund of funds A fund that invests in a number of underlying funds.

Fundamental law of active management The relation that the information ratio of a portfolio manager is approximately equal to the information coefficient multiplied by the square root of the investment discipline's breadth (the number of independent, active investment decisions made each year).

Funded status The relationship between the value of a plan's assets and the present value of its liabilities.

Funding ratio A measure of the relative size of pension assets compared to the present value of pension liabilities. Calculated by dividing the value of pension assets by the present value of pension liabilities. Also referred to as the funded ratio or funded status.

Funding risk The risk that liabilities funding long asset positions cannot be rolled over at reasonable cost.

Futures commission merchants (FCMs) Individuals or companies that execute futures transactions for other parties off the exchange.

Futures contract An enforceable contract between a buyer (seller) and an established exchange or its clearinghouse in which the buyer (seller) agrees to take (make) delivery of something at a specified price at the end of a designated period of time.

Futures exchange A legal corporate entity whose shareholders are its members. The members of the exchange have the privilege of executing transactions directly on the exchange.

Futures price The price at which the parties to a futures contract agree to exchange the underlying.

Gain-to-loss ratio The ratio of positive returns to negative returns over a specified period of time.

Gamblers' fallacy A misunderstanding of probabilities in which people wrongly project reversal to a long-term mean.

Gamma A numerical measure of the sensitivity of delta to a change in the underlying's value.

Global custodian An entity that effects trade settlement, safekeeping of assets, and the allocation of trades to individual custody accounts.

Global investable market A practical proxy for the world market portfolio consisting of traditional and alternative asset classes with sufficient capacity to absorb meaningful investment.

Global minimum-variance portfolio The portfolio on the minimum-variance frontier with smallest variance of return.

Gold standard currency system A currency regime under which currency could be freely converted into gold at established rates.

Gordon (constant) **growth model** A version of the dividend discount model for common share value that assumes a constant growth rate in dividends.

Government structural policies Government policies that affect the limits of economic growth and incentives within the private sector.

Grinold–Kroner model An expression for the expected return on a share as the sum of an expected income return, an expected nominal earnings growth return, and an expected repricing return.

Gross domestic product (GDP) The total value of final goods and services produced in the economy during a year.

Growth in total factor productivity A component of trend growth in GDP that results from increased efficiency in using capital inputs; also known as technical progress.

Growth investment style With reference to equity investing, an investment style focused on investing in high-earnings-growth companies.

Guaranteed investment contract A debt instrument issued by insurers, usually in large denominations, that pays a guaranteed, generally fixed interest rate for a specified time period.

H-model A variant of the two-stage dividend discount model in which growth begins at a high rate and declines linearly throughout the supernormal growth period until it reaches a normal growth rate that holds in perpetuity.

Hague Conference on Private International Law An intergovernmental organization working toward the convergence of private international law. Its 69 members consist of countries and regional economic integration organizations.

Halo effect An emotional bias that extends a favorable evaluation of some characteristics to other characteristics.

Heating degree day The greater of i) 65 degrees Fahrenheit minus the average daily temperature, and ii) zero.

Hedge funds A historically loosely regulated, pooled investment vehicle that may implement various investment strategies.

Hedge ratio The relationship of the quantity of an asset being hedged to the quantity of the derivative used for hedging.

Hedged return The foreign asset return in local currency terms plus the forward discount (premium).

Hedging A general strategy usually thought of as reducing, if not eliminating, risk.

Herding When a group of investors trade on the same side of the market in the same securities, or when investors ignore their own private information and act as other investors do.

High yield A value investment substyle that focuses on stocks offering high dividend yield with prospects of maintaining or increasing the dividend.

High-water mark A specified net asset value level that a fund must exceed before performance fees are paid to the hedge fund manager.

High-yield investing A distressed securities investment discipline that involves investment in high-yield bonds perceived to be undervalued.

Highest-in, first-out (HIFO) A concept related to tax loss harvesting in which investors are allowed to sell the highest cost basis lots first, which defers realizing the tax liability associated with lots having a lower cost basis.

Hindsight bias A bias with selective perception and retention aspects in which people may see past events as having been predictable and reasonable to expect.

Historical method A method of estimating VAR that uses data from the returns of the portfolio over a recent past period and compiles this data in the form of a histogram.

Historical simulation method The application of historical price changes to the current portfolio.

Holdings-based style analysis An approach to style analysis that categorizes individual securities by their characteristics and aggregates results to reach a conclusion about the overall style of the portfolio at a given point in time.

Home bias An anomaly by which portfolios exhibit a strong bias in favor of domestic securities in the context of global portfolios.

Homogenization Creating a contract with standard and generally accepted terms, which makes it more acceptable to a broader group of participants.

Human capital or **net employment capital** An implied asset; the present value of expected future labor income.

Hybrid markets Combinations of market types, which offer elements of batch auction markets and continuous auction markets, as well as quote-driven markets.

Hypothetical events A type of scenario analysis used in stress testing that involves the evaluation of performance given events that have never happened in the markets or market outcomes to which we attach a small probability.

Illiquidity premium Compensation for the risk of loss relative to an investment's fair value if an investment needs to be converted to cash quickly.

Illusion of control bias A bias in which people tend to believe that they can control or influence outcomes when, in fact, they cannot. Illusion of knowledge and self-attribution biases contribute to the overconfidence bias.

Immunization An asset/liability management approach that structures investments in bonds to match (offset) liabilities' weighted-average duration; a type of dedication strategy.

Immunization target rate of return The assured rate of return of an immunized portfolio, equal to the total return of the portfolio assuming no change in the term structure.

Immunized time horizon The time horizon over which a portfolio's value is immunized; equal to the portfolio duration.

Implementation shortfall The difference between the money return on a notional or paper portfolio and the actual portfolio return.

Implementation shortfall strategy (or arrival price strategy) A strategy that attempts to minimize trading costs as measured by the implementation shortfall method.

Implicit transaction costs The indirect costs of trading including bid–ask spreads, the market price impacts of large trades, missed trade opportunity costs, and delay costs.

Implied repo rate The rate of return from a cash-and-carry transaction implied by the futures price relative to the spot price.

Implied volatility The volatility that option traders use to price an option, implied by the price of the option and a particular option-pricing model.

Implied yield A measure of the yield on the underlying bond of a futures contract implied by pricing it as though the underlying will be delivered at the futures expiration.

Income tax structure How and when different types of income are taxed.

Incremental VAR A measure of the incremental effect of an asset on the VAR of a portfolio by measuring the difference between the portfolio's VAR while including a specified asset and the portfolio's VAR with that asset eliminated.

Index amortizing swap An interest rate swap in which the notional principal is indexed to the level of interest rates and declines with the level of interest rates according to a predefined schedule. This type of swap is frequently used to hedge securities that are prepaid as interest rates decline, such as mortgage-backed securities.

Index option An option in which the underlying is a stock index.

Indexing A common passive approach to investing that involves holding a portfolio of securities designed to replicate the returns on a specified index of securities.

Indifference curve analysis A decision-making approach whereby curves of consumption bundles, among which the decision-maker is indifferent, are constructed to identify and choose the curve within budget constraints that generates the highest utility.

Indirect commodity investment Commodity investment that involves the acquisition of indirect claims on commodities, such as equity in companies specializing in commodity production.

Individualist investors Investors who have a self-assured approach to investing and investment decision making.

Inferential statistics Methods for making estimates or forecasts about a larger group from a smaller group actually observed.

Inflation An increase in the general level of prices; a decrease in the purchasing power of a unit of currency.

Inflation hedge An asset whose returns are sufficient on average to preserve purchasing power during periods of inflation.

Inflation premium Compensation for expected inflation.

Information coefficient The correlation between forecast and actual returns.

Information ratio The mean excess return of the account over the benchmark (i.e., mean active return) relative to the variability of that excess return (i.e., tracking risk); a measure of risk-adjusted performance.

Information-motivated traders Traders that seek to trade on information that has limited value if not quickly acted upon.

Infrastructure funds Funds that make private investment in public infrastructure projects in return for rights to specified revenue streams over a contracted period.

Initial margin requirement The margin requirement on the first day of a transaction as well as on any day in which additional margin funds must be deposited.

Initial public offering The initial issuance of common stock registered for public trading by a formerly private corporation.

Input uncertainty Uncertainty concerning whether the inputs are correct.

Inside ask (or market ask) The lowest available ask price.

Inside bid (or market bid) The highest available bid price.

Inside bid–ask spread (also called market bid–ask spread, inside spread, or market spread) Market ask price minus market bid price.

Inside quote (or market quote) Combination of the highest available bid price with the lowest available ask price.

Institutional investors Corporations or other legal entities that ultimately serve as financial intermediaries between individuals and investment markets.

Interest rate call An option in which the holder has the right to make a known interest payment and receive an unknown interest payment.

Interest rate cap or **cap** A series of call options on an interest rate, with each option expiring at the date on which the floating loan rate will be reset, and with each option having the same exercise rate. A cap in general can have an underlying other than an interest rate.

Interest rate collar A combination of a long cap and a short floor, or a short cap and a long floor. A collar in general can have an underlying other than an interest rate.

Interest rate floor or **floor** A series of put options on an interest rate, with each option expiring at the date on which the floating loan rate will be reset, and with each option having the same exercise rate. A floor in general can have an underlying other than the interest rate.

Interest rate forward See *Forward rate agreement*.

Interest rate management effect With respect to fixed-income attribution analysis, a return component reflecting how well a manager predicts interest rate changes.

Interest rate option An option in which the underlying is an interest rate.

Interest rate parity A formula that expresses the equivalence or parity of spot and forward rates, after adjusting for differences in the interest rates.

Interest rate put An option in which the holder has the right to make an unknown interest payment and receive a known interest payment.

Interest rate risk Risk related to changes in the level of interest rates.

Interest rate swap A contract between two parties (counterparties) to exchange periodic interest payments based on a specified notional amount of principal.

Interest spread With respect to banks, the average yield on earning assets minus the average percent cost of interest-bearing liabilities.

Internal rate of return   The growth rate that will link the ending value of the account to its beginning value plus all intermediate cash flows; money-weighted rate of return is a synonym.

Intestate   Having made no valid will; a decedent without a valid will or with a will that does not dispose of their property is considered to have died intestate.

In-the-money   Options that, if exercised, would result in the value received being worth more than the payment required to exercise.

Intrinsic value or **exercise value**   The value obtained if an option is exercised based on current conditions.

Inventory cycle   A cycle measured in terms of fluctuations in inventories, typically lasting 2–4 years.

Inverse floater   A floating-rate note or bond in which the coupon is adjusted to move opposite to a benchmark interest rate.

Investment objectives   Desired investment outcomes, chiefly pertaining to return and risk.

Investment policy statement (IPS)   A written document that sets out a client's return objectives and risk tolerance over a relevant time horizon, along with applicable constraints such as liquidity needs, tax considerations, regulatory requirements, and unique circumstances.

Investment skill   The ability to outperform an appropriate benchmark consistently over time.

Investment strategy   An investor's approach to investment analysis and security selection.

Investment style   A natural grouping of investment disciplines that has some predictive power in explaining the future dispersion in returns across portfolios.

Investment style indices   Indices that represent specific portions of an asset category. For example, subgroups within the U.S. common stock asset category such as large-capitalization growth stocks.

Investor's benchmark   The benchmark an investor uses to evaluate performance of a given portfolio or asset class.

Irrevocable trust   A trust arrangement wherein the settlor has no ability to revoke the trust relationship.

J factor risk   The risk associated with a judge's track record in adjudicating bankruptcies and restructuring.

J-curve   The expected pattern of interim returns over the life of a successful venture capital fund in which early returns are negative as the portfolio of companies burns cash but later returns accelerate as companies are exited.

Joint ownership with right of survivorship   Jointly owned; assets held in joint ownership with right of survivorship automatically transfer to the surviving joint owner or owners outside the probate process.

Justified P/E   The price-to-earnings ratio that is fair, warranted, or justified on the basis of forecasted fundamentals.

Key rate duration   A method of measuring the interest rate sensitivities of a fixed-income instrument or portfolio to shifts in key points along the yield curve.

Lagging economic indicators   A set of economic variables whose values correlate with recent past economic activity.

Law of one price   The condition in a financial market in which two financial instruments or combinations of financial instruments can sell for only one price. Equivalent to the principle that no arbitrage opportunities are possible.

Leading economic indicators   A set of economic variables whose values vary with the business cycle but at a fairly consistent time interval before a turn in the business cycle.

Legal and regulatory factors   External factors imposed by governmental, regulatory, or oversight authorities that constrain investment decision-making.

Legal/contract risk   The possibility of loss arising from the legal system's failure to enforce a contract in which an enterprise has a financial stake; for example, if a contract is voided through litigation.

Leverage-adjusted duration gap   A leverage-adjusted measure of the difference between the durations of assets and liabilities which measures a bank's overall interest rate exposure.

Leveraged floating-rate note or **leveraged floater**   A floating-rate note or bond in which the coupon is adjusted at a multiple of a benchmark interest rate.

Liability   As used in the text, a financial obligation.

Life annuity   An annuity that guarantees a monthly income to the annuitant for life.

Lifetime gratuitous transfer   A lifetime gift made during the lifetime of the donor; also known as *inter vivos* transfers.

Limit down   A limit move in the futures market in which the price at which a transaction would be made is at or below the lower limit.

Limit move   A condition in the futures markets in which the price at which a transaction would be made is at or beyond the price limits.

Limit order   An instruction to execute an order when the best price available is at least as good as the limit price specified in the order.

Limit up   A limit move in the futures market in which the price at which a transaction would be made is at or above the upper limit.

Linear programming   Optimization in which the objective function and constraints are linear.

Liquidity   The ability to trade without delay at relatively low cost and in relatively large quantities.

Liquidity event   An event giving rise to a need for cash.

Liquidity requirement   A need for cash in excess of new contributions (for pension plans and endowments, for example) or savings (for individuals) at a specified point in time.

Liquidity risk   Any risk of economic loss because of the need to sell relatively less liquid assets to meet liquidity requirements; the risk that a financial instrument cannot be purchased or sold without a significant concession in price because of the market's potential inability to efficiently accommodate the desired trading size.

Liquidity-motivated traders   Traders that are motivated to trade based upon reasons other than an information advantage. For example, to release cash proceeds to facilitate the purchase of another security, adjust market exposure, or fund cash needs.

Locked limit   A condition in the futures markets in which a transaction cannot take place because the price would be beyond the limits.

Locked up   Said of investments that cannot be traded at all for some time.

Lock-up period   A minimum initial holding period for investments during which no part of the investment can be withdrawn.

Logical participation strategies   Protocols for breaking up an order for execution over time. Typically used by institutional traders to participate in overall market volumes without being unduly visible.

London Interbank Offer Rate (LIBOR)   The Eurodollar rate at which London banks lend dollars to other London banks; considered to be the best representative rate on a dollar borrowed by a private, high-quality borrower.

Long   The buyer of a derivative contract. Also refers to the position of owning a derivative.

Longevity risk   The risk of outliving one's financial resources.

Long-term equity anticipatory securities (LEAPS) Options originally created with expirations of several years.

Loss-aversion bias A bias in which people tend to strongly prefer avoiding losses as opposed to achieving gains.

Low P/E A value investment substyle that focuses on shares selling at low prices relative to current or normal earnings.

Lower bound The lowest possible value of an option.

M^2 A measure of what a portfolio would have returned if it had taken on the same total risk as the market index.

Macaulay duration The percentage change in price for a percentage change in yield. The term, named for one of the economists who first derived it, is used to distinguish the calculation from modified duration. (See also *modified duration*.)

Macro attribution Performance attribution analysis conducted on the fund sponsor level.

Macro expectations Expectations concerning classes of assets.

Maintenance margin requirement The margin requirement on any day other than the first day of a transaction.

Managed futures Pooled investment vehicles, frequently structured as limited partnerships, that invest in futures and options on futures and other instruments.

Manager continuation policies Policies adopted to guide the manager evaluations conducted by fund sponsors. The goal of manager continuation policies is to reduce the costs of manager turnover while systematically acting on indications of future poor performance.

Manager monitoring A formal, documented procedure that assists fund sponsors in consistently collecting information relevant to evaluating the state of their managers' operations; used to identify warning signs of adverse changes in existing managers' organizations.

Manager review A detailed examination of a manager that currently exists within a plan sponsor's program. The manager review closely resembles the manager selection process, in both the information considered and the comprehensiveness of the analysis. The staff should review all phases of the manager's operations, just as if the manager were being initially hired.

Mandate A set of instructions detailing the investment manager's task and how his performance will be evaluated.

Margin The amount of money that a trader deposits in a margin account. The term is derived from the stock market practice in which an investor borrows a portion of the money required to purchase a certain amount of stock. In futures markets, there is no borrowing so the margin is more of a down payment or performance bond.

Market bid The best available bid; highest price any buyer is currently willing to pay.

Market fragmentation A condition whereby a market contains no dominant group of sellers (or buyers) that are large enough to unduly influence the market.

Market impact (or price impact) The effect of the trade on transaction prices.

Market integration The degree to which there are no impediments or barriers to capital mobility across markets.

Market microstructure The market structures and processes that affect how the manager's interest in buying or selling an asset is translated into executed trades (represented by trade prices and volumes).

Market model A regression equation that specifies a linear relationship between the return on a security (or portfolio) and the return on a broad market index.

Market on open (close) order A market order to be executed at the opening (closing) of the market.

Market order An instruction to execute an order as soon as possible in the public markets at the best price available.

Market oriented With reference to equity investing, an intermediate grouping for investment disciplines that cannot be clearly categorized as value or growth.

Market resilience Condition where discrepancies between market prices and intrinsic values tend to be small and corrected quickly.

Market risk The risk associated with interest rates, exchange rates, and equity prices.

Market segmentation The degree to which there are some meaningful impediments to capital movement across markets.

Market timing Increasing or decreasing exposure to a market or asset class based on predictions of its performance; with reference to performance attribution, returns attributable to shorter-term tactical deviations from the strategic asset allocation.

Market-adjusted implementation shortfall The difference between the money return on a notional or paper portfolio and the actual portfolio return, adjusted using beta to remove the effect of the return on the market.

Market-not-held order A variation of the market order designed to give the agent greater discretion than a simple market order would allow. "Not held" means that the floor broker is not required to trade at any specific price or in any specific time interval.

Marking to market A procedure used primarily in futures markets in which the parties to a contract settle the amount owed daily. Also known as the *daily settlement*.

Mass affluent An industry term for a segment of the private wealth marketplace that is not sufficiently wealthy to command certain individualized services.

Matrix prices Prices determined by comparisons to other securities of similar credit risk and maturity; the result of matrix pricing.

Matrix pricing An approach for estimating the prices of thinly traded securities based on the prices of securities with similar attributions, such as similar credit rating, maturity, or economic sector.

Maturity premium Compensation for the increased sensitivity of the market value of debt to a change in market interest rates as maturity is extended.

Maturity variance A measure of how much a given immunized portfolio differs from the ideal immunized portfolio consisting of a single pure discount instrument with maturity equal to the time horizon.

Maximum loss optimization A stress test in which we would try to optimize mathematically the risk variable that would produce the maximum loss.

Mega-cap buy-out funds A class of buyout funds that take public companies private.

Mental accounting bias An information-processing bias in which people treat one sum of money differently from another equal-sized sum based on which mental account the money is assigned to.

Methodical investors Investors who rely on "hard facts."

Micro attribution Performance attribution analysis carried out on the investment manager level.

Micro expectations Expectations concerning individual assets.

Middle-market buy-out funds A class of buyout funds that purchase private companies whose revenues and profits are too small to access capital from the public equity markets.

Midquote The halfway point between the market bid and ask prices.

Minimum-variance frontier The graph of the set of portfolios with smallest variances of return for their levels of expected return.

Missed trade opportunity costs Unrealized profit/loss arising from the failure to execute a trade in a timely manner.

Model risk   The risk that a model is incorrect or misapplied; in investments, it often refers to valuation models.

Model uncertainty   Uncertainty concerning whether a selected model is correct.

Modern portfolio theory (MPT)   The analysis of rational portfolio choices based on the efficient use of risk.

Modified duration   An adjustment of the duration for the level of the yield. Contrast with *Macaulay duration.*

Monetary policy   Government activity concerning interest rates and the money supply.

Money markets   Markets for fixed-income securities with maturities of one year or less.

Moneyness   The relationship between the price of the underlying and an option's exercise price.

Money-weighted rate of return   Same as the internal rate of return; the growth rate that will link the ending value of the account to its beginning value plus all intermediate cash flows.

Monitoring   To systematically keep watch over investor circumstances (including wealth and constraints), market and economic changes, and the portfolio itself so that the client's current objectives and constraints continue to be satisfied.

Monte Carlo simulation method   An approach to estimating VAR that produces random outcomes to examine what might happen if a particular risk is faced. This method is widely used in the sciences as well as in business to study a variety of problems.

Mortality risk   The risk of loss of human capital in the event of premature death.

Multifactor model   A model that explains a variable in terms of the values of a set of factors.

Multifactor model technique   With respect to construction of an indexed portfolio, a technique that attempts to match the primary risk exposures of the indexed portfolio to those of the index.

Multiperiod Sharpe ratio   A Sharpe ratio based on the investment's multiperiod wealth in excess of the wealth generated by the risk-free investment.

Mutuals   With respect to insurance companies, companies that are owned by their policyholders, who share in the company's surplus earnings.

Natural liquidity   An extensive pool of investors who are aware of and have a potential interest in buying and/or selling a security.

Net interest margin   With respect to banks, net interest income (interest income minus interest expense) divided by average earning assets.

Net interest spread   With respect to the operations of insurers, the difference between interest earned and interest credited to policyholders.

Net worth   The difference between the market value of assets and liabilities.

Net worth tax or **net wealth tax**   A tax based on a person's assets, less liabilities.

Netting   When parties agree to exchange only the net amount owed from one party to the other.

Nominal default-free bonds   Conventional bonds that have no (or minimal) default risk.

Nominal gross domestic product (nominal GDP)   A money measure of the goods and services produced within a country's borders.

Nominal risk-free interest rate   The sum of the real risk-free interest rate and the inflation premium.

Nominal spread   The spread of a bond or portfolio above the yield of a Treasury of equal maturity.

Nondeliverable forwards (NDFs)   Cash-settled forward contracts, used predominately with respect to foreign exchange forwards.

Nonfinancial risk   Risks that arise from sources other than the external financial markets, such as changes in accounting rules, legal environment, or tax rates.

Nonparametric   Involving minimal probability-distribution assumptions.

Nonstationarity   A property of a data series that reflects more than one set of underlying statistical properties.

Normal backwardation   The condition in futures markets in which futures prices are lower than expected spot prices.

Normal contango   The condition in futures markets in which futures prices are higher than expected spot prices.

Normal portfolio   A portfolio with exposure to sources of systematic risk that are typical for a manager, using the manager's past portfolios as a guide.

Notional amount   The dollar amount used as a scale factor in calculating payments for a forward contract, futures contract, or swap.

Notional principal amount   The amount specified in a swap that forms the basis for calculating payment streams.

Objective function   A quantitative expression of the objective or goal of a process.

Off-market FRA   A contract in which the initial value is intentionally set at a value other than zero and therefore requires a cash payment at the start from one party to the other.

Offsetting   A transaction in exchange-listed derivative markets in which a party re-enters the market to close out a position.

Open market operations   The purchase or sale by a central bank of government securities, which are settled using reserves, to influence interest rates and the supply of credit by banks.

Open outcry auction market   Public auction where representatives of buyers and sellers meet at a specified location and place verbal bids and offers.

Operations risk or **operational risk**   The risk of loss from failures in a company's systems and procedures (for example, due to computer failures or human failures) or events completely outside of the control of organizations (which would include "acts of God" and terrorist actions).

Opportunistic participation strategies   Passive trading combined with the opportunistic seizing of liquidity.

Opportunity cost sell discipline   A sell discipline in which the investor is constantly looking at potential stocks to include in the portfolio and will replace an existing holding whenever a better opportunity presents itself.

Optimization   With respect to portfolio construction, a procedure for determining the best portfolios according to some criterion.

Optimizer   A heuristic, formula, algorithm, or program that uses risk, return, correlation, or other variables to determine the most appropriate asset allocation or asset mix for a portfolio.

Option   A financial instrument that gives one party the right, but not the obligation, to buy or sell an underlying asset from or to another party at a fixed price over a specific period of time. Also referred to as contingent claims.

Option price, option premium, or **premium**   The amount of money a buyer pays and seller receives to engage in an option transaction.

Option-adjusted spread (OAS)   The current spread over the benchmark yield minus that component of the spread that is attributable to any embedded optionality in the instrument.

Options on futures (futures options)   Options on a designated futures contract.

Options on physicals With respect to options, exchange-traded option contracts that have cash instruments rather than futures contracts on cash instruments as the underlying.

Order-driven markets Markets in which transaction prices are established by public limit orders to buy or sell a security at specified prices.

Ordinary income Earnings from employment.

Ordinary life insurance (also whole life insurance) A type of life insurance policy that involves coverage for the whole of the insured's life.

Orphan equities investing A distressed securities investment discipline that involves investment in orphan equities that are perceived to be undervalued.

Orphan equity Investment in the newly issued equity of a company emerging from reorganization.

Out-of-the-money Options that, if exercised, would require the payment of more money than the value received and therefore would not be currently exercised.

Output gap The difference between the value of GDP estimated as if the economy were on its trend growth path (potential output) and the actual value of GDP.

Overall trade balance The sum of the current account (reflecting exports and imports) and the financial account (consisting of portfolio flows).

Overconfidence bias A bias in which people demonstrate unwarranted faith in their own intuitive reasoning, judgments, and/or cognitive abilities.

Overconfidence trap The tendency of individuals to overestimate the accuracy of their forecasts.

Overnight index swap (OIS) A swap in which the floating rate is the cumulative value of a single unit of currency invested at an overnight rate during the settlement period.

Pairs trade (or pairs arbitrage) A basic long–short trade in which an investor is long and short equal currency amounts of two common stocks in a single industry.

Panel method A method of capital market expectations setting that involves using the viewpoints of a panel of experts.

Partial correlation In multivariate problems, the correlation between two variables after controlling for the effects of the other variables in the system.

Partial fill Execution of a purchase or sale for fewer shares than was stipulated in the order.

Participate (do not initiate) **order** A variant of the market-not-held order. The broker is deliberately low-key and waits for and responds to the initiatives of more active traders.

Passive investment approach An approach to portfolio construction in which portfolio composition does not react to changes in capital market expectations; includes indexing and buy-and-hold investing.

Passive management A buy-and-hold approach to investing in which an investor does not make portfolio changes based upon short-term expectations of changing market or security performance.

Passive traders Traders that seek liquidity in their rebalancing transactions, but are much more concerned with the cost of trading.

Payer swaption A swaption that allows the holder to enter into a swap as the fixed-rate payer and floating-rate receiver.

Payment netting A means of settling payments in which the amount owed by the first party to the second is netted with the amount owed by the second party to the first; only the net difference is paid.

Payoff The value of an option at expiration.

Pension funds Funds consisting of assets set aside to support a promise of retirement income.

Pension surplus Pension assets at market value minus the present value of pension liabilities.

Percentage-of-portfolio rebalancing Rebalancing is triggered based on set thresholds stated as a percentage of the portfolio's value.

Percentage-of-volume strategy A logical participation strategy in which trading takes place in proportion to overall market volume (typically at a rate of 5–20 percent) until the order is completed.

Perfect markets Markets without any frictional costs.

Performance appraisal The evaluation of portfolio performance; a quantitative assessment of a manager's investment skill.

Performance attribution A comparison of an account's performance with that of a designated benchmark and the identification and quantification of sources of differential returns.

Performance evaluation The measurement and assessment of the outcomes of investment management decisions.

Performance guarantee A guarantee from the clearinghouse that if one party makes money on a transaction, the clearinghouse ensures it will be paid.

Performance measurement A component of performance evaluation; the relatively simple procedure of calculating an asset's or portfolio's rate of return.

Performance netting risk For entities that fund more than one strategy and have asymmetric incentive fee arrangements with the portfolio managers, the potential for loss in cases where the net performance of the group of managers generates insufficient fee revenue to fully cover contractual payout obligations to all portfolio managers with positive performance.

Performance-based fee Fees specified by a combination of a base fee plus an incentive fee for performance in excess of a benchmark's.

Periodic (or batch) **auction markets** Auction markets where multilateral trading occurs at a single price at a prespecified point in time.

Permanent income hypothesis The hypothesis that consumers' spending behavior is largely determined by their long-run income expectations.

Personality typing The determination of an investor's personality type.

Plain vanilla swap An interest rate swap in which one party pays a fixed rate and the other pays a floating rate, with both sets of payments in the same currency.

Plan sponsor An enterprise or organization—such as a business, labor union, municipal or state government, or not-for-profit organization—that sets up a pension plan.

Pledging requirement With respect to banks, a required collateral use of assets.

Point estimate A single-valued estimate of a quantity, as opposed to an estimate in terms of a range of values.

Policy portfolio A synonym of strategic asset allocation; the portfolio resulting from strategic asset allocation considered as a process.

Policyholder reserves With respect to an insurance company, an amount representing the estimated payments to policyholders, as determined by actuaries, based on the types and terms of the various insurance policies issued by the company.

Political risk (or geopolitical risk) The risk of war, government collapse, political instability, expropriation, confiscation, or adverse changes in taxation.

Portable Moveable. With reference to a pension plan, one in which a plan participant can move his or her share of plan assets to a new plan, subject to certain rules, vesting schedules, and possible tax penalties and payments.

Portable alpha A strategy involving the combining of multiple positions (e.g., long and short positions) so as to separate the alpha (unsystematic risk) from beta (systematic risk) in an investment.

Portfolio implementation decision The decision on how to execute the buy and sell orders of portfolio managers.

Portfolio management process An integrated set of steps undertaken in a consistent manner to create and maintain an appropriate portfolio (combination of assets) to meet clients' stated goals.

Portfolio optimization The combining of assets to efficiently achieve a set of return and risk objectives.

Portfolio segmentation The creation of subportfolios according to the product mix for individual segments or lines of business.

Portfolio selection/composition decision The decision in which the manager integrates investment strategies with capital market expectations to select the specific assets for the portfolio.

Portfolio trade (also known as program trade or basket trade) A trade in which a number of securities are traded as a single unit.

Position a trade To take the other side of a trade, acting as a principal with capital at risk.

Position trader A trader who typically holds positions open overnight.

Positive active position An active position for which the account's allocation to a security is greater than the corresponding weight of the same security in the benchmark.

Post-trade transparency Degree to which completed trades are quickly and accurately reported to the public.

Potential credit risk The risk associated with the possibility that a payment due at a later date will not be made.

Potential output The value of GDP if the economy were on its trend growth path.

Preferred return With respect to the compensation of private equity fund managers, a hurdle rate.

Pre-investing The strategy of using futures contracts to enter the market without an immediate outlay of cash.

Premium Regarding life insurance, the asset paid by the policy holder to an insurer who, in turn, has a contractual obligation to pay death benefit proceeds to the beneficiary named in the policy.

Prepackaged bankruptcy A bankruptcy in which the debtor seeks agreement from creditors on the terms of a reorganization before the reorganization filing.

Prepaid swap A contract calling for payment today and delivery of the asset or commodity at multiple specified times in the future.

Present (price) value of a basis point (PVBP) The change in the bond price for a 1 basis point change in yield. Also called *basis point value* (BPV).

Present value distribution of cash flows A list showing what proportion of a portfolio's duration is attributable to each future cash flow.

Pretrade transparency Ability of individuals to quickly, easily, and inexpensively obtain accurate information about quotes and trades.

Price discovery Adjustment of transaction prices to balance supply and demand.

Price improvement Execution at a price that is better than the price quoted at the time of order placement.

Price limits Limits imposed by a futures exchange on the price change that can occur from one day to the next.

Price risk The risk of fluctuations in market price.

Price uncertainty Uncertainty about the price at which an order will execute.

Price weighted With respect to index construction, an index in which each security in the index is weighted according to its absolute share price.

Priced risk Risk for which investors demand compensation.

Primary risk factors With respect to valuation, the major influences on pricing.

Prime brokerage A suite of services that is often specified to include support in accounting and reporting, leveraged trade execution, financing, securities lending (related to short-selling activities), and start-up advice (for new entities).

Principal trade A trade with a broker in which the broker commits capital to facilitate the prompt execution of the trader's order to buy or sell.

Private equity Ownership interests in non-publicly-traded companies.

Private equity funds Pooled investment vehicles investing in generally highly illiquid assets; includes venture capital funds and buyout funds.

Private exchange A method for handling undiversified positions with built-in capital gains in which shares that are a component of an index are exchanged for shares of an index mutual fund in a privately arranged transaction with the fund.

Private placement memorandum A document used to raise venture capital financing when funds are raised through an agent.

Probate The legal process to confirm the validity of a will so that executors, heirs, and other interested parties can rely on its authenticity.

Profit-sharing plans A defined-contribution plan in which contributions are based, at least in part, on the plan sponsor's profits.

Projected benefit obligation (PBO) A measure of a pension plan's liability that reflects accumulated service in the same manner as the ABO but also projects future variables, such as compensation increases.

Prospect theory An alternative to expected utility theory, it assigns value to gains and losses (changes in wealth) rather than to final wealth, and probabilities are replaced by decision weights. In prospect theory, the shape of a decision maker's value function is assumed to differ between the domain of gains and the domain of losses.

Protective put An option strategy in which a long position in an asset is combined with a long position in a put.

Proxy hedging Hedging that involves the use of a forward contract between the home currency and a currency that is highly correlated with the foreign asset's currency.

Prudence trap The tendency to temper forecasts so that they do not appear extreme; the tendency to be overly cautious in forecasting.

Psychological profiling The determination of an investor's psychological characteristics relevant to investing, such as his or her personality type.

Public good A good that is not divisible and not excludable (a consumer cannot be denied it).

Purchasing power parity The theory that movements in an exchange rate should offset any difference in the inflation rates between two countries.

Pure sector allocation return A component of attribution analysis that relates relative returns to the manager's sector-weighting decisions. Calculated as the difference between the allocation (weight) of the portfolio to a given sector and the portfolio's benchmark weight for that sector, multiplied by the difference between the sector benchmark's return and the overall portfolio's benchmark return, summed across all sectors.

Put An option that gives the holder the right to sell an underlying asset to another party at a fixed price over a specific period of time.

Put–call parity An equation expressing the equivalence (parity) of a portfolio of a call and a bond with a portfolio of a put and the underlying, which leads to the relationship between put and call prices.

Put–call–forward parity The relationship among puts, calls, and forward contracts.

Quality control charts A graphical means of presenting performance appraisal data; charts illustrating the performance of an actively managed account versus a selected benchmark.

Quality option (or swap option) With respect to Treasury futures, the option of which acceptable Treasury issue to deliver.

Quoted depth The number of shares available for purchase or sale at the quoted bid and ask prices.

Quote-driven markets (or dealer markets) Markets that rely on dealers to establish firm prices at which securities can be bought and sold.

Rate duration A fixed-income instrument's or portfolio's sensitivity to a change in key maturity, holding constant all other points along the yield curve.

Ratio spread An option strategy in which a long position in a certain number of options is offset by a short position in a certain number of other options on the same underlying, resulting in a risk-free position.

Rational economic man A self-interested, risk-averse individual who has the ability to make judgments using all available information in order to maximize his/her expected utility.

Real estate Interests in land or structures attached to land.

Real estate investment trusts (REITs) Publicly traded equities representing pools of money invested in real estate properties and/or real estate debt.

Real option An option involving decisions related to tangible assets or processes.

Real risk-free interest rate The single-period interest rate for a completely risk-free security if no inflation were expected.

Rebalancing Adjusting the actual portfolio to the current strategic asset allocation because of price changes in portfolio holdings. Also: revisions to an investor's target asset class weights because of changes in the investor's investment objectives or constraints, or because of changes in capital market expectations; or to mean tactical asset allocation.

Rebalancing ratio A quantity involved in reestablishing the dollar duration of a portfolio to a desired level, equal to the original dollar duration divided by the new dollar duration.

Re-base With reference to index construction, to change the time period used as the base of the index.

Recallability trap The tendency of forecasts to be overly influenced by events that have left a strong impression on a person's memory.

Receiver swaption A swaption that allows the holder to enter into a swap as the fixed-rate receiver and floating-rate payer.

Recession A broad-based economic downturn, conventionally defined as two successive quarterly declines in GDP.

Reference entity An entity, such as a bond issuer, specified in a derivatives contract.

Regime A distinct governing set of relationships.

Regret The feeling that an opportunity has been missed; typically an expression of *hindsight bias*.

Regret-aversion bias An emotional bias in which people tend to avoid making decisions that will result in action out of fear that the decision will turn out poorly.

Regulatory risk The risk associated with the uncertainty of how a transaction will be regulated or with the potential for regulations to change.

Reinvestment risk The risk of reinvesting coupon income or principal at a rate less than the original coupon or purchase rate.

Relative economic strength forecasting approach An exchange rate forecasting approach that suggests that a strong pace of economic growth in a country creates attractive investment opportunities, increasing the demand for the country's currency and causing it to appreciate.

Relative return objective A return objective stated as a return relative to the portfolio benchmark's total return.

Relative strength indicators A price momentum indicator that involves comparing a stock's performance during a specific period either to its own past performance or to the performance of some group of stocks.

Remaindermen Beneficiaries of a trust; having a claim on the residue.

Replacement value The market value of a swap.

Representativeness bias A belief perseverance bias in which people tend to classify new information based on past experiences and classifications.

Repurchase agreement A contract involving the sale of securities such as Treasury instruments coupled with an agreement to repurchase the same securities at a later date.

Repurchase yield The negative of the expected percent change in number of shares outstanding, in the Grinold–Kroner model.

Required return (or return requirement) With reference to the investment policy statement, a return objective relating to the level of return that will be adequate to satisfy a need.

Resampled efficient frontier The set of resampled efficient portfolios.

Resampled efficient portfolio An efficient portfolio based on simulation.

Residence jurisdiction A framework used by a country to determine the basis for taxing income, based on residency.

Residence–residence conflict When two countries claim residence of the same individual, subjecting the individual's income to taxation by both countries.

Residence–source conflict When tax jurisdiction is claimed by an individual's country of residence and the country where some of their assets are sourced; the most common source of double taxation.

Residue With respect to trusts, the funds remaining in a trust when the last income beneficiary dies.

Retired-lives The portion of a pension fund's liabilities associated with retired workers.

Return objective An investor objective that addresses the required or desired level of returns.

Returns-based benchmarks Benchmarks that are constructed using 1) a series of a manager's account returns and 2) the series of returns on several investment style indexes over the same period. These return series are then submitted to an allocation algorithm that solves for the combination of investment style indexes that most closely tracks the account's returns.

Returns-based style analysis An approach to style analysis that focuses on characteristics of the overall portfolio as revealed by a portfolio's realized returns.

Reverse optimization A technique for reverse engineering the expected returns implicit in a diversified market portfolio.

Revocable trust A trust arrangement wherein the settlor (who originally transfers assets to fund the trust) retains the right to rescind the trust relationship and regain title to the trust assets.

Rho The sensitivity of the option price to the risk-free rate.

Risk aversion The degree of an investor's inability and unwillingness to take risk.

Risk budget The desired total quantity of risk; the result of risk budgeting.

Risk budgeting The establishment of objectives for individuals, groups, or divisions of an organization that takes into account the allocation of an acceptable level of risk.

Risk exposure A source of risk. Also, the state of being exposed or vulnerable to a risk.

Risk governance The process of setting overall policies and standards in risk management.

Risk management The process of identifying the level of risk an entity wants, measuring the level of risk the entity currently has, taking actions that bring the actual level of risk to the desired level of risk, and monitoring the new actual level of risk so that it continues to be aligned with the desired level of risk.

Risk objective An investor objective that addresses risk.

Risk premium approach An approach to forecasting the return of a risky asset that views its expected return as the sum of the risk-free rate of interest and one or more risk premiums.

Risk profile A detailed tabulation of the index's risk exposures.

Risk tolerance The capacity to accept risk; the level of risk an investor (or organization) is willing and able to bear.

Risk tolerance function An assessment of an investor's tolerance to risk over various levels of portfolio outcomes.

Risk-neutral probabilities Weights that are used to compute a binomial option price. They are the probabilities that would apply if a risk-neutral investor valued an option.

Risk-neutral valuation The process by which options and other derivatives are priced by treating investors as though they were risk neutral.

Roll return (or roll yield) The component of the return on a commodity futures contract that comes from rolling long futures positions forward through time.

Rolling return The moving average of the holding-period returns for a specified period (e.g., a calendar year) that matches the investor's time horizon.

Sample estimator A formula for assigning a unique value (a point estimate) to a population parameter.

Sample-size neglect A type of representativeness bias in which financial market participants incorrectly assume that small sample sizes are representative of populations (or "real" data).

Sandwich spread An option strategy that is equivalent to a short butterfly spread.

Satisfice A combination of "satisfy" and "suffice" describing decisions, actions, and outcomes that may not be optimal, but are adequate.

Savings–investment imbalances forecasting approach An exchange rate forecasting approach that explains currency movements in terms of the effects of domestic savings–investment imbalances on the exchange rate.

Scalper A trader who offers to buy or sell futures contracts, holding the position for only a brief period of time. Scalpers attempt to profit by buying at the bid price and selling at the higher ask price.

Scenario analysis A risk management technique involving the examination of the performance of a portfolio under specified situations. Closely related to *stress testing*.

Seats Memberships in a derivatives exchange.

Secondary offering An offering after the initial public offering of securities.

Sector/quality effect In a fixed-income attribution analysis, a measure of a manager's ability to select the "right" issuing sector and quality group.

Security selection Skill in selecting individual securities within an asset class.

Security selection effect In a fixed-income attribution analysis, the residual of the security's total return after other effects are accounted for; a measure of the return due to ability in security selection.

Segmentation With respect to the management of insurance company portfolios, the notional subdivision of the overall portfolio into sub-portfolios each of which is associated with a specified group of insurance contracts.

Self-attribution bias A bias in which people take personal credit for successes and attribute failures to external factors outside the individual's control.

Self-control bias A bias in which people fail to act in pursuit of their long-term, overarching goals because of a lack of self-discipline.

Sell side Broker/dealers that sell securities and make recommendations for various customers, such as investment managers and institutional investors.

Sell-side analysts Analysts employed by brokerages.

Semiactive management (also called enhanced indexing or risk-controlled active management) A variant of active management. In a semiactive portfolio, the manager seeks to outperform a given benchmark with tightly controlled risk relative to the benchmark.

Semiactive, risk-controlled active, or **enhanced index approach** An investment approach that seeks positive alpha while keeping tight control over risk relative to the portfolio's benchmark.

Semivariance A measure of downside risk. The average of squared deviations that fall below the mean.

Separate property regime A marital property regime under which each spouse is able to own and control property as an individual.

Settlement date or **payment date** The designated date at which the parties to a trade must transact.

Settlement netting risk The risk that a liquidator of a counterparty in default could challenge a netting arrangement so that profitable transactions are realized for the benefit of creditors.

Settlement period The time between settlement dates.

Settlement price The official price, designated by the clearinghouse, from which daily gains and losses will be determined and marked to market.

Settlement risk When settling a contract, the risk that one party could be in the process of paying the counterparty while the counterparty is declaring bankruptcy.

Settlor (or **grantor**) An entity that transfers assets to a trustee, to be held and managed for the benefit of the trust beneficiaries.

Shari'a The law of Islam. In addition to the law of the land, some follow guidance provided by Shari'a or Islamic law.

Sharpe ratio (or reward-to-variability) A measure of risk-adjusted performance that compares excess returns to the total risk of the account, where total risk is measured by the account's standard deviation of returns.

Short The seller of a derivative contract. Also refers to the position of being short a derivative.

Shortfall risk The risk that portfolio value will fall below some minimum acceptable level during a stated time horizon; the risk of not achieving a specified return target.

Shrinkage estimation Estimation that involves taking a weighted average of a historical estimate of a parameter and some other parameter estimate, where the weights reflect the analyst's relative belief in the estimates.

Shrinkage estimator The formula used in shrinkage estimation of a parameter.

Sign-constrained optimization An optimization that constrains asset class weights to be nonnegative and to sum to 1.

Single-payment loan A loan in which the borrower receives a sum of money at the start and pays back the entire amount with interest in a single payment at maturity.

Situational profiling The categorization of individual investors by stage of life or by economic circumstance.

Smart routing The use of algorithms to intelligently route an order to the most liquid venue.

Smoothing rule With respect to spending rates, a rule that averages asset values over a period of time in order to dampen the spending rate's response to asset value fluctuation.

Socially responsible investing (ethical investing) An approach to investing that integrates ethical values and societal concerns with investment decisions.

Social proof A bias in which individuals tend to follow the beliefs of a group.

Soft dollars (also called soft dollar arrangements or soft commissions) The use of commissions to buy services other than execution services.

Sole ownership Owned by one person; assets held in sole ownership are typically considered part of a decedent's estate. The transfer of their ownership is dictated by the decedent's will through the probate process.

Solow residual A measure of the growth in total factor productivity that is based on an economic growth model developed by economist Robert M. Solow.

Sortino ratio A performance appraisal ratio that replaces standard deviation in the Sharpe ratio with downside deviation.

Source jurisdiction or **territorial tax system** A framework used by a country to determine the basis for taxing income or transfers. A country that taxes income as a source within its borders imposes source jurisdiction.

Source–source conflict When two countries claim source jurisdiction of the same asset; both countries may claim that the income is derived from their jurisdiction.

Sovereign risk A form of credit risk in which the borrower is the government of a sovereign nation.

Spontaneous investors Investors who constantly readjust their portfolio allocations and holdings.

Spot return (or price return) The component of the return on a commodity futures contract that comes from changes in the underlying spot prices via the cost-of-carry model.

Spread An option strategy involving the purchase of one option and sale of another option that is identical to the first in all respects except either exercise price or expiration.

Spread duration The sensitivity of a non-Treasury security's price to a widening or narrowing of the spread over Treasuries.

Spread risk Risk related to changes in the spread between Treasuries and non-Treasuries.

Stack and roll A hedging strategy in which an existing stack hedge with maturing futures contracts is replaced by a new stack hedge with longer dated futures contracts.

Stack hedge Hedging a stream of obligations by entering futures contracts with a *single* maturity, with the number of contracts selected so that changes in the *present value* of the future obligations are offset by changes in the value of this "stack" of futures contracts.

Stale price bias Bias that arises from using prices that are stale because of infrequent trading.

Standard deviation The positive square root of variance.

Stated return desire A stated desired level of returns.

Static approach With respect to strategic asset allocation, an approach that does not account for links between optimal decisions in future time periods.

Static spread (or zero-volatility spread) The constant spread above the Treasury spot curve that equates the calculated price of the security to the market price.

Stationary A series of data for which the parameters that describe a return-generating process are stable.

Status quo bias An emotional bias in which people do nothing (i.e., maintain the "status quo") instead of making a change.

Status quo trap The tendency for forecasts to perpetuate recent observations—that is, to predict no change from the recent past.

Sterling ratio The compound annualized rate of return over a specified time period divided by the average yearly maximum drawdown over the same time period less an arbitrary 10 percent.

Stock companies With respect to insurance companies, companies that have issued common equity shares.

Stock index futures Futures contracts on a specified stock index.

Storage costs or **carrying costs** The costs of holding an asset, generally a function of the physical characteristics of the underlying asset.

Straddle An option strategy involving the purchase of a put and a call with the same exercise price. A straddle is based on the expectation of high volatility of the underlying.

Straight-through processing Systems that simplify transaction processing through the minimization of manual and/or duplicative intervention in the process from trade placement to settlement.

Strangle A variation of a straddle in which the put and call have different exercise prices.

Strap An option strategy involving the purchase of two calls and one put.

Strategic asset allocation 1) The process of allocating money to IPS-permissible asset classes that integrates the investor's return objectives, risk tolerance, and investment constraints with long-run capital market expectations. 2) The result of the above process, also known as the policy portfolio.

Stratified sampling (or representative sampling) A sampling method that guarantees that subpopulations of interest are represented in the sample.

Stress testing A risk management technique in which the risk manager examines the performance of the portfolio under market conditions involving high risk and usually high correlations across markets. Closely related to *scenario analysis*.

Strike spread A spread used to determine the strike price for the payoff of a credit option.

Strip An option strategy involving the purchase of two puts and one call.

Strip hedge Hedging a stream of obligations by offsetting each individual obligation with a futures contract matching the maturity and quantity of the obligation.

Structural level of unemployment The level of unemployment resulting from scarcity of a factor of production.

Structured note A variation of a floating-rate note that has some type of unusual characteristic such as a leverage factor or in which the rate moves opposite to interest rates.

Style drift Inconsistency in style.

Style index A securities index intended to reflect the average returns to a given style.

Stylized scenario A type of analysis often used in stress testing. It involves simulating the movement in at least one interest rate, exchange rate, stock price, or commodity price relevant to the portfolio.

Sunshine trades Public display of a transaction (usually high-volume) in advance of the actual order.

Surplus The difference between the value of assets and the present value of liabilities. With respect to an insurance company, the net difference between the total assets and total liabilities (equivalent to policyholders' surplus for a mutual insurance company and stockholders' equity for a stock company).

Surplus efficient frontier The graph of the set of portfolios that maximize expected surplus for given levels of standard deviation of surplus.

Survey method   A method of capital market expectations setting that involves surveying experts.

Survival probability   The probability an individual survives in a given year; used to determine expected cash flow required in retirement.

Survivorship bias   Bias that arises in a data series when managers with poor track records exit the business and are dropped from the database whereas managers with good records remain; when a data series as of a given date reflects only entities that have survived to that date.

Swap   A contract calling for the exchange of payments over time. Often one payment is fixed in advance and the other is floating, based upon the realization of a price or interest rate.

Swap rate   The interest rate applicable to the pay-fixed-rate side of an interest rate swap.

Swap spread   The difference between the fixed rate on an interest rate swap and the rate on a Treasury note with equivalent maturity; it reflects the general level of credit risk in the market.

Swap tenor   The lifetime of a swap.

Swap term   Another name for *swap tenor*.

Swaption   An option to enter into a swap.

Symmetric cash flow matching   A cash flow matching technique that allows cash flows occurring both before and after the liability date to be used to meet a liability; allows for the short-term borrowing of funds to satisfy a liability prior to the liability due date.

Synthetic call   The combination of puts, the underlying, and risk-free bonds that replicates a call option.

Synthetic forward contract   The combination of the underlying, puts, calls, and risk-free bonds that replicates a forward contract.

Synthetic index fund   An index fund position created by combining risk-free bonds and futures on the desired index.

Synthetic put   The combination of calls, the underlying, and risk-free bonds that replicates a put option.

Tactical asset allocation   Asset allocation that involves making short-term adjustments to asset class weights based on short-term predictions of relative performance among asset classes.

Tactical rebalancing   A variation of calendar rebalancing that specifies less frequent rebalancing when markets appear to be trending and more frequent rebalancing when they are characterized by reversals.

Tail value at risk   (or conditional tail expectation)   The VAR plus the expected loss in excess of VAR, when such excess loss occurs.

Target covariance matrix   A component of shrinkage estimation; allows the analyst to model factors that are believed to influence the data over periods longer than observed in the historical sample.

Target semivariance   The average squared deviation below a target value.

Target value   The value that the portfolio manager seeks to ensure; the value that the life insurance company has guaranteed the policyholder.

Tax alpha   The value created by using investment techniques that effectively manage tax liabilities.

Tax avoidance   Developing strategies that minimize tax, while conforming to both the spirit and the letter of the tax codes of jurisdictions with taxing authority.

Tax concerns   Concerns related to an investor's tax position.

Tax drag   The negative effect of taxes on after-tax returns.

Tax efficiency   The proportion of the expected pretax total return that will be retained after taxes.

Tax evasion   The practice of circumventing tax obligations by illegal means such as misreporting or not reporting relevant information to tax authorities.

Tax loss harvesting   The practice of realizing a loss to offset a gain or income, thereby reducing the current year's tax obligation.

Tax premium   Compensation for the effect of taxes on the after-tax return of an asset.

Tax risk   The uncertainty associated with tax laws.

Tax structures   The specifics of how governments collect taxes.

Taylor rule   A rule linking a central bank's target short-term interest rate to the rate of growth of the economy and inflation.

Tenor   The original time to maturity on a swap.

Term life insurance   A type of life insurance policy that provides coverage for a specified length of time and accumulates little or no cash values.

Termination date   The date of the final payment on a swap; also, the swap's expiration date.

Testamentary gratuitous transfer   The bequeathing or transfer of assets upon one's death. From a recipient's perspective, it is called an inheritance.

Testator   A person who makes a will.

Theta   The change in price of an option associated with a one-day reduction in its time to expiration; the rate at which an option's time value decays.

Tick   The smallest possible price movement of a security.

Time deposit   A deposit requiring advance notice prior to a withdrawal.

Time horizon   The time period associated with an investment objective.

Time to expiration   The time remaining in the life of a derivative, typically expressed in years.

Time value or **speculative value**   The difference between the market price of the option and its intrinsic value, determined by the uncertainty of the underlying over the remaining life of the option.

Time value decay   The loss in the value of an option resulting from movement of the option price toward its payoff value as the expiration day approaches.

Time-period bias   Bias that occurs when results are time-period specific.

Time-series estimators   Estimators that are based on lagged values of the variable being forecast; often consist of lagged values of other selected variables.

Time-weighted average price (TWAP) strategy   A logical participation strategy that assumes a flat volume profile and trades in proportion to time.

Time-weighted rate of return   The compound rate of growth over a stated evaluation period of one unit of money initially invested in the account.

Timing option   With respect to certain futures contracts, the option that results from the ability of the short position to decide when in the delivery month actual delivery will take place.

Tobin's q   An asset-based valuation measure that is equal to the ratio of the market value of debt and equity to the replacement cost of total assets.

Top-down   Proceeding from the macroeconomy, to the economic sector level, to the industry level, to the firm level.

Total factor productivity   A variable which accounts for that part of Y not directly accounted for by the levels of the production factors (K and L).

Total future liability   With respect to defined-benefit pension plans, the present value of accumulated and projected future service benefits, including the effects of projected future compensation increases.

Total rate of return A measure of the increase in the investor's wealth due to both investment income (for example, dividends and interest) and capital gains (both realized and unrealized).

Total return The rate of return taking into account capital appreciation/depreciation and income. Often qualified as follows: **Nominal** returns are unadjusted for inflation; **real** returns are adjusted for inflation; **pretax** returns are returns before taxes; **post-tax** returns are returns after taxes are paid on investment income and realized capital gains.

Total return analysis Analysis of the expected effect of a trade on the portfolio's total return, given an interest rate forecast.

Total return swap A swap in which one party agrees to pay the total return on a security. Often used as a credit derivative, in which the underlying is a bond.

Tracking risk (also called tracking error, tracking error volatility, or active risk) The condition in which the performance of a portfolio does not match the performance of an index that serves as the portfolio's benchmark.

Trade blotter A device for entering and tracking trade executions and orders to trade.

Trade settlement Completion of a trade wherein purchased financial instruments are transferred to the buyer and the buyer transfers money to the seller.

Trading activity In fixed-income attribution analysis, the effect of sales and purchases of bonds over a given period; the total portfolio return minus the other components determining the management effect in an attribution analysis.

Transaction exposure The risk associated with a foreign exchange rate on a specific business transaction such as a purchase or sale.

Transcription errors Errors in gathering and recording data.

Translation exposure The risk associated with the conversion of foreign financial statements into domestic currency.

Transparency Availability of timely and accurate market and trade information.

Treasury spot curve The term structure of Treasury zero coupon bonds.

Treynor ratio (or reward-to-volatility) A measure of risk-adjusted performance that relates an account's excess returns to the systematic risk assumed by the account.

Turnover A measure of the rate of trading activity in a portfolio.

Twist With respect to the yield curve, a movement in contrary directions of interest rates at two maturities; a nonparallel movement in the yield curve.

Type I error With respect to manager selection, keeping (or hiring) managers with zero value-added. (Rejecting the null hypothesis when it is correct.)

Type II error With respect to manager selection, firing (or not hiring) managers with positive value-added. (Not rejecting the null hypothesis when it is incorrect.)

Unconstrained optimization Optimization that places no constraints on asset class weights except that they sum to 1. May produce negative asset weights, which implies borrowing or shorting of assets.

Underfunded plan A pension plan in which the ratio of the value of plan assets to the present value of plan liabilities is less than 100 percent.

Underlying An asset that trades in a market in which buyers and sellers meet, decide on a price, and the seller then delivers the asset to the buyer and receives payment. The underlying is the asset or other derivative on which a particular derivative is based. The market for the underlying is also referred to as the spot market.

Underwriting (profitability) **cycle** A cycle affecting the profitability of insurance companies' underwriting operations.

Undisclosed limit order (reserve, hidden, or iceberg order) A limit order that includes an instruction not to show more than some maximum quantity of the unfilled order to the public at any one time.

Unhedged return A foreign asset return stated in terms of the investor's home currency.

Unique circumstances Internal factors (other than a liquidity requirement, time horizon, or tax concern) that may constrain portfolio choices.

Universal life insurance A type of life insurance policy that provides for premium flexibility, an adjustable face amount of death benefits, and current market interest rates on the savings element.

Unrelated business income With respect to the U.S. tax code, income that is not substantially related to a foundation's charitable purposes.

Unstructured modeling Modeling without a theory on the underlying structure.

Uptick rules Trading rules that specify that a short sale must not be on a downtick relative to the last trade at a different price.

Urgency of the trade The importance of certainty of execution.

Utility The level of relative satisfaction received from the consumption of goods and services.

Utility theory Theory whereby people maximize the present value of utility subject to a present value budget constraint.

Valuation The process of determining the value of an asset or service.

Valuation reserve With respect to insurance companies, an allowance, created by a charge against earnings, to provide for losses in the value of the assets.

Value The amount for which one can sell something, or the amount one must pay to acquire something.

Value at risk (VAR) A probability-based measure of loss potential for a company, a fund, a portfolio, a transaction, or a strategy over a specified period of time.

Value investment style With reference to equity investing, an investment style focused on paying a relatively low share price in relation to earnings or assets per share.

Value weighted (or market-capitalization weighted) With respect to index construction, an index in which each security in the index is weighted according to its market capitalization.

Value-motivated traders Traders that act on value judgments based on careful, sometimes painstaking research. They trade only when the price moves into their value range.

Variable annuity A life annuity in which the periodic payment varies depending on stock prices.

Variable life insurance (unit-linked life insurance) A type of ordinary life insurance in which death benefits and cash values are linked to the investment performance of a policyholder-selected pool of investments held in a so-called separate account.

Variable prepaid forward A monetization strategy that involves the combination of a collar with a loan against the value of the underlying shares. When the loan comes due, shares are sold to pay off the loan and part of any appreciation is shared with the lender.

Variable universal life (or flexible-premium variable life) A type of life insurance policy that combines the flexibility of universal life with the investment choice flexibility of variable life.

Variance The expected value of squared deviations from the random variable's mean; often referred to as volatility.

Variation margin Additional margin that must be deposited in an amount sufficient to bring the balance up to the initial margin requirement.

Vega A measure of the sensitivity of an option's price to changes in the underlying's volatility.

Venture capital   The equity financing of new or growing private companies.

Venture capital firms   Firms representing dedicated pools of capital for providing equity or equity-linked financing to privately held companies.

Venture capital fund   A pooled investment vehicle for venture capital investing.

Venture capital trusts   An exchange-traded, closed-end vehicle for venture capital investing.

Venture capitalists   Specialists who seek to identify companies that have good business opportunities but need financial, managerial, and strategic support.

Vested   With respect to pension benefits or assets, said of an unconditional ownership interest.

Vintage year   With reference to a private equity fund, the year it closed.

Vintage year effects   The effects on returns shared by private equity funds closed in the same year.

Volatility   Represented by the Greek letter sigma (σ), the standard deviation of price outcomes associated with an underlying asset.

Volatility clustering   The tendency for large (small) swings in prices to be followed by large (small) swings of random direction.

Volume-weighted average price (VWAP)   The average price at which a security is traded during the day, where each trade price is weighted by the fraction of the day's volume associated with the trade.

Volume-weighted average price strategy   A logical participation strategy that involves breaking up an order over time according to a prespecified volume profile.

Wealth relative   The ending value of one unit of money invested at specified rates of return.

Weather derivative   A derivative contract with a payment based on a weather-related measurement, such as heating or cooling degree days.

Wild card option   A provision allowing a short futures contract holder to delay delivery of the underlying.

Will (or testament)   A document associated with estate planning that outlines the rights others will have over one's property after death.

Within-sector selection return   In attribution analysis, a measure of the impact of a manager's security selection decisions relative to the holdings of the sector benchmark.

Worst-case scenario analysis   A stress test in which we examine the worst case that we actually expect to occur.

Yardeni model   An equity valuation model, more complex than the Fed model, that incorporates the expected growth rate in earnings.

Yield beta   A measure of the sensitivity of a bond's yield to a general measure of bond yields in the market that is used to refine the hedge ratio.

Yield curve   The relationship between yield and time to maturity.

Yield curve risk   Risk related to changes in the shape of the yield curve.

Yield spread   The difference between the yield on a bond and the yield on a default-free security, usually a government note, of the same maturity. The yield spread is primarily determined by the market's perception of the credit risk on the bond.

Yield to worst   The yield on a callable bond that assumes a bond is called at the earliest opportunity.

Zero-cost collar   A transaction in which a position in the underlying is protected by buying a put and selling a call with the premium from the sale of the call offsetting the premium from the purchase of the put. It can also be used to protect a floating-rate borrower against interest rate increases with the premium on a long cap offsetting the premium on a short floor.

Zero-premium collar   A hedging strategy involving the simultaneous purchase of puts and sale of call options on a stock. The puts are struck below and the calls are struck above the underlying's market price.

INDEX